From **Grassroots: The Writer's Workbook**, Tenth Edition
by Susan Fawcett

P9-DJU-658

If found, please return to:

Name: _____

Phone: ( ) _____

Personal Error Patterns Chart				
Error Type & Symbol	Specific Error	Correction	Rule or Reminder	Assignment & Number of Errors

Proofreading Strategies

Many writers have found that the proofreading strategies described below help them see their own writing with a fresh eye. You will learn more strategies throughout *Grassroots*. Try a number of methods and see which ones work best for you.

Proofreading Strategy: Allow enough time to proofread.

Many students don't proofread at all, or they skim their paper for grammatical errors two minutes before class. This just doesn't work. Set aside enough time to proofread slowly and carefully, searching for errors and hunting especially for your personal error patterns.

Proofreading Strategy: Work from a paper copy.

People who proofread on computers tend to miss more errors. If you write on a computer, do not proofread on the monitor. Instead, print a copy of your paper, perhaps enlarging the type to 14 point. Switching to a paper copy seems to help the brain see more clearly.

Proofreading Strategy: Read your words aloud.

Reading silently makes it easier to skip over small errors or mentally fill in missing details, whereas listening closely is a great way to hear mistakes. Listen and follow along on your printed copy, marking errors as you hear them.

   a. Read your paper aloud to *yourself*. Be sure to read *exactly* what's on the page, and read with enthusiasm.

   b. Ask a *friend* or *writing tutor* to read your paper out loud to you. Tell the reader you just want to hear your words and that you don't want any other suggestions right now.

Proofreading Strategy: Read "bottom up," from the end to the beginning.

One way to fool the brain into taking a fresh look at something you've written is to proofread the last sentence first. Read slowly, word by word. Then read the second-to-last sentence, and so on, all the way back to the first sentence.

Proofreading Strategy: Isolate your sentences.

If you write on a computer, spotting errors is often easier if you reformat so that each sentence appears isolated, on its own line. Double-space between sentences. This visual change can help the brain focus clearly on one sentence at a time.

Proofreading Strategy: Check for one error at a time.

If you make many mistakes, proofread separately all the way through your paper for each error pattern. Although this process takes time, you will catch many more errors this way and make real progress. You will begin to eliminate some errors altogether as you get better at spotting and fixing them. You will learn more recommended proofreading strategies in upcoming chapters.

Grassroots with Readings:
The Writer's Workbook

Tenth Edition

Grassroots
with Readings
The Writer's Workbook

TENTH EDITION

Susan Fawcett

WADSWORTH
CENGAGE Learning

Australia · Brazil · Japan · Korea · Mexico · Singapore · Spain · United Kingdom · United States

WADSWORTH
CENGAGE Learning

Grassroots with Readings:
The Writer's Workbook
Tenth Edition
Susan Fawcett

Senior Publisher: Lyn Uhl

Director of Developmental Studies: Annie Todd

Senior Development Editor: Judith Fifer

Assistant Editor: Melanie Opacki

Editorial Assistant: Matthew Conte

Media Editor: Amy Gibbons

Senior Marketing Manager: Kirsten Stoller

Marketing Coordinator: Ryan Ahern

Marketing Communications Manager:
    Courtney Morris

Content Project Manager:
    Aimee Chevrette Bear

Art Director: Jill Ort

Print Buyer: Betsy Donaghey

Rights Acquisition Specialist, Image:
    Jennifer Meyer Dare

Rights Acquisition Specialist, Text: Katie Huha

Cover Designer: Leonard Massiglia

Production Service: Lachina Publishing Services

Text Designer: Lachina Publishing Services

Compositor: Lachina Publishing Services

For product information and technology assistance, contact us at
Cengage Learning Customer & Sales Support, 1-800-354-9706

For permission to use material from this text or product,
submit all requests online at **cengage.com/permissions.**
Further permissions questions can be emailed to
permissionrequest@cengage.com

Library of Congress Control Number: 2010936959

Student Edition

ISBN-13: 978-0-495-90123-5

ISBN-10: 0-495-90123-7

Wadsworth
20 Channel Center Street
Boston, MA 02210
USA

Cengage Learning is a leading provider of customized learning solutions with office locations around the globe, including Singapore, the United Kingdom, Australia, Mexico, Brazil, and Japan. Locate your local office at:
international.cengage.com/region

Cengage Learning products are represented in Canada by Nelson Education, Ltd.

For your course and learning solutions, visit **www.cengage.com**

Purchase any of our products at your local college store or at our preferred online store **www.cengagebrain.com**

Printed in Canada
1 2 3 4 5 6 7 14 13 12 11 10

Brief Contents

Contents

UNIT 4   Joining Ideas Together   184

14 Coordination   186

15 Subordination   193

16 Avoiding Run-Ons and Comma Splices   203

17 Semicolons and Conjunctive Adverbs   212

UNIT 9   Reading Selections and Quotation Bank   406

Reading Strategies for the Writer   407

Quotation Bank   459

To the Student

Students from across the country have written to tell me that *Grassroots* works, that it has helped them become better writers. This note is typical: "I love *Grassroots*. Finally, I understand what a fragment is and know how to fix this big problem in my writing. I will keep *Grassroots* forever as a reference."

Grassroots with Readings grew out of my experience teaching English and directing the writing lab at Bronx Community College of the City University of New York. I am proud that *Grassroots* has won awards for excellence and has remained through every edition the top-selling basic writing text in the United States. It's designed to help students like you, who may have struggled with English courses in the past, become better, more confident writers. The all-important writing skills you gain will help you find the job of your dreams.

Grassroots provides brief, enjoyable lessons that show how to avoid the serious errors that will lower your grades in college and harm your chances at work. The colorful design, variety of visual images (photographs, cartoons, ads, and paintings), and interesting writing samples (many by students) will teach you the skills needed to improve your grades in your college courses and hone your workplace readiness. The step-by-step lessons, with frequent opportunities to practice each skill, will help you grow as a writer, just as they have helped two million college students before you.

B. Proofread the following essay for incorrect or missing capitals, commas, apostrophes, and quotation marks. Correct the errors above the lines. (You should find thirty-two individual errors.)

Most Valuable

(1) One of baseballs most feared sluggers, José albert Pujols was name greatest player of the decade by ESPN in 2010. (2) Talent, luck, and hard work helped him realize his dreams. ... was born on January 16 1980 in Santo domingo.

(4) The son of a w... raised by his grandmother.

(5) Although they ...

the dominican re...

family moved t...

PRACTICE 17

In each of these sentences, cross out any confusing prepositional phrases, locate the subject, and then circle the correct verb.

1. Greetings around the world (differs, differ) from culture to culture.
2. A resident of the United States (shakes, shake) hands firmly to say hello.
3. Kisses on each cheek (is, are) customary greetings in Latin America and southern Europe.
4. Natives of Hawaii (hugs, hug) and (exchanges, exchange) breaths in a custom called *alo ha* (sharing of life breath).
5. The Maori people of New Zealand (presses, press) noses to greet each other.
6. A person in traditional Japanese circles (bows, bow) upon meeting someone.
7. A custom among Pakistanis (is, are) the *salaam*, bowing with the right hand on the forehead.
8. Hindus in India (folds, fold) the hands and (tilts, tilt) the head forward.
9. The Hindi word for the greeting (is, are) *namaste*.

In this Tenth Anniversary Edition, I have included special new instruction on proofreading that will help you eliminate common mistakes that can reflect poorly on you as a writer.

- A new Chapter 6, "Proofreading to Correct Your Personal Error Patterns," introduces six helpful proofreading strategies, plus tools you can use to recognize, chart, and later correct your personal error patterns.

Proofreading Strategy: Read your words aloud.

Reading silently makes it easier to skip over small errors or mentally fill in missing details, whereas listening closely is a great way to hear mistakes. Listen and follow along on your printed copy, marking errors as you hear them.

  a. Read your paper aloud to *yourself*. Be sure to read *exactly* what's on the page, and read with enthusiasm.

  b. Ask a *friend* or *writing tutor* to read your paper out loud to you. Tell the reader you just want to hear your words and that you don't want any other suggestions right now.

- A removable Personal Error Patterns chart is located at the front of the book to help you keep track of your actual mistakes, one assignment at a time. Use this tool to improve your writing and your grades. It will reveal your writing patterns—what you do well and what errors you keep repeating; knowing these is key to improving your work and your grade.

- Every chapter in Units 2 through 8 now includes a specific Proofreading Strategy geared to the errors addressed in that chapter. You can try out each strategy in a companion writing assignment.

CHAPTER REVIEW

Proofread this paragraph for semicolon errors, conjunctive adverb errors, and punctuation or capitalization errors. You might use the proofreading strategy above.

(1) Shakira is a more than a gifted Colombian singer and songwriter she is also a philanthropist, determined ... brighter future. (2) By the age of 8, Shakira had decided she would su... ...d to use her fame and money to h... saw countless children s... ("Barefoot"), her breakt... the Pies Descalzos Fou... and conflict have lon...

(6) Today, Pies Des... services and classe...

Shakira works with children in Bangladesh as a UNICEF Goodwill Ambassador.

the schools aim to help students grow emotionally and socially. (8) Shakira's work with children extends beyond her foundation; she serves as a UNICEF Goodwill Ambassador and

- By the time you reach Chapter 31, Putting Your Proofreading Skills to Work, you can test yourself in a whole chapter of interesting practices with a real-world mix of errors.

Other important features of *Grassroots* include the following:

- **Readings and practices on important contemporary topics**, such as a day in the life of an emergency room nurse, video games that train soldiers, tips for first-generation college students, and stories of fascinating people who succeed despite the odds

- **Writers' Workshops** with real student compositions to evaluate and discuss

- **Clear review and interesting practice** exercises for every stage of the writing process and every crucial grammar topic

- Practice in **evaluating visual images**, such as advertisements and web pages, and critical thinking tasks, needed for college and work

A Technology Package with Additional Online Practices to Help You Succeed

Technology aids, including additional online practices, available to you include

- Exploring Online features in every chapter that refer you to interesting or important links and interactive practice opportunities

Babe is telling her parents and others that science and feminine appeal can exist during the

same person.

EXPLORING ONLINE

<http://a4esl.org/q/h/vm/prepos01.html> Interactive quiz: Select the right prepositions for each sentence.

<http://a4esl.org/q/j/ck/mc-prepositions.html> Test your preposition intuition with this 52-question quiz.

<http://grammar.ccc.commnet.edu/grammar/quizzes/cross/cross_prep3.htm> Crossword puzzle: Have you mastered prepositions?

 View an integrated eBook and chapter-specific interactive learning tools, including flashcards, quizzes, videos, and extra help tracking and correcting your Personal Error Patterns, in your Basic Writing CourseMate, accessed through <www.cengagebrain.com>.

- Online tests, games, exercises, and more through your instructor's *Grassroots* resources.

- 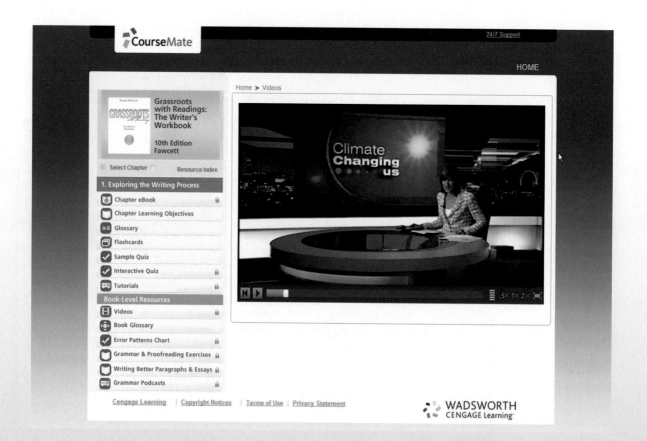 Basic Writing CourseMate, which includes:

  - an interactive eBook with highlighting, note-taking and search capabilities
  - interactive learning tools, such as

    quizzes

    flashcards

    videos

    grammar podcasts

    additional grammar and proofreading exercises

    and more!

To access Basic Writing CourseMate, please visit <www.cengagebrain.com> and search for the ISBN of your title (from the back cover of your book) using the search box at the top of the page. This will take you to the product page for the book, where these resources can be found.

Together, the *Grassroots* textbook, its online tools, and this class will provide all the support you need to break bad grammatical habits and gain command of your writing. I wish you success.

S. F.

Preface

Grassroots with Readings grew out of my experience teaching and directing the writing lab at Bronx Community College of the City University of New York. The book is designed for a range of students—native and non-native speakers, diverse in age, ethnicity, and background—who have not yet mastered the basic writing skills so crucial for success in college and most careers. The hallmarks of *Grassroots'* successful pedagogy are its clear, step-by-step, inductive lessons; inspiring student and professional models; numerous engaging practices and writing assignments; and high-quality reading selections. I am proud that *Grassroots* has won juried awards for excellence and has remained through every edition the top-selling first-level developmental writing text in the United States. My goal in every revision is to rethink the book, seeing how it can better serve the needs of today's students and instructors.

In planning this important Tenth Anniversary Edition, I was struck by the large number of instructors refocusing on the basics. They wanted more engaging grammar lessons and better ways to help students move from facility with grammar exercises to proofreading their own work. Like many English teachers, I know that this transfer of skills to student writing sometimes seems like the "missing link," but I was intrigued. Instructors also reported that students today need more visuals and charts to help them grasp basic concepts, ever-clearer practice directions, and more definitions of English terms (conjunctions, for example)—perhaps reflecting the growing numbers of ESL students in our writing classes.

These thoughtful comments inspired the two most important changes in this new edition: its greatly expanded and reimagined coverage of proofreading and its improved grammar coverage. I am especially indebted to Professor Patricia A. Dungan of Austin Community College–Rio Grande for her astute review of *Grassroots'* grammar sections and her excellent, specific suggestions for building students' proofreading skills. Successfully proofreading one's own work requires a number of skills, from time management in the writing process to the habit of disciplined self-monitoring that most experts consider an essential quality of the critical thinker. The new proofreading material, drawing on my study of brain-based learning, critical thinking, and visual literacy, now frames and permeates the grammar units—2 through 8—the heart of *Grassroots*. Specific tools build students' self awareness and skills:

- A **new Chapter 6, "Proofreading to Correct Your Personal Error Patterns"** kick-starts the grammar units. This chapter introduces six basic proofreading strategies and tools that students can use to recognize, chart, and later correct their *personal error patterns*.

- A **removable error-pattern chart**, found at the front of the book, will help students proactively track their errors, one assignment at a time, rather than just waiting for the instructor's red marks.

- Every chapter in Units 2 through 8 now concludes with a **specific proofreading strategy** geared to the errors addressed in that chapter. Students can try out each strategy in a companion writing assignment.

- Of course, *Grassroots* retains its much-praised **proofreading practices** on contemporary topics in every chapter, and the mixed-error review, **Chapter 31, Putting Your Proofreading Skills to Work**, still assesses students' cumulative gains.

The presentation of grammar in this Tenth Edition has been updated and strengthened through a careful review of every sentence, instruction, and practice. The directions for many exercises have been clarified and made more specific. Early coverage of prepositions has been expanded and enriched. A new critical viewing practice asks students to study a photo of a rock climber and list as many prepositional phrases as possible to describe the action, and additional practices have enriched the coordination chapter. A chart of subordinating conjunctions and their meanings has been added, and many fill-in exercises, especially in the verb units, have been recast as proofreading or other types of exercises.

Grassroots' much-loved photo program is expanded with more than 45 images, plus new margin photos to highlight selected content. More captions contain critical thinking questions, and some images form the basis of writing assignments. My work on critical thinking and viewing has taught me that effectively using visual images means that every photo, ad, painting, or cartoon must be thoughtfully chosen to relate to and augment written content. Thus, the visuals in this text are not just pretty pictures and even go beyond helping visual learners; they train students to view critically the advertisements, websites, and other visuals that bombard them daily.

A new, visual design punctuates *Grassroots'* pedagogy. The colors, layout, wide margins, spatial "pauses" between concepts and between items in the practices are all designed to assist developmental learners as their brains focus on and absorb new material.

Grassroots' readings have been widely praised for their ability to spark discussion, critical thinking, and strong written responses. Four new thought-provoking readings complement student and instructor favorites from the last edition, for a total of 20. New to this edition are Sherman Alexie's "Superman and Me," nurse and stand-up comedian Beve Stevenson's "A Day in the Life of an ER Nurse," Gary Soto's "The Jacket," and Deborah Rosado Shaw's "The Power to Shine."

For those students and instructors who tell me they love the practices in *Grassroots* and all that fascinating and relevant subject matter, I have once again had great fun finding subjects I hope will seduce students into wanting to do their grammar and writing homework. Forty new practices, critical thinking, and critical viewing tasks explore the challenges of first-generation college students, video games that train soldiers, theories of why we dream, Shakira's work as a champion of education, baseball great Albert Pujols, longevity on the Greek Isle of Ikaria, the animator Hayao Miyazaki, a web physicist who calls herself "Science Babe," the successful puppies in prison program, and why some exercise makes us smarter.

Flexible Organization of the Text

The range of material and flexible format of *Grassroots with Readings* make this worktext and its much-expanded technology package adaptable to almost any teaching and learning situation: classroom, laboratory, or self-teaching. Each chapter is a self-contained lesson, so instructors may teach the chapters in any sequence that fits their course design. *Grassroots* is versatile enough to support many different approaches to basic writing instruction.

Comprehensive Support

Grassroots is a complete learning and teaching program that can be used by any instructor, whether full- or part-time, and that allows instructors to incorporate as much technology support as they wish. The text itself stands alone, with its numerous practices and comprehensive coverage, but is also available as an eBook with multimedia components, online homework and automatic grading solutions, and more. Major components of the *Grassroots* program include:

- **Aplia™ for *Grassroots*** is an online learning solution that helps your students become stronger writers. Aplia's clear, succinct, and engaging instruction and practice help students build the confidence they need to master basic writing and grammar skills with ongoing individualized practice, access to an electronic version of *Grassroots* and terminology and concepts that match the textbook, high-interest examples that demonstrate the principles of writing, and engaging multimedia content that engages students in the writing process. Learn more by visiting *www.aplia.com/developmentalenglish*.

- *Grassroots* includes **Basic Writing CourseMate**, a complement to your textbook. Basic Writing CourseMate includes

    - an interactive eBook

    - interactive teaching and learning tools, such as

        quizzes

        flashcards

        videos

        grammar podcasts

        additional grammar and proofreading exercises

    - Engagement Tracker, a first-of-its-kind tool that monitors student engagement in the course

    Access these resources at *login.cengage.com*.

- **Annotated Instructor's Edition.** The **Annotated Instructor's Edition** includes answers to every practice in the text. In addition, margin annotations provide Teaching Tips with teaching suggestions for specific text sections or practice exercises, new Learning Styles Tips with suggestions for reaching students with particular learning styles, and ESL Tips with suggestions for teaching English Language Learners.

- **Instructor's Resource Manual and Test Bank.** The Instructor's Resource Manual and Test Bank offers suggestions for the new instructor looking for support or the more experienced teacher looking for ideas. Advice about instructional methods, assignments, and uses of the book's features are based on the author's many years of classroom teaching experience. Notes on the book's units provide an overview of concepts and skills addressed in each chapter along with some specific teaching suggestions. A robust Test Bank including diagnostic and mastery tests, chapter tests, and unit tests offers instructors a wide array of supplementary assessments that can be used as additional practice or a way to monitor students' progress.

- **PowerLecture.** Organized around topics covered in the book, this easy-to-use tool helps you assemble, edit, and present tailored multimedia lectures. You can create a lecture from scratch, customize the provided templates, or use the readymade Microsoft PowerPoint slides as they are. The CD-ROM also includes the Instructor's Resource Manual, the Test Bank, and web links. Available at no additional charge to adopters of this text.

● **CourseCare.** Available exclusively to Cengage Learning, **CourseCare** is a revolutionary program designed to provide you and your students with an unparalleled user experience with your Cengage Learning digital solution. Digital solutions experts provide you with one-on-one service every step of the way—from finding the right solution for your course to training to ongoing support—helping you to drive student engagement.

Acknowledgments

The author wishes to thank these reviewers and colleagues. Their thoughtful comments and suggestions helped strengthen this Tenth Edition.

Nicole Argall	*College of Menominee Nation*
Geoffrey Bellah	*Orange Coast College*
Steven J. Belluscio	*Borough of Manhattan Community College/ CUNY*
Melvin Brooks	*Baltimore City Community College*
Krysten Buchanan	*Catawba Valley Community College*
Rochelle Dahmer	*Jones County Junior College*
Beverly F. Dile	*Elizabethtown Community and Technical College*
Patricia Dungan	*Austin Community College–Rio Grande Campus*
Marianne Dzik	*Illinois Valley Community College*
Michelle D. Fields	*Big Sandy Community and Technical College*
Darius Frasure	*Mountain View College*
Deborah P. Fuller	*Bunker Hill Community College*
Steven Garcia	*Riverside City College*
Bill W. Hall	*St. Petersburg College*
Catherine Higdon	*Tarrant County College, South Campus*
Deborah Johnson-Evans	*English Language Institute at the University of Texas at Arlington*
Lisa Kern-Lipscomb	*Tidewater Community College–Portsmouth Campus*
Laura Kingston	*South Seattle Community College*
Jaquelyn S. Lyman	*Anne Arundel Community College*
Cynthia Maxson	*Rio Salado College*
Jennifer McCann	*Bay de Noc Community College*
Christopher Morelock	*Walters State Community College*
Laura Neubauer	*Saddleback College*
Karen Owen-Bogan	*Central Carolina Community College*
Michelle Van de Sande	*Arapahoe Community College*
Helena Zacharis	*Palm Beach State College*

I am indebted to the wonderful team at Cengage who helped make this the best revision of *Grassroots* yet. My deep thanks to Annie Todd, Director of Developmental Studies, for her vision, brains, creativity, and strong support of my work; Judith Fifer, Senior Development Editor, whose deep understanding of *Grassroots,* skill and grace as a problem solver, and long friendship have enriched this book; Marcy Kagan, photo researcher and artist whose eye for great images shines in *Grassroots'* pages and whose friendship I treasure; Aimee Bear, Content Product Manager, who supervised the great new design and production of the book; Kirsten Stoller, Senior Marketing Manager, for her fantastic instincts and ability to spread the word about my textbooks and their mission; and for their work on the supplements, reviews, and so much else, Melanie Opacki, Assistant Editor, Amy Gibbons, Media Editor, and Matthew Conte, Editorial Assistant.

Professor Patricia Dungan, of Austin Community College–Rio Grande, began as a reviewer and became a key contributor to this edition. Professor Dungan made wonderful suggestions for improving the text, pointed out confusing practice directions in *Grassroots,* and shared her own classroom strategies for getting students to proofread for their mistakes. She patiently read drafts of the new proofreading chapter and proofreading strategies. Meeting and working with her across the miles was one of the surprise joys of the revision. The talented Ann Marie Radaskiewicz, Dean of the Developmental Education Division at Western Piedmont Community College, North Carolina, has played a vital role, researching and drafting a number of new practices and helping me manage *Grassroots'* many supplements and online resources. Her professionalism and can-do cheer make working with her a delight. Professor Karen Cox of San Francisco City College brainstormed ideas for new high-interest topics and discussed plans for this revision with her usual intelligence and wit; discussing our mission as writing teachers and the issues we face always expands my horizon.

My love and eternal gratitude to the friends who supported me during this very difficult year—especially Maggie Smith, Colleen Huff, Trisha Nelson, Bryan Hoffman, Elaine and Jay Unkeless, Ginger Chaich, Pauline Kubic, Pat Vince, and Laraine Flemming. Through it all, this beautiful *Grassroots* managed to be born. I dedicate this Tenth Anniversary Edition to my beloved mother, the watercolor artist Harriet Fawcett, who died July 23, 2010, and to my family—my brother David Fawcett, David's partner Edward Brown, and my husband Richard Donovan, who have taught me that love is so much greater than death.

S. F.

Grassroots with Readings:
The Writer's Workbook

Tenth Edition

UNIT 1

Writing Effective Paragraphs

The goal of Grassroots *is to make you a better writer, and Unit 1 is key to your success. In this unit, you will*

- Learn the importance of subject, audience, and purpose
- Learn the parts of a good paragraph
- Practice the paragraph-writing process
- Learn how to revise and improve your paragraphs
- Apply these skills to exam questions and short essays
- Learn proofreading strategies to find and correct your own errors

Spotlight on Writing

Here, writer Alice Walker recalls her mother's extraordinary talent. If possible, read the paragraph aloud.

My mother adorned with flowers whatever shabby house we were forced to live in, and not just your typical straggly country stand of zinnias, either. She planted ambitious gardens—and still does—with over fifty different varieties of plants that bloom profusely from early March until late November. Before she left home for the fields, she watered her flowers, chopped up the grass, and laid out new beds. When she returned from the fields, she might divide clumps of bulbs, dig a cold pit, uproot and replant roses, or prune branches from her taller bushes or trees—until night came and it was too dark to see.

Alice Walker, "In Search of Our Mothers' Gardens"

- Ms. Walker's well-written paragraph brings to life her mother's passion for flowers. Are any words and details especially vivid? Why do you think Walker's mother worked so hard on her gardening?

- Good writing can make us remember, see, feel, or think in certain ways. Unit 1 will guide you through the steps of writing well and give you tools to improve your writing.

Writing Ideas

- *An activity that you or someone close to you passionately enjoys*
- *Someone who inspires you with her or his ambition or creativity*

CHAPTER 1

Exploring the Writing Process

A: The Writing Process

B: Subject, Audience, and Purpose

C: Guidelines for Submitting Written Work

D id you know that the most successful students and employees are people who write well? In fact, many good jobs today require excellent writing and communication skills in fields as varied as computer technology, health sciences, education, and social services.

The goal of this book is to help you become a better and more confident writer. You will realize that the ability to write well is not a magical talent that some people possess and others don't but rather a life skill that can be learned. I invite you now to make a decision to excel in this course. It will be one of the best investments you could ever make in yourself, your education, and your future. Let *Grassroots* be your guide, and enjoy the journey.

A. The Writing Process

This chapter will give you an overview of the writing process, as well as some tips on how to approach your writing assignments in college. Many people have the mistaken idea that good writers just sit down and write a perfect paper or assignment from start to finish. In fact, experienced writers go through a **process** consisting of steps like these:

1 Prewriting
- Thinking about possible subjects
- Freely jotting down ideas on paper or computer
- Narrowing the subject and writing it as one sentence
- Deciding which ideas to include
- Arranging ideas in a plan or outline

2 Writing
- Writing a first draft

3 Rewriting
- Rethinking, rearranging, and revising as necessary
- Writing one or more new drafts
- Proofreading for grammar and spelling errors

Writing is a personal and often messy process. Writers don't all perform these steps in the same order, and they may have to go through some steps more than once. However, most writers **prewrite**, **write**, **rewrite**—and **proofread**.

It is important that you set aside enough time to complete every step in the writing process. A technique called **backwards planning** helps many students manage their writing time. Begin with the assignment's due date and plan to complete each step on a different day. Using the calendar below, one student first wrote down the Friday deadline for her paragraph assignment. Then, working backwards, she decided to proofread on Thursday and again Friday morning, to revise her paragraph on Wednesday, write her first draft on Tuesday, and start jotting and organizing her ideas on Monday.

SUNDAY	MONDAY	TUESDAY	WEDNESDAY	THURSDAY	FRIDAY	SATURDAY
1	2	3	4	5	6	7
	Jot down and organize ideas for paragraph.	Write first draft of paragraph.	Revise paragraph.	Proofread.	Proofread again. Final draft due!	

PRACTICE 1

Self-Assessment

Choose something that you wrote recently for a class or for work and think about the *process* you followed in writing it. With a group of three or four classmates, or in your notebook, answer these questions:

1. Did I do any planning or prewriting—or did I just start writing the assignment?
2. How much time did I spend improving and revising my work?
3. Was I able to spot and correct my own grammar and spelling errors?
4. What ideas or beliefs do I have about writing? (Examples: *In my field, I won't need to write*, or *English teachers make a bigger deal about errors than anyone else*.) Do any of my beliefs get in the way of my progress?
5. What one change in my writing process would most improve my writing? Spending more time for prewriting? Spending more time revising? Improving my proofreading skills?

PRACTICE 2

Bring in several newspaper help-wanted sections. In a group with four or five classmates, study the ads in career fields that interest you. Next, count the number of ads that stress writing and communication skills. Alternately, if you have Internet access, you could visit a job-search website like ‹**http://www.monster.com**› and perform the same exercise. Be prepared to present your findings to the class.

PRACTICE 3

Using a calendar, employ the *backwards planning technique* to plan the steps needed to complete your next writing assignment.

B. Subject, Audience, and Purpose

As you begin a writing assignment, give some thought to your **subject**, **audience**, and **purpose**.

When your instructor assigns a broad **subject**, try to focus on one aspect that interests you. For example, suppose the broad subject is *music*, and you play the conga drums. You might focus on why you play them rather than some other instrument or on what drumming means to you. Whenever possible, choose subjects you know and care about: observing your neighborhood come to life in the morning, riding a dirt bike, helping a child become more confident, learning more about your computer. Your answers to such questions, like those listed below, will suggest promising writing ideas. Keep a list of the best ones.

To find or focus your subject, ask

- What special experience or knowledge do I have?
- What angers, saddens, or inspires me?
- What campus, job, or community problem do I have ideas about solving?
- What story in the news affected me recently?

How you approach your subject will depend on your **audience**, your readers. Are you writing for classmates, a professor, people who know about your subject, or people who do not? For instance, if you are writing about weight training, and your readers have never been inside a gym, you will approach your subject in a simple and basic way, perhaps stressing the benefits of weightlifting. An audience of bodybuilders, however, already knows these things; for bodybuilders, you would write in more depth, perhaps focusing on how to develop one muscle group.

To focus on your audience, ask

- For whom am I writing? Who will read this?
- Are they beginners or experts? How much do they know about the subject?
- Do I think they will agree or disagree with my ideas?

Finally, keeping your **purpose** in mind helps you know what to write. Do you want to *explain* something to your readers, *convince* them that a certain point of view is correct, *describe* something, or just *tell a good story*? If your purpose is to persuade parents to support having school uniforms, you can explain that uniforms lower clothing costs and may reduce student crime. However, if your purpose is to convince students that uniforms are a good idea, you might approach the subject differently, emphasizing how stylish the uniforms look or why students from other schools feel that uniforms improve their school atmosphere.

PRACTICE 4

List five subjects you might like to write about. Consider your audience and purpose. For whom are you writing? What do you want them to know about your subject? For ideas, reread the boxed questions.

	Subject	Audience	Purpose
EXAMPLE:	how to make a Greek salad	inexperienced cooks	to show how easy it is to make a great Greek salad

	Subject	Audience	Purpose
1.	_____	_____	_____
2.	_____	_____	_____
3.	_____	_____	_____
4.	_____	_____	_____
5.	_____	_____	_____

PRACTICE 5

With a group of three or four classmates, or on your own, jot down ideas for the following two writing tasks. Notice how your points and details differ depending on your audience and purpose. (If you are not employed, write about a job with which you are familiar.)

1. For a new co-worker, you plan to write a description of a typical day on your job. Your purpose is to help train this person, who will perform the same duties you do. Your supervisor will need to approve what you write.

2. For one of your closest friends, you plan to write a description of a typical day on your job. Your purpose is to make your friend laugh because he or she has been feeling down recently.

PRACTICE 6

Study the advertisement shown below and then answer these questions: What *subject* is the ad addressing? Who do you think is the target *audience*? What is the ad's intended *purpose*? In your view, how successful is the ad in achieving its purpose? Why or why not?

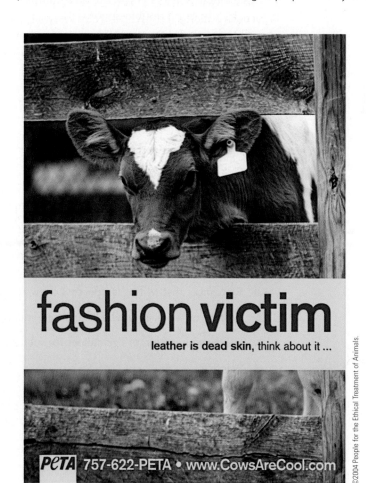

©2004 People for the Ethical Treatment of Animals.

PRACTICE 7

In a group with three or four classmates, read the following classified ads from real city newspapers around the country. The *subject* of each ad is a product or service that is for sale, the *audience* is the potential customer, and the *purpose* is to convince that customer to buy the product or service. How does each ad writer undercut his or her purpose? How would you revise each ad so that it better achieves its apparent purpose?

1. Do you need a dramatic new look? Visit our plastered surgeons.
2. We do not tear your clothing with machinery. We do it carefully by hand.
3. Now is your chance to have your ears pierced and get an extra pair to take home free.
4. Tired of cleaning yourself? Let me do it.
5. Auto repair service. Try us once, and you'll never go anywhere again.

C. Guidelines for Submitting Written Work

Learn your instructor's requirements for submitting written work, as these may vary from class to class. Here are some general guidelines. Write in any special instructions.

1. Choose sturdy, white, 8½-by-11-inch paper, lined if you write by hand, plain if you use a computer.
2. Clearly write your name, the date, and any other required information, using the format requested by your instructor.
3. If you write by hand, do so neatly in black or dark blue ink.
4. Write on only one side of the paper.
5. Double-space if you write on a computer. Some instructors also want handwriting double-spaced.
6. Leave margins of at least one inch on all sides.
7. Number each page of your assignment, starting with page 2. Place the numbers at the top of each page, either centered or in the top right corner.

Other guidelines: _____

_____

_____

Chapter Highlights

Tips for Succeeding in This Course

- Remember that writing is a process: prewriting, writing, and rewriting.
- Before you write, always be clear about your subject, audience, and purpose.
- Follow your instructor's guidelines for submitting written work.
- Practice.

EXPLORING ONLINE

Throughout this text, the Exploring Online feature will suggest ways that you can use the Internet to improve your writing and grammar skills. You will find that if you need extra writing help, online writing centers (called OWLs) can be a great resource. Many provide extra review or practice in areas in which you might need assistance. You will want to do some searching to find the best sites for your needs, but here are two excellent OWL sites to explore:

<http://owl.english.purdue.edu/> Purdue University.

<http://grammar.ccc.commnet.edu/grammar/> Capital Community College.

 View an integrated eBook and chapter-specific interactive learning tools, including flashcards, quizzes, videos, and extra help tracking and correcting your Personal Error Patterns, in your Basic Writing CourseMate, accessed through <www.cengagebrain.com>.

CHAPTER 2

Prewriting to Generate Ideas

A: Freewriting

B: Brainstorming

C: Clustering

D: Keeping a Journal

The author of this book used to teach ice skating. On the first day of class, her students practiced falling. Once they knew how to fall without fear, they were free to learn to skate.

Writing is much like ice skating: the more you practice, the better you get. If you are free to make mistakes, you'll want to practice, and you'll look forward to new writing challenges.

The problem is that many people avoid writing. Faced with an English composition or a report at work, they put it off and then scribble something at the last minute. Other people sit staring at the blank page or computer screen—writing a sentence, crossing it out, unable to get started. In this chapter, you will learn four useful prewriting techniques that will help you jump-start your writing process and generate lots of ideas: **freewriting**, **brainstorming**, **clustering**, and **keeping a journal**.

A. Freewriting

Freewriting is a method many writers use to warm up and get ideas. Here are the guidelines: For five or ten full minutes, write without stopping. Don't worry about grammar or about writing complete sentences; just set a timer and go. If you get stuck, repeat or rhyme the last word you wrote, but keep writing nonstop until the timer sounds. Afterward, read what you have written, and underline any parts you like.

Freewriting is a wonderful way to let your ideas pour out without getting stuck by worrying too soon about correctness or "good writing." Sometimes freewriting produces nonsense, but often it provides interesting ideas for further thinking and writing. **Focused freewriting** can help you find subjects to write about.

Focused Freewriting

In *focused freewriting*, you try to focus your thoughts on one subject as you freewrite. The subject can be one assigned by your instructor, one you choose, or one you discover in unfocused freewriting.

Here is one student's focused freewriting on the topic *someone who strongly influenced me.*

> Thin, thinner, weak, weaker. You stopped cooking for yourself—forced yourself to choke down cans of nutrition. Your chest caved in; your bones stuck out. You never asked, Why me? With a weak laugh you asked, Why not me? I had a wonderful life, a great job, a good marriage while it lasted. Have beautiful kids. Your wife divorced you—couldn't stand to watch you die, couldn't stand to have her life fall apart the way your body was falling apart. I watched you stumble, trip over your own feet, sink, fall down. I held you up. Now I wonder which one of us was holding the other one up. I saw you shiver in your summer jacket because you didn't have the strength to put on your heavy coat. Bought you a feather-light winter jacket, saw your eyes fill with tears of pleasure and gratitude. You said they would find you at the bottom of the stairs. When they called to tell me we'd lost you, the news wasn't unexpected, but the pain came in huge waves. Heart gave out, they said. Your daughter found you crumpled at the foot of the stairs. How did you know? What else did you guess?
>
> *Daniel Corteau, student*

- This student later used his freewriting as the basis for an excellent paragraph.

- Underline any words or lines that you find especially striking or powerful. Be prepared to discuss your choices.

- How was the writer influenced by the man he describes?

PRACTICE 1

1. Set a timer for ten minutes, or have someone time you. Freewrite without stopping for the full ten minutes. Repeat or rhyme words if you get stuck, but keep writing! Don't let your pen or pencil leave the page or your fingers leave the keyboard.

2. When you finish, write down one or two words that describe how you feel while freewriting. _____

3. Now read your freewriting. Underline any words or lines you like—anything that strikes you as powerful, moving, funny, or important. If nothing strikes you, that's okay.

PRACTICE 2

Now choose one word or idea from your freewriting or from the following list. Focus your thoughts on it, and do a ten-minute focused freewriting. Try to stick to the topic, but don't worry too much about it. Just keep writing! When you finish, read and underline any striking lines or ideas.

1. home
2. a good student
3. the biggest lie
4. a dream
5. someone who influenced you
6. your experiences with writing
7. the smell of _____
8. strength

PRACTICE 3

Try two more focused freewritings at home, each one ten minutes long. Do them at different times of the day when you have a few quiet moments. If possible, use a timer: set it for ten minutes, and then write fast until it rings. Later, read your freewritings, and underline any ideas or passages you might like to write more about.

B. Brainstorming

Brainstorming means freely jotting down ideas about a topic on paper or on a computer. As in freewriting, the purpose of brainstorming is to get as many ideas down as possible so that you will have something to work with later. Just write down everything that comes to mind about a topic—words and phrases, ideas, details, examples, little stories. Once you have brainstormed, read over your list, underlining any ideas you might want to develop further.

Here is one student's brainstorming list on *an interesting job*:

> midtown messenger
>
> frustrating but free
>
> I know the city backward and forward
>
> good bike needed
>
> fast, ever-changing, dangerous
>
> drivers hate messengers—we dart in and out of traffic
>
> old clothes don't get respect
>
> I wear the best Descent racing gear, a Giro helmet
>
> people respect you more
>
> I got tipped $100 for carrying a crystal vase from the showroom to Wall Street in 15 minutes
>
> other times I get stiffed
>
> lessons I've learned—controlling my temper
>
> having dignity
>
> staying calm no matter what—insane drivers, deadlines, rudeness
>
> weirdly, I like my job

As he brainstormed, this writer produced many interesting facts and details about his job as a bicycle messenger, all in just a few minutes. He might want to underline the ideas that most interest him—perhaps the time he was tipped $100—and then brainstorm again for more details.

PRACTICE 4

Choose one of the following topics that interests you, and write it at the top of your page. Then brainstorm! Write anything that comes into your head about the topic. Let your ideas flow.

1. a singer or a musician
2. the future
3. an intriguing job
4. a story in the news
5. the best/worst class I've ever had
6. making a difference
7. a place to which I never want to return
8. a community problem

After you fill a page with your list, read it over, underlining the most interesting ideas. Draw arrows to connect related ideas. Do you find one idea that might be the subject of a paper?

C. Clustering

Some writers find *clustering* or mapping an effective way to get ideas onto paper. To begin clustering, write one idea or topic—usually one word—in the center of your paper. Then let your mind make associations, and write those ideas down, branching out from the center. When one idea suggests other ideas, details, or examples, jot down those around it in a cluster, like this:

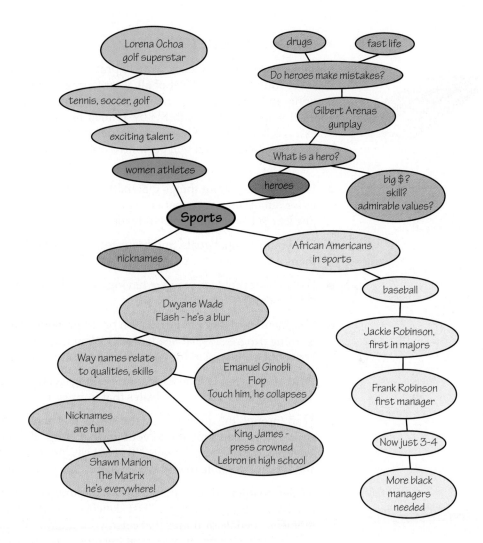

Once this student filled a page with clustered ideas about the word *sports*, his next step was choosing the cluster that most interested him and writing further. He might even have wanted to freewrite for more ideas.

PRACTICE 5

Read over the clustering map above. If you were giving advice to the writer, which cluster or branch do you think would make the most interesting paper? Why?

PRACTICE 6 Choose one of these topics or another topic that interests you. Write it in the center of a piece of paper and then try clustering. Keep writing down associations until you have filled the page.

1. movies
2. a pet
3. a lesson
4. sports

5. my hometown
6. self-esteem
7. a relative
8. someone I don't understand

D. Keeping a Journal

Keeping a journal is an excellent way to practice your writing skills and to discover ideas for future writing. Most of all, your journal is a place to record your private thoughts and important experiences. Open a journal file on your computer, or get yourself a special book with 8½-by-11-inch lined paper. Every night, or several times a week, write for at least ten minutes in your journal.

What you write about will be limited only by your imagination. Here are some ideas:

● Write in detail about things that matter to you—family relationships, falling in (or out of) love, an experience at school or work, something important you just learned, something you did well.

● List your personal goals, and brainstorm possible steps toward achieving them.

● Write about problems you are having, and "think on paper" about ways to solve them.

● Comment on classroom instruction or assignments, and evaluate your learning progress. What needs work? What questions do you need to ask? Write out a study plan for yourself and refer to it regularly.

● Write down your responses to your reading—class assignments, newspaper items, magazine articles, websites that impress or anger you.

● Read through the quotations at the end of this book until you find one that strikes you. Then copy it into your journal, think about it, and write. For example, Agnes Repplier says, "It is not easy to find happiness in ourselves, and it is not possible to find it elsewhere." Do you agree with her?

● Be alert to interesting writing topics all around you. If possible, carry a notebook during the day for "fast sketches." Jot down moving or funny moments, people or things that catch your attention—an overworked waitress in a restaurant, a scene at the day-care center where you leave your child, a man trying to persuade an officer not to give him a parking ticket.

You will soon find that ideas for writing will occur to you all day long. Before they slip away, capture them in words. Writing is like ice skating. You have to practice.

PRACTICE 7 Write in your journal for at least ten minutes three times a week.

At the end of each week, read what you have written. Underline striking passages, and mark interesting topics and ideas that you would like to explore further.

As you complete the exercises in this book and work on the writing assignments, try all four techniques—freewriting, brainstorming, clustering, and keeping a journal—and see which ones work best for you.

PRACTICE 8

From your journal, choose one or two passages that you might want to rewrite and allow others to read. Put a check beside each of those passages or mark them with sticky notes so that you can find them easily later. Underline the parts you like best. Can you already see ways you might rewrite and improve the writing?

Chapter Highlights

To get started and to discover your ideas, try these techniques.

- Focused freewriting: freewriting for five or ten minutes about one topic

- Brainstorming: freely jotting down many ideas about a topic

- Clustering: making word associations on paper

- Keeping a journal: writing regularly about things that interest and move you

EXPLORING ONLINE

<http://owl.english.purdue.edu/owl/resources/673/01> If you still feel stuck when you start to write, try these techniques from Purdue University's famous OWL (Online Writing Lab).

<http://aaweb.gallaudet.edu/CLAST/Tutorial_and_Instructional_Programs/ English_Works/Writing/Prewriting_Writing_and_Revising/Prewriting_ Strategies.html> Review or print this handy chart of prewriting strategies.

 View an integrated eBook and chapter-specific interactive learning tools, including flashcards, quizzes, videos, and extra help tracking and correcting your Personal Error Patterns, in your Basic Writing CourseMate, accessed through <www.cengagebrain.com>.

CHAPTER **3**

Developing Effective Paragraphs

A: Defining the Paragraph and the Topic Sentence

B: Narrowing the Topic and Writing the Topic Sentence

C: Generating Ideas for the Body of the Paragraph

D: Selecting and Dropping Ideas

E: Arranging Ideas in a Plan or an Outline

F: Writing and Revising the Paragraph

G: Proofreading and Writing the Final Draft

The paragraph is the basic unit of writing. This chapter will guide you through the process of writing paragraphs.

A. Defining the Paragraph and the Topic Sentence

A *paragraph* is a group of related sentences that develop one main idea. Although a paragraph has no definite length, it is often four to twelve sentences long. A paragraph usually appears with other paragraphs in a longer piece of writing—an essay, a letter, or an article, for example.

A paragraph looks like this on the page:

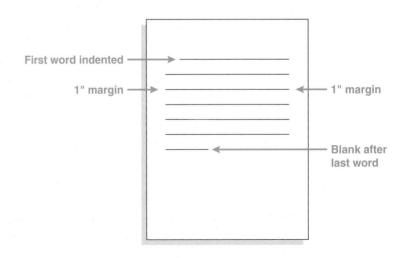

First word indented

1" margin — 1" margin

Blank after last word

- Clearly **indent** the first word of every paragraph about 1 inch (or one tab on the computer).

- Extend every line of a paragraph as close to the right-hand margin as possible.

- If the last word of the paragraph comes before the end of the line, however, leave the rest of the line blank.

Topic Sentence and Body

Most paragraphs contain one main idea to which all the sentences relate. The **topic sentence** states this main idea. The **body** of the paragraph supports this main idea with specific details, facts, and examples.

> When I was growing up, my older brother Joe was the greatest person in my world. If anyone teased me about my braces or buckteeth, he fiercely defended me. When one boy insisted on calling me "Fang," Joe threatened to knock his teeth out. It worked—no more teasing. My brother always chose me to play on his baseball teams though I was a terrible hitter. Even after he got his driver's license, he didn't abandon me. Instead, every Sunday, the two of us went for a drive. We might stop for cheeseburgers, go to a computer showroom, drive past some girl's house, or just laugh and talk. It was one of childhood's mysteries that such a wonderful brother loved me.
>
> *Jeremiah Woolrich, student*

- The first sentence of this paragraph is the *topic sentence*. It states in a general way the main idea of the paragraph: that *Joe was the greatest person in my world*. Although the topic sentence can appear anywhere in the paragraph, it is often the first sentence.

- The rest of the paragraph, the *body*, fully explains this statement with details about braces and buckteeth, baseball teams, Sunday drives, cheeseburgers, and so forth.

- Note that the final sentence provides a brief conclusion so that the paragraph *feels* finished.

PRACTICE 1

Each group of sentences below can be arranged and written as a paragraph. Circle the letter of the sentence that would be the best topic sentence. REMEMBER: The topic sentence states the main idea of the entire paragraph and includes all the other ideas.

EXAMPLE: a. Speed-walking three times a week is part of my routine.
b. Staying healthy and fit is important to me.
c. Every night, I get at least seven hours of sleep.
d. I eat as many fresh fruits and vegetables as possible.

(Sentence b is more general than the other sentences; it would be the best topic sentence.)

1. a. Some colleges are experimenting with using iPods to deliver instructional material, complete with musical clips, news, and even video.

   b. Runners, hikers, and bicyclists sometimes use their iPods as personal trainers that plan a route and then provide maps, distances, and time goals.

c. Although most people still think of the iPod as a digital music player, others are using these gadgets in creative and innovative ways.

d. Video iPod owners can search for their soul mates using PodDater software to download short video clips and profiles of available singles.

2. a. Each prisoner in the program receives a puppy, which he feeds, cares for, and trains to be a service dog for a combat veteran.

b. The convicted felons often feel, many for the first time, a sense of responsibility, compassion for other creatures, and the power of unconditional love.

c. The successful Puppies Behind Bars program improves the lives of both inmates and disabled war veterans.

d. When a dog "graduates," each trainer presents his dog to a vet who returned from Iraq or Afghanistan with brain or bodily injuries.

e. The disabled soldiers say that the dogs not only open doors, turn on lights, and dial 911 on special phones but greatly ease their anxiety and depression.

3. a. When his family moved to Los Angeles in 1974, ten-year-old Lenny won a place in the California Boys Choir and taught himself to play many instruments.

b. As a teen, he studied music at the Berkeley Hills School and created the dramatic look for which he is now famous.

c. Before he was ten, he had convinced his parents to take him to concerts by James Brown, Duke Ellington, and the Jackson 5.

d. Lenny and his father produced his first album, *Let Love Rule*, which won him a Virgin Records contract and huge numbers of fans.

e. A childhood love of performing music launched rocker and songwriter Lenny Kravitz on the path to stardom.

f. As a toddler in Brooklyn, New York, Lenny made his own drum set out of pots and pans.

4. a. Physical courage allows soldiers or athletes to endure bodily pain or danger.

b. Those with social courage dare to expose their deep feelings in order to build close relationships.

c. Those rare people who stand up for their beliefs despite public pressure possess moral courage.

d. Inventors and artists show creative courage when they break out of old ways of seeing and doing things.

e. Psychologist Rollo May claimed that there are four different types of courage.

5. a. She watched her mother and father, who had only an elementary school education, struggle to feed and clothe the family.

b. Today, Aguilera is president of the Congressional Hispanic Caucus Institute (CHCI), which supports Hispanic students with scholarships and internships.

c. For Esther Aguilera, education is the key that unlocks the American dream.

d. Esther became an excellent student, earned her bachelor's degree in public policy, and decided to help other Hispanics aim high and succeed in college.

e. Born in Mexico, five-year-old Esther arrived in California with her parents and five siblings.

6. a. Many old toys and household objects are now collectors' items.

   b. A 1959 Barbie doll still in its original box recently sold for $3,552 on the eBay auction website.

   c. Many collectors now hunt for Fiesta dinnerware, made in the 1930s, in garage sales and resale shops.

   d. Star Wars action figures and vintage baseball cards are among the ten most wanted collectibles.

7. a. You should read the ingredients on every package of food you buy.

   b. Children should not eat mandelona, which is made from peanuts soaked in almond flavoring.

   c. Avoid buying food from bins that do not list ingredients.

   d. If your child is allergic to peanuts, you need to be constantly on the alert.

   e. In a restaurant, tongs may have been used to pick up items containing peanuts.

8. a. In our increasingly global economy, employees who can communicate with non-English-speaking customers and overseas colleagues are in demand at many American companies.

   b. People who can speak and write two languages fluently possess a valuable professional, social, and mental asset.

   c. Studies confirm that bilingualism boosts brain power because adults who grew up speaking two language stay sharper and quicker later in life.

   d. Bilingualism brings personal rewards, such as the ability to bridge cultural boundaries and broaden one's social network to include people of other nationalities and ethnic groups.

B. Narrowing the Topic and Writing the Topic Sentence

The rest of this chapter will guide you through the process of writing paragraphs of your own. Here are the steps we will discuss:

1. Narrowing the topic and writing the topic sentence
2. Generating ideas for the body
3. Selecting and dropping ideas
4. Grouping ideas in a plan
5. Writing and revising the paragraph
6. Proofreading and writing the final draft

Narrowing the Topic

Often your first step as a writer will be **narrowing** a broad topic—one assigned by your instructor, one you have thought of yourself, or one suggested by a particular writing task, like a letter. That is, you must cut the topic down to size and choose one aspect that interests you.

Assume, for example, that you are asked to write a paragraph describing a person you know. The trick is to choose someone you would *like* to write about, someone who interests you and would probably also interest your audience of readers.

At this point, many writers find it helpful to think on paper by *brainstorming*, *freewriting*, or *clustering*.* As you jot down or freely write ideas, ask yourself questions. Whom do I love, hate, or admire? Who is the funniest or most unusual person I know? Is there a family member or friend about whom others might like to read?

Suppose you choose to write about your friend Beverly. *Beverly* is too broad a topic for one paragraph. Therefore, you should limit your topic further, choosing just one of her qualities or acts. What is unusual about her? What might interest others? Perhaps what stands out in your mind is that Beverly is a determined person who doesn't let difficulties defeat her. You have now *narrowed* your broad topic to *Beverly's determination*.

You might visualize the process like this:

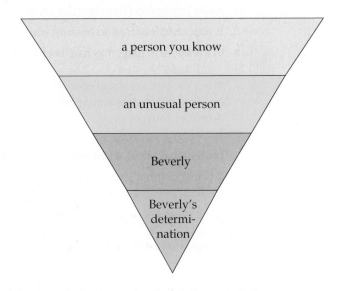

a person you know

an unusual person

Beverly

Beverly's determination

PRACTICE 2

Good writers need a clear understanding of general and specific—that is, which ideas are general and which are specific. Number the items in each group below, with 1 being the most specific and limited, 2 being the second most specific, and the highest number being the most general.

1. __ chairs
   __ furniture
   __ Grandma's oak rocking chair
   __ household contents

2. __ Malian singer Habib Koité
   __ music
   __ African music
   __ music of Mali, West Africa
   __ sound

3. __ rose
   __ flowering plants
   __ living things
   __ plants
   __ the Betty Boop rose

4. __ *Union-Tribune* sports writer Jim Jackson
   __ California
   __ North America
   __ *San Diego Union-Tribune* office building
   __ Earth

* Brainstorming is discussed further in Part C. Also see Chapter 2 for more information about prewriting.

5. ___ athletes

    ___ Brodeur's agility

    ___ hockey players

    ___ goalies

    ___ New Jersey Devils goalie
    Martin Brodeur

6. ___ actresses

    ___ movie stars

    ___ Helen Mirren

    ___ successful older actresses

    ___ human beings

Writing the Topic Sentence

The next step is to write your **topic sentence**, which clearly states, in sentence form, your narrowed topic and a point about that topic. This step helps you further focus your topic by forcing you to make a statement about it. That statement sets forth one main idea that the rest of your paragraph will support and explain. A topic sentence can be very simple (*Beverly is very determined*), or, better yet, it can state your attitude or point of view about the topic (*Beverly's determination inspires admiration*).

Think of the topic sentence as having two parts: a **topic** and a **controlling idea**. The controlling idea states the writer's attitude, angle, or point of view about the topic.

                         topic   **controlling idea**

Topic sentence: Beverly's determination inspires admiration.

All topics can have many possible topic sentences, depending on the writer's interests and point of view. The controlling idea helps you focus on just one aspect. Here are three possible topic sentences about the topic *attending college*:

(1) Attending college has revolutionized my career plans.

(2) Attending college has put me in debt.

(3) Attending college is exhausting but rewarding.

- These topic sentences all explore the same topic—attending college—but each controlling idea is different. The controlling idea in topic sentence (1) is *has revolutionized my career plans*.

- What is the controlling idea in topic sentence (2)?

    _____

- What is the controlling idea in topic sentence (3)?

    _____

● Notice the way each controlling idea lets the reader know what that paragraph will be about. By choosing different key words, a writer can angle any topic in different directions. If you were assigned the topic *attending college*, what would your topic sentence be?

_____

_____

PRACTICE 3

Read each topic sentence below. Circle the topic and underline the controlling idea.

EXAMPLE: (Computer games) improved my study skills.

1. Hybrid cars offer monetary advantages over gasoline vehicles.

2. White-water rafting increased my self-confidence.

3. Ed Bradley achieved many firsts as a television journalist.

4. Immigrants frequently are stereotyped by native-born Americans.

5. A course in financial planning should be required of all college freshmen.

Writing Limited and Complete Topic Sentences

Check to make sure your topic sentence is *limited* and *complete*. Your topic sentence should be **limited**. It should make a point that is neither too broad nor too narrow to be supported in a paragraph. As a rule, the more specific and well defined the topic sentence, the better the paragraph. Which of these topic sentences do you think will produce the best paragraph?

(1) My recent trip to Colorado was really bad.

(2) My recent trip to Colorado was disappointing because the weather ruined my camping plans.

● Topic sentence (1) is so broad that the paragraph could include almost anything.

● Topic sentence (2), on the other hand, is *limited* enough to provide the main idea for a good paragraph: how terrible weather ruined the writer's camping plans.

(3) The Each-One-Reach-One tutoring program encourages academic excellence at Chester Elementary School.

(4) Tutoring programs can be found all over the country.

- Topic sentence (3) is limited enough to provide the main idea for a good paragraph. Reading this topic sentence, what do you expect the paragraph to include?

  _____

  _____

- Topic sentence (4) lacks a limited point. Reading this sentence, someone cannot guess what the paragraph will be about.

In addition, the topic sentence must be a **complete sentence**; it must contain a subject and a verb and express a complete thought.* Do not confuse a topic with a topic sentence. For example, *the heroism of Captain "Sully" Sullenberger* cannot be a topic sentence because it is not a complete sentence. Here is one possible topic sentence: *Because Captain "Sully" Sullenberger landed a packed airplane on the Hudson River and saved 155 lives, he is a true hero.*

For now, it is best to place your topic sentence at the beginning of the paragraph. After you have mastered this pattern, you can try variations. Placed first, the topic sentence clearly establishes the focus of your paragraph and helps grab the reader's attention. Wherever the topic sentence appears, all other sentences must relate to it and support it with specific details, facts, examples, arguments, and explanations. If necessary, you can revise the topic sentence later to make it more accurately match the paragraph you have written.

Caution: Do not begin a topic sentence with *This paragraph will be about . . .* or *I am going to write about . . .* These extra words contribute nothing. Instead, make your point directly. Make every word in the topic sentence count.

PRACTICE 4

Put a check beside each topic sentence that is limited enough to be the topic sentence of a good paragraph. If you think a topic sentence is too broad, limit the topic according to your own interests; then write a new, specific topic sentence.

EXAMPLES:

✔ E-mail has changed my life in three ways.

Rewrite: _____

I am going to write about cell phones.

Rewrite: *Talking on a cell phone can distract drivers to the point of causing accidents.*

1. Working in the complaint department taught me tolerance.

   Rewrite: _____

2. A subject I want to write about is money.

   Rewrite: _____

   _____

_____

* For more work on writing complete sentences, see Chapters 7 and 8.

3. This paragraph will discuss food.

   Rewrite: _____

   _____

4. Some things about college have been great.

   Rewrite: _____

   _____

5. Living in a one-room apartment forces a person to be organized.

   Rewrite: _____

   _____

PRACTICE 5

Here is a list of topics. Choose one that interests you from this list or from your own list in Chapter 1 on page 7. Narrow the topic, and write a topic sentence limited enough to provide the main idea for a good paragraph. Make sure that your topic sentence is a complete sentence.

A talented musician	An act of courage
Why get an education?	Advertising con jobs
AIDS	Clothing styles on campus

Narrowed topic: _____

Topic sentence: _____

_____

C. Generating Ideas for the Body of the Paragraph

Rich supporting detail is one key to effective writing. A good way to generate ideas for the body of a paragraph is by *brainstorming*, freely jotting down ideas. This important step may take just a few minutes, but it gets your ideas on paper and may pull ideas out of you that you didn't even know you had.

Freely jot down anything that might relate to your topic—details, examples, little stories. Don't worry at this point if some ideas don't seem to belong. For now, just keep jotting them down.

Here is a possible brainstorming list for the topic sentence *Beverly inspires admiration because she is so determined.*

1. saved enough money for college

2. worked days, went to school nights

3. has beautiful brown eyes

4. nervous about learning to drive but didn't give up

5. failed road test twice—passed eventually

6. her favorite color—wine red
7. received degree in accounting
8. she is really admirable
9. with lots of will power, quit smoking
10. used to be a heavy smoker
11. married to Virgil
12. I like Virgil too
13. now a good driver
14. never got a ticket
15. hasn't touched another cigarette

As you saw in Part B, some writers brainstorm or use other prewriting techniques *before* they write the topic sentence. Do what works best for you.

PRACTICE 6

Now choose the topic from Practice 4 or Practice 5 that most interests you. Write your limited topic sentence here.

Topic sentence: _____

_____

Next, brainstorm, freewrite, or cluster for specific ideas to develop a paragraph. On paper or on a computer, write anything that comes to you about your topic sentence. Just let ideas pour out—details, memories, facts. Try to fill at least one page.

PRACTICE 7

Many writers adjust the topic sentence after they have finished drafting the paragraph. In a group of three or four classmates, study the body of each of the following paragraphs. Then, working together, write the most exact and interesting topic sentence you can.

1. Topic sentence: _____

_____

One challenge is a lack of knowledge about how to apply, register for classes, and obtain financial aid. Students who are first in their families to attend college often lack an experienced guide to help them navigate these procedures. After they do enroll, first-generation college students may also find that their high school classes did not adequately prepare them for the academic demands of college work. Consequently, they may have to take courses to strengthen their reading, writing, or math skills. Even as they improve academically and progress through their studies, students whose relatives and friends never attended college must deal with a range of difficult emotions. They may feel anxious about pleasing proud relatives with high hopes for their success. They may fear losing old friends who undercut or even mock their college goals. They may experience stress from the constant struggle to find enough time to study. When they finally receive their college degrees, however, they always swell with pride, knowing that their accomplishment is worth every obstacle they have overcome.

Inocencia Colon, student

2. Topic sentence: _____

_____

Despite his pressured schedule, he always found time to play with my sisters and me, tell us stories, and make us feel loved. From his example, I learned that men can be loving and show affection. In addition, he often sat with me and discussed the responsibilities of being a man. He instilled in me principles and morals that I would not have learned from the guys on the corner. My hero felt that a man should be the provider for his family. He demonstrated this by working two jobs, seven days a week. After many years, my father saved enough money to make a down payment on a three-bedroom house next to a park. He accomplished all this with only a sixth-grade education. The values on which I now base my life were given to me by my hero, an unknown man who deserves to be famous.

Robert Fields, student

3. Topic sentence: _____

_____

Frigid air would hit us in the eyes when we stepped out the door to catch the school bus. Even though our faces were wrapped in scarves and our heads covered with wool caps, the cold snatched our breath away. A thin layer of snow crunched loudly under our boots as we ran gasping out to the road. I knew that the famous Minnesota wind chill was pulling temperatures well below zero, but I tried not to think about that. Instead, I liked to see how everything in the yard was frozen motionless, even the blades of grass that shone like little glass knives.

Ari Henson, student

D. Selecting and Dropping Ideas

This may be the easiest step in paragraph writing because all you have to do is select those ideas that best support your topic sentence and drop those that do not. Also drop ideas that just repeat the topic sentence and add nothing new to the paragraph.

Here is the brainstorming list for the topic sentence *Beverly inspires admiration because she is so determined.* Which ideas would you drop? Why?

1. saved enough money for college
2. worked days, went to school nights
3. has beautiful brown eyes
4. nervous about learning to drive but didn't give up
5. failed road test twice—passed eventually
6. her favorite color—wine red
7. received degree in accounting
8. she is really admirable
9. with lots of will power, quit smoking
10. used to be a heavy smoker
11. married to Virgil
12. I like Virgil too

13. now a good driver

14. never got a ticket

15. hasn't touched another cigarette

You probably dropped ideas 3, 6, 11, and 12 because they do not relate to the topic. You also should have dropped idea 8 because it merely repeats the topic sentence.

PRACTICE 8

Read through your own brainstorming list in Practice 6. Select the ideas that best support your topic sentence, and cross out those that do not. In addition, drop ideas that merely repeat the topic sentence. You should be able to give good reasons for keeping or dropping each idea in the list.

E. Arranging Ideas in a Plan or an Outline

Next, choose an **order** in which to arrange your ideas. First, group together ideas that have something in common, that are related or alike in some way. Then decide which ideas should come first, which second, and so on. Many writers do this by numbering the ideas on their list.

Here is a plan for a paragraph about Beverly's determination.

Topic sentence: Beverly inspires admiration because she is so determined.

worked days, went to school nights
saved enough money for college
received degree in accounting

nervous about learning to drive but didn't give up
failed road test twice—passed eventually
now a good driver
never got a ticket

used to be a heavy smoker
with lots of will power, quit smoking
hasn't touched another cigarette

● How are the ideas in each group related? _____

_____

● Does it make sense to discuss college first, driving second, and smoking last?

● Why? _____

_____

Keep in mind that there is more than one way to arrange ideas. As you group your own brainstorming list, think of what you want to say; then arrange your ideas accordingly.*

PRACTICE 9

On paper or on a computer, make a plan or outline from your brainstormed list of ideas. First, group together related ideas. Then decide which ideas will come first, which second, and so on.

F. Writing and Revising the Paragraph

Writing the First Draft

By now, you should have a clear plan or outline from which to write the first draft of your paragraph. The **first draft** should contain all the ideas you have decided to use, in the order in which you have chosen to present them. Writing on every other line will leave room for later changes.

Explain your ideas fully, including details that will interest or amuse the reader. If you are unsure about something, put a check in the margin and come back to it later, but avoid getting stuck on any one word, sentence, or idea. If possible, set the paper aside for several hours or several days; this step will help you read it later with a fresh eye.

PRACTICE 10

On paper or on a computer, write a first draft of the paragraph you have been working on.

Revising

Whether you are a beginning writer or a professional, you must **revise**—that is, rewrite what you have written in order to improve it. You might cross out and rewrite words or entire sentences. You might add, drop, or rearrange details.

As you revise, keep the reader in mind. Ask yourself these questions:

- Is my topic sentence clear?
- Can the reader easily follow my ideas?
- Is the order of ideas logical?
- Will this paragraph keep the reader interested?

In addition, revise your paragraph for *support* and for *unity*.

Revising for Support

Make sure your paragraph contains excellent **support**—that is, specific details, facts, and examples that fully explain your topic sentence.

Avoid simply repeating the same idea in different words, especially the idea in the topic sentence. Repeated ideas are just padding, a sign that you need to brainstorm or freewrite again for new ideas. Which of the following two paragraphs contains the best and most interesting support?

---

* For more work on choosing an order, see Chapter 4, Part B.

A.   Every Saturday morning, Fourteenth Street is alive with activity. From one end of the street to the other, people are out doing everything imaginable. Vendors sell many different items on the street, and storekeepers will do just about anything to get customers into their stores. They will use signs, and they will use music. There is a tremendous amount of activity on Fourteenth Street, and just watching it is enjoyable.

B.   Every Saturday morning, Fourteenth Street is alive with activity. Vendors line the sidewalks, selling everything from DVD players to wigs. Trying to lure customers inside, the shops blast pop music into the street or hang brightly colored banners announcing "Grand Opening Sale" or "Everything Must Go." Shoppers jam the sidewalks, both serious bargain hunters and families just out for a stroll, munching chili dogs as they survey the merchandise. Here and there, a panhandler hustles for handouts, taking advantage of the Saturday crowd.

- The body of *paragraph A* contains vague and general statements, so the reader gets no clear picture of the activity on Fourteenth Street.

- The body of *paragraph B*, however, includes many specific *details* that clearly explain the topic sentence: *vendors selling everything from DVD players to wigs, shops blasting pop music, brightly colored banners.*

- What other details in *paragraph B* help you see just how Fourteenth Street is alive with activity?

_____

_____

_____

_____

PRACTICE 11

Check the following paragraphs for strong, specific support. Mark places that need more details or explanation, and cross out any weak or repeated words. Then revise and rewrite each paragraph *as if you had written it*, inventing and adding support when you need to.

Paragraph A: Aunt Alethia was one of the most important people in my life. She had a strong influence on me. No matter how busy she was, she always had time for me. She paid attention to small things about me that no one else seemed to notice. When I was successful, she praised me. When I was feeling down, she gave me pep talks. She was truly wise and shared her wisdom with me. My aunt was a great person who had a major influence on my life.

Paragraph B: Just getting to school safely can be a challenge for many young people. Young as he is, my son has been robbed once and bullied on several occasions. The robbery was very frightening, for it involved a weapon. What was taken was a small thing, but it meant a lot to my son. It angers me that just getting to school is so dangerous. Something needs to be done.

Revising for Unity

While writing, you may sometimes drift away from your topic and include information that does not belong in the paragraph. It is important, therefore, to revise your paragraph for **unity**—that is, to drop any ideas or sentences that do not relate to the topic sentence.

This paragraph lacks unity:

> (1) Franklin Mars, a Minnesota candy maker, created many popular candy snacks. (2) Milky Way, his first bar, was an instant hit. (3) Snickers, which he introduced in 1930, also sold very well. (4) Milton Hershey developed the very first candy bar in 1894. (5) M&Ms were a later Mars creation, supposedly designed so that soldiers could enjoy a sugar boost without getting sticky trigger fingers.

- What is the topic sentence in this paragraph? _____
- Which sentence does *not* relate to the topic sentence? _____
- Sentence (4) has nothing to do with the main idea, that *Franklin Mars created many popular candy snacks*. Therefore, sentence (4) should be dropped.

PRACTICE 12

Check the following paragraphs for unity. If a paragraph is unified, write U in the blank. If it is not, write the number of the sentence that does not belong in the paragraph.

1. ___ (1) Families who nourish their children with words as well as food at dinnertime produce better future readers. (2) Researchers at Harvard University studied the dinner conversations of sixty-eight families. (3) What they found was that parents who use a few new words in conversation with their three- and four-year-olds each night quickly build the children's vocabularies and their later reading skills. (4) The researchers point out that children can learn from eight to twenty-eight new words a day, so they need to be "fed" new words. (5) Excellent "big words" for preschoolers include *parachute, emerald, instrument,* and *education,* the researchers say.

2. ___ (1) Personalized license plates have become very popular. (2) These "vanity plates" allow car owners to express their sense of humor, marital status, pet peeves, or ethnic pride. (3) Of course, every car must display a plate on the rear bumper or in the back window. (4) Drivers have created messages such as ROCK ON, NT GUILTY, and (on a tow truck) ITZ GONE. (5) In some states, as many as one in seven autos has a personalized plate. (6) Recently, *Parade* magazine chose the nation's top ten vanity plates, including XQQSME on a Massachusetts plate, ULIV1S on an Arkansas plate, and on an SUV in Missouri, a message to be read in the rearview mirror—TI-3VOM.

3. ___ (1) Swimming is excellent exercise. (2) Swimming vigorously for just twelve minutes provides aerobic benefits to the heart. (3) Unlike jogging and many other aerobic sports, however, swimming does not jolt the bones and muscles with sudden pressure. (4) Furthermore, the motions of swimming, such as reaching out in the crawl, stretch the muscles in a healthy, natural way. (5) Some swimmers wear goggles to keep chlorine or salt out of their eyes whereas others do not.

Peer Feedback for Revising

You may wish to show your first draft or read it aloud to a respected friend or classmate. Ask this person to give an honest reader response, not to rewrite your work. Having another pair of eyes inspect your writing can alert you to issues you missed and help you think like a reader. To elicit useful responses, ask specific questions of your own, or use the Peer Feedback Sheet on the following page. You may want to photocopy the sheet rather than write on it so that you can reuse it.

PRACTICE 13   Now read the first draft of your paragraph with a critical eye. Revise and rewrite it, checking especially for a clear topic sentence, strong support, and unity.

PRACTICE 14   Exchange *revised* paragraphs with a classmate. Ask specific questions or use the Peer Feedback Sheet on page 32..

When you *give* feedback, try to be as honest and specific as possible; saying a paper is "good," "nice," or "bad" doesn't really help the writer. When you *receive* feedback, think over your classmate's responses. Do they ring true?

Now revise a second time, with the aim of writing a fine paragraph.

Did you know that even professional writers often show their work to a friend as they revise? These two college students are using the same technique, giving each other feedback on their writing.

© Hill Street Studios/Blend Images/Corbis

PEER FEEDBACK SHEET

To _____   From _____   Date _____

1. What I like about this piece of writing is _____

   _____

   _____

2. Your main point seems to be _____

   _____

   _____

3. These particular words or lines struck me as powerful.

   Words or lines: I like them because

   _____   _____

   _____   _____

   _____   _____

   _____   _____

4. Some things aren't clear to me. These lines or parts could be improved (meaning not clear; supporting points missing; order mixed up; writing not lively):

   Lines or parts: Need improving because

   _____   _____

   _____   _____

   _____   _____

   _____   _____

5. The one change you could make that would most improve this piece of writing is

   _____

   _____

   _____

   _____

G. Proofreading and Writing the Final Draft

When you are satisfied with your revisions, recopy your paper. Be sure to include all your corrections, and write neatly and legibly—a carelessly scribbled paper seems to say that you don't care about your work.

The first draft of the paragraph about Beverly, with the writer's changes, and the revised final draft follow. Compare them.

First Draft with Revisions

(1) Beverly inspires admiration because she is so determined. (2) Although

doing what? add details

she could not afford to attend college right after high school, she <u>worked</u> to save

How long?! Better support needed—show her hard work!

money. (3) It took a <u>long time</u>, but she got her degree. (4) She is now a good driver.

(5) At first, she was very nervous about getting behind the wheel and even failed

The third time,

the road test twice, but she didn't quit. (6) $\hat{}$She passed <u>eventually</u>. (7) <u>Her husband,</u>

Drop Virgil—he doesn't belong

<u>Virgil, loves to drive; he races cars on the weekend.</u> (8) Anyway, Beverly has never

how long?

gotten a ticket. (9) A year ago, Beverly quit smoking. (10) For <u>a while</u>, she had a

too general—add details here

<u>rough time</u>, but she hasn't touched a cigarette. (11) Now she says that the urge to

better conclusion needed

smoke has faded away. (12) She doesn't let <u>difficulties</u> defeat her.

Guide the reader better from point to point! Choppy—

Final Draft

(1) Beverly inspires admiration because she is so determined. (2) Although she could not afford to attend college right after high school, she worked as a cashier to save money for tuition. (3) It took her five years working days and going to school nights, but she recently received a BS in accounting. (4) Thanks to this same determination, Beverly is now a good driver. (5) At first, she was very nervous about getting behind the wheel and even failed the road test twice, but she didn't give up. (6) The third time, she passed, and she has never gotten a ticket. (7) A year ago, Beverly quit smoking. (8) For a month or more, she chewed her nails and endless packs of gum, but she hasn't touched a cigarette. (9) Now she says that the urge to smoke has faded away. (10) When Beverly sets a goal for herself, she doesn't let difficulties defeat her.

● This paragraph provides good support for the topic sentence. The writer has made sentences (2) and (3) more specific by adding *as a cashier, for tuition, five years working days and going to school nights,* and *recently received a BS in accounting.*

- What other revisions did the writer make? How do these revisions improve the paragraph? _____

_____

_____

_____

- *Transitional expressions* are words and phrases that guide the reader smoothly from point to point. In sentence (5) of the final draft, *at first* is a transitional expression showing time. What other transitional expressions of time are used?

_____

_____

- What phrase provides a transition from sentence (3) to (4)?

_____

- Note that the last sentence now provides a brief *conclusion* so that the paragraph *feels* finished.

Proofreading

Finally, carefully **proofread** your paper for grammatical and spelling errors, consulting your dictionary and this book as necessary. Errors in your writing will lower your grades in most college courses, and they may also limit your job opportunities. The more writing errors you tend to make, the more you need to proofread.

Chapter 6 of this book will teach you tools and proofreading strategies to help you find and correct your own errors. Then Units 2 through 8 will help you improve your grammar, punctuation, and spelling skills and proofread for specific errors.

Meanwhile, allow yourself enough time to proofread; read your work slowly, word by word. Some students find it useful to point to each word and read it aloud softly; others place a blank index card or ruler under the line they are reading. These methods help them catch mistakes as well as "hear" any words they might have left out as they wrote, especially little words like *and*, *at*, and *of*.

In which of these sentences have words been omitted?

(1) Texting while driving is an easy way cause accident.

(2) Plans for the new gym were on display the library.

(3) Mr. Sampson winked at his reflection in the bathroom mirror.

- Words are missing in sentences (1) and (2).
- Sentence (1) requires *to* before *cause* and *an* before *accident*.
- What word is omitted in sentence (2)? _____
- Where should this word be placed? _____

PRACTICE 15

Proofread these sentences for omitted words. Add the necessary words above the lines. Some sentences may already be correct.

> **EXAMPLE:**   People were not always able ^to^ tell time accurately.

1. People used to guess the time day by watching the sun move across the sky.

2. Sunrise and sunset were easy recognize.

3. Recognizing noon easy, too.

4. However, telling time by the position of sun was very difficult at other times.

5. People noticed that shadows lengthened during the day.

6. They found it easier to tell time by looking at the shadows than by looking the sun.

7. People stuck poles into the ground to time by the length of the shadows.

8. Those the first shadow clocks, or sundials.

9. In 300 BC, Chaldean astronomer invented a more accurate, bowl-shaped sundial.

10. Today, most sundials decorative, but they can still be used to tell time.

PRACTICE 16

Proofread the final draft of your paragraph, checking for grammar or spelling errors and omitted words.

PRACTICE 17

Writing and Revising Paragraphs

The assignments that follow will give you practice in writing and revising basic paragraphs. In each assignment, aim for (1) a clear topic sentence and (2) sentences that fully support and explain the topic sentence. As you write, refer to the checklist in the Chapter Highlights on page 37.

Paragraph 1: Describe a public place. Reread paragraph B on page 29. Then choose a place in your neighborhood that is "alive with activity"—a park, street, restaurant, or club. In your topic sentence, name the place and say when it is most active; for example, "Every Saturday night, the Blue Dog Café is alive with activity." Begin by freewriting or by jotting down as many details about the scene as possible. Then describe the scene. Arrange your observations in a logical order. Revise for support, making sure that your details are so lively and interesting that your readers will see the place as clearly as you do.

Actor Johnny Depp

Paragraph 2: Describe a portrait. Study this photograph of actor Johnny Depp. Notice his pose and expression, eyes, his hat, mouth, beard, and raised forearm. Now write a paragraph in which you describe this portrait for someone who has not seen it. In your topic sentence, state one overall impression or feeling that this portrait conveys. Support this impression with specific details. If you prefer, use Google Images or another search engine, find an expressive portrait, and describe that instead. Conclude your paragraph; don't just stop.

Paragraph 3: Evaluate your strengths as a writer. In writing as in life, it helps to know your true strengths as well as your weaknesses. You may not realize it, but you probably already possess several skills and personality traits that can nourish good writing. These include being observant and paying attention to details, imagining, feeling deep emotions, wanting to learn the truth, knowing how and where to find the answers to questions, thinking creatively, being well organized, and being persistent. Which of these abilities do you already possess? Do you possess other skills or traits that might help your writing? Describe three of your strengths as a writer. As you revise, make sure your ideas follow a logical order. Proofread carefully.

Paragraph 4: Choose your time of day. Many people have a favorite time of day—the freshness of early morning, 5 p.m. when work ends, late at night when the children are asleep. In your topic sentence, name your favorite time of day. Then develop the paragraph by explaining why you look forward to this time and exactly how you spend it. Check your work for any omitted words.

Chapter Highlights

Checklist for Writing an Effective Paragraph

- Narrow the topic: Cut the topic down to one aspect that interests you and will probably interest your readers.

- Write the topic sentence. (You may wish to brainstorm or freewrite first.)

- Brainstorm, freewrite, or cluster ideas for the body: Write down anything and everything that might relate to your topic.

- Select and drop ideas: Select those ideas that relate to your topic, and drop those that do not.

- Group together ideas that have something in common; then arrange the ideas in a plan.

- Write your first draft.

- Read what you have written, making any necessary corrections and additions. Revise for support and unity.

- Write the final draft of your paragraph neatly and legibly or print a fresh copy, using the format preferred by your instructor.

- Proofread for grammar, punctuation, spelling, and omitted words. Make neat corrections in ink.

EXPLORING ONLINE

<http://grammar.ccc.commnet.edu/grammar/paragraphs.htm> Review paragraph unity and topic sentences at this excellent OWL.

<http://owl.english.purdue.edu/owl/resource/606/01> A review of paragraph writing from the famous Purdue University OWL.

 View an integrated eBook and chapter-specific interactive learning tools, including flashcards, quizzes, videos, and extra help tracking and correcting your Personal Error Patterns, in your Basic Writing CourseMate, accessed through <www.cengagebrain.com>.

CHAPTER 4

Improving Your Paragraphs

A: More Work on Support: Examples

B: More Work on Arranging Ideas: Coherence

C: More Work on Revising: Exact and Concise Language

D: Turning Assignments into Paragraphs

In Chapter 3, you practiced the steps of the paragraph-writing process. This chapter builds on that work. It explains several skills that can greatly improve your writing: using examples; achieving coherence; choosing exact, concise language; and turning assignments into paragraphs.

A. More Work on Support: Examples

One effective way to make your writing specific is by using **examples**. Someone might write, "Divers in Monterey Bay can observe many beautiful fish. For instance, tiger-striped treefish are common." The first sentence makes a general statement about the beautiful fish in Monterey Bay. The second sentence gives a specific example of such fish: *tiger-striped treefish*.

Use one, two, or three well-chosen examples to develop a paragraph.

> Many of the computer industry's best innovators were young when they first achieved success. For example, David Filo and Jerry Yang were graduate students at Stanford when they realized that their hobby of listing the best pages on the World Wide Web might become a business. They created Yahoo!, a Web index now logging 500 million visits a month. Two more youthful examples are Google founders Larry Page and Sergey Brin. They were students in their twenties when they got the idea for one of the Internet's most popular search engines. In 2004, just six years after launching their new company, Page and Brin became multibillionaires by selling Google shares to the public. A third pair of young computer geniuses created the video-sharing website YouTube.com. Chad Hurley and Steven Chen worked in Hurley's garage to solve a personal problem: they wanted to figure out an easier way to share video clips with each other via the Internet. The popularity of their site exploded, and just one year later, Hurley and Chen sold YouTube to Google for $1.65 billion.

- The writer begins this paragraph with a topic sentence about the youth of many computer innovators.

● What three examples does the writer provide as support?

Example 1: _____

Example 2: _____

Example 3: _____

● Note that the topic sentence and the examples make a rough plan for the paragraph.

The simplest way to tell a reader that an example will follow is to say so, using a transitional expression: *For example, David Filo . . .*

Transitional Expressions to Introduce Examples	
for example	for instance
to illustrate	another example

PRACTICE 1

Each example in a paragraph must clearly relate to and explain the topic sentence. Each of the following topic sentences is followed by several examples. Circle the letter of any example that does *not* clearly illustrate the topic sentence. Be prepared to explain your choices.

EXAMPLE:

Some animals and insects camouflage themselves in interesting ways.
   a. Snowshoe rabbits turn from brown to white in winter, thus blending into the snow.
   b. The cheetah's spotted coat makes it hard to see in the dry African bush.
   c. The bull alligator smashes its tail against the water and roars during mating season.
   d. The walking stick is brown and irregular, much like the twigs among which this insect hides.

1. State troopers report that many people do dangerous and outrageous things while driving.
   a. One woman applied mascara, pressing her face close to the rearview mirror as she drove 65 miles an hour.
   b. A woman shopped in a Detroit supermarket while wearing a Queen Elizabeth mask and a crown.
   c. Another man glanced up and down as he changed lanes, writing in a spiral notebook propped against the steering wheel.
   d. A man ate scrambled eggs with a fork—from a plate on his dashboard.

2. Several players from Japanese baseball leagues have achieved success in the United States's major leagues.
   a. Outfielder Hideki Matsui, a New York Yankee since 2003, won the World Series MVP award in 2009.
   b. Pitcher Daisuke Matsuzaka of the Boston Red Sox won 18 games in 2008.
   c. The Seattle Mariners' all-star outfielder, Ichiro Suzuki, holds the single-season record for 262 hits and has won nine Gold Gloves for his stellar defense.
   d. Baseball has been played and loved in Japan for many years.

3. Mrs. Makarem is well loved in this community for her generous heart.
   a. Her door is always open to neighborhood children, who stop by for lemonade or advice.
   b. When the Padilla family had a fire, Mrs. Makarem collected clothes and blankets for them.
   c. "Hello, dear," she says with a smile to everyone she passes on the street.
   d. Born in Caracas, Venezuela, she has lived on Bay Road for thirty-two years.

4. A number of unusual, specialized scholarships are available to college students across the United States.
   a. The Icy Frost Bridge Scholarship at Indiana's DePauw University is awarded to female music students who sing or play the national anthem "with sincerity."
   b. Brighton College, a secondary school for boys and girls in England, pays the full tuition of a student with the last name of *Peyton*.
   c. Left-handed, financially needy students can get special scholarships at Juniata College in Pennsylvania.
   d. The Collegiate Inventors Competition awards $25,000 to the undergraduate with the most original, socially useful invention.

5. Throughout history, artists, scientists, and inventors have gotten new ideas or solved problems in dreams.
   a. In 1816, after a nightmare about a scientist bringing a hideous corpse back to life, Mary Shelley wrote *Frankenstein*, her famous horror story.
   b. Biologist James Watson dreamed about spiral staircases, leading him to discover the structure of DNA and win the Nobel Prize.
   c. Two weeks before he was shot and killed, President Abraham Lincoln dreamed he saw the body of a president lying in the White House.
   d. Inventor Elias Howe solved a problem with placing the needle in his invention, the sewing machine, after he dreamed of warriors holding spears with holes in the tips.

PRACTICE 2

The secret of good illustration lies in well-chosen and well-written examples. Think of one example that illustrates each of the following general statements. Write out the example in sentence form—one to three sentences—as clearly and exactly as possible.

1. Many films today have amazing special effects.

   Example: _____

   _____

2. Television programs have reached new lows in the past few years.

   Example: _____

   _____

3. Dan is always buying strange gadgets.

   Example: _____

   _____

4.   Even when she is very busy, Grace finds ways to exercise.

Example: _____

_____

5.   Children often say surprising things.

Example: _____

_____

PRACTICE 3   **Writing Assignment**

Write a paragraph developed by examples. Make sure your topic sentence can be supported by examples. Prewrite and pick the best one to three examples to explain your topic sentence. Here are some ideas for topics:

offensive "reality" television shows   ads that appeal to _____

great places to study on campus   disastrous wedding stories

B.   More Work on Arranging Ideas: Coherence

Every paragraph should have **coherence**. A paragraph *coheres*—holds together—when its ideas are arranged in a clear and logical order.

Sometimes the order of ideas flows logically from your topic. However, three basic ways to organize ideas are **time order**, **space order**, and **order of importance**.

Time Order

Time order means arranging ideas chronologically, from present to past or from past to present. Careful use of time order helps avoid such confusing writing as *Oops, I forgot to mention before that . . .*

Most instructions, histories, processes, and stories follow the logical order of time.

> The talent and drive of surfer Lisa Andersen quickly propelled her to the top of her sport. In 1983, thirteen-year-old Andersen paddled a friend's surfboard into the ocean off the coast of Florida's Ormond Beach, caught a breaking wave, and easily rode it to shore. Thrilled to discover this natural talent, she realized that she might have the potential to become a serious female surfer. Soon, in hopes of gaining a competitive edge, she began practicing with only her most skilled male counterparts. In 1987, this strategy paid off when she won the U.S. amateur women's surfing contest. Later that year, Lisa turned professional; by 1992, she was winning major competitions and training for the world championship. Almost immediately, however, news that she was pregnant put any plans to win the 1993 championship on hold. Andersen says that although it cost her one year's title, the birth of her daughter Erica motivated her to go all the way to the top. In 1994, Lisa was crowned world surfing champion, a title she won again in 1995, 1996, and 1997. Today, the four-time winner is credited with inspiring a generation of young women to enter the once male-dominated world of surfing.

● The paragraph moves in time from Lisa Andersen's first surfing experience as a teenager to her world championship victories.

● Note how some transitional expressions—*in 1983, soon, later that year, almost immediately,* and *today*—show time and connect the events in the paragraph.

Transitional Expressions to Show Time

first, second, third

then, next, finally

before, during, after

soon, the following month, the next year

PRACTICE 4

Arrange each set of sentences in time order, numbering them 1, 2, 3, and so on. Be prepared to explain your choices.

1. In eighty years, the T-shirt rose from simple underwear to fashion statement.

   ____ During World War II, women factory workers started wearing T-shirts on the job.

   ____ Hippies in the 1960s tie-dyed their T-shirts and wore them printed with messages.

   ____ Now, five billion T-shirts are sold worldwide each year.

   ____ The first American T-shirts were cotton underwear, worn home by soldiers returning from France after World War I.

2. The short life of Sadako Sasaki has inspired millions to value peace.

   ____ Sadako was just two years old in 1945 when the atom bomb destroyed her city, Hiroshima.

   ____ From her sickbed, Sadako set out to make 1,000 paper cranes, birds that, in Japan, symbolize long life and hope.

   ____ Although she died before making 1,000, classmates finished her project and published a book of her letters.

   ____ At age eleven, already a talented runner, she was crushed to learn that she had leukemia, caused by radiation from the bomb.

   ____ Now, every year, the Folded Crane Club places 1,000 cranes at the foot of a statue of Sadako, honoring her wish that all children might enjoy peace and a long life.

3. Scientists who study the body's daily rhythms can suggest the ideal time of day for different activities.

   ____ Taking vitamins with breakfast helps the body absorb them.

   ____ Allergy medication should be taken just before bedtime to combat early-morning hay fever—usually the worst of the day.

   ____ The best time to work out is 3 p.m. to 5 p.m., when strength, flexibility, and body temperature are greatest.

   ____ Ideal naptime is 1 p.m. to 3 p.m., when body temperature falls, making sleep easier.

PRACTICE 5

Writing Assignment

Have you ever been through something that lasted only a few moments but was unforgettable—for example, a sports victory, an accident, or a kiss? Write a paragraph telling about such an event. As you prewrite, pick the highlights of the experience and arrange them in time order. As you write, try to capture the drama of what happened. Use transitional expressions of time to make the story flow smoothly.

Space Order

Space order means describing a person, a place, or a thing from top to bottom, from left to right, from foreground to background, and so on.

Space order is most often used in descriptions because it moves from detail to detail, like a camera's eye.

> When the city presses in on me, I return in my mind to my hometown in St. Mary, Jamaica. I am alone, high in the mango tree on our property on the hilltop. The wind is blowing hard as usual, making a scared noise as it passes through the lush vegetation. I look down at the coconut growth with its green flooring of banana plants. Beyond that is a wide valley and then the round hills. Farther out lies the sea, and I count the ships as they pass to and from the harbor while I relax on my special branch and eat mangoes.
>
> *Daniel Dawes, student*

- The writer describes this scene from his vantage point high in a tree. His description follows space order, moving from the plants below him, farther out to the valley and the hills, and then even farther, to the sea.

- Notice how *transitional expressions* indicating space—*beyond that*, *then*, and *farther out*—help the reader follow and "see" the details.

Transitional Expressions to Show Space Order
to the left, in the center, to the right
behind, beside, in front of
next, beyond that, farther out

PRACTICE 6

Arrange each set of details according to space order, numbering them 1, 2, 3, and so on. Be prepared to explain your choices.

1. After the party, the living room was a mess.

    _____ greasy pizza boxes on the coffee table

    _____ empty soda cans on the floor

    _____ deflated balloons on the ceiling light

    _____ pictures hanging at odd angles on the wall

2. The nurse quietly strode into my aunt's hospital room.

_____ black and silver stethoscope draped around his neck

_____ crisp, white cotton pants and short-sleeved tunic

_____ reassuring smile

_____ blue paper covers on his shoes

_____ kind, dark brown eyes

3. The taxicab crawled through rush-hour traffic in the rain-drenched city.

_____ fare meter on the dashboard ticking relentlessly

_____ headlights barely piercing the stormy, gray dusk

_____ windshield wipers losing their battle with the latest cloudburst

_____ backseat passengers frantically checking their watches

_____ driver wishing hopelessly that he could be home watching the news

PRACTICE 7

Writing Assignment

Study this portrait of Dr. Mae Jemison, who in 1992 became the first woman of color ever to soar into space. Notice her facial expression, posture, clothing, equipment, and other details. Then describe the photograph to someone who has never seen it. In your topic sentence, state one feeling, impression, or message this picture conveys and then choose details that support this idea. Arrange these details in space order—from left to right, top to bottom, and so on. As you revise, make sure that your sentences flow clearly and smoothly.

To learn more about the life of this remarkable astronaut, visit ‹**http://space.about .com/cs/formerastronauts/a/jemisonbio.htm**›.

Astronaut Mae Jemison

JSC Digital Image Collection/NASA

Gehry's Disney Concert
Hall in Los Angeles

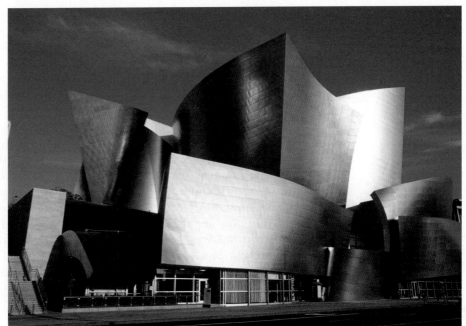

Order of Importance

Order of importance means arranging your ideas from most to least important—
or vice versa.

> Frank Gehry is one of the greatest living architects. There are at least three reasons for his worldwide influence. Most important, Gehry has created new shapes for buildings, literally moving outside the boxes in which we often live and work. He has found ways to build walls that look like mountains, sails, and wings. In addition, Gehry uses new materials—or old materials in new ways. Going beyond plaster and wood, Gehry's buildings have rounded metal walls, curves made of glass, and stone in strange places. Third, because of its striking looks, a Gehry building can bring tourist dollars and international attention to a town or city. This happened when Gehry designed the now-famous Guggenheim Museum building in the little town of Bilbao, Spain. And like the latest blockbuster movie, the Disney Concert Hall in Los Angeles recently opened to rave reviews.

- The three reasons in this paragraph are discussed from the most important reason to the least important.

- Note that the words *most important*, *in addition*, and *third* help the reader move from one reason to another.

You might visualize order of importance like this:

Point 1	MOST IMPORTANT LEAST EXPENSIVE
Point 2	IMPORTANT EXPENSIVE
Point 3	LEAST IMPORTANT MOST EXPENSIVE

Sometimes you may wish to begin with the least important idea and build toward a climax at the end of the paragraph. Paragraphs arranged from the least important idea to the most important idea can have dramatic power.

> Although my fourteen-year-old daughter learned a great deal from living with a Pennsylvania Amish family last summer, adjusting to their strict lifestyle was difficult for her. Kay admitted that the fresh food served on the farm was great, but she missed her diet colas. More difficult was the fact that she had to wear long dresses—no more jeans and baby tees. Still worse in her view were the hours. A suburban girl and self-confessed night person, my daughter had to get up at 5 a.m. to milk cows! By far the most difficult adjustment concerned boys. If an Amish woman is not married, she cannot spend time with males, and this rule now applied to Kay. Yes, she suffered and complained, but by summer's end, she was a different girl—more open-minded and proud of the fact that all these deprivations put her more in touch with herself.
>
> *Lucy Auletta, student*

● The adjustment difficulties this writer's daughter had are arranged from least to most important. How many difficulties are discussed? _____

● Note how the words *more difficult*, *still worse*, and *by far the most difficult adjustment* help the reader move from one idea to the next.

Transitional Expressions to Show Importance
first, next, finally
more, most
less, least

PRACTICE 8

Arrange the ideas that develop each topic sentence in order of importance, numbering them 1, 2, and 3. Begin with the most important idea, or reverse the order if you think that a paragraph would be more effective if it began with the least important idea. Be prepared to explain your choices. Then, on a separate sheet of paper, write the ideas in a paragraph.

1. For three reasons, joining a serious study group is an excellent idea.

    _____ A study group exposes you to new points of view and effective study habits.

    _____ Joining a study group is a good way to make new friends.

    _____ Statistics show that students who regularly attend a study group get better grades and are less likely to drop out of college.

2. A hidden epidemic of steroid use among young women—for weight control or enhanced athletic performance—is causing serious consequences.

    _____ Steroid use, which has been linked to heart attacks, strokes, and some cancers, can be fatal.

    _____ Many female steroid users not only lose hair on their heads but also grow extra body hair.

    _____ Steroids prematurely stop bones from lengthening, so developing girls who take the drug may permanently stunt their growth.

3. Undiagnosed or untreated diabetes can cause serious problems.

_____ The diabetic's craving for sweets can lead to a house littered with candy wrappers.

_____ If diabetes is not properly managed, blindness and other serious health problems, such as ulcers and gangrene, can result.

_____ Ignoring a diabetes diagnosis can result in premature death.

_____ Untreated diabetes often causes dry, itchy skin and intense thirst.

PRACTICE 9   **Writing Assignment**

Write a paragraph to persuade a certain group of people to do something they don't do now. For example, you could write to convince couch potatoes to begin exercising, senior citizens to take a free class at your college, or nonvoters to register and cast a ballot. Discuss the three most important reasons why your readers should follow your advice, and arrange these reasons in order of importance—least to most important or most to least important, whichever you think would make a better paragraph. Don't forget to use transitional expressions. If you wish, use humor to win over your audience.

C. More Work on Revising: Exact and Concise Language

Good writers do not settle for the first words that spill onto their paper or computer screen. Instead, they revise what they have written, replacing vague words with exact language and repetitious words with concise language.

Exact Language

As a rule, the more specific, detailed, and exact the language is, the better the writing. Which sentence in each of the following pairs contains the more vivid and exact language?

(1) The office was noisy.
(2) In the office, phones jangled, faxes whined, and copy machines hummed.

(3) What my tutor said made me feel good.
(4) When my tutor whispered, "Fine job," I felt like singing.

● Sentence (2) is more exact than sentence (1) because *phones jangled, faxes whined, and copy machines hummed* provide more vivid information than the general word *noisy*.

● What *exact* words does sentence (4) use to replace the general words *said* and *made me feel good*? _____

You do not need a large vocabulary to write exactly and well, but you do need to work at finding the right words to fit each sentence.

PRACTICE 10

These sentences contain vague language. Revise each one, using vivid and exact language wherever possible.

EXAMPLE: A man went through the crowd.

Revise: _A man in a blue leather jacket pushed through the crowd._

1. An automobile went down the street.

   Revise: _____

   _____

2. This apartment has problems.

   Revise: _____

   _____

3. When Allison comes home, her pet greets her.

   Revise: _____

   _____

4. This magazine is interesting.

   Revise: _____

   _____

5. The expression on his face made me feel comfortable.

   Revise: _____

   _____

6. My job is fun.

   Revise: _____

   _____

7. There was a big storm here last week.

   Revise: _____

   _____

8. The emergency room has a lot of people in it.

   Revise: _____

   _____

Concise Language

Concise writing never uses five or six words when two or three will do. It avoids repetitive and unnecessary words that add nothing to the meaning of a sentence. As you revise your writing, cross out unnecessary words and phrases.

Which sentence in each of the following pairs is more concise?

> (1) Because of the fact that Larissa owns an antiques shop, she is always poking around in dusty attics.
> (2) Because Larissa owns an antiques shop, she is always poking around in dusty attics.
>
> (3) Mr. Tibbs entered a large, dark blue room.
> (4) Mr. Tibbs entered a room that was large in size and dark blue in color.

- Sentences (2) and (3) are concise; sentences (1) and (4) are wordy.

- In sentence (1), *because of the fact that* is a wordy way of saying *because*.

- In sentence (4), *in size* and *in color* just repeat which ideas?

_____

Of course, conciseness does not mean writing short, choppy sentences. It does mean dropping unnecessary words and phrases.

PRACTICE 11

The following sentences are wordy. In a group with two or three others, make each sentence more concise by deleting unnecessary words, rewording slightly as necessary. Write your revised sentences on the lines provided, making sure not to change the meaning of the original.

EXAMPLE: Venice, an Italian city in Italy, is trying to reduce its huge number of visitors who go to see it.

Revise: *Venice, a city in Italy, is trying to reduce its huge number of visitors.*

_____

1. For a great many hundreds of years, this beautiful city of such loveliness has been a major tourist attraction.

   Revise: _____

   _____

2. The reasons why people go to Venice are because they want to see its priceless art and palaces, famous bridges, and canals that serve as streets.

   Revise: _____

   _____

3. At this time now, however, Venice is being destroyed by floods, by polluted air and water that are dirty, and by tourists who visit it.

   Revise: _____

   _____

4. Twelve million annual visitors invade Venice every year, and most of them are day-trippers who come only for the day and then go home.

   Revise: _____

   _____

5. The day-trippers, who often bring their own drinks and sandwiches with them to eat, spend little money in town, thus contributing very little to the city's economy of money.

   Revise: _____

   _____

6. However, they contribute enormously and in large amounts to the city of Venice's congestion, transportation, and sanitation nightmares.

   Revise: _____

   _____

7. Recently, the city tried to scare off day-trippers with a negative publicity campaign that gave bad publicity about the city.

   Revise: _____

   _____

8. Posters showed tourists being devoured and eaten by Venice's well-known and famous pigeons.

   Revise: _____

   _____

9. An immense giant toilet plunger became the symbol of a city that some say is the city that is the most romantic city in the world.

   Revise: _____

   _____

10. Unfortunately, the bad publicity did not work or stop tourists from pouring into Venice, so city officials are trying a new plan—asking visitors to make reservations to visit the city on a particular day.

    Revise: _____

    _____

PRACTICE 12   Review

Following are statements from real accident reports collected by an insurance company. As you will see, these writers need help with more than their fenders!

   In a group with four or five classmates, read each statement and try to understand what each writer meant to say. Then revise each statement so that it says exactly and concisely what the writer intended.

1. "The guy was all over the place. I had to swerve a number of times before I hit him."

2. "The telephone pole was approaching fast. I was attempting to swerve out of its path when it struck my front end."

3. "Coming home, I drove into the wrong house and collided with a tree I don't have."

4. "I was on my way to the doctor's with rear-end trouble when my universal joint gave way, causing me to have an accident."

5. "I was driving my car out of the driveway in the usual manner when it was struck by the other car in the same place it had been struck several times before."

PRACTICE 13   **Review**

Choose a paragraph or paper you wrote recently. Read it with a fresh eye, checking for exact and concise language. Then rewrite it, eliminating all vague or wordy language.

D. Turning Assignments into Paragraphs

In Chapter 3, Part B, you learned how to narrow a broad topic and write a specific topic sentence. Sometimes, however, your assignment may take the form of a specific question, and your job may be to answer the question in one paragraph.

For example, this question asks you to take a stand for or against a particular issue.

> Are professional athletes overpaid?

You can often turn this kind of question into a topic sentence:

> (1) Professional athletes are overpaid.
> (2) Professional athletes are not overpaid.
> (3) Professional athletes are sometimes overpaid.

- These three topic sentences take different points of view.
- The words *are*, *are not*, and *sometimes* make each writer's opinion clear.

  Sometimes you will be asked to agree or disagree with a statement:

> (4) Salary is the most important factor in job satisfaction. Agree or disagree.

- This is really a question in disguise: *Is salary the most important factor in job satisfaction?*

In the topic sentence, make your opinion clear and repeat key words.

> (5) Salary is the most important factor in job satisfaction.
> (6) Salary is not the most important factor in job satisfaction.
> (7) Salary is only one among several important factors in job satisfaction.

- The words *is*, *is not*, and *is only one among several* make each writer's opinion clear.
- Note how the topic sentences repeat the key words from the statement—*salary, important factor, job satisfaction.*

Once you have written the topic sentence, follow the steps described in Chapter 2—freewriting, brainstorming, or clustering; selecting; grouping—and then write your paragraph. Be sure that all ideas in the paragraph support the opinion you have stated in the topic sentence.

PRACTICE 14

Here are four exam questions. Write one topic sentence to answer each of them.
REMEMBER: Make your opinion clear in the topic sentence and repeat key words from
the question.

1. Should computer education be required in every public high school?

   Topic sentence: _____

   _____

2. Would you advise your best friend to buy a new car or a used car?

   Topic sentence: _____

   _____

3. Is there too much bad news on television news programs?

   Topic sentence: _____

   _____

4. How have your interests changed in the past five years?

   Topic sentence: _____

   _____

PRACTICE 15

Imagine that your instructor has just written the exam questions from Practice 14 on the
board. Choose the question that most interests you and write a paragraph answering that
question. Prewrite, select, and arrange ideas before you compose your paragraph. Then
read your work, making neat corrections in ink.

PRACTICE 16

Here are four statements. Agree or disagree, and write a topic sentence for each.

1. All higher education should be free. Agree or disagree.

   Topic sentence: _____

   _____

2. Expecting one's spouse to be perfect is the most important reason for the high
   divorce rate in the United States. Agree or disagree.

   Topic sentence: _____

   _____

3. Parents should give children money when they need it rather than give them an
   allowance. Agree or disagree.

   Topic sentence: _____

   _____

4. Silence is golden. Agree or disagree.

Topic sentence: _____

_____

PRACTICE 17

Choose the statement in Practice 16 that most interests you. Then write a paragraph in which you agree or disagree.

Chapter Highlights

To improve your writing, try these techniques:

● Use well-chosen examples to develop a paragraph.

● Organize your ideas by time order.

● Organize your ideas by space order.

● Organize your ideas by order of importance, either from the most important to the least or from the least important to the most.

● Use language that is exact and concise.

● Turn assignment questions into topic sentences.

EXPLORING ONLINE

<http://writesite.cuny.edu/projects/keywords/example/hand2.html> Online process: Develop your idea with examples.

<http://lrs.ed.uiuc.edu/students/fwalters/cohere.html> Review ways to add coherence to your writing.

 View an integrated eBook and chapter-specific interactive learning tools, including flashcards, quizzes, videos, and extra help tracking and correcting your Personal Error Patterns, in your Basic Writing CourseMate, accessed through <www.cengagebrain.com>.

CHAPTER 5

Moving from Paragraph to Essay

A: Defining the Essay and the Thesis Statement

B: The Process of Writing an Essay

So far, you have written single paragraphs, but to succeed in college and at work, you will need to handle longer writing assignments as well. This chapter will help you apply your paragraph-writing skills to planning and writing short essays.

A. Defining the Essay and the Thesis Statement

An **essay** is a group of paragraphs about one subject. In many ways, an essay is like a paragraph in longer, fuller form. Both have an introduction, a body, and a conclusion. Both explain one main idea with details, facts, and examples.

An essay is not just a padded paragraph, however. An essay is longer because it contains more ideas.

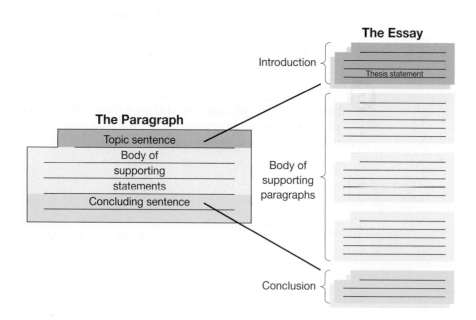

The paragraphs in an essay are part of a larger whole, so each one has a special purpose.

- The **introductory paragraph** opens the essay and tries to catch the reader's interest. It usually contains a **thesis statement**, one sentence that states the main idea of the entire essay.

- The **body** of an essay contains one, two, three, or more paragraphs, each one making a different point about the main idea.

- The **conclusion** brings the essay to a close. It might be a sentence or a paragraph long.

Here is a student essay:

Tae Kwon Do
Wineth Williams

(1) Tae kwon do is a Korean martial art. It is a way of fighting and self-defense based on an understanding of both body and mind. As a college student, I discovered tae kwon do. Even though I was physically fit and planned to become a police officer, I thought that women needed special skills to protect themselves. Tae kwon do teaches these skills and much more. The person who practices tae kwon do gains discipline, maturity, and a changed self-concept.

(2) First, the discipline of tae kwon do helps the student outfight and outsmart her opponent. For a while, I didn't appreciate the discipline. We had to move in certain ways, and we had to yell. Yelling made me laugh. Our teacher told us to shout with great force, "Keeah!" Yelling keeps the mind from focusing on being tired and helps the fighter call out the life force, or "chi," from inside her. Once we started sparring, I also had to get past not wanting to hurt anyone. Later I understood that if I punched or kicked my opponent, it meant that he or she should have been blocking and was not using good skills.

(3) Second, with practice, tae kwon do increases maturity. I have a hot temper. Before tae kwon do, I would walk dark streets and take chances, almost daring trouble. I reacted to every look or challenge. Practicing this martial art, I started to see the world more realistically. I developed more respect for the true danger in the streets. I spoke and behaved in ways to avoid trouble. My reactions became less emotional and more rational.

(4) Finally, after a year or so, tae kwon do can change the student's self-concept. This happened to me. On one hand, I became confident that I had the skills to take care of business if necessary. On the other hand, the better I got, the more I acted like a pussycat instead of a lion. That may sound strange, but inside myself, I knew that I had nothing to prove to anybody.

(5) Friends who do not work out are often surprised when I describe the way that tae kwon do changed me, but a serious exercise routine can do this for anyone. By committing to a routine or "practice," a person is setting a self-loving goal and working toward it. As I discovered firsthand, the rewards are discipline, the maturity to keep going despite discomfort, and finally, new confidence and self-respect.

- The last sentence in the introduction (underlined) is the *thesis statement*. The thesis statement must be general enough to include the topic sentence of every paragraph in the body of the essay.

- Underline the topic sentences of paragraphs (2), (3), and (4). Note that the thesis statement and the topic sentences make a rough plan of the entire essay.

- **Transitional expressions** are words and phrases that guide the reader from point to point and from paragraph to paragraph. What transition does this student use between paragraphs (1) and (2)? Between (2) and (3)? Between (3) and (4)?

  _____

- The last paragraph provides a brief *conclusion.**

PRACTICE 1

To help you understand the structure of an essay, complete this plan for "Tae Kwon Do." Under each topic sentence, jot down the writer's two or three main supporting points as if you were making a plan for the essay. (In fact, the writer probably made such a plan before she wrote her first draft.)

Paragraph 1. INTRODUCTION

Thesis statement: The person who practices tae kwon do gains discipline, maturity, and a changed self-concept.

Paragraph 2. Topic sentence: First, the discipline of tae kwon do helps the student outfight and outsmart her opponent.

Point 1: _____

Point 2: _____

Point 3: _____

Paragraph 3. Topic sentence: Second, with practice, tae kwon do increases maturity.

Point 1: _____

Point 2: _____

Paragraph 4. Topic sentence: Finally, after a year or so, tae kwon do can change the student's self-concept.

Point 1: _____

Point 2: _____

Point 3: _____

Paragraph 5. CONCLUSION

PRACTICE 2

Discuss with several classmates or write your answers to these questions.

1. Did Wineth Williams' introduction (paragraph 1) catch and hold your interest? Would this essay be just as good or better if it had no introduction but started right in with the thesis statement? Why or why not?

2. In paragraph (4), the writer says she now can "take care of business." Is this language appropriate for a college essay? Will readers know what this means?

3. Is the conclusion effective, or is it too short?

_____

* To read essays by other students, see the Writers' Workshops in Units 3, 6, 7, and 8.

4. Williams' audience was her English class. Her purpose (though not directly stated in the essay) was to let people know some of the benefits that come from practicing tae kwon do. Did she achieve her purpose?

5. What did you like best about the essay? What, if anything, would you change?

B. The Process of Writing an Essay

Whether you are writing a paragraph or an essay, the writing process is the same. Of course, writing an essay will probably take longer. In this section, you will practice these steps of the essay-writing process:

● Narrowing the subject and writing the thesis statement

● Generating ideas for the body of the essay

● Selecting and arranging ideas in a plan

● Writing and revising your essay

Narrowing the Subject and Writing the Thesis Statement

While an essay subject should be broader than a paragraph topic, a good essay subject also must be narrow enough to write about in detail. For example, the topic *jobs* is broad enough to fill a book. But the far narrower topic *driving a bulldozer at the town dump* could make a good essay. Remember to select or narrow your subject in light of your intended audience and purpose. Who are your readers, and what do you want your essay to achieve?

Writing the *thesis statement* forces you to narrow the topic further: *Driving a bulldozer for the Department of Highways was the best job I ever had.* That could be an intriguing thesis statement, but the writer could focus it even more: *For three reasons, driving a bulldozer for the Department of Highways was the best job I ever had.* The writer might discuss one reason in each of three paragraphs.

Here are two more examples of the narrowing process:

(1) Subject:	music
Narrowed subject:	Cuban singer Lucretia
Thesis statement:	In talent and style, Cuban singer Lucretia might be the next Celia Cruz.
(2) Subject:	pets
Narrowed subject:	pains and pleasures of owning a parrot
Thesis statement:	Owning a parrot will enrich your life with noise, occasional chaos, and lots of laughs.

● On the basis of each thesis statement, what do you expect the essays to discuss?

_____

_____

Although the thesis statement must include all the ideas in the body of the essay, it should also be **clear** and **specific**. Which of these thesis statements is specific enough for a good essay?

> (1) Three foolproof techniques will help you avoid disastrous first dates.
>
> (2) NBA basketball is the most exciting sport in the world.
>
> (3) Dr. Villarosa is a competent and caring physician.

- Thesis statements (1) and (3) are both specific. From (1), a reader might expect to learn about the "three foolproof techniques," each one perhaps explained in a paragraph.

- On the basis of thesis statement (3), what supporting points might the essay

  discuss? _____

  _____

- Thesis statement (2), however, is too broad for an essay—or even a book. It gives the reader (and writer) no direction.

PRACTICE 3

Choose one of these topics for your own essay. Then narrow the topic and write a clear and specific thesis statement.

> The benefits of a sport or practice
>
> The most fascinating/boring/important job I ever had
>
> Qualities of an excellent husband/wife/partner

Narrowed subject: _____

_____

Thesis statement: _____

_____

Generating Ideas for the Body of the Essay

Writers generate support for an essay just as they do for a paragraph—by prewriting to get as many interesting ideas as possible. Once you know your main point and have written a thesis statement, use your favorite prewriting method—freewriting, for example. If you feel stuck, change to brainstorming or clustering. Just keep writing.

PRACTICE 4

Generate as many good ideas as possible to support your thesis statement. Fill at least one or two pages with ideas. As you work, try to imagine how many paragraphs your essay will contain and what each will include.

Selecting and Arranging Ideas in a Plan

Next, underline or mark the most interesting ideas that support your thesis statement. Cross out the rest.

Make a rough **plan** or **outline** that includes an introductory paragraph, two or three paragraphs for the body of the essay, and a brief conclusion. Choose a logical order for presenting your ideas. Which idea will come first, second, third?

For example, the bulldozer operator might explain why that job was "the best" with three reasons, arranged in this order: 1. *On the job, I learned to operate heavy equipment.* 2. *Working alone at the controls gave me time to think.* 3. *One bonus was occasionally finding interesting items beside the road.* This arrangement moves logically from physical skills to mental benefits to a surprising bonus.

PRACTICE 5

Read over your prewriting pages, selecting your best ideas and a logical order in which to present them. Make an outline or a plan that includes an introduction and a thesis statement; two or three supporting paragraphs, each with a clear topic sentence; and a brief conclusion.

Writing and Revising Your Essay

Draft.   Now write your first draft. Try to express your ideas clearly and fully. If a section seems weak or badly written, put a check in the margin and go on; you can come back to that section later, prewriting again if necessary for fresh ideas. Set aside your draft for an hour or a day.

Revise.   Revising may be the most important step in the writing process. Reread your essay as if you were reading someone else's work, marking it up as you answer questions like these:

● Are my main idea and my thesis statement clear?

● Have I supported my thesis in a rich and convincing way?

● Does each paragraph in the body clearly explain the main idea?

● Does my essay have a logical order and good transitions?

● Are there any parts that don't belong or don't make sense?

● What one change would most improve my essay?*

You also might wish to ask a respected friend to read or listen to your essay, giving peer feedback before you revise.**

Proofread.   Now, carefully proofread your essay for errors in grammar, punctuation, and spelling. It is all-important not to skip or rush through this step. Read slowly, word by word, line by line.

The next chapter is devoted entirely to proofreading, teaching you some proven proofreading techniques that you will practice in Units 2 through 8. The units to come are your *proofreading handbook*, showing you how to spot and correct a wide range of serious errors.

PRACTICE 6

Now read your first draft to see how you can improve it. Trust your instincts about what is alive and interesting and what is dull. Take your time. As you revise, try to make this the best paper you have ever written.

Finally, write a new draft of your essay, using the format preferred by your instructor. Proofread carefully, correcting any grammar or spelling errors.

PRACTICE 7

Exchange essays with a classmate. Write a one-paragraph evaluation of each other's work, saying as specifically as possible what you like about the essay and what might be improved. If you wish, use the Peer Feedback Sheet (page 32).

---

* See Chapter 3, Part F, for more revising ideas.
** See Chapter 3, page 32, for a sample Peer Feedback Sheet

Possible Topics for Essays

1. The best/worst class I ever had

2. Two surefire ways to relax

3. Modern dating

4. A major decision

5. Tips for the new parent (college student, NBA draft pick, cell-phone user, and so forth)

6. A valuable/worthless television show

7. A good friend

8. Can anger be used constructively?

9. How I fell in love with books (German shepherds, rock climbing, video games, and so forth)

10. What childhood taught me about boys/girls in society

Chapter Highlights

Checklist for Writing an Effective Essay

- Narrow the topic in light of your audience and purpose. Be sure you can discuss the topic fully in a short essay.

- Write a clear thesis statement. If you have trouble, freewrite or brainstorm first; then narrow the topic and write the thesis statement.

- Freewrite, brainstorm, or cluster to generate facts, details, and examples to support your thesis statement.

- Plan or outline your essay, choosing two to three main ideas to support the thesis statement.

- Write a topic sentence that expresses each main idea.

- Decide on a logical order in which to present the paragraphs.

- Plan the body of each paragraph, using all you have learned about support and paragraph development.

- Write the first draft of your essay.

- Revise as necessary, checking your essay for support, unity, and coherence.

- Proofread carefully for grammar, punctuation, and spelling.

EXPLORING ONLINE

<http://www.powa.org/> Review the essay-writing process.

 View an integrated eBook and chapter-specific interactive learning tools, including flashcards, quizzes, videos, and extra help tracking and correcting your Personal Error Patterns, in your Basic Writing CourseMate, accessed through <www.cengagebrain.com>.

CHAPTER 6

Proofreading to Correct Your Personal Error Patterns

A: Identifying and Tracking Your Personal Error Patterns

B: Proofreading Strategies

The important last step in the writing process is **proofreading**: slowly reading your revised paragraph or essay in order to find and correct any errors in grammar, punctuation, and spelling.

It is essential that you proofread work before turning it in because grammatical and other mistakes distract readers and give a negative impression of your skills and even intelligence. Often, employers won't interview a candidate whose letter or résumé contains errors. Yet many new writers avoid proofreading or rush through it so quickly that they set themselves up for failure.

In fact, the more mistakes you tend to make, the more important proofreading is for you. This chapter will give you tools to enhance your skills as an error detective and writer. Then Units 2 through 8 will further develop your proofreading skills, teaching you how to understand, spot, and correct many specific errors. In every coming chapter, you will practice a proofreading strategy that targets a particular mistake.

A. Identifying and Tracking Your Personal Error Patterns

Knowing what errors you tend to make and then proofreading for these errors will boost your success in college and at work.

Learn Your Error Patterns

An **error pattern** is any error you make two, three, or more times. For example, if a teacher has noted that one of your papers has several comma splices or numerous verb errors, those are *error patterns* that you need to work on. The first step in getting rid of these errors is becoming aware of them.

Here are four ways to discover your error patterns:

Papers. Study recently returned papers, making sure you understand the errors that have been marked. Check the inside back cover of this book for proofreading symbols your instructor might use, like *frag* for sentence fragment. Count the number of times each mistake appears.

Instructor. Ask your instructor to identify your error patterns. List them. Ask which three are the most serious.

Textbook. As you work through this book, notice chapters or practices where you keep making mistakes or writing incorrect answers. These are your error patterns.

Writing lab. Go to the writing lab with a paper you recently wrote. Ask a tutor to help identify the kinds of errors you make. Ask which three are the most serious.

PRACTICE 1

Consult your instructor, or bring a recent paper to the college writing lab. Seek help in identifying your error patterns and start a written list. Ask which three error patterns most harm your written communication and your grade.

Create a Personal Error Patterns Chart

Let's say your instructor marks twelve errors on your English paper, and eight of them are verb agreement errors. This means that eight of your errors are really one error repeated eight times! Mastering this one error pattern would certainly improve your grade.

An excellent tool for tracking and beginning to master your errors is an **error chart** or **log**. This tool will show you what to study and what mistakes to watch for in your writing. Here is an example of one student's chart:

Personal Error Patterns Chart				
Error Type & Symbol	**Specific Error**	**Correction**	**Rule or Reminder**	**Assignment & Number of Errors**
Apostrophe error apos	My brothers fundraiser was a success.	My brother's fundraiser was a success.	's shows ownership by ONE brother.	Paper 1: 4 apos
Run-on ro	Jada is always late she can't decide what to wear.	Jada is always late because she can't decide what to wear.	Check for the end of each complete sentence. Join two sentences with a period or conjunction. See Ch. 15!	Paper 1: 5 ro #2: 3 ro #3: no run-ons!
Adverb adv	The patient did good.	The patient did well.	Good is an adjective; well is the adverb form.	#1: 4 adv #2: 3 adv

- Each time you receive a marked paper, write every *error name* or *type* in column 1 (like *apostrophe error* or *run-on*). Check the inside back cover to understand your instructor's proofreading symbols; for instance, *apos* for apostrophe error.

- In column 2, copy the error as you wrote it.

- In column 3, correct the error. If you have trouble understanding what you did wrong, ask the instructor, or search the index of this book for the pages you need.

- In column 4, jot the rule or ideas for fixing this type of mistake.

- In column 5, write the assignment number or date, plus the number of times you made this error. Add the error count for every later paper. Any error that appears in paper after paper will need a special plan of attack.

Continue to add errors from future papers, instructor conferences, and tests. As you work in this textbook, add to your chart any grammatical concepts that still confuse you. Whenever you master the correction of an error, cross it off the chart and celebrate your achievement.

PRACTICE 2   Using a recent paper of yours that was graded by an instructor, begin your Personal Error Patterns Chart. You can use the blank chart in this book or create your chart as a Word file, adding rows as you need them. Some students design and draw their own charts. Follow this format:

Personal Error Patterns Chart				
Error Type & Symbol	**Specific Error**	**Correction**	**Rule or Reminder**	**Assignment & Number of Errors**

B. Proofreading Strategies

Whenever you write, honor your own writing process by setting aside enough time to perform each step, including proofreading. Just as it helps to take a break of hours or days between writing your first draft and revising, taking a break *before you proofread* is beneficial. Go for a walk. Call a friend. You cannot do a good job proofreading when you are tired. You will catch more errors with a rested mind and fresh outlook.

If possible, proofread in a quiet place where you won't be distracted—not at a dance club, not standing in the kitchen fixing dinner with the kids.

Many writers have found that the **proofreading strategies** described below help them see their own writing with a fresh eye. You will learn more strategies in subsequent chapters of this book. Try a number of methods and see which ones work best for you.

Proofreading Strategy: Allow enough time to proofread.

Many students don't proofread at all, or they skim their paper for grammatical errors two minutes before class. This just doesn't work. Set aside enough time to proofread slowly and carefully, searching for errors and hunting especially for your personal error patterns.

Proofreading Strategy: Work from a paper copy.

People who proofread on computers tend to miss more errors. If you write on a computer, do not proofread on the monitor. Instead, print a copy of your paper, perhaps enlarging the type to 14 point. Switching to a paper copy seems to help the brain see more clearly.

Proofreading Strategy: Read your words aloud.

Reading silently makes it easier to skip over small errors or mentally fill in missing details, whereas listening closely is a great way to hear mistakes. Listen and follow along on your printed copy, marking errors as you hear them.

a. Read your paper aloud to *yourself*. Be sure to read *exactly* what's on the page, and read with enthusiasm.

b. Ask a *friend* or *writing tutor* to read your paper out loud to you. Tell the reader you just want to hear your words and that you don't want any other suggestions right now.

Proofreading Strategy: Read "bottom up," from the end to the beginning.

One way to fool the brain into taking a fresh look at something you've written is to proofread the last sentence first. Read slowly, word by word. Then read the second-to-last sentence, and so on, all the way back to the first sentence.

Proofreading Strategy: Isolate your sentences.

If you write on a computer, spotting errors is often easier if you reformat so that each sentence appears isolated, on its own line. Double-space between sentences. This visual change can help the brain focus clearly on one sentence at a time.

Proofreading Strategy: Check for one error at a time.

If you make many mistakes, proofread separately all the way through your paper for each error pattern. Although this process takes time, you will catch many more errors this way and make real progress. You will begin to eliminate some errors altogether as you get better at spotting and fixing them. You will learn more recommended proofreading strategies in upcoming chapters.

PRACTICE 3

Win your Academy Award! In a group with several classmates, role-play discussions between Waldo (or Wanda) and several friends. The friends are committed to getting As in their writing class, but Waldo is getting Ds and Fs. He *says* he wants to earn a nursing degree, but his actions say otherwise. Last night the friends saw him "proofreading" his paper in a Mexican restaurant over margaritas with a buddy.

Pick someone to play W. Then, one at a time, each member of the group in turn should try to persuade him to take his writing seriously, and especially to work on his proofreading skills. At the end, ask W if anyone's argument got through to him. Be prepared to report to the class.

PRACTICE 4

Print out or make a photocopy of something you wrote recently for college or work. Ask someone to read the original out loud as you listen. On your copy, underline or highlight sentences or places that sound wrong. Also mark any places where the reader stumbles verbally. Rewrite the marked sentences.

PRACTICE 5

Choose a paper you wrote recently. Select one of the proofreading strategies and try it out on this paper. Read with full attention, keenly watching for your personal error patterns. Put a check in the margin beside each error. Then correct them neatly above the lines.

Chapter Highlights

- Proofreading for errors in grammar, punctuation, and spelling is a crucial step in the writing process. Proofreading skills can be learned.

- Keeping a Personal Error Patterns Chart helps writers spot and correct the errors that they habitually make.

- Using proofreading strategies can help writers recognize the errors in their own work. These strategies helped many writers:

  - Allow enough time to proofread.
  - Work from a paper copy, not the monitor.
  - Read your words aloud.
  - Read "bottom up," from the last sentence to the first.
  - Isolate your sentences.
  - Read for one error at a time.

EXPLORING ONLINE

<http://writing.wisc.edu/Handbook/Proofreading.html> Excellent proofreading advice from the University of Wisconsin OWL.

<http://owl.english.purdue.edu/owl/resource/561/01/> Proofreading tips from the Purdue University OWL, plus advice on correcting common errors made by college students.

 View an integrated eBook and chapter-specific interactive learning tools, including flashcards, quizzes, videos, and extra help tracking and correcting your Personal Error Patterns, in your Basic Writing CourseMate, accessed through <www.cengagebrain.com>.

UNIT 1
Writing Assignments

As you complete each writing assignment, remember to perform these steps:

- Write a clear, complete topic (or thesis) sentence.
- Use freewriting, brainstorming, or clustering to generate ideas for the body of your paragraph or essay.
- Arrange your best ideas in a plan.
- Revise for support, unity, coherence, and exact language.
- Proofread for grammar, punctuation, and spelling errors.

Writing Assignment 1 *Discuss one requirement for a happy family life.* Complete this topic sentence: "A basic requirement for a happy family life is _____." What do you believe a family should have? Is it something material, like a house or a certain amount of money? Is it related to the number or types of people in the family? Does it have to do with nonmaterial things, like communication or support? Begin by jotting down all the reasons why you would require this particular thing. Then choose the three most important reasons and arrange them in order of importance—either from the least to the most important or the reverse. Explain each reason, making clear to the reader why you feel as strongly as you do.

Writing Assignment 2 *Present yourself online.* To meet people and make new friends, many computer users are creating personal Web pages on social networking sites like MySpace and Facebook. Write a description of yourself that you could post in the "About Me" section of your own page on one of these sites. To communicate who you are in just one brief paragraph, think of a one- or two-word phrase that describes you (for example, "proud mom," "daredevil," "computer geek," or "good friend"). Include that phrase in your topic sentence. Then choose details and examples to support this description.

Writing Assignment 3 *Interview a classmate about an achievement.* Write about a time your classmate achieved something important, like winning a sales prize at work, losing thirty pounds, or helping a friend through a bad time. To gather interesting facts and details, ask your classmate questions like these and take notes: *Is there one accomplishment of which you are very proud? Why was this achievement so important? Did it change the way you feel about yourself?* Keep asking questions until you feel you have enough information to give your reader a vivid sense of your classmate's triumph.

In your first sentence, state the person's achievement—for instance, *Getting her first A in English was a turning point in Jessica's life.* Then explain specifically why the achievement was so meaningful.

Writing Assignment 4 *Develop a paragraph with examples.* Below are topic sentences for possible paragraphs. Pick the topic sentence that most interests you and write a paragraph, using one to three examples to explain the topic sentence. If you prefer, choose a quotation from the Quotation Bank at the end of this book and explain it with one or more examples.

a. A sense of humor can make difficult times easier to bear.

b. Mistakes can be great teachers.

c. Television commercials often insult my intelligence.

67

UNIT 1

Review

Choosing a Topic Sentence

Each group of sentences could be unscrambled and written as a paragraph. Circle the letter of the sentence that would be the best topic sentence.

1. a. Rooftops and towers made eye-catching shapes against the winter sky.

   b. Far below, the faint sounds of slush and traffic were soothing.

   c. From the apartment-house roof, the urban scene was oddly relaxing.

   d. Stoplights changing color up and down the avenues created a rhythmic pattern invisible from the street.

2. a. Actor Andy Garcia and *CSI Miami* star Adam Rodriguez own homes in Miami.

   b. Mexican actress and singer Lucia Mendez resides there, as does Venezuelan soap opera star Jose Luis Rodriguez.

   c. Singers Ricky Martin and Enrique Iglesias call Miami home.

   d. In recent years, Miami has become the Hollywood of southern America.

Selecting Ideas

Here is a topic sentence and a brainstormed list of possible ideas for a paragraph. Check "Keep" for ideas that best support the topic sentence and "Drop" for ideas that do not.

Topic sentence: Oprah Winfrey is a force for tremendous good in the United States.

Keep   Drop

_____ _____ 1. on her TV show, often has experts who help people with relationships or finances

_____ _____ 2. through her book club, inspired millions to start reading and periodically introduces a vast audience to new and old authors

_____ _____ 3. proves that women don't need to be thin to be beautiful, popular, famous, and greatly loved

_____ _____ 4. was born in 1954 on a farm in Mississippi

_____ _____ 5. at age six was sent to Milwaukee; kept cockroaches in a jar as substitute for farm animals

_____ _____ 6. is a well-known example of someone who overcame many obstacles, including childhood abuse and racial prejudice

_____ _____ 7. another example of someone who has overcome abuse and prejudice is actress Halle Berry

68

_____ _____ 8. physical abuse by a former boyfriend caused Berry to lose 80 percent of her hearing in one ear

_____ _____ 9. Winfrey gives millions to such causes as helping South African children orphaned by AIDS

_____ _____ 10. her website, magazine, and radio network encourage women to develop their spirituality and pursue personal goals

Examining a Paragraph

Read this paragraph and answer the questions.

(1) Students at some American colleges are learning a lot from trash by studying "garbology." (2) Wearing rubber gloves, they might sift through the local dump, counting and collecting treasures that they examine back at the laboratory. (3) First, they learn to look closely and to interpret what they see, thus reading the stories that trash tells. (4) More important, they learn the truth about what Americans buy, what they eat, and how they live. (5) Students at the University of Arizona, for instance, were surprised to find that low-income families in certain areas buy more educational toys for their children than nearby middle-income families do. (6) Most important, students say that garbology courses can motivate them to be better citizens of planet Earth. (7) One young woman, for example, after seeing from hard evidence in her town's landfill how many people really recycled their glass, cans, and newspapers and how many cheated, organized an annual recycling awareness day.

1. Write the number of the topic sentence in the paragraph. _____

2. What kind of order does this writer use? _____

3. Students learn three things in garbology courses. (a) Write the numbers of the sentences stating these. (b) Which two ideas are supported by examples?

(a) _____ (b) _____

On Earth Day, garbology students at Western Kentucky University examine the contents of campus dumpsters to raise awareness about the impact of waste.

Copyright © Cengage Learning. All rights reserved.

Reprinted with permission of Western Kentucky University Office of Sustainability

Writers' Workshop

Discuss Your Name

Good writers are masters of exact language and thoughtful observation. Read this student's paragraph about her name. Underline any words or details that strike you as well written, interesting, or powerful.

In this paragraph I will write about my name. My name YuMing is made up of two Chinese characters that mean "the universe" and "the crow of a bird." This may seem like a strange name to an American, but in fact it has a special meaning for me. In ancient Chinese literature, there is a story about a bird that was owned by God. This bird was rumored to have the most beautiful voice in the universe. A greedy king wanted this bird, so he had it captured and placed in a big cage. He sat next to this cage day after day waiting for the bird to sing, but the bird stayed silent. After three years, the impatient king threw open the cage door and set the bird free. As the bird flew up toward the heavens, it made its first crow in three years. The sound shocked everyone in the kingdom because they realized the legend was true—they had never heard such a beautiful voice before! My parents told me that they gave me this name because they want me to be like the bird in the story. Though I may stay silent for a while as I establish myself in society, they hope that I will "crow" one day when it is the right time for me, and crow loudly so everyone in the universe can hear.

YuMing Lai, student

1. How effective is YuMing Lai's paragraph about the meaning of her name?

    _____ Good topic sentence?   _____ Rich supporting details?

    _____ Logical organization?   _____ Effective conclusion?

2. Underline the words, details, or sentences you like best. Put a check beside anything that needs improvement.

3. Now discuss your underlinings with your group or class. Try to explain as exactly as you can why you like something. For example, in the last sentence, the way that the writer ties her parents' wish for her to the meaning of the story is moving and surprising.

4. Is YuMing's topic sentence as good as the rest of her paragraph? If not, how might she change it?

5. Did YuMing's thoughts about her name make you think about your own name? Do you like your name? Why or why not? Do you know why your parents chose it?

6. What order does this paragraph employ?

Writing and Revising Ideas

1. Write about the meaning of your name or the name of someone close to you.

2. Visit the government's website below, which lists the most popular baby names in the United States, year by year. Do you see any patterns? How popular is your name? Your parents' names?
<http://www.ssa.gov/OACT/babynames/>

For help with writing your paragraph, see Chapter 3 and Chapter 4, Parts B and C. As you revise, pay special attention to writing a clear, catchy topic sentence supported by interesting details.

UNIT 2

Writing Complete Sentences

The sentence is the basic unit of all writing, so good writers must know how to write clear and correct sentences. In this unit, you will

- Learn to spot subjects and verbs
- Practice writing complete sentences
- Learn to avoid or correct any sentence fragments
- Learn proofreading strategies to correct your own errors

Spotlight on Writing

Notice the way this writer uses strong, correct sentences to capture a moment with her grandfather, her *abuelo*. If possible, read the paragraph aloud.

My grandfather has misplaced his words again. He is trying to find my name in the kaleidoscope of images that his mind has become. His face brightens like a child's who has just remembered his lesson. He points to me and says my mother's name. I smile back and kiss him on the cheek. It doesn't matter what names he remembers anymore. Every day he is more confused, his memory slipping back a little further in time. Today he has no grandchildren yet. Tomorrow he will be a young man courting my grandmother again, quoting bits of poetry to her. In months to come, he will begin calling her Mama.

Judith Ortiz Cofer, "The Witch's Husband"

- How does the writer feel about her grandfather? Which sentences tell you this?

- Why do you think the writer arranges the last three sentences in the order that she does?

Writing Ideas

- *A visit with a loved (or feared) relative*
- *Your relationship with someone who has a disability*

CHAPTER **7**

Subjects and Verbs

A. Defining and Spotting Subjects

The sentence is the basic unit of all writing. To write well, you need to know how to write correct and effective sentences. This chapter will show you how. A **sentence** is a group of words that expresses a complete thought about something or someone. It contains a **subject** and a **verb**.

> (1) _____ jumped over the black Buick, scaled the building, and finally reached the roof.
>
> (2) _____ needs a new coat of paint.

These sentences might be interesting, but they are incomplete.

● In sentence (1), *who* jumped, scaled, and reached? Spider-Man, Alicia Keys, the English teacher?

● Depending on *who* performed the action—jumping, scaling, or reaching—the sentence can be exciting, surprising, or strange.

● What is missing is the *who* word—the *subject*.

● In sentence (2), *what* needs a new coat of paint? The house, the car, the old rocking chair?

● What is missing is the *what* word—the *subject*.

For a sentence to be complete, it must contain a *who* or *what* word—a *subject*. The subject tells you *who* or *what* does something or exists in a certain way.

The subject is often a *noun*, a word that names a person, place, or thing (such as *Alicia Keys*, *English teacher*, or *house*).* However, a *pronoun* (*I, you, he, she, it, we,* or *they*) also can be the subject.**

_____
* For more work on nouns, see Chapter 20.
** For more work on pronoun subjects, see Chapter 21, Part F.

PRACTICE 1

In each of these sentences, the subject (the *who* or *what* word) is missing. Fill in your own subject to make the sentence complete.

EXAMPLE: A(n) _____*fox*_____ dashed across the road.

1. The _____ skidded across the ice.

2. The _____ was eager to begin the semester.

3. Because of the crowd, the _____ slipped out unnoticed.

4. For years, _____ piled up in the back of the closet.

5. The cheerful yellow _____ brightened Sheila's mood.

6. _____ and _____ were scattered all over the doctor's desk.

7. The _____ believed that his _____ would return someday.

8. The _____ was in bad shape. The _____ was falling in, and

   the _____ were all broken.

As you may have noticed, the subject can be just one noun or pronoun. This single noun or pronoun is called **the simple subject**. The subject also can include *words that describe the noun or pronoun* (such as *the, cheerful,* or *yellow*). The noun and pronoun plus the words that describe it are called **the complete subject**.

> (3) Three scarlet roses grew near the path.
>
> (4) A large box was delivered this morning.

● The complete subject of sentence (3) is *three scarlet roses*.

● The simple subject is the noun *roses*.

● What is the complete subject of (4)? _____

● What is the simple subject of (4)? _____

Try This   To find the subject, try turning the sentence into a question: *Who or what grew near the path? Three scarlet roses. Who or what was delivered this morning? A large box.*

PRACTICE 2

Circle the *simple* subject in each sentence. (A person's complete name—though more than one word—is considered a simple subject.)

EXAMPLE: (Stacie Ponder) blogs about horror movies.

(1) Many people love scary films. (2) Psychologists want to know why. (3) Dr. Leon Rappoport studies this fear factor among moviegoers. (4) Humans have always liked to explore their feelings of fear and anxiety, according to Rappoport. (5) Frightening movies allow them to master those emotions and work through them. (6) People do not wish to meet Hannibal Lecter in daily life. (7) They like to watch him onscreen, however, in

Movie poster, 1958. Horror movies allow people to face their fears in a safe way, claim psychologists.

the absence of any real danger. (8) Horror films and stories provide opportunities for such experiences. (9) Also, some moviegoers like to explore their uncivilized, antisocial nature in safe settings. (10) Many teenagers, in particular, need to test their tolerance for threatening situations. (11) In addition, parents often declare horror movies inappropriate. (12) Therefore, adolescents want to see this forbidden entertainment more than ever.

PRACTICE 3

In these sentences, the complete subject has been omitted. You must decide where it belongs and fill in a complete subject (a *who* or *what* word along with any words that describe it). Write in any complete subject that makes sense.

EXAMPLE: Raced down the street.

My worried friend raced down the street.

1. Trained day and night for the big event.

   _____

2. Has a dynamic singing voice.

   _____

3. Landed in the cornfield.

   _____

4. After the show, applauded and screamed for fifteen minutes.

   _____

5. Got out of the large gray van.

   _____

B. Spotting Singular and Plural Subjects

Besides being able to spot subjects in sentences, you need to know whether a subject is singular or plural.

> (1) The man jogged around the park.

- The subject of this sentence is *the man*.
- Because *the man* is one person, the subject is *singular*.

Singular means only one of something.

> (2) The man and his friend jogged around the park.

- The subject of sentence (2) is *the man and his friend*.
- Because *the man and his friend* refers to more than one person, the subject is *plural*.

Plural means more than one of something.*

PRACTICE 4

Here is a list of possible subjects of sentences. If the subject is singular, write *S* next to it; if the subject is plural, write *P* next to it.

EXAMPLES: an elephant   _S_

children   _P_

1. our cousins   _____   5. women   _____
2. a song and a dance   _____   6. a rock star and her band   _____
3. Kansas   _____   7. his three pickup trucks   _____
4. their website   _____   8. salad dressing   _____

PRACTICE 5

Circle the complete subjects in these sentences. Then, in the space at the right, write *S* if the subject is singular or *P* if the subject is plural.

EXAMPLE: This (young cartoonist) is getting national attention.   _S_

1. Aaron McGruder was a student at the University of Maryland.   _____
2. Comic books and hip-hop music intrigued him.   _____
3. To Aaron, existing comics did not capture racial diversity in a real way.   _____
4. McGruder decided to create a comic strip called *Boondocks*.   _____
5. The characters were African-American city kids in suburbia.   _____
6. The strip appeared in the college's student paper, *The Diamondback*, in 1997.   _____
7. Rave reviews and a few angry letters poured in.   _____
8. A major music magazine soon began publishing *Boondocks* every day.   _____

_____

* For much more on singulars and plurals, see Chapter 20, Nouns.

9. Aaron's goal is to expand racial dialogue by using humor. _____

10. The daily strip, a book, and a TV series now keep him very busy. _____

C. Spotting Prepositional Phrases

A **preposition** is a word like *on*, *through*, and *before*. Prepositions usually indicate location, direction, or time. For example, the plane sat *on the runway*, flew *through a thunderstorm*, and landed *before dark*. These humble words can be confusing, so it's important to be able to recognize them.

Common Prepositions			
about	beneath	inside	through
above	beside	into	throughout
across	between	like	to
after	beyond	near	toward
against	by	of	under
along	despite	off	underneath
among	down	on	until
around	during	onto	up
at	except	out	upon
before	for	outside	with
behind	from	over	within
below	in	past	without

One group of words that may confuse you as you look for the subjects of sentences is the prepositional phrase. A **prepositional phrase** contains a *preposition* and its *object* (the noun or pronoun that follows the preposition). Here are some prepositional phrases:*

Prepositional Phrase	=	Preposition	+	Object
at work		at		work
behind her		behind		her
of the students		of		the students
on the blue table		on		the blue table

The object of a preposition *cannot* be the subject of a sentence. Therefore, crossing out prepositional phrases can help you find the real subject.

(1) On summer evenings, girls in white dresses stroll under the trees.

(2) ~~On summer evenings~~, girls ~~in white dresses~~ stroll ~~under the trees~~.

(3) From dawn to dusk, we hiked.

(4) The president of the college will speak tonight

- In sentence (1), you may have trouble spotting the subject. Is it *evening*, *girls*, or *dresses*?

* For more work on prepositions and a list of many English expressions containing prepositions, see Chapter 23, Prepositions.

● However, once the prepositional phrases are crossed out in (2), the subject, *girls*, is easy to see.

● Cross out the prepositional phrase in sentence (3). What is the subject of the sentence? _____

● Cross out the prepositional phrase in sentence (4). What is the subject of the sentence? _____

Try This If you have trouble finding prepositional phrases, circle all the prepositions, referring to the prepositions list. Then locate the rest of the words in each prepositional phrase.

PRACTICE 6

Underline all the prepositional phrases in the following sentences. Some sentences include more than one prepositional phrase.

1. In college or the workplace, a knowledge of your learning style can help you master any subject.

2. A learning style is a person's preferred way of learning new information.

3. The four types of learning styles are visual, auditory, reading/writing, and hands-on.

4. Most people learn in all four ways, with one favored style.

5. People with a visual learning style understand best from diagrams, images, or videos.

6. Auditory learners, on the other hand, learn by reading aloud, talking, and listening.

7. Learners with a reading/writing style absorb information easily through written words.

8. After a class, they should write notes and summaries of the material.

9. Hands-on learners show a strong preference for movement and action.

10. For example, they handle objects, perform, or conduct experiments.

PRACTICE 7

Now cross out the prepositional phrase or phrases in each sentence. Then circle the *simple* subject of the sentence.

    EXAMPLE: (Millions) of people walk on the Appalachian Trail each year.

1. That famous trail stretches from Springer Mountain in Georgia to Mount Katahdin in Maine.

2. One quarter of the trail goes through Virginia.

3. The majority of walkers hike for one day.

4. Of the four million trail users, two hundred people complete the entire trail every year.

5. For most hikers, the trip through fourteen states takes four or five months.

6. In the spring, many hardy souls begin their 2,158-mile-long journey.

7. These lovers of the wilderness must reach Mount Katahdin before winter.

8. On the trail, men and women battle heat, humidity, bugs, blisters, muscle sprains, and food and water shortages.

9. After beautiful green scenery, the path becomes rocky and mountainous.

10. Hikers in the White Mountains of New Hampshire struggle against high winds.

11. A pebble from Georgia is sometimes added to the pile of stones at the top of Mount Katahdin.

12. At the bottom of the mountain, the conquerors of the Appalachian Trail add their names to the list of successful hikers.

D. Defining and Spotting Action Verbs

(1) The pears _____ on the trees.

(2) Robert _____ his customer's hand and _____ her dog on the head.

These sentences tell you what or who the subject is—*the pears* and *Robert*—but not what each subject does.

● In sentence (1), what do the pears do? Do they *grow, ripen, rot, stink,* or *glow*?

● All these *action verbs* fit into the blank space in sentence (1), but the meaning of the sentence changes depending on which action verb you use.

● In sentence (2), what actions did Robert perform? He might have *shaken, ignored, kissed, patted,* or *scratched.*

● Depending on which verb you use, the meaning of the sentence changes.

● Some sentences, like sentence (2), contain two or more action verbs.

For a sentence to be complete, it must have a *verb*. An *action verb* tells what action the subject is performing.

PRACTICE 8

Fill in each blank with an action verb.

1. Kevin Durant _____ through the air for a slam dunk.

2. An artist _____ the scene at the waterfront.

3. When the rooster _____, the dogs _____.

4. A fierce wind _____ and _____.

5. The audience _____ while the conductor _____.

6. This new kitchen gadget _____ and _____ any vegetable you can imagine.

7. When the dentist _____ his drill, Charlene _____.

8. Will Smith _____ and _____ across the stage.

PRACTICE 9

Circle the action verbs in these sentences. Some sentences contain more than one action verb.

(1) Sometimes the combination of talent and persistence explodes into well-deserved fame and fortune. (2) For almost a year, J. K. Rowling survived on public assistance in Edinburgh, Scotland. (3) Almost every day that year, she brought her baby to a coffee

shop near their damp, unheated apartment. (4) In the warmth of the café, the divorced, unemployed mother sat and wrote. (5) Almost at the end of her endurance, she finally finished her first book. (6) Today, Rowling's Harry Potter books sell hundreds of millions of copies in sixty languages. (7) Each book tells about Harry's adventures, both in the everyday world (the Muggles' world) and at a new grade level at Hogwarts School of Witchcraft and Wizardry. (8) The imaginative and very funny series about the courageous young wizard-in-training attracts and enthralls adults as well as children. (9) In fact, the *New York Times* began a children's bestseller list for the first time—after months of Harry Potter books in slots 1, 2, and 3 on the adult bestseller list!

E. Defining and Spotting Linking Verbs

The verbs you have been examining so far show action, but a second kind of verb simply links the subject to words that describe or rename it.

> (1) Aunt Claudia sometimes seems a little strange.

- The subject in this sentence is *Aunt Claudia*, but there is no action verb.
- Instead, *seems* links the subject, *Aunt Claudia*, with the descriptive words *a little strange*.

Aunt Claudia	seems	a little strange.
↓	↓	↓
subject	linking verb	descriptive words

> (2) They are reporters for the newspaper.

- The subject is *they*. The word *reporters* renames the subject.
- What verb links the subject, *they*, with the word *reporters*? _____

For a sentence to be complete, it must contain a *verb*. A *linking verb* **links the subject with words that describe or rename that subject.**

Here are some linking verbs you should know:

Common Linking Verbs	
be (am, is, are, was, were)	look
act	seem
appear	smell
become	sound
feel	taste
get	

- The most common linking verbs are the forms of *to be—am, is, are, was, were*—but verbs of the senses, such as *feel, look,* and *smell,* also may be used as linking verbs.

PRACTICE 10

The subjects and descriptive words in these sentences are boxed. Circle the linking verbs.

1. Jerry sounds sleepy today.
2. Ronda always was the best debater on the team.
3. His brother often appeared relaxed and happy.
4. By evening, Harvey felt confident about the exam.
5. Mara and Maude became talent scouts.

PRACTICE 11

Circle the linking verbs in these sentences. Then underline the subject and the descriptive word or words in each sentence.

1. The sweet potato pie tastes delicious.
2. You usually seem energetic.
3. During the summer, she looks calm.
4. Under heavy snow, the new dome roof appeared sturdy.
5. Raphael is a gifted animal trainer.
6. Lately, I feel very competent at work.
7. Luz became a medical technician.
8. Yvonne acted surprised at her baby shower.

F. Spotting Verbs of More Than One Word

All the verbs you have dealt with so far have been single words—*look, walked, saw, are, were,* and so on. However, many verbs consist of more than one word.

> (1) Sarah is walking to work.

- The subject is *Sarah.* What is *Sarah* doing?
- Sarah is walking.
- *Walking* is the *main verb. Is* is the *helping verb;* without *is, walking* is not a complete verb.

> (2) Should I have written sooner?

- The subject is *I.*
- *Should have written* is the *complete verb.*
- *Written* is the *main verb. Should* and *have* are the *helping verbs;* without *should have, written* is not a complete verb.

(3) Do you eat fish?

● What is the subject? _____
● What is the main verb? _____
● What is the helping verb? _____

The *complete verb* **in a sentence consists of all the helping verbs and the main verb**.

PRACTICE 12

The blanks following each sentence tell you how many words make up the complete verb. Fill in the blanks with the complete verb; then circle the main verb.

EXAMPLE: Language researchers at the University of Arizona have been studying parrots.

_____*have*_____ _____*been*_____ _____(*studying*)_____

1. Dr. Irene Pepperberg has worked with Alex, an African Gray parrot, for years.

   _____   _____

2. Nearly one hundred words can be used by this intelligent bird.

   _____   _____   _____

3. Alex is believed to understand the words, not just "parrot" sounds.

   _____   _____

Alex, the talking parrot, with his trainer, Dr. Irene Pepperberg

4. For example, from a tray of objects, Alex can select all the keys, all the wooden items, or all the blue items.

    _____   _____

5. Dr. Pepperberg might show Alex a fuzzy cloth ball.

    _____   _____

6. The bird will shout, "Wool!"

    _____   _____

7. Alex has been counting to six.

    _____   _____   _____

8. Currently, he and the other parrots are learning letters and their sounds.

    _____   _____

9. Can these birds really be taught to read?

    _____   _____   _____

10. Scientists in animal communication are excited by the possibility.

    _____   _____

PRACTICE 13   Box the simple subject, circle the main verb, and underline any helping verbs in each of the following sentences.

> **EXAMPLE:**   Most │people│ have ⟨wondered⟩ about the beginning of the universe.

1. Scientists have developed one theory.
2. According to this theory, the universe began with a huge explosion.
3. The explosion has been named the Big Bang.
4. First, all matter must have been packed into a tiny speck under enormous pressure.
5. Then, about 15 billion years ago, that speck burst with amazing force.
6. Everything in the universe has come from the original explosion.
7. In fact, the universe still is expanding from the Big Bang.
8. All of the planets and stars are moving away from each other at an even speed.
9. Will it expand forever?
10. Experts may be debating that question for a long time.

Chapter Highlights

- **A sentence contains a subject and a verb, and expresses a complete thought:**

  S   V
  Jennifer swims every day.

          S   V
  The two students have tutored in the writing lab.

- **An action verb tells what the subject is doing:**

  Toni Morrison *writes* novels.

- **A linking verb links the subject with words that describe or rename it:**

  Her novels *are* bestsellers.

- **Don't mistake the object of a prepositional phrase for a subject:**

         S   PP
  The red car [in the showroom] is a Corvette.

     PP   S
  [In my dream,] *a sailor and his parrot* were singing.

Proofreading Strategy

Being able to recognize subjects and verbs will help you know whether or not your sentences are complete. To test for completeness, **cross out** and **color code**:

1. Read each sentence slowly, crossing out any prepositional phrases.

2. Then either circle the subject and underline the verb or *color code your subjects and verbs,* using two different highlighters, like this:

   My hometown has been hit very hard ~~by the recession~~.

   Many ~~of my neighbors~~ have lost their jobs, including both ~~of my brothers~~.

3. Finally, read each sentence slowly to make sure it expresses a complete thought and ends with a period.

WRITING AND PROOFREADING ASSIGNMENT

Whether you have just graduated from high school or have worked for several years, the first year of college can be difficult. Imagine that you are writing to an incoming student who needs advice and encouragement. Pick one serious problem you had as a first-year student and explain how you coped with it. State the problem clearly. Use examples from your own experience or the experience of others to make your advice more vivid. After you write and revise your composition, take a break before you proofread. Then, cross out your prepositional phrases and mark or highlight every subject and verb. Check each sentence for completeness.

CHAPTER REVIEW

Circle the simple subjects, crossing out any confusing prepositional phrases. Then underline the complete verbs. If you prefer, color code the subjects and verbs. If you have difficulty with this review, consider rereading the lesson.

Target Practice: Setting Attainable Goals

(1) Successful people know an important secret about setting and reaching goals. (2) These high achievers break their big goals into smaller, more manageable steps or targets. (3) Then they hit the targets, one by one. (4) Otherwise, a huge goal might seem impossible.

(5) To turn a major goal into smaller steps, many achievers think backward. (6) Dillon, for example, wanted to lose twenty pounds by graduation. (7) That much weight must be lost gradually. (8) So Dillon decided to set smaller targets for himself. (9) First, Dillon eliminated between-meal snacks. (10) On the new plan, he might eat an occasional apple, but only in emergencies. (11) Second, Dillon gave up second helpings at any meal—no matter what. (12) His third target was a walk after dinner. (13) Every night, this purposeful dieter would check off the day's successes.

(14) Even high achievers do not complete a major goal, like losing a lot of weight, every day. (15) Yet they can feel satisfaction about moving forward one step at a time. (16) The photographer at Dillon's graduation captured his beaming smile. (17) Under that cap and gown, Dillon's weight had dropped by twenty-two pounds.

EXPLORING ONLINE

<http://grammar.ccc.commnet.edu/grammar/quizzes/subjector.htm>
Interactive quiz: Identify the subjects.

<http://grammar.ccc.commnet.edu/grammar/quizzes/verbmaster.htm>
Interactive quiz: Identify verbs of one or more words.

 View an integrated eBook and chapter-specific interactive learning tools, including flashcards, quizzes, videos, and extra help tracking and correcting your Personal Error Patterns, in your Basic Writing CourseMate, accessed through <www.cengagebrain.com>.

CHAPTER 8

Avoiding Sentence Fragments

A: Writing Sentences with Subjects and Verbs

B: Writing Sentences with Complete Verbs

C: Completing the Thought

A. Writing Sentences with Subjects and Verbs

Which of these groups of words is a sentence? Be prepared to explain your answers.

(1) People will bet on almost anything.

(2) For example, every winter the Nenana River in Alaska.

(3) Often make bets on the date of the breakup of the ice.

(4) Must guess the exact day and time of day.

(5) Recently, the lucky guess won $300,000.

- In (2), you probably wanted to know what the Nenana River *does*. The idea is not complete because there is no *verb*.

- In (3) and (4), you probably wanted to know *who* often makes bets on the date of the breakup of the ice and *who* must guess the exact day and time of day.

  The ideas are not complete. What is missing? _____

- But in sentences (1) and (5), you knew *who did what*. These ideas are complete. Why? _____

Below are the same groups of words written as complete sentences:

(1) People will bet on almost anything.

(2) For example, every winter the Nenana River in Alaska freezes.

(3) The townspeople often make bets on the date of the breakup of the ice.

(4) Someone must guess the exact day and time of day.

(5) Recently, the lucky guess won $300,000.

Every *sentence* must have both a subject and a verb—and must express a complete thought.

A *fragment* is not a complete sentence because it lacks either a subject or a complete verb—or does not express a complete thought.

PRACTICE 1

All of the following are *fragments* because they lack a subject, a verb, or both. Add a subject, a verb, or both to make the fragments into sentences.

EXAMPLE: Raising onions in the backyard.

Rewrite: _Charles is raising onions in the backyard._____

1. Melts easily.

   Rewrite: _____

2. That couple on the street corner.

   Rewrite: _____

3. One of the fans.

   Rewrite: _____

4. Manages a Software City store.

   Rewrite: _____

5. The tip of her nose.

   Rewrite: _____

6. DVD players.

   Rewrite: _____

7. Makes me nervous.

   Rewrite: _____

8. A person who likes to take risks.

   Rewrite: _____

Sentence fragments are considered a serious and distracting error in college and at work, so it is important that you learn to eliminate them from your writing.

B. Writing Sentences with Complete Verbs

Do not be fooled by incomplete verbs.

> (1) She leaving for the city.
>
> (2) We done that chapter already.

- *Leaving* seems to be the verb in (1).
- *Done* seems to be the verb in (2).

But . . .

● An *-ing* word like *leaving* is not by itself a verb.

● A word like *done* is not by itself a verb.

(1) She $\left.\begin{array}{c} is \\ was \end{array}\right\}$ leaving for the city.

(2) We $\left.\begin{array}{c} have \\ had \end{array}\right\}$ done that chapter already.

● To be a verb, an *-ing* word (called a *present participle*) must be combined with some form of the verb *to be*.*

Helping Verb		Main Verb
am	were	
is	has been	jogging
are	have been	
was	had been	

● To be a verb, a word like *done* (called a *past participle*) must be combined with some form of *to have* or *to be*.**

Helping Verb		Main Verb
am	have	
is	had	
are	has been	forgotten
was	have been	
were	had been	
has		

PRACTICE 2

All of the following are fragments; they have only a partial or an incomplete verb. Complete each verb in order to make these fragments into sentences.

EXAMPLE: Both children grown tall this year.

Rewrite: *Both children have grown tall this year.*

1. The Australian winning the tennis match.

   Rewrite: _____

2. Her friends seen her at the mall every Saturday.

   Rewrite: _____

_____

* For a detailed explanation of present participles, see Chapter 12.
** For a detailed explanation of past participles, see Chapter 11.

3. Steve's letter published in the *Miami Herald*.

   Rewrite: _____

4. My physics professor always forgetting the assignment.

   Rewrite: _____

5. This sari made of scarlet silk.

   Rewrite: _____

6. For the past two years, Joan working at a computer company.

   Rewrite: _____

7. You ever been to Hawaii?

   Rewrite: _____

8. Yesterday, Ed's wet gloves taken from the radiator.

   Rewrite: _____

PRACTICE 3

All of the following are fragments; *they lack a subject*, and they contain only a *partial verb*. Make these fragments into sentences by adding a subject and by completing the verb.

EXAMPLE: Written by Ray Bradbury.

Rewrite: *This science fiction thriller was written by Ray Bradbury.*

1. Forgotten the password.

   Rewrite: _____

2. Now running the copy center.

   Rewrite: _____

3. Making sculpture from old car parts.

   Rewrite: _____

4. Been working at the state capitol building.

   Rewrite: _____

5. Creeping along the windowsill.

   Rewrite: _____

6. Driven that tractor for years.

   Rewrite: _____

7. Worked as a web designer.

   Rewrite: _____

8. Been to a wrestling match.

Rewrite: _____

PRACTICE 4

Fragments are most likely to occur in paragraphs or longer pieces of writing. Proofread the paragraph below for fragments; check for missing subjects, missing verbs, or incomplete verbs. Circle the number of every fragment; then write your corrections above the lines.

(1) On a routine day in 1946, a scientist at the Raytheon Company his hand into his pants pocket for a candy bar. (2) The chocolate, however, a messy, sticky mass of gunk. (3) Dr. Percy Spencer had been testing a magnetron tube. (4) Could the chocolate have melted from radiation leaking from the tube? (5) Spencer sent out for a bag of popcorn kernels. (6) Put the kernels near the tube. (7) Within minutes, corn popping wildly onto the lab floor. (8) Within a short time, Raytheon working on the development of the microwave oven. (9) Microwave cooking the first new method of preparing food since the discovery of fire more than a million years ago. (10) Was the first cooking technique that did not directly or indirectly apply fire to food.

C. Completing the Thought

Can these ideas stand by themselves?

> (1) Because oranges are rich in vitamin C.
>
> (2) Although Sam is sleepy.

- These ideas have a subject and a verb (find them), but they cannot stand alone because you expect something else to follow.

- Because oranges are rich in vitamin C, *then what*? Should you *eat them, sell them*, or *make marmalade*?

- Although Sam is sleepy, what will he do? Will he *wash the dishes, walk the dog*, or *go to the gym*?

> (1) Because oranges are rich in vitamin C, *I eat one every day*.
>
> (2) Although Sam is sleepy, *he will work late tonight*.

- These sentences are now complete.

- Words like *because* and *although* make an idea incomplete unless another idea is added to complete the thought.

You will learn more about words like this, called *subordinating conjunctions*, in Chapter 15, but here is a list of the most common ones.*

Common Subordinating Conjunctions			
after	because	though	whenever
although	before	unless	where
as	if	until	whether
as if	since	when	while

Fragments often begin with these *subordinating conjunctions*. When you spot one of these words in your writing, check to make sure you have completed the thought.

PRACTICE 5

Make these fragments into sentences by adding some idea that completes the thought.

EXAMPLE: Because I miss my family, *I am going home for the weekend.*

1. As May stepped off the elevator, _____

2. If you are driving to Main Street, _____

3. While Kimi studied chemistry, _____

4. Because you believe in yourself, _____

5. Although spiders scare most people, _____

6. Unless the surgery is absolutely necessary, _____

7. Whenever I hear Macy Gray sing, _____

8. Although these air conditioners are expensive to run, _____

_____

Can these ideas stand by themselves?

(3) Graciela, who has a one-year-old daughter.

(4) A course that I will always remember.

(5) Vampire stories, which are popular now.

● In each of these examples, you expect something else to follow. Graciela, who has a one-year-old daughter, *is doing what*? Does she *attend town meetings, knit sweaters,* or *fly planes*?

● A course that I will always remember *is what*? The thought must be completed.

● Vampire stories, which are popular now, *do what*? The thought must be completed.

_____

* For more work on this type of sentence, see Chapter 15, Subordination.

(3) Graciela, who has a one-year-old daughter, *attends Gordon College.*

(4) A course that I will always remember *is documentary filmmaking.*

(5) Vampire stories, which are popular now, *exist in cultures all over the world.*

● These sentences are now complete.*

Try This Try this "fragment test," which works for some people. Ask, "Is it true that . . ." followed by the test sentence:

Is it true that ___*The horoscopes that appear in the daily papers*___? NO

Is it true that ___*The horoscopes that appear in the daily papers make me laugh*___? YES

If the answer is *no*, this is a fragment. If the answer is *yes*, the sentence is correct.

PRACTICE 6

Make these fragments into sentences by completing the thought.

EXAMPLE: Kent, who is a good friend of mine, *rarely writes to me.*___

1. The horoscopes that appear in the daily papers _____

2. Couples who never argue _____

3. Alonzo, who is a superb pole-vaulter, _____

4. Satellite radio, which offers hundreds of channels, _____

5. A person who has coped with a great loss _____

6. My dog, which is the smartest animal alive, _____

7. Libraries that are up to date _____

8. This video, which we watched last night, _____

9. A person who becomes upset easily _____

10. A country that I have always wanted to visit _____

PRACTICE 7

To each fragment, add a subject, a verb, or whatever is required to complete the thought.

1. Visiting the White House.

   Rewrite: _____

2. That digital clock blinking for hours.

   Rewrite: _____

3. People who can't say no to their children.

   Rewrite: _____

_____

* For more work on this type of sentence, see Chapter 18, Part A.

4. Make tables from driftwood they find on the beach.

   Rewrite: _____

5. Over the roof and into the garden.

   Rewrite: _____

6. Raúl completed a culinary arts program, and now he a well-known chef.

   Rewrite: _____

7. Chess, which is a difficult game to play.

   Rewrite: _____

8. Whenever Dolly starts to yodel.

   Rewrite: _____

PRACTICE 8

Proofread the paragraph for fragments. Circle the number of every fragment, and then write your corrections above the lines.

(1) Ralph Gilles won fame as the designer of the Chrysler 300C. (2) Which earned many design awards. (3) Raised in Canada by Haitian parents, Gilles was in awe of his mother. (4) Because she gave her all to various thankless jobs and still told her children success stories. (5) When he was a boy. (6) Gilles loved to draw futuristic cars in his

Designer Ralph Gilles poses with a Dodge Challenger, one of Chrysler's "muscle cars."

notebooks. (7) An aunt noticed his design gifts and urged him to write to Lee Iacocca. (8) Who was then chairman of the Chrysler Corporation. (9) Amazingly, after the embarrassed fourteen-year-old sent a letter and some sketches. (10) An executive responded with encouragement. (11) And a list of colleges from which Chrysler hired designers. (12) Later Gilles took the advice, attended Detroit's College for Creative Studies, and landed his first job at Chrysler. (13) Talent and hard work earned him promotions, the title of director of truck design, and media stardom. (14) While Gilles is designing the next generation of vehicles. (15) He is also inspiring the next generation of young people. (16) He tells the kids who write him or attend his talks, "Dream out loud."

Chapter Highlights

A sentence fragment is an incomplete sentence because it lacks

- **a subject:**

  Was buying a gold ring. (*incorrect*)

  Diamond Jim was buying a gold ring. (*correct*)

- **a verb:**

  The basketball game Friday at noon. (*incorrect*)

  The basketball game *was played* Friday at noon. (*correct*)

- **a complete thought:**

  While Teresa was swimming. (*incorrect*)

  While Teresa was swimming, she lost a contact lens. (*correct*)

  The woman who bought your car. (*incorrect*)

  The woman who bought your car is walking down the highway. (*correct*)

Proofreading Strategy

Sentence fragments are a serious error. To spot and correct them more easily in your writing, try the **bottom-up proofreading technique**. Start by reading the last sentence of your paper, slowly, word by word. Then read the second-to-last sentence, and so on, all the way from the "bottom to the top." For each sentence, ask:

1. Does this sentence have a *subject*, a *complete verb*, and express a *complete thought*?

2. Is this an incomplete thought beginning with a word like *because, although,* or *when*? If so, such fragments often can be fixed by connecting them to the sentence before or after.

3. Is this an incomplete thought containing *who, which,* or *that*? If so, such fragments often can be fixed by connecting them to the sentence before or after.

If sentence fragments are one of your error patterns, log them in your Personal Error Chart and proofread every paper once through just for fragments.

WRITING AND PROOFREADING ASSIGNMENT

Working in a small group, choose one of the sentences below that could begin a short story.

1. As soon as Sean read the text message, he knew he had to take action.
2. Suddenly, the bright blue sky turned dark.
3. The boss's heels clicked down the hallway toward my pathetic cubicle.

Next, each person in the group should write his or her own short story, starting with that sentence. First decide what type of story yours will be—science fiction, romance, action, comedy, murder mystery, and so on; perhaps each person will choose a different type. It may help you to imagine the story later becoming a TV show. As you write, be careful to avoid fragments, making sure each sentence has a subject and a complete verb—and expresses a complete thought.

Then exchange papers, using the bottom-up technique to check each other's work for fragments. If time permits, read the papers aloud to the group. Are you surprised by the different ways in which that first sentence was developed?

CHAPTER REVIEW

Circle the number of each fragment. Correct it in any way that makes sense, changing it into a separate idea or adding it to another sentence. You might try the bottom-up proofreading strategy.

A.   (1) In our fast-paced society, we often turn to multitasking. (2) Which is doing two or more things at once. (3) For example, we might check our email while talking on the phone. (4) Because we want to save time. (5) Ironically, multitasking often takes longer. (6) Than completing each task separately. (7) The reason is simple. (8) Each task requires attention, and switching our attention back and forth is time-consuming. (9) According to recent research, multitasking also can be dangerous. (10) Especially when one of the tasks is driving. (11) In laboratory studies with college students, students who simulated driving in a city and talking on a hands-free cell phone. (12) Crashed four times more often than other students. (13) An even more frightening study videotaped truck drivers on the road. (14) Some of these truck drivers sending text messages as they drove. (15) Because they switched their attention back and forth from texting to driving. (16) Their reaction times were slow. (17) The texting drivers were an amazing 23 times more likely to crash than other drivers.

B.   (1) Growing up in Alaska. (2) Marianne Cusato disliked the trashy, manmade strip malls surrounded by glorious mountain scenery. (3) She decided to be an architect. (4) Who would build practical, beautiful buildings. (5) In fact, Cusato achieved her goal. (6) After Hurricane Katrina in 2005, the young architect entered and won a contest to create an alternative to

Katrina Cottage,
448 square feet

the ugly FEMA trailers. (7) Which disaster victims often live in temporarily. (8) Her Katrina Cottage won many admirers. (9) Adapting the pastel colors and white trim of Caribbean architecture. (10) Cusato gave her Katrina Cottages compact living spaces, charming porches, and hurricane windows. (11) The smallest cottage was just 330 square feet. (12) Soon regular families wanted to build these inexpensive and attractive homes. (13) Lowe's selling the houses in prefabricated kits to the public. (14) Cusato believes that small, well-designed houses often feel cozier. (15) Than large, pricey homes. (16) Which have pushed many Americans into debt. (17) Her designs and books promote these values. (18) But not strip malls.

C.   (1) Many people seem to forget all about good manners. (2) When they use a cell phone. (3) They rudely allow the ringing phone to interrupt conversations, meetings, appointments, performances, and romantic dinner dates. (4) The ringtones, which range from roaring motorcycles to mooing cows. (5) Blare out in classrooms and concert halls. (6) Many people even answer these calls in church or at funerals. (7) And then proceed to talk loudly. (8) Forcing others to listen or wait for them to finish talking. (9) Public relations consultant Carol Page, known as the "Miss Manners of Cell Phones." (10) Believes we can stop cell rudeness. (11) We should fix a "cell glare" on any cell phone user who is behaving badly. (12) If that doesn't work. (13) We can interrupt and gently ask if the phone conversation might be postponed. (14) Setting a good example when you use your own cell phone probably the best way to teach good cellular phone manners to others.

D.   (1) As the demand for paralegals, or legal assistants, grows. (2) More students nationwide are majoring in paralegal studies. (3) Because many different types of law firms and businesses hire paralegals. (4) A paralegal's duties vary with the job setting. (5) For instance, because Denise Cunningham is the only paralegal at a small law firm in Louisville, Kentucky. (6) She has many duties. (7) Cunningham relishes being at the center of things. (8) Researching cases, doing client intake interviews, writing, and even managing the office. (9) When she was earning her associate's degree in paralegal studies from the University of Louisville. (10) Cunningham learned about immigration law, real estate law, family law, and criminal law. (11) Drawn to criminal law, she was hired in 1980 by the attorney with whom she still works today. (12) Her professional rewards include a good salary. (13) And the satisfaction of helping people. (14) In 2006, her boss nominated her for Paralegal of the Year.

EXPLORING ONLINE

<http://www.bls.gov/oco/> Visit this helpful career website, which describes the duties and future outlook for hundreds of professions. Choose one career that interests you, research it, take notes, and write a report on the pros and cons of the job for you.

E.   (1) Braille, which is a system of reading and writing now used by blind people all over the world. (2) Was invented by a fifteen-year-old French boy. (3) In 1824, when Louis Braille entered a school for the blind in Paris. (4) He found that the library had only fourteen books for the blind. (5) These books used a system that he and the other blind students found hard to use. (6) Most of them just gave up. (7) Louis Braille devoted himself to finding a better way. (8) Working with the French army method called night-writing. (9) He came up with a new system in 1829. (10) Although his classmates liked and used Braille. (11) It not widely accepted in England and the United States for another hundred years.

EXPLORING ONLINE

<http://grammar.ccc.commnet.edu/grammar/cgi-shl/quiz.pl/fragments_add2.htm> Interactive quiz: Find the correct sentence in each group.

<http://grammar.ccc.commnet.edu/grammar/quizzes/fragment_fixing.htm> Try your skills with this interactive fragment test. Can you find and fix all the fragments?

 View an integrated eBook and chapter-specific interactive learning tools, including flashcards, quizzes, videos, and extra help tracking and correcting your Personal Error Patterns, in your Basic Writing CourseMate, accessed through <www.cengagebrain.com>.

UNIT 2

Writing Assignments

As you complete each writing assignment, remember to perform these steps:

- Write a clear, complete topic sentence.
- Use freewriting, brainstorming, or clustering to generate ideas for your paragraph, essay, or memo.
- Arrange your best ideas in a plan.
- Revise for support, unity, coherence, and exact language.
- Proofread for grammar, punctuation, and spelling errors.

Writing Assignment 1 *Plan to achieve a goal*. Did you know that nearly all successful people are good goal-planners? Choose a goal you would truly love to achieve, and write it down. Next, write down three to six smaller steps or targets that will lead you to your goal. Arrange these in time order. Have you left out any crucial steps? To inspire you and help you plan, reread "Target Practice: Setting Attainable Goals" on page 86, or try out the interactive goal-planner from Paradise Valley Community College at <http://www.pvc.maricopa.edu/advisement/goalplan.html>.

Writing Assignment 2 *Describe your place in the family*. Your psychology professor has asked you to write a brief description of your place in the family— as an only child, the youngest child, the middle child, or the oldest child. Did your place provide you with special privileges or lay special responsibilities on you? For instance, youngest children may be babied; oldest children may be expected to act like parents. Does your place in the family have an effect on you as an adult? In your topic sentence, state what role your place in the family played in your development: *Being the _____ child in my family has made me _____.* Proofread for fragments.

Writing Assignment 3 *Write about someone who changed jobs*. Did you, someone you know, or someone you know about change jobs because of a new interest or love for something else? Describe the person's first job and feelings of job satisfaction (or lack of them). What happened to make the person want to make a job switch? How long did the switch take? Was it difficult or easy to accomplish? Describe the person's new job and feelings of job satisfaction (or lack of them). Proofread for fragments.

Writing Assignment 4 *Ask for a raise*. Compose a memo to a boss, real or imagined, attempting to persuade him or her to raise your pay. In your first sentence, state that you are asking for an increase. Be specific: note how the quality of your work, your extra hours, or any special projects you have been involved in have made the business run more smoothly or become more profitable. Do not sound vain, but do praise yourself honestly. Use the memo style shown here. Proofread for fragments.

MEMORANDUM

DATE: Today's date

TO: Your boss's name

FROM: Your name

SUBJECT: Salary Increase

99

UNIT 2

Review

Proofreading and Revising

Proofread the following essay to eliminate all sentence fragments. Circle the number of every fragment. (You should find nine.) Then correct the fragments in any way you choose—by connecting them to a sentence before or after, by completing any incomplete verbs, and so on. Make your corrections above the lines.

Living Without Television

(1) What would you do without your television? (2) Every spring, millions of Americans answer this question for themselves. (3) By taking part in TV Turn-Off Week. (4) They find out that they can in fact lead enjoyable lives without watching TV. (5) Begun in 1995, TV Turn-Off Week now has motivated 24 million participants to spend seven full days. (6) Engaging in activities other than TV viewing. (7) Although many Turn-Off Week participants initially fear that they will be bored without their TVs. (8) They often rediscover the joys of reading, talking to family and friends, going for walks, exercising, and learning new skills like playing the guitar.

(9) Statistics help explain the power of TV Turn-Off Week. (10) Americans watch more than four hours of TV a day. (11) That's two full months each year. (12) Simply turning off the box leaves people with lots of time to do other things. (13) Nearly half of the U.S. population watches TV while eating dinner. (14) Instead of using that time to talk to other family members. (15) Because 56 percent of children have a television set in their bedrooms. (16) They tend to watch programs alone instead of doing homework, interacting with their parents and siblings, or exercising.

(17) Interestingly, the consequences of TV Turn-Off Week seem to be lasting. (18) Many past participants say that they have changed their viewing habits. (19) While a few people go so far as to get rid of their televisions. (20) Most report that they now watch fewer shows. (21) And are less likely to leave the TV sputtering

100

as unwatched background noise. (22) Some move their televisions. (23) Taking them out of bedrooms and the family room. (24) Others cancel or reduce their cable or satellite services. (25) One major benefit is that individuals and families prove to themselves that they can find other, more engaging things to do. (26) Many parents gain confidence about limiting their children's viewing time. (27) And more important, about teaching their children how and when to watch TV.

EXPLORING ONLINE

Turn off all the TVs in your house for one week, keeping notes on any reactions or changes. Use these notes to write about the experience.

<http://www.tvturnoff.org/> Visit the website and read for ideas. See "Facts and Information." Then use this information in a composition arguing for or against watching less TV.

UNIT 2

Writers' Workshop

Discuss an Event That Influenced You

Readers of a final draft can easily forget that they are reading the *end result* of someone else's writing process. The following paragraph is one student's response to the assignment *Write about an event in history that influenced you*.

In your class or group, read it aloud if possible. As you read, underline any words or lines that strike you as especially powerful.

Though the Vietnam War ended almost before I was born, it changed my life. My earliest memory is of my father. A grizzled Vietnam warrior who came back spat upon, with one less brother. He wore a big smile playing ball with my brother and me, but even then I felt the grin was a coverup. When the postwar reports were on, his face became despondent. What haunted his heart and mind, I could not know, but I tried in my childish way to reason with him. A simple "It'll be all right, Dad" would bring a bleak smirk to his face. When he was happy, I was happy. When he was down, I was down. Soon the fatherly horseplay stopped, and once-full bottles of liquor were empty. He was there in body. Yet not there. Finally, he was physically gone. Either working a sixty-hour week or out in the streets after a furious fight with my mother. Once they divorced, she moved us to another state. I never came to grips with the turmoil inside my father. I see him as an intricate puzzle, missing one piece. That piece is his humanity, tangled up in history and blown up by a C-19.

Brian Pereira, student

1. How effective is Brian Pereira's paragraph?

   _____ Good topic sentence?   _____ Rich supporting details?

   _____ Logical organization?   _____ Effective conclusion?

2. Discuss your underlinings with the group or class. Did others underline the same parts? Explain why you feel particular words or details are effective. For instance, the strong words *bleak smirk* say so much about the father's hopeless mood and the distance between him and his young son.

102

3. The topic sentence says that the writer's life changed, yet the body of the paragraph speaks mostly about his troubled father. Does the body of the paragraph explain the topic sentence?

4. What order, if any, does this writer follow?

5. If you do not know what a "C-19" is in the last sentence, does that make the conclusion less effective for you?

6. Would you suggest any changes or revisions?

7. Proofread for grammar and spelling. Do you notice any error patterns (two or more errors of the same type) that this student should watch out for?

Brian Pereira's fine paragraph was the end result of a difficult writing process. Pereira describes his process this way:

> The floor in my room looked like a writer's battleground of crumpled papers. Before this topic was assigned, I had not the slightest idea that this influence even existed, much less knew what it was. I thought hard, started a sentence or two, and threw a smashed paper down in disgust, over and over again. After hours, I realized it—the event in history that influenced me was Vietnam, even though I was too young to remember it! That became my topic sentence.

Writing and Revising Ideas

1. Discuss an event that influenced you.

2. Choose your best recent paper and describe your own writing process—what you did well and not so well.

For help with writing your paragraph, see Chapter 3 and Chapter 4, Part B (see "Time Order"). Give yourself plenty of time to revise. Stick with it, trying to write the best possible paper. Pay special attention to fully supporting your topic with interesting facts and details.

UNIT 3

Using Verbs Effectively

Every sentence contains at least one verb. Because verbs often are action words, they add interest and punch to any piece of writing. In this unit, you will

- Learn to use present, past, and other verb tenses correctly
- Learn when to add -*s* or -*ed*
- Recognize and use past participle forms
- Recognize -*ing* verbs, infinitives, and other special forms
- Learn proofreading strategies to find and correct your own errors

---

104

Spotlight on Writing

Notice how vividly this writer describes the scene before him. His verbs are underlined.

Russell Thomas <u>places</u> the toe of his right sneaker one inch behind the three-point line. Inspecting the basket with a level gaze, he <u>bends</u> twice at the knees, <u>raises</u> the ball to shoot, then suddenly <u>looks</u> around. What <u>is</u> it? <u>Has</u> he <u>spotted</u> me, watching from the opposite end of the playground? No, something else <u>is</u> up. He <u>is</u> <u>lifting</u> his nose to the wind like a spaniel; he <u>appears</u> to be gauging air currents. Russell <u>waits</u> until the wind <u>settles</u>, bits of trash feathering lightly to the ground. Then he <u>sends</u> a twenty-five-foot jump shot arcing through the soft summer twilight. It <u>drops</u> without a sound through the dead center of the bare iron rim. So <u>does</u> the next one. So <u>does</u> the one after that. Alone in the gathering dusk, Russell <u>begins</u> to work the perimeter against imaginary defenders, unspooling jump shots from all points.

Darcy Frey, *The Last Shot*

- Simple but well-chosen *verbs* help bring this description to life. Which verbs most effectively help you see and experience the scene?

- Do you think that the writer realistically captures this young athlete at practice? What, if anything, do you learn about Russell Thomas—his abilities, personality, even his loves—from reading this short passage?

Writing Ideas

- *A person practicing or performing some sport, art, or task*
- *A time when you watched or overheard someone in a public place*

CHAPTER 9

Present Tense (Agreement)

A: Defining Agreement

B: Troublesome Verb in the Present Tense: TO BE

C: Troublesome Verb in the Present Tense: TO HAVE

D: Troublesome Verb in the Present Tense: TO DO (+ NOT)

E: Changing Subjects to Pronouns

F: Practice in Agreement

G: Special Problems in Agreement

A. Defining Agreement

A subject and a present tense verb **agree** if you use the correct form of the verb with each subject. The chart below shows which form of the verb to use for each kind of pronoun subject (we discuss other kinds of subjects later).

Verbs in the Present Tense *(example verb: to write)*				
Singular			**Plural**	
If the subject is	the verb is		If the subject is	the verb is
↓	↓		↓	↓
1st person: I	write		1st person: we	write
2nd person: you	write		2nd person: you	write
3rd person: he she it	writes		3rd person: they	write

PRACTICE 1   Fill in the correct present tense form of the verb.

1. You *ask* questions.
2. They *decide*.

1. He _____ questions.
2. She _____ .

3. I *remember.*

4. They *wear* glasses.

5. We *hope* so.

6. I *laugh* often.

7. We *study* daily.

8. He *amazes* me.

3. He _____.

4. She _____ glasses.

5. He _____ so.

6. She _____ often.

7. He _____ daily.

8. It _____ me.

Add *-s* or *-es* to a verb in the present tense only when the subject is *third person singular (he, she, it).*

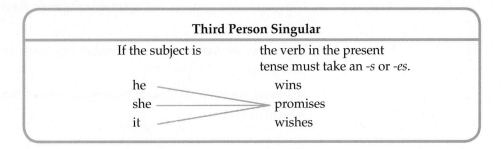

Third Person Singular	
If the subject is	the verb in the present tense must take an *-s* or *-es.*
he	wins
she	promises
it	wishes

PRACTICE 2   Write the correct form of the verb in the space to the right of the pronoun subject.

EXAMPLE: **to see**   I ___*see*___

they ___*see*___

she ___*sees*___

to find	**to ask**	**to go**
he _____	I _____	it _____
they _____	she _____	you _____
you _____	he _____	we _____

to rest	**to hold**	**to select**
I _____	it _____	she _____
they _____	we _____	he _____
she _____	you _____	I _____

PRACTICE 3   First, underline the subject (always a pronoun) in each sentence below. Then circle the correct verb form. REMEMBER: If the subject of the sentence is *he, she,* or *it* (third person singular), the verb must end in *-s* or *-es* to agree with the subject.

1. According to researcher Deborah Tannen, we sometimes (fail, fails) to understand how men and women communicate on the job.

2. When working together, they sometimes (differ, differs) in predictable ways.

3. In Tannen's book *Talking from 9 to 5: Women and Men at Work*, she (describe, describes) the following misunderstanding between Amy, a manager, and Donald, her employee.

4. She (read, reads) Donald's report and (find, finds) it unacceptable.

5. She (meet, meets) with him to discuss the necessary revisions.

6. To soften the blow, she (praise, praises) the report's strengths.

7. Then, she (go, goes) on to explain in detail the needed revisions.

8. The next day, he (submit, submits) a second draft with only tiny changes.

9. She (think, thinks) that Donald did not listen to her.

10. He (believe, believes) that Amy first liked his report, then changed her mind.

11. According to the author, they (represent, represents) different communication styles.

12. Like many women supervisors, she (criticize, criticizes) gently, adding positive comments to protect the other person's feelings.

13. Like many male employees, he (expect, expects) more direct—and to him, more honest—criticism.

14. Tannen says that both styles make sense, but they (cause, causes) confusion if not understood.

15. Stereotypes or truth? You (decide, decides) for yourself about the accuracy of Tannen's analysis.

B. Troublesome Verb in the Present Tense: TO BE

A few present tense verbs are formed in special ways. The most common of these verbs is *to be*.

Reference Chart: TO BE
(present tense)

Singular		**Plural**	
If the subject is	the verb is	If the subject is	the verb is
↓	↓	↓	↓
1st person: I	am	1st person: we	are
2nd person: you	are	2nd person: you	are
3rd person: he / she / it	is	3rd person: they	are

This chart can also be read like this:

Pronoun	Verb
I	am
you	
we	are
they	
he	
she	is
it	

PRACTICE 4   Use the charts to fill in the present tense form of *to be* (*am, is, are*) that agrees with the subject.

1. She _____ a member of the Olympic softball team.

2. We _____ both carpenters, but he _____ more skilled than I am.

3. I _____ sorry about your accident; you _____ certainly unlucky with rollerblades.

4. They _____ salmon fishermen.

5. He _____ a gifted website designer.

6. Because she _____ a native of Morocco, she _____ able to speak both Arabic and French.

7. I _____ too nervous to sleep because we _____ having an accounting exam tomorrow.

8. So you _____ the one we have heard so much about!

9. It _____ freezing outside, but he _____ opening all the windows.

10. If it _____ sunny tomorrow, they _____ going hot-air ballooning.

C. Troublesome Verb in the Present Tense: TO HAVE

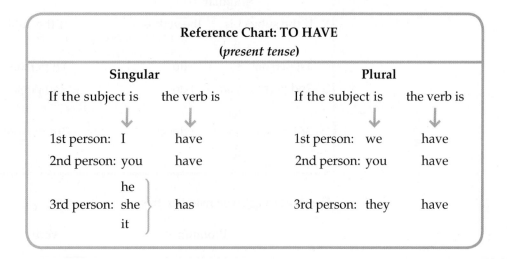

Reference Chart: TO HAVE
(present tense)

Singular			Plural		
If the subject is	the verb is		If the subject is	the verb is	
1st person: I	have		1st person: we	have	
2nd person: you	have		2nd person: you	have	
3rd person: he she it	has		3rd person: they	have	

This chart can also be read like this:

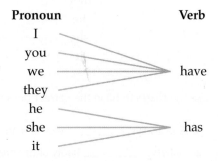

PRACTICE 5

Fill in the present tense form of *to have* (*have, has*) that agrees with the subject. Use the charts.

1. He _____ a cabin on Lake Superior.
2. You _____ a wonderful sense of style.
3. We _____ to taste these pickled mushrooms.
4. It _____ to be spring because the cherry trees _____ pink blossoms.
5. She _____ the questions, and he _____ the answers.
6. You _____ a suspicious look on your face, and I _____ to know why.
7. They _____ plans to build a fence, but we _____ plans to relax.
8. You _____ one ruby earring, and she _____ the other.
9. It _____ to be repaired, and I _____ just the person to do it for you.
10. If you _____ $50, they _____ an offer you can't refuse.

D. Troublesome Verb in the Present Tense: TO DO (+ NOT)

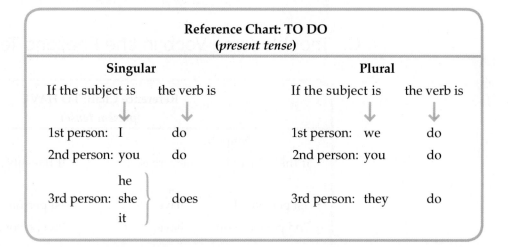

Reference Chart: TO DO
(*present tense*)

Singular		Plural	
If the subject is	the verb is	If the subject is	the verb is
1st person: I	do	1st person: we	do
2nd person: you	do	2nd person: you	do
3rd person: he she it	does	3rd person: they	do

The chart can also be read like this:

Pronoun	Verb
I	
you	
we	do
they	
he	
she	does
it	

PRACTICE 6

Use the charts to fill in the correct present tense form of *to do* (*do, does*).

1. She always _____ well in math courses.
2. I always _____ badly under pressure.

3. It _____ matter if you forget to vote.

4. They most certainly _____ sell muscle shirts.

5. You _____ the nicest things for people!

6. If you _____ the dishes, I'll _____ the laundry.

7. He _____ seem sorry about forgetting your dog's birthday.

8. You sometimes _____ surprise me.

9. _____ they dance the tarantella?

10. _____ she want to be a welder?

To Do + Not

Once you know how to use *do* and *does*, you are ready for *don't* and *doesn't*.

$$\begin{bmatrix} do + not = don't \\ does + not = doesn't \end{bmatrix}$$

PRACTICE 7

In the Positive column, fill in the correct form of *to do* (*do* or *does*) to agree with the pronoun. In the Negative column, fill in the correct form of *to do* with the negative *not* (*don't* or *doesn't*).

Pronoun	Positive	Negative
1. he	_____	_____
2. we	_____	_____
3. I	_____	_____
4. they	_____	_____
5. she	_____	_____
6. it	_____	_____
7. they	_____	_____
8. you	_____	_____

PRACTICE 8

Fill in either *doesn't* or *don't* in each blank.

1. If they _____ turn down that music, I'm going to scream.

2. It just _____ make sense.

3. You _____ have to reply in writing.

4. He _____ always lock his door at night.

5. We _____ mind the rain.

6. If she _____ stop calling collect, I _____ want to talk to her.

7. He _____ know the whole truth, and they _____ want to know.

8. They _____ want to miss Larry King Live tonight.

9. Although you _____ like biking five miles a day to work, it _____ do your health any harm.

10. When I _____ try, I _____ succeed.

PRACTICE 9 | Review

As you read this paragraph, fill in the correct present tense form of *to be*, *to have*, or *to do* in each blank. Make sure all your verbs agree with their subjects.

(1) He _____ the expertise of an action hero, but he _____ a real-life member of the U.S. Navy SEALs. (2) After 35 weeks of brutal "adversity" training, he _____ whatever the mission requires. (3) Right now, he _____ calm although he _____ ready to leap from the open door of a Navy aircraft. (4) On his back, he _____ an oversized parachute capable of supporting both him and the extra hundred pounds of special equipment packed in his combat vest. (5) When he _____ hit the water, he _____ ready to face the real challenge: finding and defusing a bomb sixty feet under rough and frigid seas. (6) He _____ a mission and a tight time frame, and he _____ not want to let the enemy know he _____ there. (7) Swimming underwater in special scuba gear, he _____ not release any air bubbles to mark the water's surface. (8) Working in semi-darkness, performing dangerous technical tasks, he quickly _____ the job. (9) However, unlike video heroes, he _____n't work alone. (10) It _____ precise teamwork for which the SEALs _____ famous. (11) Among the most respected special forces in the world, they _____ commando divers prepared for hazardous duty on sea, air, and land.

E. Changing Subjects to Pronouns

So far, you have worked on pronouns as subjects (*I, you, he, she, it, we, they*) and on how to make verbs agree with them. Often, however, the subject of a sentence is not a pronoun but a noun—like *dog, banjo, Ms. Callas, José and Robert, swimming* (as in *Swimming keeps me fit*).

To be sure that your verb agrees with your subject, *mentally* change the subject into a pronoun and then select the correct form of the verb. The chart on the next page will show you how.

Reference Chart: Subject-Verb Agreement

If the subject is	it can be changed to the pronoun
1. the speaker himself or herself ──────────────▶	I
2. masculine and singular ──────────────▶ (*Bill, one man*)	he
3. feminine and singular ──────────────▶ (*Sondra, a woman*)	she
4. neither masculine nor feminine and singular (a thing or an action) ──────────────▶ (*this pen, love, running*)	it
5. a group that includes the speaker (I) ──────────────▶ (*the family and I*)	we
6. a group of persons or things not including the speaker ──────────────▶ (*Jake and Wanda, several pens*)	they
7. the person or persons spoken to ──────────────▶	you

PRACTICE 10

Change the subjects into pronouns. REMEMBER: If you add *I* to a group of people, the correct pronoun for the whole group is *we*; if you add *you* to a group, the correct pronoun for the whole group is *you*.

Possible Subject	Pronoun		Possible Subject	Pronoun
EXAMPLE: Frank	*he*			
1. a huge moose	_____		6. the silk scarf	_____
2. a calculator and a checkbook	_____		7. Frank and Ted	_____
3. Sheila	_____		8. her son	_____
4. my buddies and I	_____		9. their power drill	_____
5. you and the other actors	_____		10. scuba diving	_____

PRACTICE 11   Review

Change each subject into a pronoun. Then circle the present tense verb that agrees with that subject. (Use the reference chart on this page if you need to.)

EXAMPLES: Harry = ___*he*___   Harry (whistle, (whistles)).

Sam and I = ___*we*___   Sam and I ((walk,) walks).

1. Camilla = _____   1. Camilla (own, owns) a horse farm.

2. Their concert = _____   2. Their concert (is, are) sold out.

3. You and Ron = _____

3. You and Ron (seem, seems) exhausted.

4. The men and I = _____

4. The men and I (repair, repairs) potholes.

5. This blender = _____

5. This blender (grate, grates) cheese.

6. This beach = _____

6. This beach (is, are) deserted.

7. Our printer = _____

7. Our printer (jam, jams) too often.

8. Folk dancing = _____

8. Folk dancing (is, are) our current passion.

9. The museum and garden = _____

9. The museum and garden (is, are) open.

10. Aunt Lil and I = _____

10. Aunt Lil and I (like, likes) Swedish massages.

F. Practice in Agreement

PRACTICE 12 **Review**

First identify the subject in each sentence. Then circle the correct verb, making sure it agrees with its subject.

Project Runway: Keeping It (Sort of) Real

(1) *Project Runway* (entertains, entertain) viewers, but the television show also (teaches, teach) some valuable life and work lessons. (2) This combination (does, do) not occur often in American television, especially in "reality" TV. (3) On *Project Runway*, designers, tailors, and dressmakers (competes, compete) for the ultimate $100,000 prize. (4) For every new challenge, they (tries, try) to design the winning outfit. (5) Sometimes contestants (creates, create) clothes out of paper or leaves, or they (redesigns, redesign) U.S. postal uniforms. (6) Fashion expert Tim Gunn (serves, serve) as the designers' mentor, cheerleader, and guide. (7) Professionals like designer Michael Kors, editor Nina Garcia, and host Heidi Klum (judges, judge) the work. (8) At home, the viewer (guesses, guess) the outcome as contestants (reacts, react) to brutally honest criticism.

(9) *Project Runway* (differs, differ) from other "reality" shows because the contestants (are, is) talented professionals. (10) They already (knows, know) how to design and sew. (11) The challenges (tests, test) their ability to rise to another level. (12) The show (tells,

Project Runway designer Jay Nicolas Sario thanks the audience during Fashion Week in New York.

AP Images/Stephen Chernin

tell) the personal story of each designer, so the viewer (observes, observe) contestants dealing with low self-esteem, anger problems, or even addiction. (13) Week after week, the designers (struggles, struggle) to turn criticism into improvement. (14) The viewer (sees, see) how hard professionals work, even in a glamorous field. (15) According to critics, *Project Runway* (feeds, feed) unrealistic dreams of quick success, but for admirers, the show (exposes, expose) the creative process in a realistic and helpful way.

PRACTICE 13

Review

In each blank, write the *present tense* form of one of the verbs from this list. Your sentences can be funny; just make sure that each verb agrees with each subject.

> leap   spin   yip   woof   attend   win   compete
>
> go   love   try   prance   wiggle   fly   encourage

(1) Dogs of every size and shape, their owners, and visitors all _____ the Great American Mutt Show. (2) Sponsored by Tails in Need, the Mutt Show _____ people to adopt mixed-breed dogs instead of buying pure breeds. (3) Pooches _____ in categories like Mostly Terrier, Most Misbehaved,

Best Kisser, and Best Lap Dog Over 50 Pounds. (4) In one event, a shepherd mix named

Top Gun _____ through the air to be crowned Best Jumper while a beagle

named Jack _____ his stumpy tail, energetically claiming the coveted trophy

for Best Wag. (5) Four-legged hopefuls _____ and _____ trying to

snag the award for Best Bark. (6) The proud winner of Best in Show _____ with

a trophy designed by Michael Graves—a red fire hydrant topped by a golden bone.

PRACTICE 14 **Review**

The sentences that follow have singular subjects and verbs. To gain skill in verb agreement, rewrite each sentence, changing the subject from *singular* to *plural*. Then make sure the verb agrees with the new subject. Keep all verbs in the present tense.

EXAMPLE: The train stops at Cold Spring.

Rewrite: *The trains stop at Cold Spring.* _____

1. The movie ticket costs too much.

   Rewrite: _____

2. The pipeline carries oil from Alaska.

   Rewrite: _____

3. A white horse grazes by the fence.

   Rewrite: _____

4. My brother knows American Sign Language.

   Rewrite: _____

5. The family needs good health insurance.

   Rewrite: _____

6. The backup singer wears green contact lenses.

   Rewrite: _____

7. My niece wants an iguana.

   Rewrite: _____

8. A wave laps softly against the dock.

   Rewrite: _____

PRACTICE 15   Review

The sentences that follow have plural subjects and verbs. Rewrite each sentence, changing the subject from *plural* to *singular*. Then make sure the verb agrees with the new subject. Keep all verbs in the present tense.

1. My cousins raise sheep.

   Rewrite: _____

2. The engines roar loudly.

   Rewrite: _____

3. The students manage money wisely.

   Rewrite: _____

4. The inmates watch *America's Most Wanted*.

   Rewrite: _____

5. Overhead, seagulls ride on the wind.

   Rewrite: _____

6. Good card players know when to bluff.

   Rewrite: _____

7. On Saturday, the pharmacists stay late.

   Rewrite: _____

8. The jewels from Bangkok are on display.

   Rewrite: _____

PRACTICE 16   Review

This paragraph is written in the past tense. Rewrite it in the present tense by changing all the verbs. Write the present tense form of each verb above the lines. (Hint: You should change seventeen verbs.)

(1) At a rink in Chicago's inner city, two-year-old Shani Davis put on his first pair of roller skates. (2) Before long, he skated so fast that the rink guards chased him and warned him to slow down. (3) Then, at 6, Davis discovered ice skating, and the future star took off. (4) His mother recognized her son's gifts, moving the family to be near a speed skating rink. (5) With his huge talent and grueling work ethic, Davis soon became the first U.S. junior to make both the short-track and long-track national teams. (7) He not only flew across frozen finish

lines winning medals, but he was the first African American to join the U.S. Olympic speed-skating team. (8) Fans around the world praised his fine technique and form. (9) Taller than other U.S. skaters, he bent low and held his upper body very still. (10) At the 2006 Winter Olympics in Turin, Italy, Davis scored a gold medal in the 1000-meter and a silver in the 1500. (11) At the Vancouver Olympics in 2010, he earned gold again in the 1000-meter. (12) In addition to his achievements on ice, Shani Davis was a founder of Inner City Excellence, a skating program for urban children, and he found time to attend Northern Michigan University.

G. Special Problems in Agreement

So far, you have learned that if the subject of a sentence is third person singular (*he, she, it*) or a word like *Sasha*, *sister*, or *car* that mentally can be changed into *he, she,* or *it*, the verb takes -*s* or -*es* in the present tense.

In special cases, however, you will need to know more before you can make your verb agree with your subject.

Focusing on the Subject

(1) A box of chocolates sits on the table.

- *What* sits on the table?

- Don't be confused by the prepositional phrase before the verb—*of chocolates.**

- Just one *box* sits on the table.

- *A box* is the subject. *A box* takes the third person singular verb—*sits.*

$$
\begin{array}{ccc}
\text{A box (of chocolates) sits on the table.} \\
\downarrow \qquad\qquad\qquad\qquad \downarrow \\
\text{subject} \qquad\qquad\qquad \text{verb} \\
\text{(singular)} \qquad\qquad\qquad \text{(singular)}
\end{array}
$$

(2) The children in the park play for hours.

---

* For a detailed explanation of prepositional phrases, see Chapter 7, Part C, and Chapter 23.

- *Who* play for hours?

- Don't be confused by the prepositional phrase before the verb—*in the park*.

- *The children* play for hours.

- *The children* is the subject. *The children* takes the third person plural verb—*play*.

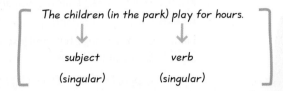

---

(3) The purpose of the exercises is to improve your spelling.

- *What* is to improve your spelling?

- Don't be confused by the prepositional phrase before the verb—*of the exercises*.

- *The purpose* is to improve your spelling.

- *The purpose* is the subject. *The purpose* takes the third person singular verb—*is*.

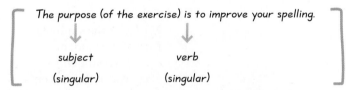

    As you can see from these examples, sometimes what seems to be the subject is really not the subject. Prepositional phrases (groups of words beginning with *of*, *in*, *at*, and so on) *cannot* contain the subject of a sentence. One way to find the subject of a sentence that contains a prepositional phrase is to ask yourself *what makes sense as the subject.*

My friends from the old neighborhood often visits / visit } me.

- Which makes sense as the subject of the sentence: *my friends* or *the old neighborhood*?

(a) My friends . . . visit me.

(b) The old neighborhood . . . visits me.

- Obviously, sentence (a) makes sense; it clearly expresses the intention of the writer.

PRACTICE 17

In each of these sentences, cross out any confusing prepositional phrases, locate the subject, and then circle the correct verb.

1. Greetings around the world (differs, differ) from culture to culture.

2. A resident of the United States (shakes, shake) hands firmly to say hello.

3. Kisses on each cheek (is, are) customary greetings in Latin America and southern Europe.

4. Natives of Hawaii (hugs, hug) and (exchanges, exchange) breaths in a custom called *alo ha* (sharing of life breath).

5. The Maori people of New Zealand (presses, press) noses to greet each other.

6. A person in traditional Japanese circles (bows, bow) upon meeting someone.

7. A custom among Pakistanis (is, are) the *salaam*, bowing with the right hand on the forehead.

8. Hindus in India (folds, fold) the hands and (tilts, tilt) the head forward.

9. The Hindi word for the greeting (is, are) *namaste*.

10. This word (means, mean) "The divine in me (salutes, salute) the divine in you."

Spotting Special Singular Subjects

> *Either* of the students
> *Neither* of the students
> *Each* of the students   }   seems happy.
> *One* of the students
> *Every one* of the students

- *Either*, *neither*, *each*, *one*, and *every one* are the real subjects of these sentences.

- *Either*, *neither*, *each*, *one*, and *every one* are special singular subjects. They always take a singular verb.

- REMEMBER: The subject is never part of a prepositional phrase, so *of the students* cannot be the subject.

PRACTICE 18

Mentally cross out the prepositional phrases and then circle the correct verb.

1. One of the forks (is, are) missing.

2. Each of my brothers (wear, wears) cinnamon after-shave lotion.

3. Each of us (carry, carries) a snakebite kit.

4. Neither of those excuses (sound, sounds) believable.

5. One of the taxi drivers (see, sees) us.

6. Either of the watches (cost, costs) about $30.

7. Neither of those cities (is, are) the capital of Brazil.

8. One of the butlers (commit, commits) the crime, but which one?

9. One of the desserts in front of you (do, does) not contain sugar.

10. Each of the cars (have, has) a CD player.

PRACTICE 19   On a separate sheet of paper, write five sentences using the special singular subjects. Make sure your sentences are in the present tense.

Using THERE to Begin a Sentence

(1) *There* is a squirrel in the yard.
(2) *There* are two squirrels in the yard.

- Although sentences sometimes begin with *there*, *there* cannot be the subject of a sentence.

- Usually, the subject *follows* the verb in sentences that begin with *there*.

   To find the real subject (so you will know how to make the verb agree), mentally drop the word *there* and rearrange the sentence to put the subject at the beginning.

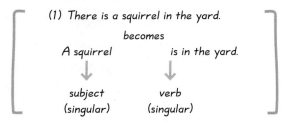

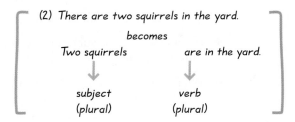

   BE CAREFUL: Good writers avoid using *there* to begin a sentence. Whenever possible, they write more directly: *Two squirrels are in the yard*.

PRACTICE 20   In each sentence, mentally drop the word *there* and rearrange the sentence to put the subject at the beginning. Then circle the verb that agrees with the subject of the sentence.

1. There (is, are) a daycare center on campus.

2. There (is, are) a scarecrow near the barn.

3. There (is, are) two scarecrows near the barn.

4. There (is, are) one good reason to quit this job—my supervisor.

5. There (is, are) six customers ahead of you.

6. There (is, are) a water fountain in the lounge.

7. There (is, are) a house and a barn in the wheat field.

8. There (is, are) only two shopping days left before my birthday.

9. There (is, are) thousands of plant species in the rain forest.

10. There (is, are) a single blue egg in the nest over the kitchen door.

PRACTICE 21

On paper or on a computer, rewrite each sentence in Practice 20 so that it does not begin with *there is* or *there are*. (You may add or change a word or two if you like.) Sentences (1) and (2) are done for you.

EXAMPLES: 1. *A daycare center is on campus.*

2. *A scarecrow hangs near the barn.*

Choosing the Correct Verb in Questions

(1) Where is Lucas?

(2) Where are Lucas and Jay?

(3) Why are they singing?

(4) Have you painted the hall yet?

● In questions, the subject usually *follows* the verb.

● In sentence (1), the subject is *Lucas*. *Lucas* takes the third person singular verb *is*.

● In sentence (2), the subject is *Lucas and Jay*. *Lucas and Jay* takes the third person plural verb *are*.

● What is the subject in sentence (3)? _____ What verb does it take?

_____

● What is the subject in sentence (4)? _____ What verb does it take?

_____

If you can't find the subject, mentally turn the question around:

(1) Lucas is . . .

(2) Lucas and Jay are . . .

PRACTICE 22

Circle the correct verb.

1. Where (is, are) my leather bomber jacket?

2. (Have, Has) our waiter gone to lunch?

3. How (is, are) your children enjoying computer camp?

4. Who (is, are) those people on the fire escape?

5. Which (is, are) your day off?

6. Why (do, does) she want to buy another motorcycle?

7. (Have, Has) you considered taking a cruise next year?

8. Where (is, are) Don's income tax forms?

9. (Have, Has) the groundhog raided the zucchini patch today?

10. Well, what (do, does) you know about that?

PRACTICE 23 On paper or on a computer, write five questions of your own. Make sure that your questions are in the present tense and that the verbs agree with the subjects.

Using WHO, WHICH, and THAT as Relative Pronouns

When you use a **relative pronoun**—*who, which,* or *that*—to introduce a dependent idea, make sure you choose the correct verb.*

> (1) I know a woman *who* plays expert chess.

- Sentence (1) uses the singular verb *plays* because *who* relates or refers to *a woman* (singular).

> (2) Suede coats, *which* stain easily, should not be worn in the rain.

- Sentence (2) uses the plural verb *stain* because *which* relates to the subject *suede coats* (plural).

> (3) Dishwashers *that* talk make me nervous.

- Sentence (3) uses the plural verb *talk* because *that* relates to what word?

_____

PRACTICE 24 Write the word that *who, which,* or *that* relates or refers to in the blank at the right; then circle the correct form of the verb.

  EXAMPLE: I like people who (is, are) creative.   _____*people*_____

1. My office has a robot that (fetch, fetches) the mail.   _____

2. Never buy food in cans that (have, has) dents in them.   _____

3. My husband, who (take, takes) marvelous photographs, won the Nikon Prize.   _____

4. He likes women who (is, are) very ambitious.   _____

5. The old house, which (sit, sits) on a cliff above the sea, is called Balston Heights.   _____

6. Students who (love, loves) to read usually write well.   _____

_____

* For work on relative pronouns, see Chapter 18.

7. I like a person who (think, thinks) for himself or herself. _____

8. The only airline that (fly, flies) to Charlottesville is booked solid. _____

9. People who (live, lives) in glass houses should invest in blinds. _____

10. Most students want jobs that (challenge, challenges) them. _____

PRACTICE 25

Review

Proofread the following paragraph for a variety of verb agreement errors. First, locate the subject in each sentence. Then underline all present tense verbs and correct any errors above the lines.

(1) Each year, millions of people watches the films that Lauren Lazin produces and directs. (2) Her name is not well known, but her TV shows and movies certainly is. (3) Lazin, a documentary filmmaker, works for MTV. (4) Her creative spark bring popular shows to the network each season, including the wildly successful *Cribs* and *True Life*. (5) Her work explore the lives of high-profile celebrities, but she also champions important causes for the network, such as racial justice and AIDS awareness. (6) There are a long list of MTV shows on Lazin's resume, but she also makes films independently. (7) *Tupac: Resurrection* probe the complex life of rapper Tupac Shakur. (8) Many considers it one of Lazin's best movies. (9) Another powerful film, *I'm Still Here*, weaves together diary excerpts from teenagers during the Holocaust. (9) Lazin wants to create documentary films that appeals to young adults and makes them think. (10) She hope that each of her films engage and educates her viewers.

Chapter Highlights

- **A subject and a present tense verb must agree:**

    The light flickers. (*singular subject, singular verb*)

    The lights flicker. (*plural subject, plural verb*)

- **Only third person singular subjects (*he, she, it*) take verbs ending in *-s* or *-es*.**

- **Three troublesome present tense verbs are *to be, to have,* and *to do*.**

- **When a prepositional phrase comes between a subject and a verb, the verb must agree with the subject.**

    The *chairs* on the porch *are* painted white.

- **The subjects *either, neither, each, one,* and *every one* are always singular.**

    Neither of the mechanics *repairs* transmissions.

- **In a sentence beginning with** *there is* **or** *there are*, **the subject follows the verb.**

    There are three *oysters* on your plate.

- **In questions, the subject usually follows the verb.**

    Where are *Kimi and Fred*?

- **Relative pronouns (***who***,** ***which***,** **and** ***that***) refer to the word with which the verb must agree.**

    A *woman who* has children must manage time skillfully.

Proofreading Strategy

If present tense verb agreement is one of your error patterns, you might **isolate and color code**. First, if you are writing on a computer, *isolate each sentence* on its own line. This will help your brain and eye focus on one sentence at a time. Next, find the subject and verb in each sentence; use highlighters to *color code* subjects yellow and verbs green. Cross out any confusing prepositional phrases.

Now check each color-coded pair for subject-verb agreement. 1. If you aren't sure, *change the subject to a pronoun*, and see if it agrees with the verb. 2. Do a final "audio check" and read the sentence aloud. Here are two examples:

> *it*   *serves*
> The cafeteria ~~at my son's school~~ serve sweet-potato fries.

> *they   want*
> Most parents wants the cafeteria to offer more fresh vegetables and fruits.

WRITING AND PROOFREADING ASSIGNMENT

In a group of three or four classmates, choose an area of the building or campus that contains some interesting action—the hallway, the cafeteria, or a playing field. Go there now and observe what you see, recording details and using verbs in the present tense. Choose as many dynamic action verbs as you can. Keep observing and writing for ten minutes. Then head back to the classroom and write a first draft of a paragraph. Proofread for subject-verb agreement, using the strategy described above.

Next, exchange papers within your group. The reader should check for verb agreement and tell the writer what he or she liked about the writing and what could be improved.

CHAPTER REVIEW

Proofread this essay carefully for verb agreement. First, underline all present tense verbs. Then correct each verb agreement error.

Advantages and Disadvantages of Online Dating

(1) Every month, about 40 million Americans visits online dating sites like Match.com and

Matchmaker.com. (2) In fact, these sites now make more money than any other paid service on the Web. (3) Clearly, many people no longer feels embarrassed about using a dating service. (4) But are websites really good places to find a mate? (5) You decide. (6) There is both advantages and disadvantages to cyberdating.

(7) Some busy people likes the convenience of online dating and the chance to meet people at any time of day or night. (8) The Web makes a better meeting place than bars, they argue. (9) In addition, the sites allow individuals to search for mates with certain qualities or characteristics. (10) According to supporters of cyberdating, this method also encourage people to get to know possible romantic partners better. (11) In cyberspace, they are less likely to be swept away by physical attraction alone.

(12) On the other hand, computer dating also have dangers and drawbacks. (13) Online, many people tends to lie about their physical appearance, age, profession, or personality traits. (14) According to a recent study, about three out of ten people using online sites are married. (15) Others has criminal backgrounds. (16) Therefore, safety remain a constant concern for cyberdaters. (17) Getting to know each other online takes more time. (18) Consequently, the online environment actually slow down the dating process instead of speeding it up.

EXPLORING ONLINE

<http://english-zone.com/verbs/thereisare1.html> Interactive quiz: *There is* or *there are*? Test your verb agreement skills.

<http://www.new.towson.edu/ows/exercisesub-verb.htm> This interactive quiz from Towson University is a tricky one. Test yourself.

 View an integrated eBook and chapter-specific interactive learning tools, including flashcards, quizzes, videos, and extra help tracking and correcting your Personal Error Patterns, in your Basic Writing CourseMate, accessed through <www.cengagebrain.com>.

CHAPTER **10**

Past Tense

A: Regular Verbs in the Past Tense

B: Irregular Verbs in the Past Tense

C: Troublesome Verb in the Past Tense: TO BE

D: Review

A. Regular Verbs in the Past Tense

Verbs in the past tense express actions that occurred in the past. The italicized words in the following sentences are verbs in the past tense.

(1) They *noticed* a dent in the fender.
(2) She *played* the guitar very well.
(3) For years I *studied* yoga.

- What ending do all these verbs take? _____
- In general, what ending do you add to put a verb in the past tense? _____
- Verbs that add -*d* or -*ed* to form the past tense are called regular verbs.

PRACTICE 1

Some of the verbs in these sentences are in the present tense; others are in the past tense. Circle the verb in each sentence. Write *present* in the column at the right if the verb is in the present tense; write *past* if the verb is in the past tense.

1. Ricardo stroked his beard. _____
2. Light travels 186,000 miles in a second. _____
3. They donate blood every six months. _____
4. Magellan sailed around the world. _____
5. The lake looks as calm as glass. _____
6. Yesterday, Rover buried many bones. _____
7. Mount St. Helens erupted in 1980. _____
8. That chemical plant pollutes our water. _____
9. A robin nested in the mailbox. _____
10. He owns two exercise bikes. _____

PRACTICE 2

Change the verbs in this paragraph to past tense by writing the past tense form above each italicized verb.

(1) Again this year, Carnival *transforms* Rio de Janeiro, Brazil, into one of the most fantastic four-day parties on the planet. (2) On the Friday before Ash Wednesday, thousands of visitors *pour* into the city. (3) They *watch* all-night parades and *admire* the glittering costumes. (4) They *cheer, sweat,* and *dance* the samba. (5) Of course, preparation *starts* long before. (6) For months, members of the samba schools (neighborhood dance clubs) *plan* their floats, *practice* samba steps, and *stay* up for nights making their costumes. (7) Using bright fabrics, sequins, feathers, and chains, both men and women *create* spectacular outfits. (8) Each samba school *constructs* a float that *features* a smoke-breathing dragon or a spouting waterfall. (9) During Carnival, judges *rate* the schools on costumes, dancing, and floats, and then they *award* prizes. (10) Together, Brazilians and their visitors *share* great music, drink, food, fun, and the chance to go a little bit crazy.

As you can see from this exercise, many verbs form the past tense by adding either -d **or** -ed.

Furthermore, in the past tense, agreement is not a problem, except for the verb to be **(see Part C of this chapter). This is because verbs in the past tense have only one form, no matter what the subject is.**

PRACTICE 3

The verbs have been omitted from this paragraph. Choose verbs from the list below and write a past tense form in each blank space. Do not use any of the verbs twice.

arrive	cry	walk	help
install	climb	pound	learn
grab	hug	smile	work
paint	thank	shout	hurry

(1) Last month, Raoul and I _____ build a Habitat for Humanity house as part of our college's service learning program. (2) On the first day, we _____ at the construction site at dawn. (3) With three other volunteers, we _____ our hammers and _____ onto the roof. (4) We _____ nails for hours while other volunteers _____ the Sheet-rock walls. (5) For three weeks, we _____ hard and _____ a lot about plumbing, wiring, and

interior finishes. (6) On our last day, the new homeowners _____ with joy and

_____ the whole crew.

PRACTICE 4   Fill in the past tense of each verb.

1. Erik Weihenmayer, blinded at age thirteen, _____ (dream) for years of climbing Mount Everest.

2. Mountaineers _____ (laugh) at the idea of a blind man scaling the world's tallest peak—a death trap of rock, wind, and cold.

3. But in 2001, Erik _____ (gather) a climbing team and _____ (start) the trek up Everest.

4. Before the climbers _____ (reach) the first of several camps on the way to the top, Erik _____ (slip) into a crevasse, but he _____ (survive).

5. When he finally _____ (stumble) into the first camp, weak and dehydrated, Erik _____ (wonder) whether he had made a serious mistake.

6. Nevertheless, he and his teammates _____ (vow) to continue the climb.

7. The group _____ (battle) upward through driving snow and icy winds.

8. Erik _____ (manage) to keep up and even _____ (edge) across the long, knife-blade ridge just below the peak, taking tiny steps and using his ice ax as an anchor.

9. Months after he began his journey, the blind mountaineer _____ (step) onto Everest's summit and _____ (stay) for ten minutes to savor his victory.

10. For many people around the world, this achievement _____ (symbolize) the nearly unstoppable human power to reach a goal.

Blind mountaineer
Erik Weihenmayer
successfully scaled
Mount Everest.

Didrick Johnck/CORBIS/Sygma

B. Irregular Verbs in the Past Tense

Instead of adding *-d* or *-ed*, some verbs form the past tense in other ways.

> (1) He *threw* a knuckle ball.
> (2) She *gave* him a dollar.
> (3) He *rode* from his farm into the town.

● The italicized words in these sentences are also verbs in the past tense.

● Do these verbs form the past tense by adding *-d* or *-ed*? _____

● *Threw, gave,* and *rode* are the past tense of verbs that do not add *-d* or *-ed* to form the past tense.

● Verbs that do not add *-d* or *-ed* to form the past tense are called *irregular verbs*.

A chart listing common irregular verbs follows.

Reference Chart: Irregular Verbs

Simple Form	Past	Simple Form	Past
be	was, were	lose	lost
become	became	make	made
begin	began	mean	meant
blow	blew	meet	met
break	broke	pay	paid
bring	brought	put	put
build	built	quit	quit
burst	burst	read	read
buy	bought	ride	rode
catch	caught	ring	rang
choose	chose	rise	rose
come	came	run	ran
cut	cut	say	said
dive	dove (dived)	see	saw
do	did	seek	sought
draw	drew	sell	sold
drink	drank	send	sent
drive	drove	set	set
eat	ate	shake	shook
fall	fell	shine	shone (shined)
feed	fed	shrink	shrank (shrunk)
feel	felt	sing	sang
fight	fought	sit	sat
find	found	sleep	slept
fly	flew	speak	spoke
forget	forgot	spend	spent
forgive	forgave	spring	sprang
freeze	froze	stand	stood
get	got	steal	stole
give	gave	strike	struck
go	went	swim	swam
grow	grew	swing	swung

Reference Chart: Irregular Verbs (*continued*)

Simple Form	Past	Simple Form	Past
have	had	take	took
hear	heard	teach	taught
hide	hid	tear	tore
hold	held	tell	told
hurt	hurt	think	thought
keep	kept	throw	threw
know	knew	understand	understood
lay	laid	wake	woke
lead	led	wear	wore
leave	left	win	won
let	let	wind	wound
lie	lay	write	wrote

Learn the unfamiliar past tense forms by grouping together verbs that change from present tense to past tense in the same way. For example, some irregular verbs change *ow* in the present to *ew* in the past:

blow	blew	know	knew
grow	grew	throw	threw

Another group changes from *i* in the present to *a* in the past:

begin	began	sing	sang
drink	drank	spring	sprang
ring	rang	swim	swam

As you write, refer to the chart. If you are unsure of the past tense form of a verb that is not in the chart, check a dictionary. For example, if you look up the verb *go* in the dictionary, you will find an entry like this:

go \ went \ gone \ going

The first word listed is used to form the *present* tense of the verb (I *go*, he *goes*, and so on). The second word is the *past* tense (I *went*, he *went*, and so on). The third word is the *past participle* (*gone*), and the last word is the *present participle* (*going*).

Some dictionaries list different forms only for irregular verbs. If no past tense is listed, you know that the verb is regular and that its past tense ends in *-d* or *-ed*.

PRACTICE 5

Circle the correct past tense form of each verb. If you aren't sure, check the chart.

(1) Emma (began, begun) her job search in an organized way. (2) She (thought, thinked) carefully about her interests and abilities. (3) She (spended, spent) time in the library and (readed, read) books like *What Color Is Your Parachute?* and *Job Hunting Online.* (4) She (did, done) online research about interesting professions at sites like Career InfoNet (‹**http://www.acinet.org/acinet/**›). (5) She (spoke, spoken) to people with jobs that (had, have) special appeal for her. (6) After Emma (understanded, understood) her own goals, she (writed, wrote) a straightforward, one-page, error-free résumé. (7) Her clear objectives

statement (telled, told) prospective employers about her job preferences. (8) After listing her educational experience, she (gave, gived) her past employment, with the most recent job first. (9) She (choosed, chose) lively action verbs like *organized, filed, oversaw,* and *inspected* to describe her responsibilities at each job. (10) Her references (was, were) four people who (knowed, knew) her work well. (11) At last, Emma (felt, feeled) ready to answer newspaper ads, search for jobs online, and explore every lead she (got, gotten). (12) She (putted, put) her résumé on the *monster.com* site so that hundreds of companies would see it. (13) Then, she (took, taked) a friend's good suggestion that they interview each other to practice their skills. (14) A few days later, the phone (rang, ringed) and Emma (made, maked) preparations for her first job interview.

PRACTICE 6   Look over the list of irregular verbs on pages 130–131. Pick out the ten verbs that give you the most trouble and list them here.

Simple	**Past**	**Simple**	**Past**
_____	_____	_____	_____
_____	_____	_____	_____
_____	_____	_____	_____
_____	_____	_____	_____
_____	_____	_____	_____

Now, on paper or on a computer, write one paragraph using *all ten* verbs. Your paragraph may be humorous; just make sure your verbs are correct.

C. Troublesome Verb in the Past Tense: TO BE

Reference Chart: TO BE *(past tense)*		
	Singular	**Plural**
1st person:	I was ————————→	we were
2nd person:	you were ————————→	you were
3rd person:	he she } was ————————→ it	they were

● Note that the first and third person singular forms are the same—*was*.

PRACTICE 7

In each sentence, circle the correct past tense of the verb *to be*—either *was* or *were*.

1. Our instructor (was, were) a pilot and skydiver.
2. You always (was, were) a good friend.
3. Jorge Luis Borges (was, were) a great twentieth-century writer.
4. Why (was, were) they an hour early for the party?
5. I (was, were) seven when my sister (was, were) born.
6. Carmen (was, were) a Republican, but her cousins (was, were) Democrats.
7. The bride and groom (was, were) present, but where (was, were) the ring?
8. (Was, Were) you seasick on your new houseboat?
9. Either they (was, were) late, or she (was, were) early.
10. At this time last year, Sarni and I (was, were) in Egypt.

To Be + Not

Be careful of verb agreement if you use the past tense of *to be* with *not* as a contraction.

$$
\begin{array}{l}
was + not = wasn't \\
were + not = weren't
\end{array}
$$

PRACTICE 8

In each sentence, fill in the blank with either *wasn't* or *weren't*.

1. The printer cartridges _____ on sale.
2. That papaya _____ cheap.
3. He _____ happy about the opening of the nuclear power plant.
4. This fireplace _____ built properly.
5. The parents _____ willing to tolerate drug dealers near the school.
6. That _____ the point!
7. My pet lobster _____ in the aquarium.
8. That history quiz _____ so bad.
9. He and I liked each other, but we _____ able to agree about music.
10. Many young couples _____ able to afford homes.

D. Review

PRACTICE 9

Review

All main verbs in this paragraph are underlined to help you spot them. Proofread the paragraph, checking every verb in this paragraph and correcting any past tense errors or incorrect verbs above the lines.

(1) Mohawk Indians <u>played</u> a major role in constructing American cities. (2) They <u>builded</u>

skyscrapers all over the United States and Canada, earning fame as skillful ironworkers.

(3) Almost 150 years ago, Mohawks first <u>began</u> to "walk high steel" when they <u>work</u> on a

Mohawk Indians and other ironworkers eat lunch on a beam during construction of Rockefeller Center. New York City, 1932.

bridge over the St. Lawrence River in Canada. (4) They <u>done</u> well at this dangerous job. (5) Some people <u>sayed</u> that Mohawks <u>haved</u> no fear, but in fact they just <u>handled</u> their fear better than others. (6) Mohawk ironworking families <u>move</u> where the jobs <u>was</u>. (7) They <u>putted</u> up the Sears Tower in Chicago (now the Willis Tower) and the San Francisco Bay Bridge. (8) In New York City, they proudly <u>taked</u> their place in history, working on the Chrysler Building, the Empire State Building, and the George Washington Bridge. (9) In the 1960s, the call <u>wented</u> out for ironworkers willing to climb the tallest buildings in the world. (10) Five hundred Mohawks <u>signed</u> up to build the World Trade Center. (11) In 2001, after the Twin Towers <u>falled</u>, a new generation of Mohawk steelworkers <u>come</u> back to dismantle the twisted beams.

PRACTICE 10 Review

This paragraph is written in the present tense. Underline every main verb. Then change the paragraph to the past tense by changing all the verbs, writing the past tense form of every verb above the lines.*

   (1) Above the office where I work is a karate studio. (2) Every day as I go through my email, make out invoices, and write letters, I hear loud shrieks and crashes from the studio above

---

* See also Chapter 24, "Consistent Tense," for more practice.

me. (3) All day long, the walls tremble, the ceiling shakes, and little pieces of plaster fall like snow onto my desk. (4) Sometimes, the noise does not bother me; at other times, I wear earplugs. (5) If I am in a very bad mood, I stand on my desk and pound out reggae rhythms on the ceiling with my shoe. (6) However, I appreciate one thing. (7) The job teaches me to concentrate no matter what.

Chapter Highlights

- **Regular verbs add** -d **or** -ed **to form the past tense:**

  We *decided.*

  The frog *jumped.*

  He *outfoxed* the fox.

- **Irregular verbs in the past tense change in irregular ways:**

  We *took* a marketing course.

  Owen *ran* fast.

  Jan *brought* pineapples.

- *To be* **is the only verb that takes more than one form in the past tense:**

I *was*	we *were*
you *were*	you *were*
he she it } *was*	they *were*

Proofreading Strategy

To proofread for past tense verb errors, especially if these are one of your error patterns, **highlight** and **read aloud**. First, read slowly through the text, underlining or highlighting the *main verb* in every sentence.

- Make sure that every *regular past tense verb* ends in –d or –ed.

- Carefully consider every *irregular past tense verb* to make sure it is in the correct form. If you aren't sure, check the past tense chart. Here are two examples:

  became

  In 2008, Barack Obama become the first African-American president of the United

  voted

  States. Almost 53 percent of Americans who participated in the election vote for him.

WRITING AND PROOFREADING ASSIGNMENT

With three or four classmates, invent a group fairy tale. Take five minutes to decide on a subject for your story. On a clean sheet of paper, the first student should write the first sentence—in the past tense, of course. Use vivid action verbs. Each student should write a sentence in turn until the fairy tale is finished.

Now proofread. Underline or highlight every main verb. Then have a group member read your story aloud. As you listen, make sure the verbs are correct. Should any verbs be replaced with livelier ones?

CHAPTER REVIEW

Proofread carefully for past tense verbs. Check every verb in this essay, correcting any past tense errors or incorrect verbs above the lines.

Homegrown Warrior

(1) Majora Carter growed up in a rough neighborhood of New York's South Bronx. (2) When she gone to college, she vowed never to return. (3) Like many inner-city areas, it was an industrial wasteland, with decaying buildings and gray air. (4) Yet a strange twist of fate bringed Carter home and inspire an amazing career.

(5) For financial reasons, Majora have to move back with her parents while she work on a master's degree in writing. (6) She soon heard about the city's plan to build yet another solid waste treatment plant in the South Bronx. (7) She and her neighbors discuss this pattern of dumping unwanted waste in poor areas. (8) They learnt that the toxic effects of sewage plants already in the South Bronx added to the plague of local health problems, especially asthma. (9) Angry and determined, Carter rallyed the residents to fight. (10) Incredibly, they defeated the city's plan.

(11) Inspired by this success, Carter seen how much more need to be done. (12) Her group want clean air, waterfront development, and environmentally friendly jobs. (13) In 2001, she created Sustainable South Bronx (SSB), an organization dedicated to community restoration. (14) The group assemble a workforce, built a park on the site of an old cement plant, and explores the idea of a four-mile-long greenway along the waterfront. (15) With new respect from local officials and businesses, SSB push for economic development, too. (16) The slow but sure revival attracted other activists and artists to the neighborhood.

(17) Carter further studied the connection between environment and health. (18) Her group taked steps to improve residents' fitness, recreation, and nutrition. (19) But the "green roof" become one of her proudest achievements. (20) Carter demonstrate how growing plants on

Green roofs like this
one in New York City
reduce urban heat and
pollution.

city roofs cleans the air, cools buildings, provides healthy food, and reduces water pollution.

(21) The idea of green roofs catched on and got national attention.

(22) In 2005, at age 38, Majora Carter received a MacArthur "Genius" Grant for profoundly

improving her community's quality of life. (23) A career she never plan just keeped blooming.

EXPLORING ONLINE

<http://iteslj.org/cw/1/em-past3.html> Past tense crossword. Write the
correct verbs and solve the puzzle.

<http://grammar.ccc.commnet.edu/grammar/quizzes/chute.htm> Change
present tense verbs to past in this passage from a famous book.

 View an integrated eBook and chapter-specific interactive learning tools,
including flashcards, quizzes, videos, and extra help tracking and correcting
your Personal Error Patterns, in your Basic Writing CourseMate, accessed
through <www.cengagebrain.com>.

CHAPTER 11

The Past Participle in Action

A: Defining the Past Participle

B: Past Participles of Regular Verbs

C: Past Participles of Irregular Verbs

D: Using the Present Perfect Tense

E: Using the Past Perfect Tense

F: Using the Passive Voice

G: Using Past Participles as Adjectives

A. Defining the Past Participle

Every verb has one form that can be combined with helping verbs like *has* and *have* to make verbs of more than one word. This form is called the **past participle**.

> (1) She has solved the problem.
>
> (2) I have solved the problem.
>
> (3) He had solved the problem already.

- Each of these sentences contains a two-part verb. Circle the first part, or *helping verb*, in each sentence, and write each helping verb in the blanks that follow:

    (1) _____

    (2) _____

    (3) _____

- Underline the second part, or *main verb*, in each sentence. This word, a form of the verb *to solve*, is the same in all three. Write it here: _____

- *Solved* is the past participle of *to solve*.

The past participle never changes, no matter what the subject is and no matter what the helping verb is.

138

B. Past Participles of Regular Verbs

Fill in the past participle in each series below:

Present Tense	Past Tense	Helping Verb + Past Participle
(1) Beth dances.	(1) Beth danced.	(1) Beth has _____.
(2) They decide.	(2) They decided.	(2) They have _____.
(3) He jumps.	(3) He jumped.	(3) He has _____.

● Are the verbs *to dance, to decide,* and *to jump* regular or irregular?

_____ How do you know? _____

● What ending does each verb take in the past tense? _____

● Remember that any verb that forms its past tense by adding *-d* or *-ed* is a *regular* verb. What past participle ending does each verb take? _____

The past participle forms of regular verbs look exactly like the past tense forms. Both end in *-d* or *-ed*.

PRACTICE 1

The first sentence in each of these pairs contains a one-word verb in the past tense. Fill in the past participle of the same verb in the blank in the second sentence.

EXAMPLE: She designed jewelry all her life.

She has _____*designed*_____ jewelry all her life.

1. Several students worked in the maternity ward.

   Several students have _____ in the maternity ward.

2. The pot of soup boiled over.

   The pot of soup has _____ over.

3. The chick hatched.

   The chick has _____.

4. We congratulated Jorgé.

   We have _____ Jorgé.

5. Nelson always studied in the bathtub.

   Nelson has always _____ in the bathtub.

6. Many climbers scaled this mountain.

   Many climbers have _____ this mountain.

7. The landlord asked for a rent increase.

   The landlord has _____ for a rent increase.

8. Sylvia located her long-lost cousin in New Jersey.

   Sylvia has _____ her long-lost cousin in New Jersey.

9. The satellite circled Jupiter.

   The satellite has _____ Jupiter.

10. They signed petitions to save the seals.

    They have _____ petitions to save the seals.

PRACTICE 2

Write the missing two-part verb in each of the following sentences. Use the helping verb *has* or *have* and the past participle of the verb written in parentheses.

> **EXAMPLE:** _____*Have*_____ you ever _____*wished*_____ (to wish) for a new name?

1. Some of us _____ _____ (to want) new names at one time or another.

2. Many famous people _____ _____ (to fulfill) that desire.

3. Some _____ _____ (to use) only their first names.

4. Madonna Louise Ciccone _____ _____ (to drop) everything but Madonna.

5. Beyoncé Knowles _____ _____ (to shorten) her name to Beyoncé.

6. Other celebrities _____ _____ (to retain) their first names and taken new last names.

7. For example, comedian Jonathan Leibowitz _____ _____ (to rename) himself Jon Stewart.

8. Changing both names, Eric Bishop _____ _____ (to turn) himself into Jamie Foxx.

9. Replacing all her names, Stefani Joanne Angelina Germanotta _____ _____ (to transform) herself into Lady Gaga.

10. What new name would you _____ _____ (to pick) for yourself?

C. Past Participles of Irregular Verbs

Present Tense	Past Tense	Helping Verb + Past Participle
(1) He sees.	(1) He saw.	(1) He has seen.
(2) I take vitamins.	(2) I took vitamins.	(2) I have taken vitamins.
(3) We sing.	(3) We sang.	(3) We have sung.

- Are the verbs *to see, to take,* and *to sing* regular or irregular? _____

- Like all irregular verbs, *to see, to take,* and *to sing* do not add *-d* or *-ed* to show past tense.

- Most irregular verbs in the past tense are also irregular in the past participle—like *seen, taken,* and *sung.*

BE CAREFUL: past participles must be used with helping verbs.*

Because irregular verbs change their spelling in irregular ways, there are no easy rules to explain these changes. Here is a list of some common irregular verbs.

Reference Chart: Irregular Verbs

Simple Form	Past	Past Participle
be	was, were	been
become	became	become
begin	began	begun
blow	blew	blown
break	broke	broken
bring	brought	brought
build	built	built
burst	burst	burst
buy	bought	bought
catch	caught	caught
choose	chose	chosen
come	came	come
cut	cut	cut
dive	dove (dived)	dived
do	did	done
draw	drew	drawn
drink	drank	drunk
drive	drove	driven
eat	ate	eaten
fall	fell	fallen
feed	fed	fed
feel	felt	felt
fight	fought	fought
find	found	found
fly	flew	flown
forget	forgot	forgotten
forgive	forgave	forgiven
freeze	froze	frozen
get	got	gotten (got)
give	gave	given
go	went	gone
grow	grew	grown
have	had	had
hear	heard	heard
hide	hid	hidden
hold	held	held
hurt	hurt	hurt
keep	kept	kept
know	knew	known
lay	laid	laid
lead	led	led
leave	left	left
let	let	let
lie	lay	lain

(continued)

---

* For work on incomplete verbs, see Chapter 8, Part B.

Reference Chart: Irregular Verbs (*continued***)**

Simple Form	Past	Past Participle
lose	lost	lost
make	made	made
mean	meant	meant
meet	met	met
pay	paid	paid
put	put	put
quit	quit	quit
read	read	read
ride	rode	ridden
ring	rang	rung
rise	rose	risen
run	ran	run
say	said	said
see	saw	seen
seek	sought	sought
sell	sold	sold
send	sent	sent
set	set	set
shake	shook	shaken
shine	shone (shined)	shone (shined)
shrink	shrank (shrunk)	shrunk
sing	sang	sung
sit	sat	sat
sleep	slept	slept
speak	spoke	spoken
spend	spent	spent
spring	sprang	sprung
stand	stood	stood
steal	stole	stolen
strike	struck	struck
swim	swam	swum
swing	swung	swung
take	took	taken
teach	taught	taught
tear	tore	torn
tell	told	told
think	thought	thought
throw	threw	thrown
understand	understood	understood
wake	woke (waked)	woken (waked)
wear	wore	worn
win	won	won
wind	wound	wound
write	wrote	written

You already know many of these past participle forms. One way to learn the unfamiliar ones is to group together verbs that change from the present tense to the past tense to the past participle in the same way. For example, some irregular verbs change from *ow* in the present to *ew* in the past to *own* in the past participle.

bl<u>ow</u>	bl<u>ew</u>	bl<u>own</u>
gr<u>ow</u>	gr<u>ew</u>	gr<u>own</u>
kn<u>ow</u>	kn<u>ew</u>	kn<u>own</u>
thr<u>ow</u>	thr<u>ew</u>	thr<u>own</u>

Another group changes from *i* in the present to *a* in the past to *u* in the past participle:

beg<u>i</u>n	beg<u>a</u>n	beg<u>u</u>n
dr<u>i</u>nk	dr<u>a</u>nk	dr<u>u</u>nk
r<u>i</u>ng	r<u>a</u>ng	r<u>u</u>ng
s<u>i</u>ng	s<u>a</u>ng	s<u>u</u>ng
spr<u>i</u>ng	spr<u>a</u>ng	spr<u>u</u>ng
sw<u>i</u>m	sw<u>a</u>m	sw<u>u</u>m

As you write, refer to the chart. If you are unsure of the past participle form of a verb that is not on the chart, check a dictionary. For example, if you look up the verb *see* in the dictionary, you will find an entry like this:

see \ saw \ seen \ seeing

The first word listed is the present tense form of the verb (I *see*, she *sees*, and so on). The second word listed is the past tense form (I *saw*, she *saw*, and so on). The third word is the past participle form (I *have seen*, she *has seen*, and so on), and the last word is the present participle form.

Some dictionaries list different forms only for irregular verbs. If no past tense or past participle form is listed, you know that the verb is regular and that its past participle ends in *-d* or *-ed*.

PRACTICE 3

The first sentence in each pair contains an irregular verb in the past tense. Fill in *has* or *have* plus the past participle of the same verb to complete the second sentence.

EXAMPLE: I ate too much.

I _____*have*_____ _____*eaten*_____ too much.

1. The river rose over its banks.

   The river _____ _____ over its banks.

2. She sold her 1956 Buick.

   She _____ _____ her 1956 Buick.

3. For years, we sang in a barbershop quartet.

   For years, we _____ _____ in a barbershop quartet.

4. Crime rates fell recently.

   Crime rates _____ _____ recently.

5. Ralph gave me a red satin bowling jacket.

   Ralph _____ _____ me a red satin bowling jacket.

6. They thought carefully about the problem.

   They _____ _____ carefully about the problem.

7. I kept all your love letters.

   I _____ _____ all your love letters.

8. The Joneses forgot to confirm the reservation.

The Joneses _____ _____ to confirm the reservation.

9. The pond froze solid.

The pond _____ _____ solid.

10. The children knew about those caves for years.

The children _____ _____ about those caves for years.

PRACTICE 4

Now you will be given only the first sentence with its one-word verb in the past tense. Rewrite the entire sentence, changing the verb to a two-word verb—*has* or *have* plus the past participle of the main verb.

EXAMPLE: He took his credit cards with him.

He has taken his credit cards with him.

1. They brought their Great Dane to the party.

_____

2. T. J. drove a city bus for two years.

_____

3. She chose a Romare Bearden poster for the hallway.

_____

4. I saw a white fox near the barn.

_____

5. A tornado tore through the shopping center.

_____

6. Margo became more self-confident.

_____

7. Councilman Gomez ran a fair campaign.

_____

8. The old barn stood there for years.

_____

9. Sam read about the islands of Fiji.

_____

10. Our conversations were very helpful.

_____

PRACTICE 5

Review

For each verb in the chart that follows, fill in the present tense (third person singular form), the past tense, and the past participle. BE CAREFUL: Some of the verbs are regular, and some are irregular.

Simple	Present Tense (he, she, it)	Past Tense	Past Participle
know	*knows*	*knew*	*known*
catch			
stop			
break			
reach			
bring			
fly			
fall			
feel			
take			
go			

PRACTICE 6 · Review

Carefully proofread for verb errors in this essay, which contains both *regular* and *irregular verbs.* In every sentence, find and check any verbs containing a *helping verb* (*has* or *have*) and a *past participle.* Cross out the errors and make your corrections above the lines. Hint: thirteen verbs are incorrect.

EXAMPLES: Millions has [*have*] heard them sing.

They have use [*used*] words and music to connect with others.

Latinas Break Through

(1) Recently, a new generation of Latina crossover stars has broke musical barriers, bringing to American music and films new talent and a Latin flavor. (2) The performer who started it all, Cuban-born Gloria Estefan, now has establish herself as a hugely successful crossover singer. (3) Her albums, with hits like "Conga" and "Rhythm of the Night," have sell millions of copies. (4) In fact, "Conga" was the first song to appear on the pop, soul, Latin, and dance music charts all at the same time. (5) In her long career, Estefan have blaze many trails. (6) In addition to being the first Latina to win Broadcast Music's "Songwriter of the Year" award, she have receive five Grammies. (7) Estefan was the first person ever to sing in Spanish at the Grammy Awards.

Jennifer Lopez as Selena

(8) Since then, many young singers has crossed over to English from a range of Spanish-speaking backgrounds. (9) Selena, for instance, established herself as the first female superstar of Tejano music, a Tex-Mex style that has came to blend rock, country, conjunto, norteno, and blues. (10) Selena's 1991 hit "Ven Conmigo" was the first Tejano record to go gold, and in 1993, she became the first Tejano artist to win a Grammy. (11) In addition, five Spanish-language albums on the *Billboard 200* have earn her another first. (12) Although her tragic murder in 1995 cut short a brilliant career, Selena's recordings have encourage North Americans to appreciate the beauty, exuberance, and variety of Latino music.

(13) Ironically, a film about Selena's life launched the next Latina superstar into the spotlight. (14) Since her 1997 role as the slain Tejana singer, Puerto Rican Jennifer Lopez have win acclaim in both her acting and singing careers. (15) In fact, she was the first U.S. performer to have the number 1 album (*Love Don't Cost a Thing*) and the number 1 movie (*The Wedding Planner*) during the same week. (16) Today, commanding top fees for her films and creating her own perfume and clothing lines, JLo has became the highest paid Latina actress in history.

(17) These breakthrough stars has help to blend Hispanic and Anglo cultures and have open doors for a new crop of singers and actresses.

PRACTICE 7

Review

Check your work in the preceding exercises or have it checked. Do you see any *patterns* in your errors? Do you tend to miss regular or irregular verbs? To help yourself learn, copy all four forms of each verb that you missed into your notebook in a chart like the one below. Add specific mistakes to your personal error patterns chart.

Personal Review Chart

Simple	Present Tense (he, she, it)	Past Tense	Past Participle
go	goes	went	gone

D. Using the Present Perfect Tense

The **present perfect tense** is composed of the present tense of *to have* (*has* or *have*) plus the past participle.

<table>
<tr><td colspan="2" align="center">**Present Perfect Tense**</td></tr>
</table>

Singular	**Plural**
I *have* spoken	we *have* spoken
you *have* spoken	you *have* spoken
he she *has* spoken it	they *have* spoken

Let us see how this tense is used.

(1) They *sang* together last Saturday.

(2) They *have sung* together for three years now.

● In sentence (1), the past tense verb *sang* tells us that they sang together on one occasion, Saturday, but are no longer singing together. The action began and ended in the past.

● In sentence (2), the present perfect verb *have sung* tells us something entirely different: that they have sung together in the past and *are still singing together now*.

(3) Janet *sat* on the beach for three hours.

(4) Valerie *has* just *sat* on the beach for three hours.

● Which woman is probably still sunburned? _____

● In sentence (3), Janet's action began and ended at some time in the past. Perhaps it was ten years ago that she sat on the beach.

● In (4), the present perfect verb *has sat* implies that although the action occurred in the past, it *has just happened*, and Valerie had better put some lotion on her sunburn *now*.

● Notice how the word *just* emphasizes that the action occurred very recently.

Use the *present perfect tense* to show either (1) that an action began in the past and has continued until now or (2) that an action has just happened.

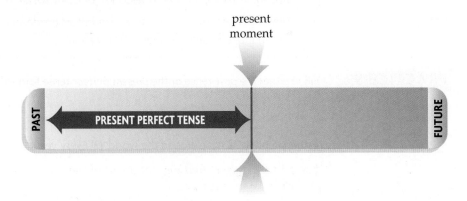

In writing about an action that began in the past and is still continuing, you will often use time words like *for* and *since*.

> (5) We have watched the fireworks *for* three hours.
>
> (6) John has sung in the choir *since* 2002.

In writing about an action that has just happened, you will often use words like *just*, *recently*, *already*, and *yet*.

> (7) I have *just* finished the novel.
>
> (8) They have *already* gone to the party.

PRACTICE 8

Paying close attention to meaning, circle the verb that best completes each sentence.

> **EXAMPLES:** Years ago, he (wanted, has wanted) to know how things worked. Since then, not much (changed, has changed).

1. Even as a young boy in New York City, Dean Kamen (loved, has loved) science and invention.

2. While just a teenager, he (got, has gotten) the job of automating the Times Square ball drop for New Year's Eve.

3. Since that time, Kamen (invented, has invented) many amazing machines, including a stair-climbing wheelchair, a robotic scooter, and a small dialysis machine.

4. For several years now, he (lived and worked, has lived and worked) in a huge, six-sided house in New Hampshire.

5. Inside and out, the house (began, has begun) to look like a fabulous science museum.

6. The collection (expanded, has expanded) to include helicopters, a steam engine, a special Humvee, and a wind turbine.

7. Some years ago, Kamen (decided, has decided) to encourage children to enter science careers.

8. In the 1990s, he (created, has created) FIRST—For Inspiration and Recognition of Science and Technology—to spark kids' interest in science and to sponsor robot-building contests.

9. In a recent speech, Kamen (said, has said), "Teenagers think they will become NBA stars and make millions, but their odds [of doing so] are less than 1 percent."

10. "However, many, many scientists and inventors (made, have made) big money and big contributions as well," he added. "Think about it."

PRACTICE 9

Fill in either the *past* tense or the *present perfect* tense form of each verb in parentheses.

(1) In 1976, the town of Twinsburg, Ohio, _____ (to begin) hosting a gathering of twins from around the world. (2) Every year since then, more and more twins

_____ (to attend), wearing matching outfits, crazy hats, and posing for photographers. (3) Last year, 2,064 sets of twins from the United States, Africa, Europe, and South America _____ (to register) for Twins Days. (4) Over the years, fascinated tourists _____ (to double) the fun. (5) More important, the annual event _____ (to offer) scientists a rare research opportunity. (6) For example, researchers _____ (to study) identical twins (with identical genes) to see how DNA and environment affect diseases, hair loss, and even personality traits like shyness. (7) By the way, in the 1990s, researchers _____ (to find) that shyness is inherited. (8) Many twins _____ (to assist) scientists by standing in line for hours to answer questions, take tests, and donate their DNA. (9) The twins festival _____ (to afford) them the chance not only to meet other twins but also to contribute to human knowledge.

E. Using the Past Perfect Tense

The **past perfect tense** is composed of the past tense of _to have_ (_had_) plus the past participle.

Past Perfect Tense	
Singular	**Plural**
I _had_ spoken	we _had_ spoken
you _had_ spoken	you _had_ spoken
he	
she } _had_ spoken	they _had_ spoken
it	

Let us see how this tense is used.

> (1) Because Bob _had broken_ his leg, he _wore_ a cast for six months.

- The actions in both parts of this sentence occurred entirely in the past, but one occurred before the other.
- At some time in the past, Bob _wore_ (past tense) a cast on the leg that he _had broken_ (past perfect tense) at some time before that.

When you are writing in the past tense, use the _past perfect tense_ **to show that something happened at an even earlier time.**

	past perfect tense	past tense	present moment

He *had* broken his leg. | He *wore* a cast. | Now he *thinks* twice before he climbs a ladder.

As a general rule, the present perfect tense is used in relation to the present tense, and the past perfect tense is used in relation to the past tense. Read the following pairs of sentences and note the time relation.

> (2) Sid *says* (present) he *has found* (present perfect) a good job.
>
> (3) Sid *said* (past) he *had found* (past perfect) a good job.
>
> (4) Grace *tells* (present) us she *has won* (present perfect) first prize.
>
> (5) Grace *told* (past) us she *had won* (past perfect) first prize.

PRACTICE 10

Choose either the present perfect or the past perfect tense of the verb in parentheses to complete each sentence. Match present perfect tense with present tense and past perfect tense with past tense.

1. The newspaper reports that the dictator _____ _____ (to leave) the country.

2. The newspaper reported that the dictator _____ _____ (to leave) the country.

3. I plan to buy a red convertible; I _____ _____ (to want) a convertible for three years now.

4. Last year, I bought a red convertible; I _____ _____ (to want) a convertible for three years before that.

5. Mel _____ _____ (to choose) the steepest trail up the mountain; he was thoroughly worn out.

6. Mel _____ _____ (to choose) the steepest trail up the mountain; he is thoroughly worn out.

7. I am worried about my cat; she _____ _____ (to drink) bubble bath.

8. I was worried about my cat; she _____ _____ (to drink) bubble bath.

9. Sam told us that he _____ _____ (to decide) to major in restaurant management.

10. Sam tells us that he _____ _____ (to decide) to major in restaurant management.

F. Using the Passive Voice

So far in this chapter, you have combined the past participle with forms of *to have*. But the past participle can also be used with forms of *to be* (*am, is, are, was, were*).

> (1) That jam was made by Aunt Clara.

- The subject of the sentence is *that jam*. The verb has two parts: the helping verb *was* and the past participle *made*.

- Note that the subject, *that jam*, does not act but is acted on by the verb. *By Aunt Clara* tells us who performed the action.

That jam *was made* by Aunt Clara.

When the subject is acted on or receives the action, it is passive, and the verb (*to be + past participle*) **is in the** *passive voice.*

Now compare the passive voice with the active voice in these pairs of sentences:

> (2) **Passive voice:** Free gifts are given by the bank.
> (3) **Active voice:** The bank gives free gifts.
>
> (4) **Passive voice:** We were photographed by a tourist.
> (5) **Active voice:** _____.

- In sentence (2), the subject, *free gifts*, is passive; it receives the action. In sentence (3), *the bank* is active; it performs the action.

- Note the difference between the passive verb *are given* and the active verb *gives*.

- However, the tense of both sentences is the same. The passive verb *are given* is in the present tense, and so is the active verb *gives*.

- Rewrite sentence (4) in the active voice. Be sure to keep the same verb tense in the new sentence.

Write in the *passive voice* **only when you want to emphasize the receiver of the action rather than the doer. Usually, however, write in the** *active voice* **because sentences in the active voice are livelier and more direct.**

PRACTICE 11

Underline the verb in each sentence. In the blank to the right, write *A* if the verb is written in the active voice and *P* if the verb is in the passive voice.

EXAMPLE: Nelson Mandela is respected worldwide as a leader. _____P_____

1. Nelson Mandela was born in South Africa on July 18, 1918, a member of the Xhosa tribe. _____

2. Under the apartheid government, only whites, not the black majority, enjoyed basic rights. _____

3. As a young lawyer, Mandela defended many black clients. _____

4. They were charged with such crimes as "not owning land" or "living in the wrong area." _____

5. Several times, Mandela was arrested for working with the African National Congress, a civil rights group. _____

6. In 1961, he sadly gave up his lifelong belief in nonviolence. _____

7. Training guerrilla fighters, he was imprisoned again, this time with a life sentence. _____

8. Twenty-seven years in jail did not break Mandela. _____

9. Offered freedom to give up his beliefs, he said no. _____

10. Finally released in 1990, this man became a symbol of hope for a new South Africa. _____

11. In 1994, black and white South Africans lined up to vote in the first free elections. _____

12. Gray-haired, iron-willed Nelson Mandela was elected president of his beloved country. _____

PRACTICE 12

In each sentence, underline both parts of the passive verb and circle the complete subject. Then draw an arrow from the verb to the word or words it acts on.

EXAMPLE: I was approached by Professor Martin.

1. The skaters were applauded vigorously by the crowd.

2. The corn is picked fresh every morning.

3. These flowered bowls were imported from Mexico.

4. Milos, my cat, was ignored by the mouse.

5. Hasty promises are often broken.

6. An antique train set was sold at the auction.

7. The speech was memorized by both actors.

8. Customers are lured into the store by loud music and bright signs.

9. Dutch is spoken on Curaçao.

10. Our quarrel was quickly forgotten.

PRACTICE 13

Whenever possible, write in the active, not the passive, voice. Rewrite each sentence, changing the verb from the passive to the active voice. Make all necessary verb and subject changes. Be sure to keep each sentence in the original tense.

EXAMPLE: Good medical care is deserved by all human beings.

All human beings deserve good medical care.

1. Doctors Without Borders was created by a small group of French doctors in 1971.

_____

Two physicians from Doctors Without Borders care for a baby in an evacuation camp in the Philippines.

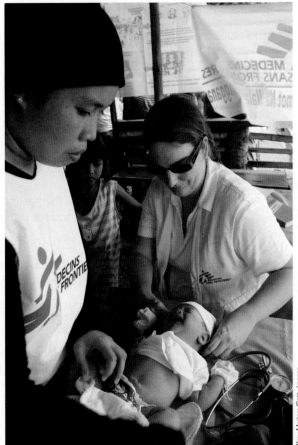

Jeoffrey Maitem/Getty Images

2. Excellent health care was provided by them to people in poor or isolated regions.

_____

3. Soon they were joined by volunteer doctors and nurses from all over the world.

_____

4. Today drugs and medical supplies are brought by the organization to people in need.

_____

5. Vaccinations are received by children in eighty countries.

_____

6. Crumbling hospitals and clinics are restored by volunteers.

_____

7. Victims of wars also are treated by the DWB staff.

_____

8. Information about humanitarian crises is gotten by the world.

_____

9. Each year, thousands are given the gifts of health and life by these traveling experts.

_____

G. Using Past Participles as Adjectives

Sometimes a past participle is not a verb at all but an *adjective*, a word that describes a noun or pronoun.*

> (1) Jay is *married*.
>
> (2) The *broken* window looks terrible.
>
> (3) Two *tired* students slept in the hall.

- In sentence (1), *married* is the past participle of the verb *to marry*, but here it is not a verb. Instead, it describes the subject, *Jay*.

- *Is* links the subject, *Jay*, with the descriptive word, *married*.

- In sentence (2), *broken* is the past participle form of *to break*, but it is used as an adjective to describe the noun *window*.

- In sentence (3), what past participle is an adjective? _____

- Which word does it describe? _____

Past participles like *married*, *broken*, and *tired* are often used as adjectives.

Some form of the verb *to be* usually links descriptive past participles with the subjects they describe, but here are a few other common linking verbs that you learned in Chapter 7, Part E.

PRACTICE 14   Underline the linking verb in each sentence. Then circle the descriptive past participle or participles that complete the sentences.

EXAMPLES: The window was (polish, polished).

Paolo seems very (worry, worried) these days.

1. This product is (guarantee, guaranteed) not to explode.

2. Nellie seems (qualify, qualified) for the job.

3. Your aunt appears (delight, delighted) to see you again.

4. After we read the chapter, we were still (confuse, confused).

5. The science laboratory is (air-condition, air-conditioned).

_____

*For more work on adjectives, see Chapter 22.

6. Dwayne feels (appreciate, appreciated) in his new job.

7. Did you know that one out of two American couples gets (divorce, divorced)?

8. We were (thrill, thrilled) to meet Venus and Serena Williams.

9. During the holidays, Paul feels (depress, depressed).

10. Are the potatoes (fry, fried), (bake, baked), or (boil, boiled)?

PRACTICE 15

Below is a list of verbs. Use the past participles of the verbs as adjectives to describe each noun in the exercise. Then use your adjective-noun combination in a sentence. Use a different past participle for each noun.

bore	freeze	park	train
delight	hide	pollute	wear
dry	lose	tire	worry
embarrass	daze	toast	wrinkle

EXAMPLE: the _____*dried*_____ fruit

We served the dried fruit for dessert.

1. a(n) _____ man

   _____

2. the _____ emeralds

   _____

3. these _____ muffins

   _____

4. a(n) _____ nurse

   _____

5. two _____ passengers

   _____

PRACTICE 16

Proofread the following ad copy for past participle errors. First, underline all the past participles. Then make any corrections above the line.

(1) First create in 1959, Barbie is the world's best-selling doll. (2) Changes in society have been reflect in Barbie's looks, clothes, and career options. (3) Although ethnically diverse Barbies were introduce over the years by Mattel, many parents grew tire of seeing brown-skinned dolls with Caucasian features. (4) They wanted dolls design to look more like their daughters. (5) Stacey McBride-Irby was an experienced designer working at Mattel. (6) She also happened to be African American and the mother of a young girl.

(7) Motivate by what she wanted for her own child, McBride-Irby pitched an idea to Mattel executives. (8) They were immediately interest. (9) The result is McBride-Irby's "So in Style" line of Barbies with fuller lips, wider noses, and more pronounce cheekbones. (10) One doll's skin is tint caramel and another's, chocolate brown. (11) Their hair ranges from curly to straight. (12) The dolls are name Grace, Kara, and Trichelle. (13) Each one has a little sister she mentors, because, says McBride-Irby, "I want girls to be inspire and dream big." (14) Like all Barbies, these can be dress and accessorize until parents wince, and some critics aren't please that their long hair and plastic-surgery proportions send harmful messages. (15) Despite the controversy, these Barbies are love by a new group of girls.

PRACTICE 17

Combine each pair of short sentences. First, find and underline the past participle. Then rewrite the two short sentences as one smooth sentence, using the past participle as an adjective.

> **EXAMPLE:** The book is lost. It is worth $1,000.
>
> _The lost book is worth $1,000._

1. This rug has been dry-cleaned. It looks new.

   _____

2. His grades have fallen. He can bring them up.

   _____

3. The envelope was sealed. Harriet opened it.

   _____

4. The weather forecast was revised. It calls for sunshine.

   _____

5. These gold chains are overpriced. Do not buy them.

   _____

PRACTICE 18

The sentences in the left column are in the present tense; those in the right column are in the past tense. If the sentence is shown in the present tense on the left, write the sentence in the past tense on the right, and vice versa. REMEMBER: Only the *linking verb,* never the past participle, changes to show tense.

> **EXAMPLES:** Smoking is forbidden.   _Smoking was forbidden._
>
> _Lunches are served._   Lunches were served.

Present Tense	Past Tense
1. Your car is repaired.	1. _____
2. _____	2. The store looked closed.
3. _____	3. My feelings were hurt.
4. The seats are filled.	4. _____
5. She is relaxed.	5. _____
6. _____	6. You seemed qualified for the job.
7. He is supposed to meet us.*	7. _____
8. They are used to hard work.*	8. _____
9. _____	9. It was written in longhand.
10. You are expected at noon.	10. _____

Chapter Highlights

- **Past participles of regular verbs add -d or -ed, just like their past tense forms:**

Present	Past	Past Participle
decide	decided	decided
jump	jumped	jumped

- **Past participles of irregular verbs change in irregular ways:**

Present	Past	Past Participle
bring	brought	brought
see	saw	seen
take	took	taken

- **Past participles can combine with** *to have***:**

    He *has edited* many articles for us. (*present perfect tense*)

    He *had edited* many articles for us. (*past perfect tense*)

- **Past participles can combine with** *to be***:**

    The report *was edited* by Mary. (*passive voice*)

- **Past participles can be used as adjectives:**

    The *edited* report arrived today. (*adjective*)

---

* For more work on *supposed* and *used*, see Chapter 33, "Look-Alikes/Sound-Alikes."

Proofreading Strategy

If past participle problems are among your error patterns, read your draft one word at a time and **search for the helping verbs *has, have, had, is, am, are, was, and were***. Every time you find a helping verb, highlight or underline it. If you are using a computer, use the *"Find"* feature to locate these words in your draft. Whenever these helping verbs are part of a past participle verb, **check the past participle form**. If it's a regular verb, it should end in *-d* or *-ed*. If it's an irregular verb and you aren't sure, check the verb chart. How should the writer correct the two incorrect past participles in these examples?

CORRECT   INCORRECT
I have registered for classes next semester, but I haven't yet buy my textbooks.

INCORRECT   CORRECT
The floor was stain a rich brown and polished to a high gloss.

WRITING AND PROOFREADING ASSIGNMENT

In a group of four or five classmates, write a wacky restaurant menu, using all the past participles that you can think of as adjectives: *steamed* fern roots, *fried* cherries, *caramel-coated* hamburgers, and so forth. Brainstorm. Get creative. Then arrange your menu in an order that makes sense (if that is the correct term for such a menu!). Don't forget to proofread.

CHAPTER REVIEW

Proofread this student's essay for past participle errors. Correct each error above the line.

Three Ways to Be a Smarter Learner

(1) Once in a great while, a person is born with a photographic memory, allowing him or her to memorize a lot of information with almost no effort. (2) However, most of us have struggle on our own to find the best ways to learn. (3) We have stayed up all night studying. (4) We have mark up our textbooks, highlighting and underlining like skill tattoo artists. (5) Maybe, in frustration, we have even questioned our own intelligence. (6) Although everyone has his or her own learning style, three techniques have make me and others better learners.

(7) The first technique is simple—sit at the front of the class! (8) A student who has choose to sit up front is more likely to stay alert and involve than students at the back and sides. (9) By sitting away from windows or talkative friends, many students discover that they take a greater interest in the classroom subject and take better notes. (10) An extra

benefit of sitting up front is that teachers are often impress by students with whom they make eye contact, students whose behavior says, "I care about this class."

(11) Second, make a smart friend. (12) During the first week of class, exchange phone numbers with another front-row student. (13) You are looking for an intelligent, responsible classmate who seems committed to learning—not for a pizza buddy or a date. (14) Students who have agree in advance to help each other can call if they miss a class. (15) What was discuss that day? (16) Was homework assign or a test announced? (17) Two students who "click" might want to become study partners, meeting regularly to review material and prepare for tests.

(18) Third, ask questions. (19) The student who has sit up front, made a study friend, and pay close attention in class should not be worried about asking the professor questions. (20) Learning a subject is like building a tower. (21) Each new level of understanding must be build solidly on the level below. (22) If an important point or term is unclear, ask for help, in or after class.

(23) Students who use these techniques will be rewarded with increase understanding and better grades—even before they have pull out their pastel highlighters.

Maurice Jabbar, student

EXPLORING ONLINE

<http://itech.pjc.edu/writinglab/vbcross.htm> Solve this crossword puzzle and test your past tense and past participle skills.

<http://grammar.ccc.commnet.edu/grammar/quizzes/passive_quiz.htm> Interactive quiz: Revise these passive sentences. Make them active.

 View an integrated eBook and chapter-specific interactive learning tools, including flashcards, quizzes, videos, and extra help tracking and correcting your Personal Error Patterns, in your Basic Writing CourseMate, accessed through <www.cengagebrain.com>.

CHAPTER 12

Progressive Tenses
(TO BE + -*ING* Verb Form)

A: Defining and Writing the Present Progressive Tense

B: Defining and Writing the Past Progressive Tense

C: Using the Progressive Tenses

D: Avoiding Incomplete Progressives

A. Defining and Writing the Present Progressive Tense

Verbs in the *present progressive tense* have two parts: the present tense form of *to be* (*am, is, are*) plus the *-ing* (or present participle) form of the main verb.

<table>
<tr><td colspan="2" align="center">Present Progressive Tense
(example verb: to play)</td></tr>
<tr><td>Singular</td><td>Plural</td></tr>
<tr><td>I am playing</td><td>we are playing</td></tr>
<tr><td>you are playing</td><td>you are playing</td></tr>
<tr><td>he
she   is playing
it</td><td>they are playing</td></tr>
</table>

Compare the present tense with the present progressive tense below.

(1) Larry works at the bookstore.

(2) Larry is working at the bookstore.

● Sentence (1) is in the present tense. Which word tells you this? _____

● Sentence (2) is also in the present tense. Which word tells you this? _____

● Note that the main verb in sentence (2), *working*, has no tense. Only the helping verb *is* shows tense.

PRACTICE 1

Change each one-word present tense verb in the left-hand column to a two-part present progressive verb in the right-hand column. Do this by filling in the missing helping verb (*am, is,* or *are*).

EXAMPLES: I fly.   I _____*am*_____ flying.

He wears my sweater.   He _____*is*_____ wearing my sweater.

Present Tense | **Present Progressive Tense**

1. Elsa and I set goals together.
2. They eat quickly.
3. He plans the wedding.
4. Our work begins to pay off.
5. We pose for the photographer.
6. Maryann smiles.
7. Sal does his Elvis impression.
8. I speak Portuguese to Manuel.
9. My grandson gets silly.
10. You probably wonder why.

1. Elsa and I _____ setting goals together.
2. They _____ eating quickly.
3. He _____ planning the wedding.
4. Our work _____ beginning to pay off.
5. We _____ posing for the photographer.
6. Maryann _____ smiling.
7. Sal _____ doing his Elvis impression.
8. I _____ speaking Portuguese to Manuel.
9. My grandson _____ getting silly.
10. You _____ probably wondering why.

REMEMBER: **Every verb in the present progressive tense must have two parts: a helping verb (*am, is,* or *are*) and a main verb ending in *-ing*. The helping verb must agree with the subject.**

PRACTICE 2

Below are sentences in the regular present tense. Rewrite each one in the present progressive tense by changing the verb to *am, is,* or *are* plus the *-ing* form of the main verb.

EXAMPLE: We play cards.

We are playing cards. _____

1. The telephone rings.

   _____

2. Dexter wrestles with his math homework.

   _____

3. James and Sylvia work in the emergency room.

   _____

4. I keep a journal of thoughts and observations.

   _____

5. We polish all our old tools.

   _____

B. Defining and Writing the Past Progressive Tense

Verbs in the *past progressive tense* have two parts: the past tense form of *to be* (*was* or *were*) plus the *-ing* form of the main verb.

Past Progressive Tense (example verb: to play)	
Singular	**Plural**
I *was playing*	we *were playing*
you *were playing*	you *were playing*
he ⎫	
she ⎬ *was playing*	they *were playing*
it ⎭	

Compare the past tense with the past progressive tense below.

(1) Larry worked at the bookstore.

(2) Larry was working at the bookstore.

● Sentence (1) is in the past tense. Which word tells you this? _____

● Sentence (2) is also in the past tense. Which word tells you this? _____

● Notice that the main verb in sentence (2), *working*, has no tense. Only the helping verb *was* shows tense.

PRACTICE 3

Change each one-word past tense verb in the left-hand column to a two-part past progressive verb in the right-hand column. Do this by filling in the missing helping verb (*was* or *were*).

EXAMPLES: I flew.   I _____*was*_____ flying.

He wore my sweater.   He _____*was*_____ wearing my sweater.

Past Tense	**Past Progressive Tense**
1. Elsa and I set goals together.	1. Elsa and I _____ setting goals together.
2. They ate quickly.	2. They _____ eating quickly.
3. He planned the wedding.	3. He _____ planning the wedding.
4. Our work began to pay off.	4. Our work _____ beginning to pay off.
5. We posed for the photographer.	5. We _____ posing for the photographer.
6. Maryann smiled.	6. Maryann _____ smiling.
7. Sal did his Elvis impression.	7. Sal _____ doing his Elvis impression.
8. I spoke Portuguese to Manuel.	8. I _____ speaking Portuguese to Manuel.

9. My grandson got silly.

10. You probably wondered why.

9. My grandson _____ getting silly.

10. You _____ probably wondering why.

PRACTICE 4

Below are sentences in the past tense. Rewrite each sentence in the past progressive tense by adding the helping verb *was* or *were* and changing the form of the main verb to the *-ing* form.

EXAMPLE: You cooked dinner.

You were cooking dinner.

1. The two linebackers growled at each other.

   _____

2. Leroy examined his bank receipt.

   _____

3. We watched the news.

   _____

4. Marsha read the *Wall Street Journal* online.

   _____

5. He painted like a professional artist.

   _____

C. Using the Progressive Tenses

As you read these sentences, do you hear the differences in meaning?

(1) Lenore *plays* the piano.

(2) Dave *is playing* the piano.

- Which person is definitely at the keyboard right now?

- If you said Dave, you are right. He is *now in the process of playing* the piano. Lenore, on the other hand, *does* play the piano; she may also paint, write novels, and play center field, but we do not know from the sentence what she *is doing right now*.

- The present progressive verb *is playing* tells us that the action is *in progress*.

  Here is another use of the present progressive tense:

(3) Tony *is coming* here later.

- The present progressive verb *is coming* shows *future* time: Tony is going to come here.

(4) Linda *washed* her hair last night.

(5) Linda *was washing* her hair when we arrived for the party.

- In sentence (4), *washed* implies a completed action.

- The past progressive verb in sentence (5) has a special meaning: that Linda was *in the process* of washing her hair when something else happened (we arrived).

- To say, "Linda *washed* her hair *when* we arrived for the party" means that first we arrived, and then Linda started washing her hair.

Writers in English use the progressive tenses *much less often* than the present tense and past tense. Use the progressive tense only when you want to emphasize that something is or was in the process of happening.

Use the *present progressive tense* (*am, is, are* + *-ing*) to show that an action is in progress now or that it is going to occur in the future.

Use the *past progressive tense* (*was, were* + *-ing*) to show that an action was in progress at a certain time in the past.

PRACTICE 5

Read each sentence carefully. Then circle the verb or verbs that best express the meaning of the sentence.

EXAMPLE: Right now, we (write, (are writing)) letters.

1. Thomas Edison (held, was holding) 1,093 patents.
2. Where is Ellen? She (drives, is driving) to Omaha.
3. Most mornings we (get, are getting) up at seven.
4. Believe it or not, I (thought, was thinking) about you when you phoned.
5. My dog Gourmand (eats, is eating) anything.
6. At this very moment, Gourmand (eats, is eating) the sports page.
7. Max (fried, was frying) onions when the smoke alarm (went, was going) off.
8. Please don't bother me now; I (study, am studying).
9. Newton (sat, was sitting) under a tree when he (discovered, was discovering) gravity.
10. The *Andrea Doria*, a huge pleasure ship, (sank, was sinking) on July 25, 1956.

D. Avoiding Incomplete Progressives

Now that you can write both present and past progressive verbs, avoid mistakes like this one:

We having fun. (*incomplete*)

- Can you see what is missing?

- All by itself, the *-ing* form *having* is not a verb. It has to have a helping verb.

- Because the helping verb is missing, *we having fun* has no time. It could mean *we are having fun* or *we were having fun*.
- *We having fun* is not complete. It is a fragment of a sentence.*

PRACTICE 6   Each group of words below is an incomplete sentence. Put an X over the exact spot where a word is missing. Then, in the Present Progressive column, write the word that would complete the sentence in the *present progressive tense*. In the Past Progressive column, write the word that would complete the sentence in the *past progressive tense*.

	Present Progressive	**Past Progressive**
EXAMPLE: He ⤬ having fun.	*is*	*was*
	(He is having fun.)	(He was having fun.)

1. Fran and I watching the sunrise. _____ _____
2. You taking a computer course. _____ _____
3. A big log floating down the river. _____ _____
4. Her study skills improving. _____ _____
5. I trying to give up caffeine. _____ _____
6. Fights about money getting me down. _____ _____
7. Thick fog blanketing the city. _____ _____
8. That child reading already. _____ _____
9. Your pizza getting cold. _____ _____
10. They discussing the terms of the new contract. _____ _____

Chapter Highlights

- **The progressive tenses combine** *to be* **with the** *-ing* **verb form:**

  present progressive tense: I *am reading*. He *is reading*.

  past progressive tense: I *was reading*. He *was reading*.

- **The** *-ing* **verb form must have a helping verb to be complete:**

  She playing the tuba. (*incorrect*)

  She *is playing* the tuba. (*correct*)

- **The present progressive tense shows that an action is in progress now:**

  Aunt Belle *is waxing* her van.

- **The present progressive tense can also show that an action will take place in the future:**

  Later today, Aunt Belle *is driving* us to the movies.

- **The past progressive tense shows that an action was in progress at a certain time in the past:**

  Aunt Belle *was waxing* her van when she heard thunder.

_____

* For more on this type of fragment, see Chapter 8, Part B.

Proofreading Strategy

If you make progressive tense errors, you are probably leaving out one of the verb's two parts: either the helping verb (*am, is, are, was,* or *were*) or the main verb ending in *–ing*.

First, check for sentences in which the verb needs to express ongoing, continuous action. **Underline or highlight** those verbs and make sure that the **main verb ends in** *–ing*.

CORRECT   INCORRECT

The clock was striking midnight, but they still moving furniture into the house.

Then, check the helping verb. If the **helping verb** is missing, add one, making sure that it **agrees** with the subject of the sentence.

                   were

The clock was striking midnight, but they still moving furniture into the house.

WRITING AND PROOFREADING ASSIGNMENT

Write a brief account that begins, "We are watching an amazing scene on TV. A man/woman/child/couple/group/animal is trying to _____." Fill in the blank, and then write four or five more sentences describing the unfolding action in the *present progressive* tense—as if the action is taking place right now. Now carefully proofread what you have written, checking the verbs.

Now rewrite the whole account in the *past progressive* tense. The new version will begin, "We were watching an amazing scene on TV. A man/woman/child/couple/group/animal was trying to _____."

CHAPTER REVIEW

Proofread this paragraph for incomplete progressive verbs. Write the missing verbs above the lines.

(1) The sluggish economy prompting many people to seek new career directions. (2) They hoping to find jobs with bright futures. (3) By checking trusted sources like the U.S. Bureau of Labor Statistics at ‹http://www.bls.gov/oco/›, job-seekers learning about opportunities in fields like health care. (4) People always need doctors, nurses, and other medical professionals to help them stay healthy, but now, as baby boomers are aging, many jobs in the health sciences experiencing higher than average growth. (5) Some of these require only a two-year degree. (6) One example is the position of dental hygienist. (7) After they pass biology, science, and other courses, dental hygienists earn an associate's degree and must pass a certification exam. (8) Then they work in dentists' offices, cleaning patients' teeth and teaching them how to maintain oral health. (9) A typical full-time dental hygienist

now earning an annual income of about $60,000 or less in some areas. (10) The number of

positions will likely increase by 36 percent before 2018, so economists predicting excellent

employment opportunities for these technicians.

EXPLORING ONLINE

<http://ww2.college-em.qc.ca/prof/epritchard/verblis9.htm> Interactive
quiz: Practice progressive tense verbs as you visit old Montreal.

<http://ww2.college-em.qc.ca/prof/epritchard/presconf.htm> Present tense
or present progressive? Take the Used Car quiz and hone your skills.

 View an integrated eBook and chapter-specific interactive learning tools,
including flashcards, quizzes, videos, and extra help tracking and correcting
your Personal Error Patterns, in your Basic Writing CourseMate, accessed
through <www.cengagebrain.com>.

CHAPTER 13

Fixed-Form Helping Verbs and Verb Problems

A: Defining and Spotting the Fixed-Form Helping Verbs

B: Using the Fixed-Form Helping Verbs

C: Using CAN and COULD

D: Using WILL and WOULD

E: Writing Infinitives

F: Revising Double Negatives

A. Defining and Spotting the Fixed-Form Helping Verbs

You already know the common—and changeable—helping verbs: *to have, to do,* and *to be*. Here are some helping verbs that do not change:

Fixed-Form Helping Verbs	
can	could
will	would
may	might
shall	should
must	

The fixed-form helping verbs do not change, no matter what the subject is. They always keep the same form.

PRACTICE 1

Fill in each blank with a fixed-form helping verb.

1. You _____ do it!

2. This _____ be the most exciting presidential debate ever held.

3. I _____ row while you watch for crocodiles.

4. Rico _____ go to medical school.

5. In South America, the elephant beetle _____ grow to twelve inches in length.

6. If the committee _____ meet today, we _____ have a new budget on time.

7. We _____ rotate the crops this season.

8. Violent films _____ cause children to act out violently.

9. You _____ have no difficulty finding a sales position.

10. Janice _____ teach users to do research on the Internet.

B. Using the Fixed-Form Helping Verbs

> (1) Al will stay with us this summer.
>
> (2) Susan can shoot a rifle well.

- *Will* is the fixed-form helping verb in sentence (1). What main verb does it help? _____

- *Can* is the fixed-form helping verb in sentence (2). What main verb does it help? _____

- Notice that *stay* and *shoot* are the simple forms of the verbs. They do not show tense by themselves.

When a verb has two parts—a fixed-form helping verb and a main verb—the main verb keeps its simple form.

PRACTICE 2

In the left column, each sentence contains a verb made up of some form of *to have* (the changeable helping verb) and a past participle (the main verb).

Each sentence in the right column contains a fixed-form helping verb and a blank. Write the form of the main verb from the left column that correctly completes each sentence.

Have + **Past Participle**	**Fixed-Form Helping Verb** + **Simple Form**
EXAMPLES:	
I have talked to him.	I may ____talk____ to him.
She has flown to Ireland.	She will ____fly____ to Ireland.
1. Irena has written a song.	1. Irena must _____ a song.
2. We have begun.	2. We can _____.
3. Joy has visited Graceland.	3. Joy will _____ Graceland.
4. He has slept all day.	4. He could _____ all day.
5. I have run three miles.	5. I will _____ three miles.

6. We have seen an eclipse.

7. It has drizzled.

8. Fred has gone on vacation.

9. Has he studied?

10. Della has been promoted.

6. We might _____ an eclipse.

7. It may _____.

8. Fred could_____ on vacation.

9. Should he _____?

10. Della might _____ promoted.

C. Using CAN and COULD

(1) He says that I *can* use any tools in his garage.

(2) He said that I *could* use any tools in his garage.

- What is the tense of sentence (1)? _____
- What is the tense of sentence (2)? _____
- What is the helping verb in sentence (1)? _____
- What is the helping verb in sentence (2)? _____
- As you can see, *could* may be used as the past tense of *can*.

Present tense: Today, I *can* touch my toes.

Past tense: Yesterday, I *could* touch my toes.

Can **means** *am/is/are able*. **It may be used to show present tense.**

Could **means** *was/were able* **when it is used to show the past tense of** *can.*

(3) If I went on a diet, I *could* touch my toes.

(4) Rod wishes he *could* touch his toes.

- In sentence (3), the speaker *could* touch his toes *if* . . . . Touching his toes is a possibility, not a certainty.
- In sentence (4), Rod *wishes* he *could* touch his toes, but probably he cannot. Touching his toes is a wish, not a certainty.

Could **also means** *might be able*, **a possibility, a wish, or a request.**

PRACTICE 3

Fill in the present tense helper *can* or the past tense helper *could*, whichever is needed. To determine whether the sentence is in the present or the past, look at the other verbs in the sentence or look for words like *now* and *yesterday*.

1. When I am rested, I _____ study for hours.

2. When I was rested, I _____ study for hours.

3. Jorge insists that he _____ play the trumpet.

4. Jorge insisted that he _____ play the trumpet.

5. A year ago, Zora _____ jog for only five minutes at a time.

6. Now Zora _____ jog for nearly an hour at a time.

7. If you're so smart, how come you _____ never find your own socks?

8. If you were so smart, how come you _____ never find your own socks?

9. When the air was clear, you _____ see the next town.

10. When the air is clear, you _____ see the next town.

PRACTICE 4   Circle either *can* or *could*.

1. Sue thinks that she (can, could) carry a tune.

2. Yesterday, we (can, could) not go to the town meeting.

3. I wish I (can, could) pitch like Johan Santana.

4. You should meet Tony: he (can, could) lift a two-hundred-pound weight.

5. Everyone I meet (can, could) do a cartwheel.

6. Until the party, everyone thought that Harry (can, could) cook.

7. She (can, could) ice skate better now than she (can, could) last year.

8. On the night that Smithers disappeared, the butler (can, could) not be found.

9. When my brother was younger, he (can, could) name every car on the road.

10. I hope that the snow leopards (can, could) survive in captivity.

PRACTICE 5   On a separate paper, write five sentences using *can* to show present tense and five sentences using *could* to show past tense.

D. Using WILL and WOULD

(1) You know you *will* do well in that class.

(2) You knew you *would* do well in that class.

- Sentence (1) says that *you know* now (present tense) that you *will* do well in the future. *Will* points to the future from the present.

- Sentence (2) says that *you knew* then (past tense) that you *would* do well after that. *Would* points to the future from the past.

Would **may be used as the past tense of** *will*, **just as** *could* **may be used as the past tense of** *can*.

(3) *If* you studied, you *would* pass physics.

(4) Juanita wishes she *would* get an A in French.

- In sentence (3), the speaker *would* pass physics *if* . . . . Passing physics is a possibility, not a certainty.

● In sentence (4), Juanita *wishes* she *could* get an A, but this is a wish, not a certainty.

Would **can also express a possibility, a wish, or a request.**

PRACTICE 6

Fill in the present tense *will* or the past tense *would*.

1. The meteorologist predicts that it _____ snow on Friday.

2. The meteorologist predicted that it _____ snow on Friday.

3. Hernan said that he _____ move to Colorado.

4. Hernan says that he _____ move to Colorado.

5. Roberta thinks that she _____ receive financial aid.

6. Roberta thought that she _____ receive financial aid.

7. I _____ marry you if you propose to me.

8. Unless you stop adding salt, no one _____ want to eat that chili.

9. Hugo thinks that he _____ be a country and western star someday.

10. Because she wanted to tell her story, she said that she _____ write an autobiography.

PRACTICE 7

Circle either *will* or *would*.

1. You (will, would) find the right major once you start taking courses.

2. When the house is painted, you (will, would) see how lovely the old place looks.

3. Yolanda wishes that her neighbor (will, would) stop raising ostriches.

4. The instructor assumed that everyone (will, would) improve.

5. They insisted that they (will, would) pick up the check.

6. The whole town assumed that they (will, would) live happily ever after.

7. When we climb the tower, we (will, would) see for miles around.

8. If I had a million dollars, I (will, would) buy a big house on the ocean.

9. Your flight to Mars (will, would) board in fifteen minutes.

10. Because we hated waiting in long lines, we decided that we (will, would) shop somewhere else.

E. Writing Infinitives

Every verb can be written as an **infinitive.** An infinitive has two parts: *to* + the simple form of the verb—*to kiss, to gaze, to sing, to wonder, to help.* Never add endings to the infinitive form of a verb: no *-ed*, no *-s*, no *-ing*.

> (1) Erin has *to take* a course in environmental law.
>
> (2) Neither dictionary seems *to contain* the words I need.

● In sentences (1) and (2), the infinitives are *to take* and *to contain.*

● *To* is followed by the simple form of the verb: *take, contain.*

Don't confuse an infinitive with the preposition *to* followed by a noun or a pronoun.

(3) Tamara spoke *to Sam.*

(4) I gave the award *to her.*

- In sentences (3) and (4), the preposition *to* is followed by the noun *Sam* and the pronoun *her.*

- *To Sam* and *to her* are prepositional phrases, not infinitives.*

PRACTICE 8

Find the infinitives in the following sentences and write them in the blanks at the right.

Infinitive

EXAMPLE: Many people don't realize how hard it is to write a funny essay.

to write
_____

1. Our guests started to leave at midnight.

_____

2. Marlena has decided to run for mayor.

_____

3. Han has to get a B on his final exam or he will not transfer to Wayne State.

_____

4. It is hard to think with that radio blaring!

_____

5. The man wanted to buy a silver watch to give to his son.

_____

PRACTICE 9

Write an infinitive in each blank in the following sentences. Use any verb that makes sense. Remember that the infinitive is made up of *to* plus the simple form of the verb.

1. They began _____ in the cafeteria.

2. Few people know how _____ well.

3. Would it be possible for us _____ again later?

4. He hopes _____ an operating-room nurse.

5. It will be easy_____ _____.

F. Revising Double Negatives

The most common **negatives** are *no, none, not, nowhere, no one, nobody, never,* and *nothing.*

The negative *not* is often joined to a verb to form a contraction: *can't, didn't, don't, hasn't, haven't,* and *won't,* for example.

However, a few negatives are difficult to spot. Read these sentences:

(1) There are hardly any beans left.

(2) By noon, we could scarcely see the mountains on the horizon.

- The negatives in these sentences are *hardly* and *scarcely.*

_____

* For more work on prepositions, see Chapter 7, Part C, and Chapter 23.

● They are negatives because they imply that there are *almost* no beans left and that we *almost couldn't* see the mountains.

Use only one negative in each idea. The double negative is an error you should avoid.

(3) **Double negative:** I can't eat *nothing*.

● There are two negatives in this sentence—*can't* and *nothing*—instead of one.
● Double negatives cancel each other out.

To revise a double negative, simply drop one of the negatives.

(4) **Revised:** I can't eat anything.

(5) **Revised:** I can eat *nothing*.

● In sentence (4), the negative *nothing* has been changed to the positive *anything*.
● In sentence (5), the negative *can't* has been changed to the positive *can*.

When you revise double negatives that include the words *hardly* and *scarcely*, keep those words and change the other negatives to positives.

(6) **Double negative:** They couldn't hardly finish their papers on time.

● The two negatives are *couldn't* and *hardly*.

(5) **Revised:** They could hardly finish their papers on time.

● Change *couldn't* to *could*.

PRACTICE 10   Revise the double negatives in the following sentences.

EXAMPLE: I don't have no more homework to do.

Revised: _I don't have any more homework to do._

1. I can't hardly wait for Christmas vacation.

   Revised: _____

2. Ms. Chandro hasn't never been to Los Angeles.

   Revised: _____

3. Fido was so excited that he couldn't scarcely sit still.

   Revised: _____

4. Nat won't talk to nobody until he's finished studying.

    Revised: _____

5. Yesterday's newspaper didn't contain no ads for large-screen television sets.

    Revised: _____

6. Alice doesn't have no bathing suit with her.

    Revised: _____

7. If Vasily were smart, he wouldn't answer no one in that tone of voice.

    Revised: _____

8. Kylie claimed that she hadn't never been to a rodeo before.

    Revised: _____

9. Some days, I can't seem to do nothing right.

    Revised: _____

10. Umberto searched, but he couldn't find his gold bow tie nowhere.

    Revised: _____

Chapter Highlights

- **Fixed-form verbs do not change, no matter what the subject is:**

    I *can.*

    He *can.*

    They *can.*

- **The main verb after a fixed-form helping verb keeps the simple form:**

    I will *sleep.*

    She might *sleep.*

    Sarita should *sleep.*

- **An infinitive has two parts,** *to* **+ the simple form of a verb:**

    to drive

    to exclaim

    to read

- **Do not write double negatives:**

    I didn't order no soup. (*incorrect*)

    I didn't order any soup. (*correct*)

    They couldn't hardly see. (*incorrect*)

    They could hardly see. (*correct*)

Proofreading Strategy

To proofread for the errors discussed in this chapter, **isolate your sentences** and **find key words.** If you write on a computer, reformat your draft to isolate your sentences, one sentence on each line. This can trick your eye and brain into seeing your words anew.

Now use your eyes or the *"Find"* feature to focus on terms related to your problem areas. For instance, if you have trouble with **fixed-form helping verbs** like *can, could, will,* and *would,* search for and highlight these words; then check the main verb following each one. If you write **double negatives,** find all the "negatives" in your paper (words like *no, none, not, nowhere, no one, nobody, never, nothing*) and check for correctness. Here is an example:

any
Make sure your paper doesn't have no fixed-form errors or double negatives.

WRITING AND PROOFREADING ASSIGNMENT

Review this chapter briefly. What part was most difficult for you? Write a paragraph explaining the difficult material to someone who is having the same trouble you had. Your purpose is to make the lesson crystal clear to him or her. As you proofread, search for key words that help you see your trouble spots.

CHAPTER REVIEW

Proofread the following essay for errors in fixed-form verbs, infinitives, and double negatives. Cross out each incorrect word and correct the error above the line.

Man of Honor

(1) According to public opinion polls, the most influential Hispanic American in the country is Edward James Olmos. (2) Olmos is someone who couldn't never be happy promoting only himself. (3) He has tried to setting an example for others through his choice of movie roles. (4) Olmos decided early in his career that he would not take no parts in *Rambo*- and *Terminator*-style movies just to get rich. (5) Instead, he wanted his life's work to be something that he and his descendants will be proud of.

(6) As a result, his film projects have included *American Me*, an examination of gang members and life in prison. (7) Young people have told him that this film convinced them that they should not have nothing to do with gangs. (8) Olmos is also famous for his portrayal of teacher Jaime Escalante in *Stand and Deliver*. (9) Other projects, from an anti–domestic violence documentary to a film about Brazilian political activist Chico Mendes called *The Burning Season*, aimed to educating the public.

Actor Edward James Olmos helps raise funds for the arts program at a Los Angeles youth center.

(10) Olmos also hopes that he would change lives through his community activism. (11) He gives antidrug speeches. (12) In addition, Olmos visits public schools and promotes projects that help Latinos. (13) For example, he cofounded and now codirects the Los Angeles Latino International Film Festival. (14) The actor also supports the Latino Book and Family Festival and oversees Latino Public Broadcasting. (15) Olmos knows from experience that one person could make a difference.

EXPLORING ONLINE

<http://grammar.ccc.commnet.edu/grammar/cgi-shl/quiz.pl/modal_quiz.htm>
Interactive verb quiz. Test your skills.

<http://www.bbc.co.uk/skillswise/words/grammar/texttypes/negatives/quiz
.shtml> Double negatives game: Try all three levels.

 View an integrated eBook and chapter-specific interactive learning tools, including flashcards, quizzes, videos, and extra help tracking and correcting your Personal Error Patterns, in your Basic Writing CourseMate, accessed through <www.cengagebrain.com>.

UNIT 3

Writing Assignments

As you complete each writing assignment, remember to perform these steps:

- Write a clear, complete topic sentence.
- Use freewriting, brainstorming, or clustering to generate ideas for the body of your paragraph, essay, or letter.
- Arrange your best ideas in a plan.
- Revise for support, unity, coherence, and exact language.
- Proofread for grammar, punctuation, and spelling errors.

Writing Assignment 1 *Tell a family story*. Many of us heard family stories as we were growing up—how our great-grandmother escaped from Poland, how Uncle Chester took his sister for a joy ride in the Ford when he was six. Assume that you have been asked to write such a story for a scrapbook that will be given to your grandmother on her eightieth birthday. Choose a story that reveals something important about a member of your family. As you revise, make sure that all your verbs are correct. Consider sharing your story online at a website that invites viewers to share their personal experiences. Try <http://www.africanaheritage.com/familystories.asp> or <http://www.ellisisland.org/Story/tellstory.asp>.

Writing Assignment 2 *Describe a giraffe (a person who sticks his or her neck out to help others)*. In this unit, you might have read about Majora Carter, who vastly improved the quality of life for her South Bronx neighbors. Carter could be described as a "giraffe," a person who goes out of his or her way for the common good. Visit the Giraffe Heroes Project at <http://www.giraffe.org/> and read some of the stories. Do you know (or know of) a giraffe? Submit your own "Giraffe Sighting Report" by describing someone you know (in person or from word of mouth or the media) who deserves to be honored as a giraffe.

Writing Assignment 3 *Describe a lively scene*. To practice choosing and using verbs, go where the action is—to a sports event, a busy store, a club, a public park, even the woods or a field. Observe carefully as you take notes and freewrite. Capture specific sounds, sights, colors, actions, and smells. Then write a description of what takes place, using lively verbs. Choose either present or past tense and make sure to use that tense consistently throughout.

Writing Assignment 4 *Describe a few intense moments*. Read paragraph A on page 179, which uses lively verbs to describe the saving of someone's life at a health club. This writer uses the present tense, as if the action is happening now. Describe some brief but dramatic event—the birth of a child, the opening of an important letter, the arrival of a blind date, or the reaction of the person to whom you just proposed. Decide whether present or past tense would be better, and choose varied, interesting verbs. As you revise, make sure the verbs are correct.

178

UNIT 3

Review

Transforming

A. Rewrite this paragraph, changing every *I* to *she*, every *me* to *her*, and every *us* to *them*. Do not change any verb tenses. Be sure all verbs agree with their new subjects, and make any other necessary changes.

(1) I am at the gym, training a client. (2) A man near us gets off the treadmill and suddenly collapses onto the floor. (3) I know that I must act quickly. (4) I shout, "Call 911!" (5) I dash to the portable defibrillator on the wall, open the box, and remove the device. (6) I press the green start button and quickly tear off the unconscious man's T-shirt. (7) I place the two electrode pads on his chest and plug them into the machine. (8) The defibrillator analyzes the man's heartbeat to determine whether his heart needs to be shocked. (9) It does. (10) The machine charges itself and warns me not to touch the patient. (11) When I press the orange button, the machine delivers a jolt and then checks to see if the patient needs another. (12) One is enough. (13) The man's skin almost instantly turns from gray to pink, and he has a pulse. (14) When the paramedics arrive, they tell me that the defibrillator and I probably saved his life.

Marcel Alfonso, student

B. Rewrite this paragraph, changing the verbs from present tense to past tense.

(1) It is the morning of August 29, 2005. (2) Hurricane Katrina churns over the warm waters of the Gulf of Mexico and bears down on the coasts of Louisiana and Mississippi. (3) When it makes landfall at 6:10 a.m., it is a monster storm, packing 125-mile-an-hour winds and dumping 10 to 15 inches of rain. (4) Hurricane-force winds rage 120 miles outward from its center. (5) In the city of New Orleans, the storm whips up huge waves in Lake Pontchartrain. (6) These waves slam into the levees around the city, causing the levees to break. (7) Lake water pours into the city and floods low-lying areas. (8) Winds and torrents rip down telephone and power lines, wash away streets and bridges, and level whole neighborhoods. (9) Many of the people still in their homes swim for their lives. (10) Others scramble to their rooftops, where they wait, sometimes in vain, for rescue. (11) One of the greatest disasters in U.S. history, Hurricane Katrina costs

179

What story does this picture tell?

over $100 billion in damages. (12) Far worse, it leaves over 1,800 people dead, shatters millions of lives, and raises deeply disturbing questions.

Proofreading

The following essay contains both past tense errors and past participle errors. First, proofread for verb errors, underlining all the incorrect verbs. Then correct the errors above the lines. (You should find a total of thirteen errors.)

Protector of the Chimps

(1) Dr. Jane Goodall, DBE*, has did more than anyone else to understand the lives of chimpanzees. (2) Always an animal lover, she was too poor to go to college to study animals. (3) She worked as a waitress until the age of twenty-five. (4) Then she fufilled a lifelong dream and gone to East Africa. (5) There she was thrilled by the beauty of the land and the wild animals.

(6) In Africa, she meet Louis Leakey, a famous naturalist. (7) Leakey recognize Goodall's curiosity, energy, and passion for the natural world. (8) He hired her for a six-month study of the wild chimpanzees in a national park in Tanzania. (9) Despite malaria, primitive living conditions, and hostile wildlife, this determined woman followed the activities of a group of chimps in the Gombe Forest. (10) For months, she watch the chimps through binoculars. (11) She moved closer and closer until she eventually become part of their lives. (12) Dr. Goodall named the chimps and recorded their

---

* DBE: Dame of the British Empire, an honorary title in England, like "Knight."

Jane Goodall communicates with a chimpanzee.

daily activities. (13) She learned that chimps was capable of feeling happiness, anger, and pain. (14) They formed complex societies with leaders, politics, and tribal wars. (15) One of her most important discoveries were that chimps made and used tools. (16) Dr. Goodall expected to stay in Gombe for six months; instead she studied the chimps there for almost forty years. (17) Her studies lead to a totally new understanding of chimps, and she became world famous.

(18) However, her life changed completely in 1986. (19) She attend a conference in Chicago, where she heard horrible stories about the fate of chimps outside Gombe. (20) She learned about the destruction of the forests and the wildlife of Africa. (21) From that day on, Dr. Goodall committed herself to education and conservation. (22) Since then, she has traveled, lectured, gave interviews, and met with people. (23) She established both the Jane Goodall Institute and a young people's group, Roots & Shoots, and is a UN Messenger of Peace. (24) These worldwide organizations have already carry out many important conservation and educational projects. (25) The author of remarkable books and the subject of inspiring television specials, Dr. Goodall is knowed for her total commitment to chimps and to a healthy natural world.

EXPLORING ONLINE

<http://www.janegoodall.org>

<http://www.worldwildlife.org> Visit the Jane Goodall Institute or the World Wildlife Fund to learn more about endangered species.

UNIT 3

Writers' Workshop

Tell a Family Story

A **narrative** tells a story. It presents the most important events in the story, usually in time order. Here, a student tells of her mother-in-law's inspiring journey to self-realization.

In your group or class, read this narrative essay aloud, if possible. As you read, underline any words or details that strike you as vivid or powerful.

Somebody Named Seeta

(1) Someone I deeply admire is my mother-in-law, Seeta, who struggled for years to become her best self. She was born in poverty on the sunny island of Trinidad. Seeta's father drank and beat his wife, and sadly, her mother accepted this lifestyle. Her parents did not believe in sending girls to school, so Seeta's daily chores began at 4:00 a.m. when she milked the cows. Then she fed the hens, scrubbed the house, cooked, and tended babies (as the third child in a family of ten children). During stolen moments, she taught herself to read. At age sixteen, this skinny girl with long black hair ran away from home.

(2) Seeta had nowhere to go, so her friend's family took her in. They believed in education, yet Seeta struggled for years to catch up and finish school. Even so, she calls this time her "foot in the door." She married my father-in-law and had four children, longing inside to become "somebody" someday. When their oldest was nine and the youngest two months, Seeta's husband died. She had to get a job fast. She cut sugar cane in the fields, wrapping her baby in a sheet on the ground. In the evenings, she hiked home to care for the other children. Word got around on the sugar estate that she was bringing a baby to work, so she was given a job indoors. All the while, Seeta stayed patient and hopeful that God would help her someday.

(3) In fact, after seven years, she moved with her children to America. She was so poor that she owned only one pot and one spoon. After she finished

182

cooking, the children would all gather around the pot, and sitting on the floor, they passed the spoon from one to another. My mother-in-law got a job at a department store, selling by day and cleaning offices at night. All the time, in the back of her head, she wanted to be somebody. A plan was taking shape. Eight years ago, my mother-in-law enrolled at this college, first for her GED and then for a college degree. She graduated and became a registered nurse.

(4) When I first met Seeta, I thought she did not like me. Was I wrong! She was just checking me out to see what I was made of. Did I too have goals to be conquered? She taught me that patience is a virtue but that one should never give up. She told me that even in modern America where women have their independence, she had to fight to hold on to hers. Today my mother-in-law is attending Lehman College at night for her master's degree in surgical nursing.

Rosalie Ramnanan, student

1. How effective is Rosalie Ramnanan's essay?
   _____ Clear thesis statement?   _____ Rich supporting details?
   _____ Logical organization?   _____ Effective conclusion?

2. Underline the thesis statement (main idea sentence) for the whole essay. The rest of the paper—a narrative—develops this idea.

3. Ramnanan uses different action verbs to help the reader see and hear the story, especially in paragraphs (1), (2), and (3). Can you identify them?

4. Why do you think the writer chose the title she did? How effective is it?

5. Proofread for grammar and spelling. Do you notice any error patterns (two or more errors of the same type) that this student should watch out for?

Writing And Revising Ideas

1. Tell an inspiring story about one or more of your family members.

2. Use narrative to develop this topic or thesis sentence: Poverty or difficult circumstances can make some people stronger and more ambitious.

For help writing your paragraph or essay, see Chapters 4 and 5. As you revise, make sure that your main idea is clear and that your paper explains it. To add punch to your writing as you revise, replace *is*, *was*, *has*, and *had* with action verbs whenever possible.

UNIT 4

Joining Ideas Together

Too many short, simple sentences can make your writing sound monotonous. This unit will show you five ways to create interesting sentences. In this unit, you will

- Join ideas through *coordination* and *subordination*
- Use semicolons and conjunctive adverbs correctly
- Spot and correct run-ons or comma splices
- Join ideas with *who*, *which*, and *that*
- Join ideas by using *-ing* modifiers
- Learn proofreading strategies to find and correct your own errors

---

Spotlight on Writing

Here, writer Brent Staples uses several methods of joining ideas as he describes his first passionate kiss (at least, he was passionate). If possible, read the paragraph aloud.

I stepped outside and pulled the door closed behind me, and in one motion encircled her waist, pulled her to me, and whispered breathlessly that I loved her. There'd been no rehearsing this; the thought, deed, and word were one. "You do? You love me?" This amused her, but that didn't matter. I had passion enough for the two of us. When I closed in for the kiss, she turned away her lips and offered me her cheek. I kissed it feverishly and with great force. We stood locked this way until I came up for air. Then she peeled me from her and went inside for the flour.

Brent Staples, *Parallel Time*

- Brent Staples mixes simple sentences with sentences that join ideas in different ways. Sentences 2, 4, 6, and 8, for example, combine ideas in ways you will learn in this unit.

- Can you recognize what any of these methods are?

- How do you think the writer now feels about this incident from his youth? Does his tone seem angry, frustrated, or amused? Which sentences tell you?

Writing Ideas

- *Your first crush or romantic encounter*

- *A time you discovered that a loved one's view of the relationship was very different from your view of it*

CHAPTER 14

Coordination

As a writer, you will sometimes want to join short, choppy sentences to form longer sentences. One way to join two ideas is to use a comma and a **coordinating conjunction**.

> (1) This car has many special features, and it costs less than $20,000.
>
> (2) The television picture is blurred, but we will watch the football game anyway.
>
> (3) She wants to practice her Italian, so she is going to Italy.

- Can you break sentence (1) into two complete and independent ideas or thoughts? What are they? Underline the subject and verb in each.

- Can you do the same with sentences (2) and (3)? Underline the subjects and verbs.

- In each sentence, circle the word that joins the two parts of the sentence together. What punctuation mark comes before that word?

- *And*, *but*, and *so* are called *coordinating conjunctions* because they coordinate, or join together, ideas. Other coordinating conjunctions are *for*, *nor*, *or*, and *yet*.

To join two complete and independent ideas, use a coordinating conjunction preceded by a comma. To help you remember these words, just think FANBOYS (the first letter of *for*, *and*, *nor*, *but*, *or*, *yet*, **and** *so*).

Now let's see just how coordinating conjunctions connect ideas:

Coordinating Conjunctions		
and	*means*	in addition
but, yet	*mean*	in contrast
for	*means*	because
nor	*means*	not either
or	*means*	either, a choice
so	*means*	as a result

BE CAREFUL: *Then*, *also*, and *plus* are not coordinating conjunctions. By themselves, they cannot join two ideas.

> **Incorrect:** He studied, then he went to work.
>
> **Correct:** He studied, and then he went to work.

Read this paragraph, aloud if possible.

> Lucky found me over the Thanksgiving holiday. She was a gray and white tabby. She looked like a skeleton cat wearing a fur blanket. It was clear that she was starving. Her ribs and rump bone were sticking out. I got to work. I cut up some leftover turkey from the fridge. I popped it into the microwave for thirty seconds. My scrawny visitor ate every bit. I made a second plate and a third. Finally, she curled up on the kitchen mat. That day, Lucky joined our family.

This might have been a good paragraph, but all the short sentences sound monotonous, even childish. Here is the same paragraph, rewritten:

> Lucky found me over the Thanksgiving holiday. She was a gray and white tabby, **but** she looked like a skeleton cat wearing a fur blanket. It was clear that she was starving, **for** her ribs and rump bone were sticking out. I got to work. I cut up some leftover turkey from the fridge, **and** I popped it into the microwave for thirty seconds. My scrawny visitor ate every bit, **so** I made a second plate and a third. Finally, she curled up on the kitchen mat. That day, Lucky joined our family.

- Can you hear the difference? This paragraph sounds smoother and more sophisticated because it uses coordinating conjunctions to connect ideas.

- This writer has joined some of the short sentences into longer ones, using *but*, *for*, *and*, and *so*.

- Because these conjunctions join two complete ideas, a comma precedes the conjunction.

- Twice in this paragraph, *and* is used to join words that are *not* complete ideas. No comma is needed because they are not complete ideas. Find these two *ands*.

REMEMBER: Coordinating conjunctions can join not just two independent ideas but also two words, two phrases, and two dependent clauses. **A comma goes before the conjunction *only* if it links two independent ideas.**

PRACTICE 1

Read these sentences for meaning. Then fill in the coordinating conjunction (FANBOY) that best expresses the relationship between the two complete thoughts. REMEMBER: Do you want to *add*, *contrast*, *give a reason*, *show a result*, or *indicate a choice*?

EXAMPLE: War is no game, _____*yet*_____ games are transforming modern warfare.

1. Young men and women today grew up playing computer games, _____ the U.S. Army is using video games to recruit and train soldiers.

Soldiers train for combat on a new simulator that uses video game technology.

AP Images/Sue Ogrocki

2. Since 2002, an online version of "America's Army" has attracted 6.5 million registered players, _____ the game has been used for real combat training.

3. Video games can teach many skills needed in battle, _____ they expose players to lifelike war zones such as deserts, jungles, and bombed-out villages.

4. Flashes, explosions, and deadly surprises are part of war, _____ similar computer effects help players adjust to stressful conditions.

5. Some games teach the soldier to load, aim, and fire realistic weapons, _____ he or she must engage in "deadly" combat with other players.

6. Virtual soldiers gain rewards for showing teamwork and bravery, _____ they are penalized for sloppy preparation or safety violations.

7. In one scenario, a Humvee driver and gunner must work together, _____ they both will "die."

8. The Army started its own $50 million video game division in 2010, _____ its programmers can create even better and more realistic training games.

9. Critics say that military-themed video games are morally dangerous, _____ they make killing a human enemy less real.

10. Some object to using games to sharpen the skills of shooters and snipers, _____ for now, these games—like war—are here to stay.

EXPLORING ONLINE

<http://www.americasarmy.com/> Explore the America's Army website and perhaps play a video game. Do you think this site would encourage young men and women to enlist in the military? Why or why not? Jot down three reasons for your opinion, and write specifically about why this website would or would not inspire volunteers to enlist.

PRACTICE 2

Punctuate these sentences correctly by adding any missing commas. Write a C for "correct" next to a sentence that does not need a comma. To determine if a comma is needed, first locate the coordinating conjunction(s) in each sentence. Any coordinating conjunction that joins *two independent ideas* must be preceded by a comma.

1. Residents of the Greek island of Ikaria live longer, healthier lives than most humans and scientists want to know why.

2. Many Ikarians thrive well into their 90s but the average American lives only to 78.

3. Americans lose years of life to heart disease and cancers yet these diseases are rare in Ikaria.

4. A key factor in Ikarians' longevity seems to be a diet packed with beans and vegetables but low in meat and sugar.

5. Ikarians consume wild local greens, herbal teas, and goat's milk so their risk of high blood pressure and heart disease is reduced.

6. This healthy diet is essential but regular exercise is another key factor.

7. Ikaria is a mountainous island so its steep terrain gives inhabitants a workout every time they leave home.

8. In addition, Ikarians refuse to rush through life and get lots of rest, including daily naps.

9. Ikarian natives are lucky to share a strong sense of community for close bonds with family and friends promote longevity.

10. Ikarians may be some of the healthiest people on earth but adopting the right habits can help anyone lead a longer, better life.

PRACTICE 3

Each of these thoughts is complete by itself, but you can join them together to make more interesting sentences. Combine pairs of these thoughts, using *and, but, for, nor, or, so,* or *yet,* and write six new sentences on the lines that follow. Punctuate correctly.

babies need constant supervision
Rico overcame his disappointment
in the 1840s, American women began to fight for the right to vote
I will write my essay at home tonight
the ancient Chinese valued peaches
he decided to try again
they are the best Ping-Pong players on the block
you should never leave them by themselves
I will write it tomorrow in the computer lab
they did not win that right until 1920
they can't beat my cousin from Cleveland
they believed that eating peaches made a person immortal

1. _____

_____

2. _____

_____

3. _____

_____

4. _____

_____

5. _____

_____

6. _____

_____

PRACTICE 4   Finish these sentences by adding a second complete idea after the coordinating conjunction.

1. She often interrupts me, but _____

_____

2. Yuri has lived in the United States for ten years, so _____

_____

3. Len has been married three times, and _____

_____

4. I like owning a car, for _____

_____

5. I like owning a car, but_____

_____

PRACTICE 5   On the lines below or on a computer, write seven sentences of your own, using each of the coordinating conjunctions—*and, but, for, nor, or, so,* and *yet*—to join two independent ideas. Punctuate correctly.

1. _____

2. _____

3. _____

4. _____

5. _____

6. _____

7. _____

Chapter Highlights

- **A comma and a coordinating conjunction join two independent ideas:**

  The fans booed, *but* the umpire paid no attention.

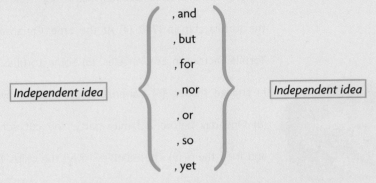

- **Note:** *Then, also,* and *plus* **are not coordinating conjunctions.**

Proofreading Strategy

Using coordination will improve your writing. Just proofread to make sure that you punctuate correctly.

1. Search for the seven coordinating conjunctions, or FANBOYS, and **highlight or underline** each one. If you are using a computer, use the *Find feature* to locate these words in your draft.

2. Check to see if each coordinating conjunction joins two complete ideas. Can the words on either side of it stand alone as complete sentences? If so, put a *comma* before the conjunction. Make sure you understand these examples.

   CORRECT   CORRECT
   The boss and his partner were very supportive but intolerant of those who arrived late for work.

   INCORRECT   CORRECT
   We paid but later Blanca and I regretted sending that check.

WRITING AND PROOFREADING ASSIGNMENT

Whether you are a teenager, a young adult, middle-aged, elderly, single, or part of a couple, there are characters in TV sitcoms who are supposed to represent you. Do these characters correctly portray the kind of person you are, or are you seeing one or more irritating exaggerations?

Write a letter of praise or complaint to a network that broadcasts one of these sitcoms. Make clear why you think a certain character does or does not correctly portray someone like you. Use examples and specific details. As you revise and proofread, avoid choppy sentences by joining ideas with coordinating conjunctions.

CHAPTER REVIEW

Read this paragraph of short, choppy sentences. Then rewrite it, using different coordinating conjunctions to combine some pairs of sentences. Keep some short sentences for variety. Copy your revised paragraph on a fresh sheet of paper. Punctuate with care.

(1) Super Bowl parties everywhere owe a debt to Rebecca Webb Carranza. (2) Most people don't even know her name. (3) This Mexican-born entrepreneur invented the tortilla chip in 1948. (4) At the time, Carranza and her husband ran the El Zarape Tortilla Factory in Los Angeles. (5) Some tortillas always came off the conveyor belt in strange shapes. (6) Carranza threw them away. (7) She hated this waste of food. (8) One day before a family party, she cut some discarded tortillas into triangles and fried them. (9) The relatives loved the chips. (10) They could easily grab a handful or dip the crunchy morsels in sauce. (11) Carranza began selling her chips for 10 cents a bag in her Mexican delicatessen and factory. (12) By the 1960s, she had named them Tort Chips. (13) Her factory now manufactured nothing but this irresistible snack. (14) Demand for the chips took off. (15) Carranza is now recognized as a snack-food industry pioneer. (16) She received awards for her work, including, appropriately, two Golden Tortillas.

EXPLORING ONLINE

<http://web2.uvcs.uvic.ca/elc/studyzone/330/grammar/coconj1.htm> Fill in the right coordinating conjunction; the computer checks your answers.

<http://grammar.ccc.commnet.edu/grammar/quizzes/nova/nova1.htm> Interactive quiz: Place commas in sentences with coordinating conjunctions.

 View an integrated eBook and chapter-specific interactive learning tools, including flashcards, quizzes, videos, and extra help tracking and correcting your Personal Error Patterns, in your Basic Writing CourseMate, accessed through <www.cengagebrain.com>.

Subordination

A: Defining and Using Subordinating Conjunctions

B: Punctuating Subordinating Conjunctions

A. Defining and Using Subordinating Conjunctions

Another way to join ideas together is with a **subordinating conjunction**.
Read this paragraph:

> A great disaster happened in 1857. The SS *Central America* sank. This steamship was carrying six hundred wealthy passengers from California to New York. Many of them had recently struck gold. Battered by a storm, the ship began to flood. Many people on board bailed water. Others prayed and quieted the children. Thirty hours passed. A rescue boat arrived. Almost two hundred people were saved. The rest died. Later, many banks failed. Three tons of gold had gone down with the ship.

This could have been a good paragraph, but notice that all the sentences are short and choppy.

Here is the same paragraph, rewritten to make it more interesting:

> A great disaster happened in 1857 *when* the SS *Central America* sank. This steamship was carrying six hundred wealthy passengers from California to New York. Many of them had recently struck gold. Battered by a storm, the ship began to flood. Many people on board bailed water *while* others prayed and quieted the children. *After* thirty hours passed, a rescue boat arrived. Almost two hundred people were saved *although* the rest died. Later, many banks failed *because* three tons of gold had gone down with the ship.

- Note that the paragraph now reads more smoothly and is more interesting because the following words were used to join some of the choppy sentences: *when, while, after, although,* and *because.*

- *When, while, after, although,* and *because* are part of a large group of words called *subordinating conjunctions.* As you can see from the paragraph, these conjunctions join ideas.

BE CAREFUL: Once you add a *subordinating conjunction* to an idea, that idea can no longer stand alone as a complete and independent sentence. It has become a subordinate or dependent idea; it must rely on an independent idea to complete its meaning.*

(1) He is tired.

(2) Because he is tired, _____

(3) I left the room.

(4) As I left the room, _____

(5) You speak Spanish.

(6) If you speak Spanish, _____

- (1), (3), and (5) are all complete sentences, but once a subordinating conjunction is added, they become dependent ideas. They must be followed by something else—a complete and independent thought.

- (2), for example, could be completed like this: Because he is tired, *he won't go out to eat with us.*

- Add an independent idea to complete each dependent idea on the lines above.

  Below is a partial list of subordinating conjunctions.

Common Subordinating Conjunctions		
after	even though	when
although	if	whenever
as	since	where
as if	so that	whereas
as though	though	wherever
because	unless	whether
before	until	while

Each subordinating conjunction expresses a specific *relationship* between two ideas in a sentence. Let's look at some of these relationships:

Subordinating Conjunctions	Meaning	One Example
after, as, before, since, until, when, whenever, while	To show different time relationships	*When* her son was diagnosed with autism, Monique started her research.

---

* For more work on sentence fragments of this type, see Chapter 8, Part C.

although, even though, though, whereas, while	To show a contrast or contradiction	I love classical music *even though* my parents did not.
as though, as if	To show something *seems* true but is not	He acts *as if* he owned the club.
because, since, so that	To show a reason, a cause, or an effect	He told the truth *because* he respects you.
even if, if, unless, whether	To show a condition for something to happen	*Even if* one has a college degree, good jobs can be hard to find.

PRACTICE 1

Read these sentences for meaning. Then fill in the subordinating conjunction that best expresses the relationship between the two ideas.

1. _____ you are like most people, you resist admitting mistakes or hurtful actions.

2. _____ it is commonly thought that apologizing shows weakness, an apology actually requires great strength.

3. A genuine apology is a powerful tool _____ it can repair damaged relationships, heal humiliation, and encourage forgiveness.

4. _____ we learn to apologize sincerely, psychologists say, we can prevent grudges, revenge, and a lot of pain.

5. _____ you apologize to someone, remember the key ingredients of a successful apology.

6. _____ you have hurt someone's feelings or betrayed that person, you must first admit your wrongdoing.

7. Specifically describe what you did _____ you reveal an understanding of your offense and its impact.

8. Say, for example, "I'm sorry for hurting you _____ I criticized you in front of your friends."

9. _____ you apologize, you must communicate remorse with both your words and your body language.

10. The other person will question your sincerity _____ you seem truly distressed and sorry.

11. _____ you admit your transgression, you should explain your actions.

12. For instance, "My behavior occurred _____ I was feeling stressed (or tired, frustrated, angry)."

13. _____ you end your apology, reassure the offended person.

14. Explain that you did not intend to wound him or her _____ you did so.

15. _____ it is difficult, an apology will be worth the effort.

PRACTICE 2

Now that you understand how subordinating conjunctions join thoughts together, try these sentences. Here you have to supply one idea. Make sure that the ideas you add have subjects and verbs.

1. The cafeteria food improved when _____

   _____

2. Because Damon and Luis both love basketball, _____

   _____

3. If _____

   Adolph plans to get legal advice.

4. I was repairing the roof while _____

   _____

5. Before _____

   you should get all the facts.

B. Punctuating Subordinating Conjunctions

As you may have noticed in the preceding exercises, some sentences with subordinating conjunctions use a comma whereas others do not. Here is how it's done.

> (1) Because it rained very hard, we had to leave early.
>
> (2) We had to leave early because it rained very hard.

● Sentence (1) has a comma because the dependent idea comes before the independent idea.

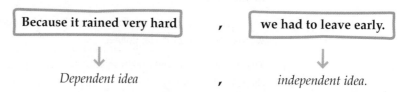

● Sentence (2) has no comma because the dependent idea follows the independent idea.

Use a comma after a dependent idea; do not use a comma before a dependent idea.

PRACTICE 3

If a sentence is punctuated correctly, write *C* in the blank. If it is not, punctuate it correctly by adding or deleting a comma.

1. Whenever Americans get hungry they want to eat quickly. _____

2. When McDonald's opened in 1954 it started a trend that continues today. _____

3. Whether you are talking about pizza or hamburgers fast food is big business— earning more than $110 billion a year. _____

4. Fast food is appealing because it is cheap, tasty, and—of course—fast. _____

5. While it has many advantages fast food also presents some health hazards. _____

6. Although the industry is booming many people are worried about the amount of fat in fast foods. _____

7. Whereas some nutritionists recommend eating only thirty-five grams of fat a day you often eat more than that in just one fast-food meal. _____

8. If you order a Burger King Double Whopper with cheese you take in a whopping sixty-three grams of fat. _____

9. That goes up to sixty-seven fat grams whenever you devour a McDonald's Big Mac, large fries, and chocolate shake. _____

10. Now some fast-food restaurants are claiming to serve low-fat items so that they can attract health-conscious customers. _____

11. However, you still must pay attention to the ingredients, if you want to make sure that your meal is healthy. _____

12. For example, most grilled or roasted chicken sandwiches are relatively low in
fat before they are slathered with mayonnaise and special sauces.   _____

13. Because just one tablespoon of mayonnaise or salad dressing contains eleven
fat grams these tasty toppings add gobs of extra fat and calories.   _____

14. Although they might taste delicious cheese and cheese sauces also add
surprising quantities of fat to a meal.   _____

15. When you next order your favorite fast food don't forget to say,
"Hold the sauce!"   _____

PRACTICE 4

Correctly combine each pair of ideas in two ways: with the subordinating conjunction at the beginning of the sentence and with the subordinating conjunction in the middle. For each pair, write in the subordinating conjunction that expresses the relationship between these ideas. Then make sure you punctuate each sentence correctly.

EXAMPLE: _____*Although*_____ marriage exists in all societies, every culture has unique wedding customs.

Every culture has unique wedding customs _____*although*_____ marriage exists in all societies.

1. _____ young couples in India marry the ceremony may last for days.
The ceremony may last for days _____ young couples in India marry.

2. _____ the wedding takes place at the bride's home everyone travels to the groom's home for more celebrating.
Everyone travels to the groom's home for more celebrating _____ the wedding takes place at the bride's home.

3. Ducks are often included in Korean wedding processions _____ they mate for life.
_____ they mate for life ducks are often included in Korean wedding processions.

4. Iroquois brides gave grain to their mothers-in-law _____ mothers-in-law gave meat to the brides.
_____ Iroquois brides gave grain to their mothers-in-law mothers-in-law gave meat to the brides.

5. _____ the food was exchanged the bride and groom were considered married.
The bride and groom were considered married _____ the food was exchanged.

6. _____ the tradition went out of style Finnish brides and grooms used to exchange wreaths.
Finnish brides and grooms used to exchange wreaths _____ the tradition went out of style.

7. A Zulu wedding is not complete _____ the bride, groom, and bridal party dance special dances.
_____ the bride, groom, and bridal party dance special dances a Zulu wedding is not complete.

8. The bride stabs at imaginary enemies with a knife _____ she dances wildly and gloriously.

   _____ the bride dances wildly and gloriously she stabs at imaginary enemies with a knife.

9. _____ the wedding ring is a very old symbol the elaborate wedding cake is even older.

   The wedding ring is a very old symbol _____ the elaborate wedding cake is even older.

10. _____ the ring symbolizes the oneness of the new couple the cake represents fertility.

    The cake represents fertility _____ the ring symbolizes the oneness of the new couple.

PRACTICE 5   Now try writing sentences of your own. Fill in the blanks, being careful to punctuate correctly. Do not use a comma before a dependent idea.

1. _____ because

   _____.

2. Although _____

   _____.

3. _____ whenever

   _____.

4. Unless _____

   _____

Chapter Highlights

● A subordinating conjunction joins a dependent idea and an independent idea:

   When I registered, all the math courses were closed.

   All the math courses were closed *when* I registered.

● **Use a comma after a dependent idea.**

   After
   Because
   Before
   If
   Since
   Unless
   When
   While
   } *dependent idea, independent idea.*

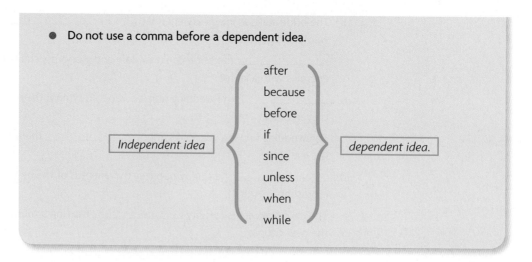

- Do not use a comma before a dependent idea.

Independent idea { after / because / before / if / since / unless / when / while } dependent idea.

Proofreading Strategy

Joining ideas with subordinating conjunctions will add sophistication to your writing, but be sure to proofread for correct punctuation.

1. **First, search the document for any subordinating conjunctions** (like *although, because, before, when,* etc.). **Highlight or underline** these words.

2. If a dependent idea comes first in the sentence, **use a comma to separate the dependent from the independent idea.** You know you have the comma in the right spot if there is a complete sentence *after* the comma. Here are two examples:

   Independent idea   dependent idea
   Lia enrolled in classes every semester until she finished her associate degree.

   Dependent idea   independent idea
   When Jorge gets home from work, he takes his dogs for a walk.

WRITING AND PROOFREADING ASSIGNMENT

Imagine that you are a teacher planning a lesson on courtesy for a class of young children. Use a personal experience, either positive or negative, to illustrate your point. Brainstorm, freewrite, or cluster to generate details for the lesson. Then write what—and how—you plan to teach. Keeping in mind that you are trying to reach young children, make sure that the significance of the experience you will describe is clear. When you finish drafting, read over your lesson and look for ideas you can join with subordinating conjunctions. Underline the subordinating conjunctions you use, and check your punctuation.

Form small groups to discuss one another's lessons. Which are most convincing? Why? Would children learn more from examples of good behavior or from examples of bad behavior?

CHAPTER REVIEW

Read this paragraph of short, choppy sentences. Then revise it by making changes above the lines, using different subordinating conjunctions to combine pairs of sentences. Keep some short sentences for variety. Punctuate with care.

(1) Jacob Lawrence was a great American painter, a powerful teller of stories on canvas. (2) Young Jacob joined his mother in Harlem in 1930. (3) He began to paint the people around him. (4) Luckily, he found excellent art classes in Harlem. (5) The big art academies often excluded blacks then. (6) He was only 23. (7) He gained fame for his sixty-picture *Migration Series*. (8) A New York gallery displayed these paintings. (9) No major commercial gallery had showcased an African American artist before. (10) The *Migration Series* depicts southern blacks journeying north to find work after World War I. (11) The paintings show people searching for a better life. (12) Lawrence's work portrays the poverty and prejudice the migrants endured. (13) He also wanted viewers of his work "to experience the beauty of life." (14) During his long career, Lawrence painted many more energetic canvases and series. (15) His work reminds us that we are all migrants. (16) We are always on the move. (17) We are seeking something more.

EXPLORING ONLINE

See Lawrence's paintings at the Whitney Museum of Art online. <http://www.whitney.org/Collection/JacobLawrence/> Click on "Jacob Lawrence's Art." Describe your favorite painting to someone who has never seen it. More writing ideas appear under "Explore" and "Tell Your Own Story."

Brownstones, 1958, by Jacob Lawrence.

EXPLORING ONLINE

<http://a4esl.org/q/h/vm/conj02.html> Quiz with answers: combine sentences with a conjunction.

<http://web2.uvcs.uvic.ca/elc/studyzone/330/grammar/subcon.htm> Explanation of subordination followed by interactive practice sets

View an integrated eBook and chapter-specific interactive learning tools, including flashcards, quizzes, videos, and extra help tracking and correcting your Personal Error Patterns, in your Basic Writing CourseMate, accessed through <www.cengagebrain.com>.

CHAPTER 16

Avoiding Run-Ons and Comma Splices

Now that you have had practice in joining ideas together, here are two serious errors to watch out for: the **run-on** and the **comma splice**. If run-ons and comma splices are among your personal error patterns, pay close attention to this chapter.

> **Run-on:** Herb talks too much nobody seems to mind.

- There are two complete ideas here: *Herb talks too much* and *nobody seems to mind*.
- A *run-on* incorrectly runs together two complete ideas without using a conjunction or punctuation.

> **Comma splice:** Herb talks too much, nobody seems to mind.

- A *comma splice* incorrectly joins two complete ideas with a comma but no conjunction.

BE CAREFUL: Run-ons and comma splices are considered serious mistakes in college and the workplace because they force readers to stop, back up, and try to figure out where one idea ends and another begins.

Here are three ways to correct a run-on or a comma splice.

1. **Write two separate sentences, making sure each is complete.**	Herb talks too much. Nobody seems to mind.
2. **Use a comma and a coordinating conjunction or FANBOY** (*for, and, nor, but, or, yet, so*).*	Herb talks too much, *but* nobody seems to mind.
3. **Use a subordinating conjunction** (for example, *although, because, if,* or *when*).**	*Although* Herb talks too much, nobody seems to mind.

---

* For more work on coordinating conjunctions, see Chapter 14.
** For more work on subordinating conjunctions, see Chapter 15.

Try This Try this "run-on" test, which works for some people. Ask **"Is it true that . . ."** followed by the test sentence. If the answer is *yes*, the sentence is correct; if the answer is *no*, it is a run-on or comma splice.

Is it true that <u>*Many drivers in my city don't use their blinkers to warn the driver behind*</u>

<u>*them that they are going to turn this reckless behavior really frustrates me*</u> **?** **NO**

This confusing example gets a *no*, so try breaking it into possible sentences:

Is it true that <u>*Many drivers in my city don't use their blinkers to warn the driver behind*</u>

<u>*them that they are going to turn*</u> **?** **YES**

Is it true that <u>*this reckless behavior really frustrates me*</u> **?** **YES**

PRACTICE 1

Many of these sentences contain run-ons or comma splices. If a sentence is correct, write *C* in the right-hand column. If it contains a run-on or a comma splice, write either *RO* or *CS*. Then correct the error in any way you wish. Use each method at least once.

EXAMPLE:
When a
A talented celebrity like actor Heath Ledger dies of a drug

overdose, we remember the dreadful price of addiction.   *CS*

1. A number of celebrities struggle with addiction public awareness of addiction has increased.   _____

2. Often politicians, athletes, and actors hide their addiction and their recovery, they do not want to risk ruining their careers.   _____

3. Other celebrities are forced to go public in their battles with alcohol or drugs.   _____

4. A few feel that their struggles may help others, they want to act as positive role models.   _____

5. One such person was Betty Ford, a former first lady with her family's help, she became sober at age sixty.   _____

6. Her recovery was successful she agreed to help several friends create a treatment center in Rancho Mirage, California.   _____

7. At the Betty Ford Center, celebrities like Keith Urban as well as everyday people receive support for their new way of life.   _____

8. Treatment centers now exist around the country, the problem of addiction seems to be increasing, especially among the young.   _____

9. For example, Drew Barrymore was famous at age six for her role in the film *E.T.*, by age nine she was addicted to drugs and alcohol.   _____

10. Forced into rehab at age thirteen, Drew was able to get her acting career back on track.   _____

11. Fergie kicked her addiction to crystal methamphetamine and Ecstasy this lead vocalist for the Black Eyed Peas went on to become one of music's biggest stars.   _____

12. Actress Eva Mendes and actor Robert Downey Jr. likewise developed
    addictions getting treatment helped them stay on top in their profession. _____

13. Legendary athlete and NBA coach John Lucas went through detox, turned
    his life around, and now helps athletes recover. _____

14. Alcohol and drugs might seem glamorous, especially to the young, they
    can destroy relationships, careers, and self-esteem. _____

15. Millions of Americans are affected, when someone returns from substance
    abuse, his or her triumph can encourage others to seek help. _____

PRACTICE 2

Label each sentence *RO* or *CS*. Then correct each run-on (RO) or comma splice (CS) in
two ways. Be sure to punctuate correctly.

EXAMPLE: Technology will change the way we shop will we like the new way? *RO*

   a. *Technology will change the way we shop. Will we like the new way?*

   b. *Technology will change the way we shop, but will we like the new way?*

1. For instance, you want to purchase a car, you may walk up to an outdoor booth.

   a. _____

   _____

   b. _____

   _____

2. You select the options on a computer screen, you press an order entry key.

   a. _____

   _____

   b. _____

   _____

3. A factory assembles your car it is later delivered to your local dealer.

   a. _____

   _____

   b. _____

   _____

4. You go to a store to buy jeans, none are on the shelf.

   a. _____

   _____

   b. _____

   _____

5. Instead, you look at different styles onscreen you make your choice.

   a. _____

   _____

   b. _____

   _____

6. Taking measurements is not new now they can be taken by a three-dimensional camera.

   a. _____

   _____

   b. _____

   _____

7. Your measurements have been taken electronically your jeans will fit perfectly.

   a. _____

   _____

   b. _____

   _____

8. Your selection and measurements are transmitted to a factory your jeans are made to order.

   a. _____

   _____

   b. _____

   _____

9. You want to experiment with changing your hairstyle, a computer screen will show you with long, short, or differently colored hair.

   a. _____

   _____

   b. _____

   _____

10. You can leave the way you came in you can leave with a new look.

   a. _____

   _____

   b. _____

   _____

Chapter Highlights

Avoid run-ons and comma splices:

> **Error:** Her house faces the ocean the view is breathtaking. (*run-on*)

> **Error:** Her house faces the ocean, the view is breathtaking. (*comma splice*)

Use these techniques to avoid run-ons and comma splices:

- Write two complete sentences.

  Her house faces the ocean. The view is breathtaking.

- Use a coordinating conjunction (*for, and, nor, but, or, yet, so*).

  Her house faces the ocean, *so* the view is breathtaking.

- Use a subordinating conjunction (*although, before, because, when*, etc.).

  Because her house faces the ocean, the view is breathtaking.

Proofreading Strategy

Proofread your work very carefully if comma splices are among your error patterns.

1. Go back through your draft and **circle every comma** in every sentence.
2. For each comma, ask yourself, *"Would substituting a period for this comma create a complete sentence that could stand alone?"*

   NO   YES
   Before he joined the Army, he completed his associate's degree, he also married his high-school sweetheart.

3. If the answer is yes, you have written a comma splice and will need to replace the comma with **a period or keep the comma and add a coordinating conjunction after it**.

   Before he joined the Army, he completed his associate's degree, and he married his high-school sweetheart.

WRITING AND PROOFREADING ASSIGNMENT

A letter of application, which is a vital job-search tool, always includes a paragraph that summarizes the applicant's qualifications for a particular job. Write a summary of your work experience, beginning with your very first job and moving in chronological order from that job to your current job. Include both paid and volunteer positions. For each job, provide your dates of employment and a brief description of your major responsibilities. A letter of application must be error-free, so proofread it carefully. Exchange papers with a classmate and check each other's work, especially for comma splices and run-ons.

CHAPTER REVIEW

Run-ons and comma splices are most likely to occur in paragraphs or longer pieces of writing. Proofread each of the following paragraphs for run-ons and comma splices. Correct them in any way that makes sense: make two separate sentences, add a coordinating conjunction, or add a subordinating conjunction. Make your corrections above the lines. Punctuate with care.

A. (1) Many people are creating personal pages on social networking websites like Facebook, MySpace, and Friendster, these sites offer an enjoyable way to make new friends with common interests. (2) Yet surprising numbers of people post intimate, extreme, or even invented information about themselves. (3) They might think that their new online identities will be fun, hip, or outrageous they probably do not realize that their peers are not the only ones visiting their sites. (4) College admissions officials and potential employers now routinely view the personal pages of promising applicants these pages often provide additional information. (5) For example, one recruiter for a tutoring company was shocked, she checked a young job applicant's page on the Facebook site. (6) The candidate had posted detailed descriptions of his love of late-night partying and drinking. (7) He had illustrated his descriptions with explicit photographs, one picture showed him apparently passed out. (8) The recruiter questioned both the behavior and the judgment of a person who would post this kind of information, she declined to hire the applicant.

B. (1) Skateboarder Tony Hawk has not only dramatically changed his sport, he also has contributed to the popularity of all extreme sports. (2) The wholesome Hawk is responsible for cleaning up skateboarding's early reputation as the pastime of rebels and hoodlums now it's an acceptable, mainstream activity. (3) Hawk is also famous for defying the laws of physics to create amazing new aerial acrobatics. (4) In 1999, at the age of thirty-one, he was the first skater ever to complete a 900, this is a 360-degree spin done two-and-a-half times in midair. (5) As a result, he is called "the Michael Jordan of skateboarding." (6) Today, although he has retired from competition, he performs in exhibitions all over the country surveys of young people reveal that he is more popular than Shaquille O'Neal or Tiger Woods. (7) Hawk's fame has created a huge interest in skateboarding. (8) In 2005, 10.3 million Americans six years old or older played baseball, 11.4 million skateboarded. (9) Today, these young athletes roll into skate parks that have sprung up all over the country, thanks to Hawk's influence.

C.   (1) What do you do every night before you go to sleep and every morning when you wake up? (2) You probably brush your teeth, most people in the United States did not start brushing their teeth until after the 1850s. (3) People living in the nineteenth century did not have toothpaste, Dr. Washington Wentworth Sheffield developed a tooth-cleaning substance, which soon became widely available. (4) With the help of his son, this Connecticut dentist changed our daily habits by making the first toothpaste it was called Dr. Sheffield's Creme Dentifrice. (5) The product was not marketed cleverly enough, the idea of using toothpaste caught on slowly. (6) Then toothpaste was put into tin tubes everyone wanted to try this new product. (7) Think of life without tubes of mint-flavored toothpaste then thank Dr. Sheffield for his idea.

D.   (1) The first semester of college is difficult for many students they must take on many new responsibilities. (2) For instance, they must create their own schedules. (3) New students get to select their courses in addition, they have to decide when they will take them. (4) Students also must purchase their own textbooks, colleges do not distribute textbooks each term as high schools do. (5) No bells ring to announce when classes begin and end students are supposed to arrive on time. (6) Furthermore, many professors do not call the roll they expect students to attend classes regularly and know the assignments. (7) Above all, new students must be self-disciplined. (8) No one stands over them telling them to do their homework or to visit the writing lab for extra help, they must balance the temptation to have fun and the desire to build a successful future.

Last Words

E.   (1) Every fourteen days, a language somewhere in the world dies. (2) For example, the last fluent speaker of the Alaskan language of Eyak was Chief Marie Jones, when she passed away in 2008, Eyak died with her. (3) Languages are disappearing on every continent. (4) North America has two hundred Native American languages, only about fifty now

A teacher at the Nixyaawii Charter School in Mission, Oregon, gives a lesson in an endangered Native American language.

have more than a thousand speakers. (5) The endangered Gaelic language is undergoing a revival in Ireland, the other Celtic languages in northwestern Europe have been declining for generations. (6) The death of languages is most noticeable in isolated communities in Asia, South America, and Australia, however. (7) Each tiny community might have its own language only few people speak it.

(8) In such small communities, a whole language can die if one village perishes. (9) When Westerners explored a rain forest in Venezuela in the 1960s they carried a flu virus into a tiny community. (10) The virus killed all the villagers, their language disappeared with them. (11) However, most languages fade out when a smaller community comes into close contact with a larger, more powerful one, people begin to use the "more important" language. (12) A language that gives better access to education, jobs, and new technology usually prevails over a native mother tongue.

(13) According to scholars who study languages, almost half of the world's 7,000 languages are in danger of extinction. (14) That statistic represents more than the loss of specific languages, every language represents a way of looking at the world. (15) Whenever a language disappears, we lose a unique point of view. (16) No other language can really take its place.

EXPLORING ONLINE

<http://depts.dyc.edu/learningcenter/owl/exercises/run-ons_ex1.htm>
Interactive quiz: Correct the run-ons and click for your score.

<http://grammar.ccc.commnet.edu/grammar/quizzes/nova/nova4.htm>
Interactive quiz: Find and fix the comma splices in these sentences.

<http://www.uvu.edu/owl/infor/test_n_games/games/fragments/gameshow/
gameshow/index.html> Game show! Win fake cash and real pride as you
identify the worst sentence errors.

 View an integrated eBook and chapter-specific interactive learning tools,
including flashcards, quizzes, videos, and extra help tracking and correcting
your Personal Error Patterns, in your Basic Writing CourseMate, accessed
through <www.cengagebrain.com>.

CHAPTER 17

Semicolons and Conjunctive Adverbs

A: Defining and Using Semicolons
B: Defining and Using Conjunctive Adverbs
C: Punctuating Conjunctive Adverbs

A. Defining and Using Semicolons

So far you have learned to join ideas together in two ways.

Coordinating conjunctions (*and, but, for, nor, or, so, yet*) can join ideas:

> (1) This is the worst food we have ever tasted, *so* we will never eat in this restaurant again.

Subordinating conjunctions (for example, *although, as, because, if,* and *when*) also can join ideas:

> (2) *Because* this is the worst food we have ever tasted, we will never eat in this restaurant again.

Another way to join ideas is with a **semicolon**:

> (3) This is the worst food we have ever tasted; we will never eat in this restaurant again.

A *semicolon* **joins two related independent ideas without a conjunction; do not capitalize the first word after a semicolon unless it is a word that is always capitalized, like someone's name.**

Use the semicolon for variety. In general, use no more than one or two semicolons in a paragraph.

PRACTICE 1

Each independent idea below is the first half of a sentence. Add a semicolon and a second complete idea, one that can stand alone.

EXAMPLE: Domingo was a cashier at Food City _; now he manages the store._

1. My cat spotted a mouse _____

_____

2. The garage became an art studio _____

_____

3. Beatrice has an unlisted phone number _____

_____

4. I felt sure someone had been in the room _____

_____

5. Roslyn's first car had a stick shift _____

_____

Semicolons should connect two *related independent ideas*. If two ideas do not have a close relationship—such as a cause and its effect, a comparison of two like things, or a time order relationship—the sentences probably should be separated with a period.

BE CAREFUL: Do not use a semicolon between a dependent idea and an independent idea.

> Although he is never at home, he is not difficult to reach at the office.

● You cannot use a semicolon in this sentence because the first idea (*although he is never at home*) cannot stand alone.

● The word *although* requires that another idea be added in order to make a complete sentence.*

PRACTICE 2

Which of these ideas can be followed by a semicolon and an independent thought? Check them (✔).

1. When Molly peered over the counter _____
2. The library has installed new computers _____
3. After he finishes cleaning the fish _____
4. She suddenly started to laugh _____
5. My answer is simple _____
6. I cannot find my car keys _____
7. The rain poured down in buckets _____
8. Before the health fair is over _____
9. Unless you arrive early _____
10. Because you understand, I feel better _____

_____

* For work on subordinating conjunctions, see Chapter 15.

Now copy the sentences you have checked, add a semicolon, and complete each sentence with a second independent idea. You should have checked sentences 2, 4, 5, 6, 7, and 10.

2. _____

_____

4. _____

_____

5. _____

_____

6. _____

_____

7. _____

_____

10. _____

_____

PRACTICE 3

Proofread for incorrect semicolons and capital letters. Make your corrections above the lines.

(1) The Swiss Army knife is carried in the pockets and purses of millions of travelers, campers, and just plain folks. (2) Numerous useful gadgets are folded into its famous red handle; These include knife blades, tweezers, scissors, toothpick, screwdriver, bottle opener, fish scaler, and magnifying glass. (3) Because the knife contains many tools; it is also carried by explorers, mountain climbers, and astronauts. (4) Lives have been saved by the Swiss Army knife. (5) It once opened the iced-up oxygen system of someone climbing Mount Everest; It saved the lives of scientists stranded on an island, who used the tiny saw on the knife to cut branches for a fire. (6) The handy Swiss Army knife was created for Swiss soldiers in 1891; and soon became popular all over the world. (7) It comes in many models and colors many people prefer the classic original. (8) The Swiss Army knife deserves its reputation for beautiful design and usefulness; a red one is on permanent display in New York's famous Museum of Modern Art.

B. Defining and Using Conjunctive Adverbs

Another excellent method of joining ideas is to use a semicolon and a special kind of adverb. This special adverb is called a **conjunctive adverb** because it is part *conjunction* and part *adverb*.

(1) (a) He received an A on his term paper; *furthermore,*

(b) the instructor exempted him from the final.

- *Furthermore* adds idea (b) to idea (a).
- The sentence might have been written, "He received an *A* on his term paper, *and* the instructor exempted him from the final."
- However, *furthermore* is stronger and more emphatic.
- Note the punctuation.

(2) (a) Luzette has never studied finance; *however,*

(b) she plays the stock market like a pro.

- *However* contrasts ideas (a) and (b).
- The sentence might have been written, "Luzette has never studied finance, *but* she plays the stock market like a pro."
- However, the word *however* is stronger and more emphatic.
- Note the punctuation.

(3) (a) The complete dictionary weighs thirty pounds; *therefore,*

(b) I bring my pocket edition to school.

- *Therefore* shows that idea (a) is the cause of idea (b).
- The sentence might have been written, "*Because* the complete dictionary weighs thirty pounds, I bring my pocket edition to school."
- However, *therefore* is stronger and more emphatic.
- Note the punctuation.

A *conjunctive adverb* may be used with a semicolon only when both ideas are independent and can stand alone.

Here are some common conjunctive adverbs and their meanings:

Common Conjunctive Adverbs		
consequently	*means*	as a result
for example	*means*	as one example
furthermore	*means*	in addition
however	*means*	in contrast
in fact	*means*	in truth, to emphasize
instead	*means*	in place of
meanwhile	*means*	at the same time
nevertheless	*means*	in contrast
otherwise	*means*	as an alternative
therefore	*means*	for that reason

Conjunctive adverbs are also called **transitional expressions**. They help the reader see the transitions, or changes in meaning, from one idea to the next.

PRACTICE 4

Add an idea after each conjunctive adverb. The idea you add must make sense in terms of the entire sentence, so keep in mind the meaning of each conjunctive adverb. If necessary, refer to the chart.

EXAMPLE: Several students had questions about the final; therefore, _they stayed after class to chat with the instructor._

1. Aunt Bessie did a handstand; meanwhile, _____

   _____

2. Anna says whatever is on her mind; consequently, _____

   _____

3. I refuse to wear those red cowboy boots again; furthermore, _____

   _____

4. Travis is a good role model; otherwise, _____

   _____

5. Kim wanted to volunteer at the hospital; however, _____

   _____

6. My mother carried two bulky pieces of luggage off the plane; furthermore, _____

   _____

7. I have many chores to do today; nevertheless, _____

   _____

8. The gas gauge on my car does not work properly; therefore, _____

   _____

C. Punctuating Conjunctive Adverbs

Notice the punctuation pattern:

> Complete idea; conjunctive adverb, complete idea.

- The conjunctive adverb is preceded by a semicolon.
- It is followed by a comma.

PRACTICE 5   Highlight or underline the conjunctive adverb in each sentence. Then punctuate each sentence correctly.

1. For centuries, humans have tried to understand why we dream consequently many different theories have been proposed.

2. To the ancients, dreams had divine meaning for example the Greeks thought a god actually entered the sleeper and delivered a message.

3. The ancient Egyptians also looked for divine guidance in dreams furthermore, they built dream temples for this purpose.

4. In 1899, Sigmund Freud brought attention to dreams again in fact his book *Interpretation of Dreams* helped create modern psychology.

5. According to Freud, dreams don't deal with conscious problems at all instead they reveal our *unconscious* thoughts, desires, and fears.

6. A dream about being fired might reveal a hidden wish for a new career therefore analyzing such a dream might expand one's self-knowledge.

7. In the last ten years, brain scientists have proposed many new theories about why we dream furthermore two of these have become widely accepted.

Fantastic images like this ship appear to us in dreams. Do dreams send messages, solve problems, or are they just brain static?

© Vladimir Kush. All rights reserved.

8. The first idea is that we dream to exercise our brains, consequently our minds will be alert in the morning.

9. The second idea is that we dream to solve problems from the day before in fact college students given a logic problem right before bed often discovered the answers in their sleep.

10. We may not study or even remember our dreams, however; dreaming seems to play an important role in our lives.

PRACTICE 6   Writing Assignment

Have you ever had a dream that sparked a new idea or new insights? Has a dream ever helped you find a solution to a problem you faced? Have you ever gained new awareness of your hidden thoughts and feelings because of a dream?

Write a description of an important dream you have had, and then explain the effects, if any, this dream had on your actions and decisions.

PRACTICE 7

Combine each set of sentences into one, using a conjunctive adverb. Choose a conjunctive adverb that expresses the relationship between the two ideas. Punctuate with care.

1. (a) Belkys fell asleep on the train.
   (b) She missed her stop.

   Combination: _____

   _____

2. (a) Last night Channel 20 televised a special about gorillas.
   (b) I did not get home in time to see it.

   Combination: _____

   _____

3. (a) Roberta writes to her nephew every month.
   (b) She sends a gift with every letter.

   Combination: _____

   _____

4. (a) It takes me almost an hour to get to school each morning.
   (b) The scenery makes the drive a pleasure.

   Combination: _____

   _____

5. (a) Luke missed work on Monday.
   (b) He did not proofread the quarterly report.

   Combination: _____

   _____

BE CAREFUL: Never use a semicolon and a conjunctive adverb when the conjunctive adverb does not join two independent ideas.

(1) *However,* I don't climb mountains.

(2) I don't, *however,* climb mountains.

(3) I don't climb mountains, *however.*

- Why aren't semicolons used in sentences (1), (2), and (3)?
- These sentences contain only one independent idea; therefore, a semicolon cannot be used.

Never use a semicolon to join two ideas if one of the ideas is subordinate to the other.

(4) If I climbed mountains, *however,* I would hike in the Rockies.

- Are the two ideas in sentence (4) independent?
- *If I climbed mountains* cannot stand alone as an independent idea; therefore, a semicolon cannot be used.

Chapter Highlights

- **A semicolon joins two related independent ideas:**

  I like hiking; she prefers fishing.

- **Do not capitalize the first word after a semicolon unless it is always capitalized.**

  | Independent idea | ; | independent idea. |

- **A semicolon and a conjunctive adverb join two independent ideas:**

  We can't go rowing now; *however,* we can go on Sunday.

  Lou earned an 83 on the exam; *therefore,* he passed physics.

  | Independent idea | ; consequently,
; furthermore,
; however,
; instead,
; meanwhile,
; nevertheless,
; therefore, | independent idea. |

- **Use a semicolon only when the conjunctive adverb joins two independent ideas:**

  I wasn't sorry; however, I apologized. (*two independent ideas*)

  I apologized, however. (*one independent idea*)

  If you wanted to go, however, you should have said so. (*one dependent idea + one independent idea*)

Proofreading Strategy

Use semicolons and conjunctive adverbs to add style and variety to your writing; just proofread with care, especially for punctuation errors. **Highlight or underline any conjunctive adverbs** (like *however, consequently,* and *for example*). Make sure the ideas on both sides of the conjunctive adverb are complete. Add any missing semicolons and commas.

Now **circle the semicolons.** Make sure the ideas on both sides are complete, closely related thoughts. No word after a semicolon should be capitalized unless it is always capitalized, like the pronoun "I" or someone's name. Here are two examples:

My dog Garbo badly needed a bath; She was sprayed by a skunk.

Randy grabbed the dog shampoo and filled the wading pool with water however; Garbo had other ideas.

WRITING AND PROOFREADING ASSIGNMENT

Many people find that certain situations make them nervous or anxious—for example, taking a test or meeting strangers at a social gathering. Have you ever conquered such an anxiety yourself or even learned to cope with it successfully?

Write to someone who has the same fear you have had; encourage him or her with your success story, explaining how you managed the anxiety. Describe what steps you took.

Use one or two semicolons and at least one conjunctive adverb in your paper. Make sure that you are joining together two independent ideas. Finally, highlight your conjunctive adverbs and circle your semicolons. Check for correctness.

CHAPTER REVIEW

Proofread this paragraph for semicolon errors, conjunctive adverb errors, and punctuation or capitalization errors. You might use the proofreading strategy above.

(1) Shakira is a more than a gifted Colombian singer and songwriter she is also a philanthropist, determined to give children a brighter future. (2) By the age of 8, Shakira had decided she would succeed as a professional musician; In addition she vowed to use her fame and money to help children. (3) In her hometown of Barranquilla, Colombia, she saw countless children struggle in poverty consequently; at 18, she released *Pies Descalzos* ("Barefoot"), her breakthrough album in Latin America. (4) As her fame grew, Shakira started the Pies Descalzos Foundation to provide education for poor children. (5) Because violence and conflict have long plagued Colombia; many families have lost their stable communities. (6) Today, Pies Descalzos sponsors six schools throughout that country, offering family services and classes for children. (7) Subjects include reading, writing, and art, furthermore,

Shakira works with children in Bangladesh as a UNICEF Goodwill Ambassador.

Sheltzad Noorani/UNICEF via Getty Images

the schools aim to help students grow emotionally and socially. (8) Shakira's work with children extends beyond her foundation; she serves as a UNICEF Goodwill Ambassador and honorary chairperson of the Global Campaign for Education. (9) This exceptional woman wants education and a bright future for every child, meanwhile; she is writing songs and producing her next album. (10) Once asked what part of her body she likes best, Shakira replied, "My brain."

EXPLORING ONLINE

<http://owl.english.purdue.edu/owl/resource/607/04/> Comma or semicolon? Review the rules.

<http://grammar.ccc.commnet.edu/grammar/cgi-shl/quiz.pl/run-ons_add1 .htm> Interactive quiz: Bring your semicolon style to these frumpy run-ons!

 View an integrated eBook and chapter-specific interactive learning tools, including flashcards, quizzes, videos, and extra help tracking and correcting your Personal Error Patterns, in your Basic Writing CourseMate, accessed through <www.cengagebrain.com>.

CHAPTER 18

Relative Pronouns

A: Defining and Using Relative Pronouns

B: Punctuating Ideas Introduced by WHO, WHICH, or THAT

A. Defining and Using Relative Pronouns

To add variety to your writing, you sometimes may wish to use **relative pronouns** to combine two sentences.

> (1) My grandfather is eighty years old.
>
> (2) He collects stamps.

- Sentences (1) and (2) are grammatically correct.
- They are so short, however, that you may wish to combine them.

> (3) My grandfather, *who* is eighty years old, collects stamps.

- Sentence (3) is a combination of (1) and (2).
- *Who* has replaced *he,* the subject of sentence (2). *Who* introduces the rest of the idea, *is eighty years old.*
- *Who* is called a *relative pronoun* because it *relates* "is eighty years old" to "my grandfather."*

BE CAREFUL: An idea introduced by a relative pronoun cannot stand alone as a complete and independent sentence. It is dependent; it needs an independent idea (like "My grandfather collects stamps") to complete its meaning.

Here are some more combinations:

> (4) He gives great singing lessons.
>
> (5) All his pupils love them.
>
> (6) He gives great singing lessons, *which* all his pupils love.

---

* For work on subject-verb agreement with relative pronouns, see Chapter 9, Part G.

(7) I have a large dining room.

(8) It can seat twenty people.

(9) I have a large dining room *that* can seat twenty people.

- As you can see, *which* and *that* can also be used as relative pronouns.

- In sentence (6), what does *which* relate or refer to? _____

- In sentence (9), what does *that* relate or refer to? _____

When *who, which,* and *that* are used as relative pronouns, they usually come directly after the words they relate to.

My grandfather, who . . .

. . . singing lessons, which . . .

. . . dining room that . . .

Relative Pronouns
BE CAREFUL: *Who, which,* and *that* cannot be used interchangeably.
Who **refers to people.**
Which **refers to things.**
That **refers to things.**

PRACTICE 1

Combine each set of sentences into one sentence. Make sure to use *who, which,* and *that* correctly.

EXAMPLE: a. The garden is beginning to sprout.

b. I planted it last week.

Combination: *The garden that I planted last week is beginning to sprout.*

1. a. My uncle is giving me diving lessons.
    b. He was a state champion.

    Combination: _____

    _____

2. a. Our marriage ceremony was quick and sweet.
    b. It made our nervous parents happy.

    Combination: _____

    _____

3. a. The manatee is a sea mammal.
    b. It lives along the Florida coast.

    Combination: _____

    _____

4. a. Donna bought a new backpack.
   b. The backpack has thickly padded straps.

   Combination:_____

   _____

5. a. This walking tour has thirty-two stops.
   b. It is a challenge to complete.

   Combination:_____

   _____

6. a. Hockey is a fast-moving game.
   b. It often becomes violent.

   Combination:_____

   _____

7. a. Andrew Jackson was the seventh U.S. president.
   b. He was born in South Carolina.

   Combination:_____

   _____

8. a. At the beach, I always use sunscreen.
   b. It prevents burns and lessens the danger of skin cancer.

   Combination:_____

   _____

B. Punctuating Ideas Introduced by WHO, WHICH, or THAT

Ideas introduced by relative pronouns can be one of two types, **restrictive** or **nonrestrictive.** Punctuating them must be done carefully.

Restrictive

> Never eat peaches *that are* green.

- A *relative clause* has (1) a subject that is a relative pronoun and (2) a verb.
- What is the relative clause in the sentence in the box? _____
- Can you leave out *that are green* and still keep the basic meaning of the sentence?
- No! You are not saying *don't eat peaches;* you are saying don't eat *certain kinds* of peaches—*green* ones.
- Therefore, *that are green* is *restrictive;* it restricts the meaning of the sentence.

A *restrictive clause* **is not set off by commas because it is necessary to the meaning of the sentence.**

Nonrestrictive

My guitar, *which is a Martin,* was given to me as a gift.

- In this sentence, the relative clause is _____.

- Can you leave out *which is a Martin* and still keep the basic meaning of the sentence?

- Yes! *Which is a Martin* merely adds a fact. It does not change the basic idea of the sentence, which is *my guitar was given to me as a gift.*

- Therefore, *which is a Martin* is *nonrestrictive;* it does not restrict or change the meaning of the sentence.

A *nonrestrictive clause* **is set off by commas because it is not necessary to the meaning of the sentence.**

Note: *Which* is often used as a nonrestrictive relative pronoun.

PRACTICE 2

Underline or highlight the relative pronoun in each sentence. Punctuate correctly. Write a C next to each correct sentence.

1. People who need help are often embarrassed to ask for it.   _____

2. Ovens that clean themselves are the best kind.   _____

3. Paint that contains lead can be dangerous to children.   _____

4. The anaconda which is the largest snake in the world can weigh 550 pounds.   _____

5. Edward's watch which tells the time and the date was a gift from his wife.   _____

6. Carol who is a flight attendant has just left for Pakistan.   _____

7. Joel Upton who is a dean of students usually sings in the yearly talent show. _____

8. Exercise that causes severe dehydration is dangerous.   _____

PRACTICE 3

Complete each sentence by completing the relative clause.

   EXAMPLE: Boxing is a sport that _*upsets me.*_____.

1. My aunt, who _____, rescued a cat last week.

2. A family that _____ can solve its problems.

3. I never vote for candidates _____.

4. This T-shirt, which _____, was a gift.

5. Paris, _____, is an exciting city to visit.

6. James, who _____, just enlisted in the Air Force.

7. I cannot resist stores that _____.

8. This company, which _____, provides health benefits and retirement plans for employees.

PRACTICE 4

On paper or on a computer, write four sentences using restrictive relative clauses and four using nonrestrictive relative clauses. Punctuate with care.

Chapter Highlights

- **Relative pronouns (*who*, *which*, and *that*) can join two independent ideas:**

    We met Krizia Stone. She runs an advertising agency.

    We met Krizia Stone, *who* runs an advertising agency.

    My favorite radio station is WQDF. It plays mostly jazz.

    My favorite radio station is WQDF, *which* plays mostly jazz.

    Last night, I had a hamburger. It was too rare.

    Last night, I had a hamburger *that* was too rare.

- **Restrictive relative clauses change the meaning of the sentence. They are not set off by commas:**

    The uncle *who is helping me through college* lives in Texas.

    The car *that we saw Ned driving* was not his.

- **Nonrestrictive relative clauses do not change the meaning of the sentence. They are set off by commas:**

    My uncle, *who lives in Texas,* owns a supermarket.

    Ned's car, *which is a 1992 Mazda,* was at the repair shop.

Proofreading Strategy

If *who, which, that* errors are one of your error patterns, **search your drafts for the words *who, which,* and *that*** and **highlight or underline** them. If you are using a computer, use the *"Find"* feature to locate these words. Whenever *who, which,* or *that* is being used as a relative pronoun, ask yourself, **"*Have I selected the correct relative pronoun?*"** *Who* is for people, *which* and *that* for things.

Now check your punctuation. Would omitting the *who, which,* or *that* clause *change* the meaning of the sentence? If the answer is "No," then use commas to set off this *restrictive* clause. Here is an example:

YES   NO
The man who caused the accident did not see the stop sign, which was hidden under thick vines.

WRITING AND PROOFREADING ASSIGNMENT

In a small group, discuss a change that would improve life in your neighborhood—a new traffic light or more police patrols, for instance. Your task is to write a flier that will convince neighbors that this change is important; your purpose is to win them over to your side. The flier might note, for instance, that a child was killed at a certain intersection or that several burglaries could have been prevented. Each group member should write his or her own flier, including two sentences with relative pronouns and correct punctuation. Then read the fliers aloud; decide which are effective and why. Finally, exchange papers and check for correct relative pronoun use.

CHAPTER REVIEW

Proofread the following paragraph for relative pronoun errors and punctuation errors. Correct each error above the line.

(1) Charles Anderson is best known as the trainer of the Tuskegee Airmen who were the first African-American combat pilots. (2) During a time when African Americans were prevented from becoming pilots, Anderson was fascinated by planes. (3) He learned about flying from books. (4) At age twenty-two, he bought a used plane which, became his teacher. (5) Eventually he met someone, who helped him become an expert flyer. (6) Battling against discrimination, Anderson became the first African American to earn an

Seven of the famous African-American pilots of World War II, the Tuskegee Airmen.

air transport pilot's license. (7) He and another pilot made the first round-trip flight across America by black Americans. (8) In 1939, Anderson started a civilian pilot training program at Tuskegee Institute in Alabama. (9) One day Eleanor Roosevelt, which was first lady at the time insisted on flying with him. (10) Soon afterward, Tuskegee Institute was chosen by the Army Air Corps for a special program. (11) Anderson who was chief flight instructor gave America's first African-American World War II pilots their initial training. (12) During the war, the Tuskegee Airmen showed great skill and heroism which were later recognized by an extraordinary number of honors and awards.

EXPLORING ONLINE

<http://grammar.ccc.commnet.edu/grammar/quizzes/which_quiz.htm>
Interactive quiz: Choose *who*, *which*, or *that*.

<http://wwwedu.ge.ch/cptic/prospective/projets/anglais/exercises/
whowhich.htm> Test your relatives (*who*, *which* and *that*, that is).

 View an integrated eBook and chapter-specific interactive learning tools, including flashcards, quizzes, videos, and extra help tracking and correcting your Personal Error Patterns, in your Basic Writing CourseMate, accessed through <www.cengagebrain.com>.

CHAPTER 19

-*ING* Modifiers

A: Using -*ING* Modifiers

B: Avoiding Confusing Modifiers

A. Using -*ING* Modifiers

Another way to join ideas together is with an **-*ing* modifier,** or **present participle.**

> (1) Beth was learning to ski. She broke her ankle.
>
> (2) Learning to ski, Beth broke her ankle.

- It seems that *while* Beth was learning to ski, she had an accident. Sentence (2) emphasizes this time relationship and also joins two short sentences in one longer one.

- In sentence (2), *learning* without its helping verb, *was*, is not a verb. Instead, *learning to ski* refers to or modifies *Beth*, the subject of the new sentence.

> Learning to ski, Beth broke her ankle.

- Note that a comma follows the introductory -*ing* modifier, setting it off from the independent idea.

PRACTICE 1

Combine the two sentences in each pair, using the -*ing* modifier to connect them. Drop unnecessary words. Draw an arrow from the -*ing* word to the word or words to which it refers.

EXAMPLE: Tom was standing on the deck. He waved good-bye to his family.

Standing on the deck, Tom waved good-bye to his family.

1. Kyla was searching for change. She found her lost earring.

   _____

2. The children worked all evening. They completed the jigsaw puzzle.

   _____

3. They were hiking cross-country. They made many new friends.

_____

4. She was visiting Santa Fe. She decided to move there.

_____

5. You are replacing the battery pack in your camera. You spot a grease mark on the lens.

_____

6. Seth was mumbling to himself. He named the fifty states.

_____

7. Judge Smithers was pounding his gavel. He called a recess.

_____

8. The masons built the wall carefully. They were lifting huge rocks and cementing them in place.

_____

B. Avoiding Confusing Modifiers

Be sure that your -*ing* modifiers say what you mean!

(1) Hanging by the toe from the dresser drawer, Joe found his sock.

- Probably the writer did not mean that Joe spent time hanging by his toe. What, then, was hanging by the toe from the dresser drawer?
- *Hanging* refers to the *sock*, of course, but the order of the sentence does not show this. We can clear up the confusion by turning the ideas around.

Joe found his sock hanging by the toe from the dresser drawer.

Read your sentences in Practice 1 to make sure the order of the ideas is clear, not confusing.

(2) Visiting my cousin, our house was robbed.

- Does the writer mean that *our house* was visiting my cousin? To whom or what, then, does *visiting my cousin* refer?
- *Visiting* seems to refer to *I*, but there is no *I* in the sentence. To clear up the confusion, we would have to add or change words.

Visiting my cousin, I learned that our house was robbed.

PRACTICE 2

Rewrite the following sentences to clarify any confusing *-ing* modifiers.

1. Biking and walking daily, Cheryl's commuting costs were cut.

   Rewrite: _____

2. Leaping from tree to tree, Professor Fernandez spotted a monkey.

   Rewrite: _____

3. Painting for three hours straight, the bathroom and the hallway were finished by Theresa.

   Rewrite: _____

4. My son spotted our dog playing soccer in the schoolyard.

   Rewrite: _____

5. Lying in the driveway, Tonya discovered her calculus textbook.

   Rewrite: _____

PRACTICE 3

On paper or on a computer, write three sentences of your own, using *-ing* modifiers to join ideas.

Chapter Highlights

- **An *-ing* modifier can join two ideas:**

  (1) Sol was cooking dinner.

  (2) He started a small fire.

  (1) + (2) *Cooking* dinner, Sol started a small fire.

- **Avoid confusing modifiers:**

  I finally found my cat riding my bike. (*incorrect*)

  Riding my bike, I finally found my cat. (*correct*)

Proofreading Strategy

If confusing *-ing* modifiers are one of your error patterns:

1. **Search your draft for *–ing* words or phrases**, and circle them. If you are using a computer, use the "*Find*" feature to locate these words.

2. If an *–ing* word or phrase is used as a modifier, ask yourself, "**What word in the sentence is being modified?**" Draw an arrow to that word.

3. Ask yourself, *"Does the −ing word or phrase come immediately before or after the word it modifies?"* If the answer is no, rewrite to move the modifier to its rightful place. Is the modifier in the sentence below positioned correctly?

INCORRECT

The seal delighted the children performing tricks for fish treats.

CORRECT

Performing tricks for fish treats, the seal delighted the children.

WRITING AND PROOFREADING ASSIGNMENT

Some people feel that much popular music degrades women and encourages drug abuse and violence. Others feel that popular songs expose many of the social ills we suffer from today. What do you think?

Prepare to take part in a debate to defend or criticize popular music. Your job is to convince the other side that your view is correct. Use specific song titles and artists as examples to support your argument. After you write, take a break. Then revise to use one or two −ing modifiers to join ideas. Proofread for correct punctuation.

CHAPTER REVIEW

Highlight or underline all the −ing modifiers in this paragraph. Then proofread the following paragraph for comma errors and confusing modifiers. Correct each error above the line.

(1) What happened in the shed behind Patrick O'Leary's house to start the Great Chicago Fire of 1871? (2) No one knows for sure. (3) Smoking in the shed some people say the fire was started by careless boys. (4) In another story, poker-playing youngsters accidentally kicked over an oil lamp. (5) The blame, however, usually is placed on Mrs. O'Leary's cow. (6) At 8:45 p.m., swinging a lantern at her side Mrs. O'Leary went out to milk the unruly cow. (7) The cow tipped the lantern switching its tail. (8) Recalling the incident Mrs. Nellie Hayes branded the cow theory "nonsense." (9) In fact, she said that the O'Learys' neighbors were having a party on the hot night of October 7. (10) Looking for some fresh milk a thirsty guest walked into the shed and dropped a lighted candle along the way. (11) Whatever happened, the fire was the greatest calamity of nineteenth-century America. (12) Killing three hundred people and destroying more than three square miles of buildings it left ninety thousand people homeless.

EXPLORING ONLINE

<http://grammar.ccc.commnet.edu/grammar/cgi-shl/quiz.pl/modifier_quiz.htm>
Are your modifiers misplaced? Take this quiz and improve your skills.

View an integrated eBook and chapter-specific interactive learning tools, including flashcards, quizzes, videos, and extra help tracking and correcting your Personal Error Patterns, in your Basic Writing CourseMate, accessed through <www.cengagebrain.com>.

UNIT 4

Writing Assignments

As you complete each writing assignment, remember to perform these steps:

- Write a clear, complete topic sentence.
- Use freewriting, brainstorming, or clustering to generate ideas for the body of your paragraph, essay, or letter.
- Arrange your best ideas in a plan.
- Revise for support, unity, coherence, and exact language.
- Proofread for grammar, punctuation, and spelling errors.

Writing Assignment 1 *Post your thoughts online.* Many websites and blogs invite viewers to respond by posting their comments or opinions. Find a blog or website forum that focuses on a topic you find interesting, such as music, sports, health/fitness, politics, the media, art, or technology. Select a site you already know and like, or find one in a list of the best websites (<http://www .100bestwebsites.org/>) or blogs (<http://blogs.botw.org/>). Then, contribute your thoughts or feedback. For example, you could post your thoughts about a favorite television show at <http:// www.televisionwithoutpity.com/>, contribute to a spiritual discussion at <http://www .beliefnet.com/boards/index.asp>, or comment on current events at <http://ireport .cnn.com/community/assignment>. Use as many techniques for joining ideas as you can, and proofread for run-ons and comma splices.

Writing Assignment 2 *Be a witness.* You have just witnessed a fender-bender involving a car and an ice cream truck. No one was hurt, but the insurance company has asked you to write an eyewitness report. First, visualize the accident and how it occurred. Then jot down as many details as possible to make your description of the accident as vivid as possible. Use subordinating conjunctions that indicate time (*when*, *as*, *before*, *while*, and so on) to show the order of events. Use as many techniques for joining ideas as you can, being careful about punctuation. Proofread for run-ons and comma splices.

Writing Assignment 3 *Evaluate so-called reality TV shows.* A newspaper has asked readers to respond to the question "Has reality television gone too far?" Think about popular reality programs—*Survivor*, *Biggest Loser*, and similar shows in which contestants are often humiliated and forced to do bizarre things. State whether reality TV has, or has not, gone too far. Then explain why you feel this way, using vivid details and examples from programs to support your point. Use a variety of techniques for joining ideas; proofread for run-ons and comma splices.

Writing Assignment 4 *React to a quotation.* From the "Work and Success" section of the Quotation Bank at the end of this book, choose a quotation that you strongly agree or disagree with. For instance, do you think it is true that "most of us are looking for a calling, not a job" or that "money is like manure"? In your first sentence, repeat the entire quotation, explaining whether you do or do not agree with it. Then brainstorm, freewrite, or cluster to generate examples and facts supporting your view. Use your own or other people's experiences to strengthen your argument. Use as many techniques for joining ideas as you can. Proofread for run-ons and comma splices.

233

UNIT 4

Review

Five Useful Ways to Join Ideas

In this unit, you have combined simple sentences by means of a **coordinating conjunction**, a **subordinating conjunction**, a **semicolon**, and a **semicolon** and **conjunctive adverb.** Here is a review chart of the sentence patterns discussed in this unit.

Coordination

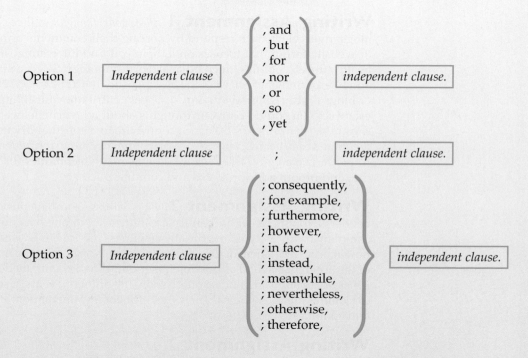

Option 1 | Independent clause | , and / , but / , for / , nor / , or / , so / , yet | independent clause.

Option 2 | Independent clause | ; | independent clause.

Option 3 | Independent clause | ; consequently, / ; for example, / ; furthermore, / ; however, / ; in fact, / ; instead, / ; meanwhile, / ; nevertheless, / ; otherwise, / ; therefore, | independent clause.

Subordination

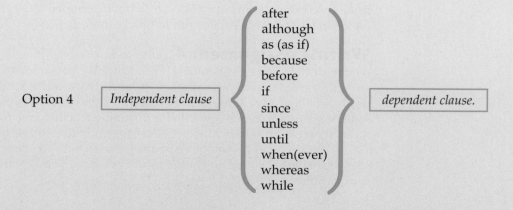

Option 4 | Independent clause | after / although / as (as if) / because / before / if / since / unless / until / when(ever) / whereas / while | dependent clause.

	After	
	Although	
	As (as if)	
	Because	
	Before	
Option 5	If	*dependent clause, independent clause.*
	Since	
	Unless	
	Until	
	When(ever)	
	Whereas	
	While	

Proofreading

The student composition below has been changed to contain run-ons, comma splices, and misused semicolons. Proofread for these errors. Then correct them above the lines in any way you choose. (You should find eight errors.)

Managing Time in College

(1) When I started college, time was a problem. (2) I was always desperately reading an assignment just before class or racing to get to work on time. (3) The stress became too much. (4) It took a while now I know how to manage my time. (5) The secret of my success is flexible planning.

(6) At the beginning of each semester, I mark a calendar with all the due dates for the term these include deadlines for assignments, papers, and tests. (7) I also write in social events and obligations, therefore; I know at a glance when I need extra time during the next few months.

(8) Next, I make out a model weekly study schedule. (9) First, I block in the hours when I have to sleep, eat, work, go to class, and tend to my family then I decide what time I will devote to study and relaxation. (10) Finally, I fill in the times I will study each subject, making sure I plan at least one hour of study time for each hour of class time. (11) Generally, I plan some time just before or after a class that way I can prepare for a class or review my notes right after a lecture.

(12) In reality, I don't follow this schedule rigidly, I vary it according to the demands of the week and day. (13) In addition, I spend more time on my harder subjects and less time on the easy ones. (14) I also try to study my harder subjects in the morning; when I am most awake.

(15) I find that by setting up a model schedule but keeping it flexible, I can accomplish all I have to do with little worry. (16) This system may not help everyone, it has certainly worked for me.

Jesse Rose, student

Combining

Read each pair of sentences below to determine the relationship between them. Then join each pair in two different ways, using the conjunctions shown. Punctuate correctly.

1. The tide had not yet come in.
   We went swimming.

   (although) _____

   _____

   (but) _____

   _____

2. Michael enjoys drinking coffee.
   He needs to limit his caffeine intake.

   (yet) _____

   _____

   (nevertheless) _____

   _____

3. Alexis plays the trumpet very well.
   She hopes to have her own band someday.

   (and) _____

   _____

   (furthermore) _____

   _____

4. The lecture starts in five minutes.
   We had better get to our seats.

   (because) _____

   _____

   (so) _____

   _____

5. He knows how to make money.
   He doesn't want to start another company.

   (although) _____

   _____

   (however) _____

   _____

Revising

Read through this essay of short, choppy sentences. Then revise it, combining some sentences. Use one coordinating conjunction, one subordinating conjunction, and any other ways you have learned to join ideas together. Keep some short sentences for variety. Make your corrections above the lines, and punctuate with care.

Control Your Credit

(1) One-fourth of all Americans want to get out of debt. (2) Many college students are among them. (3) These students graduate. (4) They owe more than $2,000 in credit-card debt. (5) Good credit habits can be learned. (6) You may have abused your plastic and gotten into trouble. (7) You might be using credit cards for the first time. (8) You can develop three habits to help control your credit-card debt.

(9) First, have and carry just one credit card. (10) Using two or more can quickly lead to overspending. (11) Choose your card wisely. (12) Some cards are better than others. (13) The best card offers the lowest interest rate. (14) It should not charge an annual fee.

(15) A second good habit is to use a credit card only as a last resort. (16) Whenever possible, use cash, a debit card, or a check. (17) Save your credit cards for true emergencies. (18) When cash is low, don't grab a card. (19) Reduce spending instead. (20) Experts also offer this rule of thumb: "If you can eat it or drink it, don't charge it!"

(21) Finally, get in the habit of thinking of credit cards as just another form of cash. (22) You never let your charges exceed your available funds. (23) You will be able to pay your full balance each month. (24) As a result, you'll avoid expensive interest charges that only increase your debt.

(25) You develop good credit card habits. (26) You will stay in control of debt. (27) It will not take control of you.

UNIT 4

Writers' Workshop

Describe a Detour off the Main Highway

When a writer really cares about a subject, often the reader will care too. In your group or class, read this student's paragraph, aloud if possible. As you read, underline any words or details that strike you as vivid or powerful.

> Sometimes detours off the main highway can bring wonderful surprises, and last week this happened to my husband and me. On the Fourth of July weekend, we decided to drive home the long way, taking the old dirt farm road. Pulling over to admire the afternoon light gleaming on a field of wet corn we saw a tiny farm stand under a tree. No one was in sight, but a card table covered with a red checkered cloth held pints of tomatoes, jars of jam, and a handwritten price list. Next to these was a vase full of red poppies and tiny American flags. We bought tomatoes, leaving our money in the tin box stuffed with dollar bills. Driving home we both felt so happy—as if we had been given a great gift.
>
> *Kim Lee, student*

1. How effective is Kim Lee's paragraph?
   _____ Clear topic sentence?   _____ Rich supporting details?
   _____ Logical organization?   _____ Effective conclusion?

2. Discuss your underlinings with one another, explaining as specifically as possible why a particular word or sentence is effective. For instance, the "red poppies and tiny American flags" are so exact that you can see them.

3. This student supports her topic sentence with a single *example,* one brief story told in detail. If you were to support the same topic sentence, what example from your own life might you use?

4. The concluding sentence tells the reader that she and her husband felt they had been given "a great gift." Do you think that the gift was being trusted to be honest?

5. Proofread for grammar and spelling. Do you notice any error patterns (two or more errors of the same type) that this student should watch out for?

About her writing process, Kim Lee says:

> I wrote this paper in my usual way—I sort of plan, and then I freewrite on the subject. I like freewriting—I pick through it for certain words or details, but of course it is also a mess. From my freewriting I got "light gleaming on a field of wet corn" and the last sentence, about the gift.

Writing and Revising Ideas

1. Develop the topic sentence "Sometimes detours off the main highway can bring wonderful [disturbing] surprises."

2. Write about a time when you were trusted or distrusted by a stranger. What effect did this have on you?

As you plan your paragraph, try to angle the subject toward something that interests *you*—chances are, it will interest your readers too. Consider using one good example to develop your paragraph. As you revise, make sure that the body of your paragraph perfectly fits the topic sentence.

Choosing the Right Noun, Pronoun, Adjective, Adverb, or Preposition

Choosing the right form of many words in English can be tricky. This unit will help you avoid some common errors. In this unit, you will

- Learn about singular and plural nouns
- Choose correct pronouns
- Use adjectives and adverbs correctly
- Choose the right prepositions
- Learn proofreading strategies to find and correct your own errors

Spotlight on Writing

Here, two researchers set forth new findings about happiness. If possible, read the paragraph aloud.

In study after study, four traits characterize happy people. First, especially in individualistic Western cultures, they like themselves. They have high self-esteem and usually believe themselves to be more ethical, more intelligent, less prejudiced, better able to get along with others, and healthier than the average person. Second, happy people typically feel personal control. Those with little or no control over their lives—such as prisoners, nursing home patients, severely impoverished groups or individuals, and citizens in totalitarian regimes—suffer lower morale and worse health. Third, happy people are usually optimistic. Fourth, most happy people are extroverted. Although one might expect that introverts would live more happily in the serenity of their less stressed lives, extroverts are happier—whether alone or with others.

David G. Myers and Ed Diener, "The Pursuit of Happiness," *Scientific American*

- This well-organized paragraph tells us the traits of happy people. They see themselves as "more *ethical*, more *intelligent*, less *prejudiced*, better *able . . .*, and *healthier . . .*" Does this sound true to you?

- All five parts of speech discussed in this unit are used here: nouns, pronouns, adjectives, adverbs, and prepositions. Can you identify one of each?

- If you don't know the meaning of the words *extrovert* and *introvert*, look them up. Which refers to you?

Writing Ideas

- *Analyze how happy you are, based on the four traits mentioned above.*

- *Describe an extrovert or an introvert you have observed.*

CHAPTER 20

Nouns

A: Defining Singular and Plural

B: Signal Words: Singular and Plural

C: Signal Words with OF

A. Defining Singular and Plural

A **noun** names a person, a place, or a thing. Nouns may be **singular** or **plural**. *Singular* means one. *Plural* means more than one.

Singular	Plural
a reporter	the reporters (person nouns)
a forest	the forests (place nouns)
a couch	the couches (thing nouns)

● Most nouns in English form the plural by adding *-s* or *-es*.

Other nouns form their plurals in unusual ways. Learning them is easier if they are divided into groups.

Some nouns form their plurals by changing their spelling:

Singular	Plural
child	children
foot	feet
goose	geese
man	men
mouse	mice
person	people
tooth	teeth
woman	women

Many nouns ending in *-f* or *-fe* change their endings to *-ves* in the plural:

Singular	Plural
half	halves
knife	knives
leaf	leaves
life	lives

scarf	scarves
shelf	shelves
wife	wives
wolf	wolves

Most nouns that end in *o* add *–es* in the plural.

echo + *es* = echoes	potato + *es* = potatoes
hero + *es* = heroes	veto + *es* = vetoes

● Here are some exceptions to memorize:

pianos	solos
radios	sopranos

Other nouns do not change at all to form the plural. Here is a partial list:

Singular	Plural
deer	deer
fish	fish
moose	moose
sheep	sheep

Hyphenated nouns usually form plurals by adding *-s* or *-es* to the first word:

Singular	Plural
brother-in-law	brothers-in-law
maid-of-honor	maids-of-honor
mother-to-be	mothers-to-be
runner-up	runners-up

If you are ever unsure about the plural of a noun, check a dictionary. For example, if you look up the noun *woman* in the dictionary, you will find an entry like this:

woman / women

The first word listed, *woman,* is the singular form of the noun; the second word, *women,* is the plural. Some dictionaries list the plural form of a noun only if the plural is unusual. If no plural is listed, the noun probably adds *-s* or *-es.*

PRACTICE 1

Make the following nouns plural.* If you are not sure of a particular plural, check the charts on this page and the previous page.

Singular	Plural	Singular	Plural
1. notebook	_____	4. brother-in-law	_____
2. hero	_____	5. technician	_____
3. man	_____	6. shelf	_____

* For help with spelling, see Chapter 32.

7. half   _____   14. potato   _____

8. bridge   _____   15. mouse   _____

9. deer   _____   16. child   _____

10. runner-up   _____   17. flight   _____

11. woman   _____   18. wife   _____

12. radio   _____   19. place   _____

13. tooth   _____   20. maid-of-honor   _____

REMEMBER: **Do not add an** -*s* **to words that form plurals by changing an internal letter or letters. For example, the plural of** *man* **is** *men*, **not** *mens*; **the plural of** *woman* **is** *women*, **not** *womens*; **the plural of** *foot* **is** *feet*, **not** *feets*.

PRACTICE 2

Proofread the following paragraph for incorrect plural nouns. Cross out the errors and correct them above the lines.

(1) Many peoples consider Glacier National Park the jewel of the National Park Service. (2) Its many mountains, glaciers, waterfalls, blue-green lake, and amazing wildlifes are in the remote Rocky Mountains in the northwest corner of Montana. (3) Several road take visitors into the park, especially Going-to-the-Sun Road, which clings to the mountainside and offers spectacular, stomach-churning views. (4) At Logan Pass—6,646 foot high—the road crosses the Continental Divide. (5) From this line along the spine of the Rocky, all river flow either west to the Pacific Ocean, south to the Gulf, or east. (6) Because Glacier is truly a wilderness park, it is best seen by hikers, not drivers. (7) Most men, woman, and childs who hike the park's 700 miles of trails come prepared—with hats, long-sleeved shirts, and on their feets, proper hiking shoes. (8) Their equipments includes bottled water and, just in case, bear spray. (9) Glacier has a large population of grizzly bears, which can weigh up to 1,400 pounds, have four-inch claws, and dislike surprises. (10) Besides grizzlies, one might glimpse mountain lions, wolfs, black bear, white mountain goats, moose, bighorn sheeps, elk, and many smaller mammals. (11) Salmon, trouts, and other fishs swim in the ice-cold rivers and lakes. (12) Scientist worry that the glaciers are melting too quickly, but Glacier Park remains a treasure.

EXPLORING ONLINE

<http://www.nps.gov/findapark/> Visit the National Park Service website. Use the find-a-park search tool to explore the many parks the public can visit and select one (Glacier National Park or some other) that you might like to learn about. Read, explore, and jot down any writing—or travel—ideas.

B. Signal Words: Singular and Plural

A *signal word* **tells you whether a singular or a plural noun usually follows.**
These **signal words** tell you that a *singular noun* usually follows:

Signal Words

a(n)
another
a single
each   } motorboat
every
one

These signal words tell you that a *plural noun* usually follows:

all
both
few
many   } motorboats
several
some
two (or more)

PRACTICE 3

In the blank following each signal word, write either a singular or a plural noun. Use as many different nouns as you can think of.

EXAMPLES: a single ___stamp___

most ___fabrics___

1. a(n)   _____
2. some   _____
3. few   _____
4. nine   _____
5. one   _____
6. all   _____

7. another   _____
8. each   _____
9. a single _____
10. every   _____
11. both   _____
12. many   _____

PRACTICE 4

Read the following essay and underline or highlight the signal words. Then check for incorrect singular or plural nouns. Cross out the errors and correct them above the lines.

The Best Medicine

(1) Many researcher believe that laughter is good for people's health. (2) In fact, some doctor have concluded that laughter actually helps patients heal faster. (3) To put this theory into practice, several hospital have introduced humor routines into their treatment programs. (4) One programs is a children's clown care unit that operates in seven New York City hospitals. (5) Thirty-five clown from the Big Apple Circus go to the hospitals three times every weeks. (6) Few child can keep from laughing at the "rubber chicken soup" and

"red nose transplant" routines. (7) Although the program hasn't been studied scientifically,

many observer have witnessed its positive effects.

(8) However, some specialist are conducting strictly scientific research on health and

laughter. (9) One study, carried out at Loma Linda University in California, has shown the

positive effects of laughter on the immune system. (10) Another tests, done at the College

of William and Mary in Virginia, has confirmed the California findings. (11) Other studies in

progress are suggesting that all physiological system may be affected positively by laughter.

(12) Finally, research also is backing up a claims made by Norman Cousins, author of the

book *Anatomy of an Illness*. (13) While he was fighting a life-threatening diseases, Cousins

maintained that hearty laughter took away his pain. (14) Several recent study have shown

that pain does become less intense when the sufferer responds to comedy.

PRACTICE 5

On paper or on a computer, write three sentences using signal words that require singular nouns. Then write three sentences using signal words that require plural nouns.

C. Signal Words with OF

Many signal words are followed by *of . . .* or *of the. . . .* Usually, these signal words are followed by a *plural* noun (or a collective noun) because you are really talking about one or more from a larger group.*

$$\left.\begin{array}{l} \text{many of the} \\ \text{a few of the} \\ \text{lots of the} \end{array}\right\} \text{ houses are } \dots$$

BE CAREFUL: The signal words *one of the* and *each of the* are followed by a *plural* noun, but the verb is *singular* because only the signal word (*one, each*) is the real subject.**

$$\left.\begin{array}{l} \text{one of the} \\ \text{each of the} \end{array}\right\} \text{ houses is } \dots$$

(1) *One* of the apples *is* spoiled.

(2) *Each* of the trees *grows* quickly.

- In sentence (1), *one* is the subject, not *apples*.
- In sentence (2), *each* is the subject, not *trees*.

---

* For more work on collective nouns, see Chapter 21, Part C.
** For more work on this type of construction, see Chapter 9, Part G.

PRACTICE 6

Fill in your own nouns in the following sentences. Use a different noun in each sentence.

1. Many of the _____ enrolled in Chemistry 202.

2. Sipho lost one of his _____ at the beach.

3. This is one of the _____ that everyone liked.

4. Each of the _____ carried a sign.

5. You are one of the few _____ who can do somersaults.

6. Few of the _____ produced calves.

PRACTICE 7

Write five sentences, using the signal words with *of* provided in parentheses. Use a different noun in each sentence.

EXAMPLE: (many of those . . .) _____ *I planted many of those flowers myself.* _____

1. (one of my . . .) _____

_____

2. (many of the . . .) _____

_____

3. (lots of the . . .) _____

_____

4. (each of these . . .)_____

_____

5. (a few of your . . .) _____

_____

PRACTICE 8

Proofread the following paragraph for correct plural nouns. Underline or highlight any signal words. Then cross out the errors and correct them above the lines.

(1) In 1782, the bald eagle became the national symbol of the United States. (2) Sadly, over the years, many of these magnificent bird suffered destruction of their habitat, poisoning of their food sources, and illegal extermination by farmers, ranchers, and hunters. (3) By the 1960s, these majestic raptors were declared an endangered species. (4) Today, however, eagles are back in American skies, thanks to some of the new recovery method used by wildlife specialists. (5) In one such method, scientists remove each of the egg from a wild eagle's nest and place it in an incubator. (6) Baby eagles must not attach themselves to people, so all of the hatchling are fed first with tweezers and later with eagle puppets.

Eagle puppet feeding a three-day-old bald eaglet.

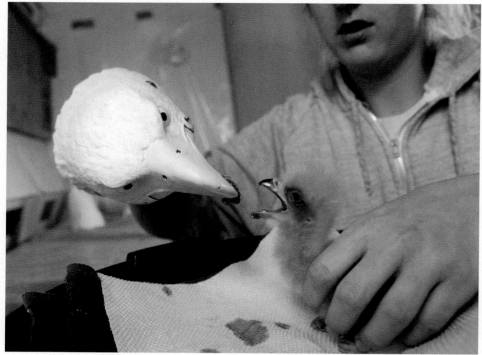

(7) In this way, they learn to recognize Mom and Dad. (8) Protected and well fed, lots of the chick grow strong enough to be placed in the nests of adult eagles. (9) Instinct kicks in, and the adults adopt and raise the chicks as their own. (10) Today, many of our wild eagle got their start in eaglet nurseries.

Chapter Highlights

- **Most plural nouns are formed by adding -s or -es to the singular noun:**

   job/jobs   watch/watches

- **Some plurals are formed in other ways:**

   child/children   woman/women   wolf/wolves

- **Some nouns ending in o add -es; others add -s:**

   echo/echoes   solo/solos

- **Some nouns have identical singular and plural forms:**

   fish/fish   equipment/equipment

- **Hyphenated nouns usually add -s or -es to the first word:**

   father-in-law/fathers-in-law

- **Signal words, with and without of, indicate whether a singular or a plural noun usually follows:**

   another musician   *many of the* musicians

Proofreading Strategy

Incorrect singular and plural nouns are considered serious errors, so proofread with care if these are among your error patterns.

First, **search each sentence for signal words and phrases** (such as *an, each, one, many, several, a few*) that "announce" the need for either a singular or a plural noun. Underline or color code these signal words. Code in a different color all phrases like *one of the . . .* and *a few of the . . .* that are *always* followed by a plural. **Locate the noun** following each signal word and check for correctness.

Notice how the color-coded signal words in this example make it easier to see if the nouns are correct.

ideas
suggestions

The teams generated several ~~idea,~~ but only a few of the ~~suggestion~~ seemed like workable solutions.

WRITING AND PROOFREADING ASSIGNMENT

For some families, shopping—whether for food, clothing, or electronics—is a delightful group outing, a time to be together and share. For other families, it is an ordeal, a time of great stress, with arguments about what to purchase and how much to spend.

Describe a particularly enjoyable or awful family shopping experience. Your first sentence might read, "Shopping for _____ was (is) a(n) _____ experience." Explain what made it so good or so bad: Was it what you were shopping for or where you were shopping? Were there arguments? Why?

Proofread your work for the correct use of singular and plural nouns. Be especially careful of nouns that follow signal words.

CHAPTER REVIEW

Proofread the following essay for incorrect singular and plural nouns. First underline or highlight the signal words. Then cross out the errors and correct them above the lines.

The Effects of Alcohol on Pregnancy

(1) All mother-to-bes who drink alcohol run the risk of harming an innocent children.

(2) When a pregnant women takes a drink, the alcohol goes straight from her bloodstream into the bloodstream of her child. (3) When she has several drink, the blood-alcohol level of her child rises as high as her own.

(4) Newborns can be harmed by alcohol in many way. (5) Some infant are born addicted to alcohol. (6) Other children are born mentally retarded. (7) In fact, most doctor believe that exposure to alcohol before birth is one of the major cause of mental retardation.

(8) In the worst cases, babies are born with a disease called fetal alcohol syndrome.

(9) These unfortunate children not only are mentally retarded but also can have many

physical deformity. (10) In milder cases, the children's problems don't show up until they go to school. (11) For instance, they may have poor memories and short attention spans. (12) Later, they may have trouble holding a jobs.

(13) Too many young life have been ruined before birth because of alcohol consumption. (14) All unborn child need and deserve a chance to have a healthy, normal futures. (15) If you are a women who is expecting a baby, stop drinking alcohol now!

EXPLORING ONLINE

<http://a4esl.org/q/h/vf004-bp.html> Interactive quiz: Click on the correct singular or plural.

<http://grammar.ccc.commnet.edu/grammar/quizzes/cross/plurals_gap.htm> Tricky plurals quiz. Drill, baby, drill.

<http://grammar.ccc.commnet.edu/grammar/noun_exercise2.htm> Art Class! Study Bruegel's famous painting and hunt for nouns.

 View an integrated eBook and chapter-specific interactive learning tools, including flashcards, quizzes, videos, and extra help tracking and correcting your Personal Error Patterns, in your Basic Writing CourseMate, accessed through <www.cengagebrain.com>.

CHAPTER 21

Pronouns

A. Defining Pronouns and Antecedents

Pronouns take the place of or refer to nouns or other pronouns. The word or words that a pronoun refers to are called the **antecedent** of the pronoun.

(1) *Tory* said that *he* was tired.

- *He* refers to *Tory*.
- *Tory* is the antecedent of *he*.

(2) *Sonia* left early, but I did not see *her* until later.

- *Her* refers to *Sonia*.
- *Sonia* is the antecedent of *her*.

(3) *Robert and Tyrone* have been good friends ever since *their* college days.

- *Their* refers to *Robert and Tyrone*.
- *Robert and Tyrone* is the antecedent of *their*.

A pronoun must agree with its antecedent. In sentence (1), the antecedent *Tory* requires the singular, masculine pronoun *he*. In sentence (2), the antecedent *Sonia* requires the singular, feminine pronoun *her*. In sentence (3), the antecedent *Robert and Tyrone* requires the plural pronoun *their*.

PRACTICE 1

In each of the following sentences, circle the pronoun. In the columns on the right, write the pronoun and its antecedent as shown in the example.

	Pronoun	**Antecedent**
EXAMPLE: Susan B. Anthony promoted women's rights before (they) were popular.	*they*	*rights*

1. Susan B. Anthony deserves praise for her accomplishments.

2. Anthony became involved in the antislavery movement because of her principles.

3. She helped President Lincoln develop his plans to free the slaves during the Civil War.

4. Eventually, Anthony realized that women wouldn't be fully protected by law until they could vote.

5. When Anthony voted in the presidential election of 1872, she was arrested.

6. She was found guilty and given a $100 fine, but she refused to pay it.

7. The judge did not sentence Anthony to jail because a sentence would have given her grounds for an appeal.

8. If the Supreme Court had heard her appeal, it might have ruled that women had the right to vote.

9. Audiences in England and Germany showed their appreciation of Anthony's work with standing ovations.

10. Unfortunately, women in the United States had to wait until 1920 before they could legally vote.

INTERFOTO/Alamy

PRACTICE 2

Read this paragraph for meaning; then circle each pronoun you find and write its antecedent above the pronoun.

(1) In 1935, a Hungarian journalist got tired of the ink blotches his fountain pen made.

(2) So László Biro and his brother developed a pen with a rolling ball at the point. (3) It wrote without making blotches. (4) Their pen wasn't the first ballpoint, but it was the first

one that worked well. (5) The new pens got a big boost during World War II. (6) Pilots

needed a pen they could use at high altitudes. (7) Only ballpoints did the job. (8) In 1945,

a department store in New York City introduced these pens to its shoppers. (9) The store

sold ten thousand ballpoints the first day. (10) They cost $12.50 each! (11) Today, people buy

almost two *billion* ballpoints a year, for as little as ten cents apiece.

B. Referring to Indefinite Pronouns

Indefinite pronouns do not point to a specific person.

anybody anyone each everybody everyone no one nobody somebody someone	Indefinite pronouns are usually *singular*. A pronoun that refers to an indefinite pronoun should also be singular.

(1) *Everyone* should do what *he* or *she* can to help.

- *Everyone* is a singular antecedent and must be used with the singular pronoun *he* or *she*.

(2) *Each* wanted to read *his* or *her* composition aloud.

- *Each* is a singular antecedent and must be used with the singular pronoun *his* or *her*.

(3) If *someone* smiles at you, give *him* or *her* a smile in return.

- *Someone* is a singular antecedent and must be used with the singular pronoun *him* or *her*.

In the past, writers used *he, his,* or *him* to refer to both men and women. Now, however, many writers use *he or she, his or her,* or *him or her.* Of course, if *everyone* is a woman, use *she* or *her*; if *everyone* is a man, use *he, his,* or *him.**

Someone left *her* purse in the classroom.

Someone left *his* wallet on the bus.

Someone left *his or her* glasses on the back seat.

---

* For more work on pronoun reference, see Chapter 25, "Consistent Person."

It is often best to avoid the repetition of *his or her* and *he or she* by changing the indefinite pronoun to a plural.

> (4) *Everyone* in the club agreed to pay *his* or *her* dues on time.
>
> *or*
>
> (5) The club *members* agreed to pay *their* dues on time.

PRACTICE 3

Fill in the blanks with the correct pronouns. Then write the antecedent of each pronoun in the column on the right.

Antecedent

EXAMPLE: Everyone should do ____*his or her*____ best.   ____*everyone*____

1. The average citizen does not take _____ right to vote seriously enough.   _____

2. If a person chooses a career in accounting,

   _____ must enjoy working with numbers.   _____

3. Each player gave _____ best in the women's basketball finals.   _____

4. Anyone can learn to do research on the Internet if

   _____ will put the time into it.   _____

5. Fred and Nina always do _____ housecleaning on Tuesday.   _____

6. Someone left _____ fingerprints on the windshield.   _____

7. The sales managers asked me to attend _____ meeting tomorrow.   _____

8. Everyone should see _____ dentist at least once a year.   _____

9. Nobody wanted to waste _____ money on a singing stapler.   _____

10. Everybody is welcome to try _____ luck in the lottery.   _____

PRACTICE 4

Some of the following sentences contain errors in pronoun reference. Revise the incorrect sentences. Write a *C* in the blank next to each correct sentence.

EXAMPLE: Everyone must provide ~~their~~ *his or her* lunch.   _____

1. Somebody left their bag of popcorn on the seat.   _____

2. A child should not carry heavy items in his or her backpack.   _____

3. Everybody can take their choice of two dishes from column A
   and one from column B.   _____

4. No one works harder at their paramedic job than my brother-in-law. _____

5. Each state has their own flag.   _____

6. Anyone can conquer his or her fear of speaking in public.   _____

PRACTICE 5   On paper or on a computer, write three sentences using indefinite pronouns as antecedents.

C. Referring to Collective Nouns

Collective nouns imply more than one person but are generally considered *singular*. Here is a partial list:

Common Collective Nouns		
board	family	panel
class	flock	school
college	government	society
committee	group	team
company	jury	tribe

(1) The *jury* meets early today because *it* must decide on a verdict.

- *Jury* is a singular antecedent and is used with the singular pronoun *it*.

(2) *Society* must protect *its* members from violence.

- *Society* is a singular antecedent and is always used with the singular pronoun *it*.
- Use *it* or *its* when referring to collective nouns.
- Use *they* or *their* only when referring to collective nouns in the plural (*schools*, *companies*, and so forth).

PRACTICE 6   Write the correct pronoun in the blank. Then write the antecedent of the pronoun in the column on the right.

Antecedent

EXAMPLE: The committee sent _____*its*_____ best
             recommendations to the president of the college.   ____*committee*____

1. Wanda's company will have _____ annual picnic
   next week.   _____

2. The two teams picked up _____ gloves and bats
   and walked off the field.   _____

3. My high school class will soon have _____ tenth
   reunion.   _____

4. The city is doing _____ best to build a new stadium.   _____

5. Many soap operas thrive on _____ viewers'
   enjoyment of "a good cry."   _____

6. Each band has _____ guitar player and drummer.   _____

7. The panel made _____ report public.   _____

8. This college plans to train _____ student
   teachers in classroom management.   _____

PRACTICE 7

Some of the following sentences contain errors in pronoun reference. Cross out the incorrect pronoun and write the correct pronoun above the line. Write a *C* in the blank next to each correct sentence.

> *its*
> **EXAMPLES:** The committee will present ~~their~~ report today.   _____
>   The jury has reached its verdict.   __*C*__

1. The computer company retrains their employees for new jobs.   _____

2. Central Technical College wants to double their enrollment by 2015. _____

3. That rock group has changed their name for the third time.   _____

4. The plumbing crew did its best to finish by 4 a.m.   _____

5. The gas company plans to move their headquarters again.   _____

6. The Robinson family held its yearly reunion last week.   _____

PRACTICE 8

On paper or on a computer, write three sentences using collective nouns as antecedents.

D. Referring to Special Singular Constructions

each of . . .
either of . . .
every one of . . .   } Each of these constructions is *singular*.
neither of . . .   Pronouns that refer to them must also
one of . . .   be singular.

(1) *Each* of the women did her work.

- *Each* is a singular antecedent and is used with the singular pronoun *her*.
- Do not be confused by the prepositional phrase *of the women*.

(2) *Neither* of the men finished his meal.

- *Neither* is a singular antecedent and is used with the singular pronoun *his*.
- Do not be confused by the prepositional phrase *of the men*.

(3) *One* of the bottles is missing from its place.

- *One* is a singular antecedent and is used with the singular pronoun *its*.
- Do not be confused by the prepositional phrase *of the bottles*.*

PRACTICE 9

Fill in the blanks with the correct pronouns. Then write the antecedent of each pronoun in the column on the right.

Antecedent

EXAMPLE: Each of my nephews did ___*his*___ homework.   ___*each*___

1. One of the hikers filled _____ canteen.   _____

2. Every one of the women scored high on _____ entrance examination.   _____

3. Each of the puzzles has _____ own solution.   _____

4. Either of them should be able to learn _____ lines before opening night.   _____

5. One of my brothers does not have a radio in _____ car.   _____

6. Neither of the dental technicians has had _____ lunch yet.   _____

7. Every one of the children sat still when _____ photograph was taken.   _____

8. Lin Li and her mother opened _____ boutique in 1998.   _____

PRACTICE 10

Some of the following sentences contain errors in pronoun reference. Cross out the incorrect pronoun and write the correct pronoun above it. Write a *C* in the blank next to each correct sentence.

EXAMPLE: One of my uncles made ~~their~~ *his* opinion known.   _____

1. One of the women at the hardware counter hasn't made their purchase yet.   _____

2. Each of the birds has their distinctive mating ritual.   _____

* For more work on these special constructions, see Chapter 9, Part G.

3. Most public speakers rehearse their speeches beforehand.   _____

4. I hope that neither of the men will change their vote.   _____

5. Both supermarkets now carry Superfizz Carrot Juice for their
    health-conscious customers.   _____

6. Neither of the women bought their toe ring at Toes R Us.   _____

7. One of the televisions was still in its box.   _____

8. Each of my grandchildren has their own bedroom.   _____

PRACTICE 11   On paper or on a computer, write three sentences that use special singular constructions as antecedents.

E. Avoiding Vague and Repetitious Pronouns

Vague Pronouns

Be sure that all pronouns *clearly* refer to their antecedents. Be especially careful of the pronouns *they* and *it*. If *they* or *it* does not refer to a *specific* antecedent, change *they* or *it* to the exact word you have in mind.

> (1) **Vague pronoun:** At registration, they said I should take Math 101.
>
> (2) **Revised:** At registration, an adviser said I should take Math 101.

- In sentence (1), who is *they*? The pronoun *they* does not clearly refer to an antecedent.

- In sentence (2), the vague *they* has been replaced by *an adviser*.

> (3) **Vague pronoun:** On the beach, it says that no swimming is allowed.
>
> (4) **Revised:** On the beach, a sign says that no swimming is allowed.

- In sentence (3), what is *it*? The pronoun *it* does not clearly refer to an antecedent.

- In sentence (4), the vague *it* has been replaced by *a sign*.

Repetitious Pronouns

Don't repeat a pronoun directly after its antecedent. Use *either* the pronoun *or* the antecedent—not both.

> (1) **Repetitious Pronoun:** The doctor, she said that my daughter is in perfect health.

- The pronoun *she* unnecessarily repeats the antecedent *doctor*, which is right before it.

(2) **Revised:** *The doctor* said that my daughter is in perfect health.

or

She said that my daughter is in perfect health.

● Use either *the doctor* or *she,* not both.

PRACTICE 12

Rewrite the sentences that contain vague or repetitious pronouns. If a sentence is correct, write C.

EXAMPLE: Dyslexia, it is a learning disorder that makes reading difficult.

Revised: <u>*Dyslexia is a learning disorder that makes reading difficult.*</u>

1. Many dyslexic persons, they have achieved success in their chosen professions.

   Revised: _____

   _____

2. For example, Albert Einstein, he was dyslexic.

   Revised: _____

   _____

3. In his biography, it says that he couldn't interpret written words the way others could.

   Revised: _____

   _____

4. At his elementary school, they claimed that he was a slow learner.

   Revised: _____

   _____

5. However, this slow learner, he changed the way science looked at time and space.

   Revised: _____

   _____

6. Even politics has had its share of dyslexic leaders.

   Revised: _____

   _____

7. American history, it teaches us that President Woodrow Wilson and Vice President Nelson Rockefeller, they were both dyslexic.

   Revised: _____

   _____

8. Authors can have this problem too; the well-known mystery writer Agatha Christie, she had trouble reading.

   Revised: _____

   _____

9. Finally, in several magazines, they report that both Jay Leno and Cher are dyslexic.

   Revised: _____

   _____

10. Cher, she wasn't able to read until she was eighteen years old.

    Revised: _____

    _____

F. Using Pronouns as Subjects, Objects, and Possessives

Pronouns have different forms, depending on how they are used in a sentence. Pronouns can be *subjects* or *objects* or *possessives*. They can be in the *subjective case*, *objective case*, or *possessive case*.

Pronouns as Subjects

A pronoun can be the *subject* of a sentence:

(1) *He* loves the summer months.

(2) By noon, *they* had reached the top of the hill.

● In sentences (1) and (2), the pronouns *he* and *they* are subjects.

Pronouns as Objects

A pronoun can be the *object* of a verb:

(1) Graciela kissed *him*.

(2) Sheila moved *it* to the corner.

● In sentence (1), the pronoun *him* tells whom Graciela kissed.

● In sentence (2), the pronoun *it* tells what Sheila moved.

● These objects answer the questions *kissed whom?* and *moved what?*

A pronoun can also be the *object* of a preposition (a word like *to*, *for*, or *at*).*

(3) The umpire stood between *us*.

(4) Near *them*, the children played.

- In sentences (3) and (4), the pronouns *us* and *them* are the objects of the prepositions *between* and *near*.

 Sometimes the prepositions *to* and *for* are understood, usually after words like *give*, *send*, *tell*, and *bring*.

(5) I gave *her* the latest sports magazine.

(6) Carver bought *him* a cowboy hat.

- In sentence (5), the preposition *to* is understood before the pronoun *her*: I gave *to* her . . .

- In sentence (6), the preposition *for* is understood before the pronoun *him*: Carver bought *for* him . . .

Pronouns That Show Possession

A pronoun can show *possession* or ownership.

(1) Bill took *his* report and left.

(2) The climbers spotted *their* gear on the slope.

- In sentences (1) and (2), the pronouns *his* and *their* show that Bill owns *his* report and that the climbers own *their* gear.

 The chart below can help you review all the pronouns discussed in this part.

Pronoun Case Chart					
Singular Pronouns			**Plural Pronouns**		
Subjective	**Objective**	**Possessive**	**Subjective**	**Objective**	**Possessive**
1st person: I	me	my (mine)	we	us	our (ours)
2nd person: you	you	your (yours)	you	you	your (yours)
3rd person: he	him	his	they	them	their (theirs)
she	her	her (hers)			
it	it	its			

* See the list of prepositions on page 283.

PRACTICE 13

In the sentences below, underline the pronouns. Then, over each pronoun, write an *S* if the pronoun is in the subjective case, an *O* if it is in the objective case, and a *P* if it is in the possessive case.

      EXAMPLE: These days, iReporters all over the world help bring the news to *us*.

1. My friend Mahit and I have joined the thousands of iReporters, or citizen reporters, who share stories from their communities.

2. We capture important or strange events as they unfold near us before the professional media even knows they are happening.

3. Using the cameras and Internet connections in our mobile phones, we take pictures or videos, add our words, and send them anywhere.

4. News organizations such as CNN and CBS post our reports in special sections of their websites.

5. They don't screen or edit the submissions before posting them.

6. Mahit became a CNN iReporter when he took photographs of a deadly tornado here in Mississippi and posted them online.

7. Sending in my video of citizens protesting taxes in Washington, D.C., to *YouTube* made me proud.

8. Some people claim that our reports are nothing more than gossip and unverified stories.

9. They say that journalism cannot keep its integrity and ethical standards unless it is practiced only by trained professionals.

10. Others praise us as "citizen journalists," but we are hooked on iReporting and wouldn't dream of leaving home without our phones.

G. Choosing the Correct Case After AND or OR

When nouns or pronouns are joined by *and* or *or*, be careful to use the correct pronoun case after the *and* or the *or*.

(1) **Incorrect:** *Carlos* and *her* have to leave soon.

- In sentence (1), the pronoun *her* should be in the *subjective case* because it is part of the subject of the sentence.

(2) **Revised:** *Carlos* and *she* have to leave soon.

- Change *her* to *she*.

(3) **Incorrect:** The dean congratulated *Charles* and *I*.

- In sentence (3), the pronoun *I* should be in the *objective case* because it is the object of the verb *congratulated*.
- The dean congratulated *whom*? The dean congratulated *me*.

(4) **Revised:** The dean congratulated *Charles* and *me*.

- Change *I* to *me*.

(5) **Incorrect:** Is that letter for *them* or *he*?

- In sentence (5), both objects of the preposition *for* must be in the *objective case*.
  What should *he* be changed to? _____

One simple way to make sure that you have the right pronoun case is to leave out the *and* or the *or*, and the word before it. You probably would not write these sentences:

(6) **Incorrect:** *Her* have to leave soon.

(7) **Incorrect:** The dean congratulated *I*.

(8) **Incorrect:** Is that letter for *he*?

These sentences look and sound strange, and you would know that they have to be corrected.

PRACTICE 14

In the sentences below, circle the correct pronoun in the parentheses. If the pronoun is a *subject*, use the *subjective case*. If the pronoun is the *object* of a verb or a preposition, use the *objective case*.

1. Frieda and (I, me) were born in Bogotá, Colombia.
2. (We, Us) girls are determined to make an A on the next exam.
3. For (we, us), a swim in the ocean on a hot day is one of life's greatest joys.
4. If it were up to Angelo and (he, him), they would spend all their time snow skiing.
5. Our lab instructor expects Dan and (I, me) to hand in our report today.
6. I'm going to the movies tonight with Yolanda and (she, her).
7. The foreman chose Ellen and (they, them).
8. Between you and (I, me), I don't like spinach.
9. Robert and (they, them) have decided to go to Rocky Mountain National Park with Jacinto and (she, her).
10. Either (he, him) or (she, her) must work overtime.

PRACTICE 15 Revise the sentences in which the pronouns are in the wrong case. Write a C in the blank next to each sentence that is correct.

1. Annie and me enjoy going to the gym every day. _____

2. Her and me have tried every class, from kickboxing to spinning. _____

3. Between you and I, I favor hydroboxing, or kickboxing in water. _____

4. Us and our friends also use the pool for water aerobics. _____

5. On cold days, however, they and I prefer step classes to keep warm. _____

6. Stationary cycling sometimes feels boring to Annie and I. _____

7. On the other hand, it is a good time for she and I to daydream. _____

8. Annie favors body pump classes, but I think she likes the instructor. _____

9. I am not sure whether him or weightlifting makes her sweat so much. _____

10. Talking while we work out gives her and me mouth and jaw exercise too. _____

H. Choosing the Correct Case in Comparisons

Pronouns in comparisons usually follow *than* or *as*.

> (1) Ferdinand is taller *than* I.
>
> (2) These guidelines help you as much *as* me.

- In sentence (1), the comparison is completed with a pronoun in the subjective case, *I*.

- In sentence (2), the comparison is completed with a pronoun in the objective case, *me*.

> (1) Ferdinand is taller than I . . . (am tall).
>
> (2) These guidelines help you as much as . . . (they help) . . . me.

- A comparison is really a kind of shorthand that omits repetitious words.

By completing the comparison mentally, you can choose the correct case for the pronoun.

BE CAREFUL: The case of the pronoun you place after *than* or *as* can change the meaning of the sentence.

> (3) Diana likes Tom more than *I* . . . (more than *I* like him).
>
> *or*
>
> (4) Diana likes Tom more than *me* . . . (more than she likes *me*).

- Sentence (3) says that Diana likes Tom more than I like Tom.
- Sentence (4) says that Diana likes Tom more than she likes me.*

PRACTICE 16

Circle the correct pronoun in these comparisons.

1. You study more often than (I, me).
2. The movie scared us more than it did (he, him).
3. Diego eats dinner earlier than (I, me).
4. She ran a better campaign for the local school board than (he, him).
5. Stan cannot memorize vocabulary words faster than (he, him).
6. The ringing of a telephone disturbs her more than it disturbs (they, them).
7. They may think they are sharper than (she, her), but wait until they tangle with her and find out the truth.
8. I hate doing laundry more than (they, them).
9. Sometimes our children are more mature than (we, us).
10. Remembering birthdays seems easier for me than for (he, him).

PRACTICE 17

Revise only those sentences in which the pronoun after the comparison is in the wrong case. Write a *C* in the blank next to each correct sentence.

1. Ben learned to operate this program more slowly than us. _____
2. Jean can sing Haitian folk songs better than me. _____
3. Nobody, but nobody, can whistle louder than she. _____
4. Sarah was surprised that Joyce paid more than her for a ticket. _____
5. In a crisis, you can reach us sooner than you can reach them. _____
6. Before switching jobs, I wanted to know if Rose would be as good a supervisor as him. _____
7. The night shift suits her better than I. _____
8. Antoinette is six feet tall; no one on the loading dock is taller than her. _____

PRACTICE 18

On paper or on a computer, write three sentences using comparisons that are completed with pronouns. Choose each pronoun case carefully.

I. Using Pronouns with -*SELF* and -*SELVES*

Pronouns with -*self* and -*selves* are used in two ways.

> (1) José admired *himself* in the mirror.

- In sentence (1), José did something to *himself*; he admired *himself*. In this sentence, *himself* is called a **reflexive pronoun**.

---

* For more work on comparisons, see Chapter 22, Part C.

(2) The teacher *herself* thought the test was too difficult.

● In sentence (2), *herself* emphasizes the fact that the teacher—much to her surprise—found the test too hard. In this sentence, *herself* is called an **intensive pronoun**.

This chart will help you choose the right reflexive or intensive pronoun.

	Antecedent		Reflexive or Intensive Pronoun
Singular	I	_____	myself
	you	_____	yourself
	he	_____	himself
	she	_____	herself
	it	_____	itself
Plural	we	_____	ourselves
	you	_____	yourselves
	they	_____	themselves

Note that in the plural -*self* is changed to -*selves*.

PRACTICE 19

Write the correct reflexive or intensive pronoun in each sentence. Be careful to match the pronoun with the antecedent.

EXAMPLES: I should have stopped _____*myself*_____.

Roberta _____*herself*_____ made this bracelet.

1. We built all the cabinets _____.

2. He _____ was surprised to discover that he had a green thumb.

3. Did you give _____ a party after you graduated?

4. Rick, look at _____ in the mirror!

5. Don't bother; Don and André will hang the pictures _____.

6. The trainer _____ was amazed at the progress the athletes had made.

7. Tameca found _____ in a difficult situation.

8. These new lamps turn _____ on and off.

9. The oven cleans _____.

10. Because he snores loudly, he wakes _____ up several times each night.

PRACTICE 20

On paper or on a computer, write three sentences, using either a reflexive or an intensive pronoun in each.

Chapter Highlights

- **A pronoun takes the place of or refers to a noun or another pronoun**:

  Louise said that *she* would leave work early.

- **The word that a pronoun refers to is its antecedent**:

  I have chosen *my* seat for the concert.

  (*I* is the antecedent of *my*.)

- **A pronoun that refers to an indefinite pronoun or a collective noun should be singular**:

  Everyone had cleared the papers off *his* or *her* desk.

  The *committee* will give *its* report Friday.

- **A pronoun after *and* or *or* is usually in the subjective or objective case**:

  Dr. Smythe and *she* always work as a team. (*subjective*)

  The bus driver wouldn't give the map to Ms. Tallon or *me*. (*objective*)

- **Pronouns in comparisons usually follow *than* or *as***:

  Daisuke likes Sally more than *I*.
  (*subjective*: . . . more than I like Sally)

  Daisuke likes Sally more than *me*.
  (*objective*: . . . more than he likes me)

- **A pronoun ending in *-self* (singular) or *-selves* (plural) may be used as a reflexive or an intensive pronoun. A reflexive pronoun shows that someone did something to himself or to herself; an intensive pronoun is used for emphasis**:

  On his trip, Martin bought nothing for *himself*.

  The musicians *themselves* were almost late for the street fair.

Proofreading Strategy

One of the most common pronoun errors is using the plural pronouns *they*, *them*, or *their* incorrectly to refer to a singular antecedent. If this is one of your error patterns, **search your draft for *they*, *them*, and *their*** and **highlight or underline** them. If you are using a computer, use the "*Find*" feature to locate these words.

Take a moment to **identify the antecedent** for each of these highlighted words by drawing an arrow from the highlighted word to its antecedent. Do the two words agree?

The **people** who work here usually clean up their messes, but

his or her

somebody let their lunch splatter in the microwave and didn't wipe it up.

(*Somebody* means *one*, so *their* must be changed to *his or her*.)

WRITING AND PROOFREADING ASSIGNMENT

In a small group, discuss the factors that seem absolutely necessary for a successful marriage or long-term relationship. As a group, brainstorm to identify four or five key factors.

Now imagine that a friend with very little experience has asked you for written advice about relationships. Each member of the group should choose just one of the factors and write a letter to this person. Explain in detail why this factor—for example, honesty or mutual respect—is so important to a good relationship.

Read the finished letters to one another. Which letters give the best advice or are the most convincing? Why? Exchange letters with a partner, proofreading for the correct use of pronouns.

CHAPTER REVIEW

Proofread the following essay for pronoun errors. Cross out any incorrect, vague, or repetitious pronouns and make your corrections above the lines. Use nouns to replace vague pronouns. Hint: There are twelve errors.

A New Beginning

(1) Martha Andrews, she was a good student in high school. (2) After graduation, she found a job as a bank teller to save money for college. (3) She liked her job because she knew her regular customers and enjoyed handling his or her business. (4) When she was nineteen, Patrick Kelvin, another teller, and her fell in love and married. (5) By the time she was twenty-two, she was the mother of three children. (6) Martha's plans for college faded.

(7) As her fortieth birthday approached, Martha began thinking about going to college to study accounting; however, she had many fears. (8) Would she remember how to study after so many years? (9) Would the younger students be smarter than her? (10) Would she feel out of place with them? (11) Worst of all, her husband, he worried that Martha would neglect him. (12) He thought that everyone who went to college forgot their family. (13) He also feared that Martha would be more successful than him.

(14) One of Martha's children, who attended college hisself, encouraged her. (15) With his help, Martha got the courage to visit Middleton College. (16) In the admissions office, they told her that older students were valued at Middleton. (17) Older students often enriched

classes because he or she brought a wealth of life experiences with them. (18) Martha also learned that the college had a special program to help their older students adjust to school.

(19) Martha enrolled in college the next fall. (20) To their credit, her and her husband soon realized that they had made the right decision.

EXPLORING ONLINE

<http://grammar.ccc.commnet.edu/grammar/cgi-shl/quiz.pl/pronouns_add2.htm> Interactive quizzes: Choose the correct pronoun or verb.

<http://aliscot.com/bigdog/agrpa_exercise.htm> Take Big Dog's pronoun quiz to see how well you have mastered pronoun use.

 View an integrated eBook and chapter-specific interactive learning tools, including flashcards, quizzes, videos, and extra help tracking and correcting your Personal Error Patterns, in your Basic Writing CourseMate, accessed through <www.cengagebrain.com>.

CHAPTER 22

Adjectives and Adverbs

A. Defining and Writing Adjectives and Adverbs

Adjectives and adverbs are two kinds of descriptive words. An **adjective** describes a noun or a pronoun. It tells *which one*, *what kind*, or *how many*.

(1) The *red* coat belongs to me.

(2) He looks *healthy*.

- In sentence (1), the adjective *red* describes the noun *coat*.

- In sentence (2), the adjective *healthy* describes the pronoun *he*.

An **adverb** describes a verb, an adjective, or another adverb. Adverbs often end in *-ly*. They tell *how, to what extent, why, when*, or *where*.

(3) Laura sings *loudly*.

(4) My biology instructor is *extremely* short.

(5) Lift this box *very* carefully.

- In sentence (3), *loudly* describes the verb *sings*. How does Laura sing? She sings *loudly*.

- In sentence (4), *extremely* describes the adjective *short*. How short is the instructor? *Extremely* short.

- In sentence (5), *very* describes the adverb *carefully*. How carefully should you lift the box? *Very* carefully.

10. Flightless cormorants, which live only in the Galapagos, dive (graceful, gracefully) into the sea, searching for eel and octopus.

11. Tiny Galapagos penguins, the only ones north of the equator, hop (easy, easily) into and out of the ocean.

12. During his voyage of 1831, Charles Darwin visited the Galapagos Islands and gathered evidence to support his (famous, famously) theory of natural selection.

13. Today, the islands are still the (perfect, perfectly) place for scientists to conduct research.

14. Ecotourists, too, are drawn to the (spectacular, spectacularly) scenery and (fabulous, fabulously) animals.

15. If we tread very (gentle, gently) on this fragile ecosystem, we might preserve it for future generations.

EXPLORING ONLINE

Using Google or your favorite search engine, look up "Galapagos, animals, birds" or "Galapagos, Darwin's voyage" to see pictures and learn more about these islands.

PRACTICE 5

Using paper or on a computer, write sentences using the following adjectives and adverbs: *quick/quickly, bad/badly, glad/gladly, real/really, easy/easily.*

EXAMPLES: (*cheerful*) You are cheerful this morning.

(*cheerfully*) You make breakfast cheerfully.

B. A Troublesome Pair: GOOD/WELL

Unlike most adjectives, *good* does not add *-ly* to become an adverb; it changes to *well*.

(1) **Adjective**: Peter is a *good* student.

(2) **Adverb**: He writes *well*.

- In sentence (1), the adjective *good* describes or modifies *student*.

- In sentence (2), the adverb *well* describes or modifies *writes*.

Note, however, that *well* can be used as an adjective to mean *in good health*—for example, *He felt well after his long vacation.*

PRACTICE 6

Write either *good* or *well* in each blank.

EXAMPLE: Charles plays ball very _____well_____.

1. Lorelle is a _____ pilot.

2. She handles a plane _____.

3. How _____ do you understand virtual reality?

4. Pam knows my bad habits very _____.

5. It is a _____ thing we ran into each other.

6. Brian works _____ with other people.

7. How _____ or how badly did you do at the tryouts?

8. Were the cherry tarts _____ or tasteless?

9. Denzel Washington is not just a _____ actor; he's a great one.

10. These plants don't grow very _____ in the sunlight.

11. Carole doesn't look as though she takes _____ care of herself.

12. He asked _____ questions at the meeting, and she answered them _____.

C. Writing Comparatives

> (1) John is *tall*.
>
> (2) John is *taller* than Mike.

●　Sentence (1) describes John with the adjective *tall*, but sentence (2) *compares* John and Mike in terms of how tall they are: John is the *taller* of the two.

Taller **is called the** *comparative* **of** *tall*.

Use the comparative when you want to compare two people or things.

To Form Comparatives
Add *-er* to adjectives and adverbs that have *one syllable*:*

short	shorter
fast	faster
thin	thinner

Place the word *more* before adjectives and adverbs that have *two or more syllables*:

foolish	more foolish
rotten	more rotten
happily	more happily

Use either *more* **or** *-er* **to show a comparison—never both.**

Example: Your voice is *louder* **than mine. (**not *more louder*)

PRACTICE 7

Write the comparative form of each word. Either add *-er* to the word or write *more* before it. Never add both *-er* and *more*!

EXAMPLES:　_____ fresh _*er*_____

_____*more*_____ willing _____

1. _____ fast _____　　　3. _____ thick _____

2. _____ interesting _____　　4. _____ modern _____

---

* For questions about spelling, see Chapter 32, Part D.

5. _____ hopeful _____   7. _____ valuable _____

6. _____ sweet _____   8. _____ cold _____

Here is one important exception to the rule that two-syllable words use *more* to form the comparative:

> To show the comparative of two-syllable adjectives ending in *-y*, change the *y* to *i* and add *-er*.*
>
> cloudy   cloudier
> sunny   sunnier

PRACTICE 8

Write the comparative form of each adjective.

EXAMPLE: happy _____ *happier* _____

1. shiny _____   5. fancy _____
2. friendly _____   6. lucky _____
3. lazy _____   7. lively _____
4. easy _____   8. crazy _____

PRACTICE 9

The following incorrect sentences use both *more* and *-er*. Decide which one is correct and write your revised sentences on the lines provided.

REMEMBER: Write comparatives with either *more* or *-er*—not both!

EXAMPLES: Jan is more younger than her brother.
Jan is younger than her brother.

I feel more comfortabler in this chair than on the couch.
I feel more comfortable in this chair than on the couch.

1. Her new boss is more fussier than her previous one.

   _____

2. The trail was more rockier than we expected.

   _____

3. The people in my new neighborhood are more friendlier than those in my old one.

   _____

4. Magda has a more cheerfuler personality than her sister.

   _____

5. I have never seen a more duller TV program than this one.

   _____

_____

* For questions about spelling, see Chapter 32, Part G.

6. The audience at this theater is more noisier than usual.

_____

7. His jacket is more newer than Rudy's.

_____

8. If today is more warmer than yesterday, we'll picnic on the lawn.

_____

PRACTICE 10   On paper or on a computer, write sentences using the comparative form of the following adjectives or adverbs: *dark, cloudy, fortunate, slowly, wet.*

   EXAMPLE: (*funny*) *This play is funnier than the one we saw last week.*

D. Writing Superlatives

(1) Niko is the *tallest* player on the team.

(2) Juan was voted the *most useful* player.

- In sentence (1), Niko is not just *tall* or *taller than* someone else; he is the *tallest* of all the players on the team.

- In sentence (2), Juan was voted the *most useful* of all the players.

Tallest **and** *most useful* **are called** *superlatives*.

Use the superlative when you wish to compare more than two people or things.

To Form Superlatives
Add *-est* to adjectives and adverbs of *one syllable*:   short   shortest
Place the word *most* before adjectives and adverbs that have *two or more syllables*:   foolish   most foolish
Exception: With two-syllable adjectives ending in *-y*, change the *y* to *i* and add *-est*.*   happy   happiest

Use either *most* **or** *-est* **to compare three or more things—never both.**

Example: Jaden is the most creative web designer. (not *most creativest***)**

_____

* For questions about spelling, see Chapter 32, Part G.

PRACTICE 11 Write the superlative form of each word. Either add -est to the word or write *most* before it; do not do both.

EXAMPLES: _____ tall _est_____

___most_____ ridiculous _____

1. _____ loud _____   6. _____ wild _____
2. _____ colorful _____ 7. _____ practical _____
3. _____ brave _____   8. _____ frightening _____
4. _____ strong _____   9. _____ green _____
5. _____ brilliant _____ 10. _____ hazy _____

PRACTICE 12 The following incorrect sentences use both *most* and -est. Decide which one is correct and write your revised sentences on the lines provided.

REMEMBER: Write superlatives with either *most* or -est—not both!

EXAMPLES: Emmy is the most youngest of my three children.
Emmy is the youngest of my three children.

He is the most skillfulest guitarist in the band.
He is the most skillful guitarist in the band.

1. My nephew is the most thoughtfulest teenager I know.

_____

2. Mercury is the most closest planet to the sun.

_____

3. This baby makes the most oddest gurgling noises we have ever heard.

_____

4. Jackie always makes us laugh, but she is most funniest when she hasn't had enough sleep.

_____

5. When I finally started college, I was the most eagerest student on campus.

_____

6. Ms. Dross raises the most strangest reptiles in her basement.

_____

7. This peach is the most ripest in the basket.

_____

8. He thinks that the most successfulest people are just lucky.

_____

E. Troublesome Comparatives and Superlatives

These comparatives and superlatives are some of the trickiest you will learn:

		Comparative	Superlative
Adjective:	good	better	best
Adverb:	well	better	best
Adjective:	bad	worse	worst
Adverb:	badly	worse	worst

PRACTICE 13

Fill in the correct comparative or superlative form of the word in parentheses.
REMEMBER: *Better* and *worse* compare *two* persons or things. *Best* and *worst* compare three or more persons or things.

EXAMPLES: Is this report _____*better*_____ (good) than my last one?
(Here two reports are compared.)

It was the _____*worst*_____ (bad) movie I have ever seen.
(Of *all* movies, it was the *most* awful.)

1. He likes jogging _____ (well) than running.

2. I like country and western music _____ (well) of all.

3. Bob's motorcycle rides _____ (bad) now than it did last week.

4. That is the _____ (bad) joke Molly has ever told!

5. The volleyball team played _____ (badly) than it did last year.

6. He plays the piano _____ (well) than he plays the guitar.

7. The traffic is _____ (bad) on Fridays than on Mondays.

8. That was the _____ (bad) cold I have had in years.

9. Sales are _____ (good) this year than last.

10. Do you take this person for _____ (good) or for _____ (bad)?

F. Demonstrative Adjectives: THIS/THAT and THESE/THOSE

This, that, these, and *those* are called **demonstrative adjectives** because they point out, or demonstrate, which noun is meant.

(1) I don't trust *that* wobbly front wheel.

(2) *Those* toys are not as safe as their makers claim.

- In sentence (1), *that* points to a particular wheel, the wobbly front one.

- In sentence (2), *those* points to a particular group of toys.

Demonstrative adjectives are the only adjectives that change to show singular and plural:

Singular	Plural
this book	these books
that book	those books

This and *that* are used before singular nouns; *these* and *those* are used before plural nouns.

PRACTICE 14

In each sentence, circle the correct form of the demonstrative adjective in parentheses.

1. (This, These) corn flakes taste like cardboard.
2. Mr. Lathorpe is sure (this, these) address is correct.
3. You can find (that, those) maps in the reference room.
4. Can you catch (that, those) waiter's eye?
5. I can't imagine what (that, those) gadgets are for.
6. We prefer (this, these) tennis court to (that, those) one.
7. The learning center is in (that, those) gray building.
8. (These, This) biography tells the story of Charles Curtis, the first Native American elected to the Senate.

Chapter Highlights

- **Most adverbs are formed by adding -*ly* to an adjective:**

  quick/quickly   bright/brightly   *but* good/well

- **Comparative adjectives and adverbs compare two persons or things:**

  I think that Don is *happier* than his brother.

  Laura can balance a checkbook *more quickly* than I can.

- **Superlative adjectives and adverbs compare more than two persons or things:**

  Last night, Ingrid had the *worst* headache of her life.

  That was the *most carefully* prepared speech I have ever heard.

- **The adjectives *good* and *bad* and the adverbs *well* and *badly* require special care in the comparative and the superlative:**

  good/better/best
  bad/worse/worst

  well/better/best
  badly/worse/worst

- **Demonstrative adjectives can be singular or plural:**

  this/that (chair)
  these/those (chairs)

Proofreading Strategy

To help you proofread for *adjective* and *adverb* errors, use two highlighters to code the text. Read slowly, and **mark every adjective purple and every adverb gray** (or colors of your choice), like these sentences below from one student's paper.

Next check every purple and gray word, one by one. **Ask yourself what word each one describes.** For example, *What word do gold and purple describe?* (*Gold* and *purple* describe *jersey*, a noun. Thus, the adjectives *gold* and *purple* are correct.) *What does the word proudly describe?* (*Proudly* describes *wears*, a verb. Thus, the adverb *proudly* is correct.)

My son wears his gold and purple jersey proudly. He longs to be real tall, like his
                                                                                really
favorite players. He tells me he will have the most amazingest jump shot in the NBA.
                                                 most amazing

WRITING AND PROOFREADING ASSIGNMENT

Sports figures and entertainers can be excellent role models. Sometimes, though, they teach the wrong lessons. For example, an athlete or entertainer might take drugs, have affairs, or get in trouble with the law; another might set a bad example through lifestyle or even dress.

Assume that you are concerned that your child or young sibling is being negatively influenced by one of these figures. Write a "fan letter" to this person, explaining the bad influence he or she is having on young people—in particular, on your child or sibling. Convince him or her that being in the spotlight is a serious responsibility and that a positive change in behavior could help young fans.

Brainstorm, freewrite, or cluster to generate ideas and examples to support your concern. After you revise your letter, take time to proofread: color code your adjectives and adverbs. Then check the word each one refers to and make sure your choices are correct.

CHAPTER REVIEW

Proofread these paragraphs for adjective and adverb errors. Cross out the errors and correct them above the lines.

A.   (1) The Hubble Space Telescope is the world's famousest telescope and one of the

most important in history. (2) Launched into space in 1990, it orbits regular around the

Earth and takes incredibly photographs. (3) Named for astronomer Dr. Edwin Hubble, it

carries real sensitive equipment that captures more better and sharp images than Earth-

based telescopes do. (4) This extreme detailed pictures of planets, galaxies, nebulas, and

black holes have helped scientists solve age-old riddles, such as the age of the universe.

(5) Hubble has helped find new galaxies and the most old planet known—3 billion years.

(6) Many people log on to the Hubble website every day just to gaze at beautiful close-ups

The Hubble Telescope
orbiting in space

of Mars or brilliantly gas towers rising from a nebula. (7) For them, viewing the universe through Hubble's eyes is inspirational, even spiritually. (8) In 2013, NASA plans to let the Hubble telescope burn up in Earth's atmosphere. (9) Some say that its demise won't be the baddest thing that could happen because plans to launch an even more big telescope are already under way.

EXPLORING ONLINE

<http://hubblesite.org/> Go to the Hubble website, click on Gallery, and take notes as you look at the images. Why do you think so many people log on to gaze? Why do some call the pictures "spiritual"?

B. (1) One of the real inspirational stories of recent years is the story of Lance Armstrong. (2) In 1993, Armstrong became the World Cycling champion. (3) In 1999, he won the 2,287-mile Tour de France, the world's most greatest bike race. (4) Between those two events, however, he won something that was even more importanter.

(5) In 1996, Lance Armstrong was diagnosed with testicular cancer. (6) The cancer spread to his brain, abdomen, and lungs. (7) He was given only a 40 percent chance of surviving and even worser odds of ever returning to cycling. (8) According to his doctors,

however, he approached his cancer with the same skills he used for competitive sports: discipline, persistence, sacrifice. (9) Armstrong courageous went through brain surgery and incredibly painful chemotherapy, but he also continued training. (10) Two years later, he became only the second American to win the twenty-one-day Tour de France. (11) More stronger than ever, Armstrong finished seven minutes and thirty-seven seconds ahead of his most nearest competitor. (12) Astonishingly enough, he went on to win the Tour de France the following year and an Olympic bronze medal in 2000.

(13) Although some people believe that cancer is the worstest thing that can happen, Armstrong maintains that cancer is the most best thing that ever happened to him. (14) In his book, *It's Not About the Bike*, he writes that without those disease he would not have married or had a child. (15) When you face death, he says, your focus becomes really clear.

EXPLORING ONLINE

<http://a4esl.org/q/f/z/zz60fck.htm> Interactive quiz: Choose the adjective or the adverb.

<http://www.dailygrammar.com/066to070.shtml> Five tests with answers: Choose the correct form: adjective or adverb.

<http://a4esl.org/q/h/vm/compsup2.html> Interactive quiz: Pick the correct comparatives and superlatives.

 View an integrated eBook and chapter-specific interactive learning tools, including flashcards, quizzes, videos, and extra help tracking and correcting your Personal Error Patterns, in your Basic Writing CourseMate, accessed through <www.cengagebrain.com>.

Prepositions

A: Defining and Working with Prepositional Phrases

B: Troublesome Prepositions: IN, ON, and LIKE

C: Prepositions in Common Expressions

A. Defining and Working with Prepositional Phrases

A **preposition** is a word like *at*, *beside*, *from*, *of*, or *with* that shows the *relationship* between other words in a sentence. Prepositions usually show *location*, *direction*, or *time*. Here are a few examples:

Prepositions of location	above, against, around, behind, beside, between, beyond, in, under
Prepositions of direction	across, down, through, to, toward, up
Prepositions of time	after, before, during, until

Because there are so many prepositions in English, these words can be confusing, especially to nonnative speakers. Here is a partial list of common prepositions.*

Common Prepositions			
about	beneath	inside	through
above	beside	into	throughout
across	between	like	to
after	beyond	near	toward
against	by	of	under
along	despite	off	underneath
among	down	on	until
around	during	onto	up
at	except	out	upon
before	for	outside	with
behind	from	over	within
below	in	past	without

---

* For more work on prepositions, see Chapter 7, Part C.

A preposition is usually followed by a noun or pronoun. The noun or pronoun is called the **object** of the preposition. Together, the preposition and its object are called a **prepositional phrase**.

Here are some prepositional phrases:

Prepositional Phrase	=	Preposition	+	Object
after the movie		after		the movie
at Kean College		at		Kean College
beside them		beside		them
between you and me		between		you and me

The preposition shows a relationship between the object of the preposition and some other word in the sentence. Below are some sentences with prepositional phrases:

(1) Ms. Kringell arrived *at noon*.

(2) A man *in a gray suit* bought thirty lottery tickets.

(3) The huge moving van sped through the tunnel.

- In sentence (1), the prepositional phrase *at noon* tells when Ms. Kringell arrived. It describes *arrived*.

- In sentence (2), the prepositional phrase *in a gray suit* describes how the man was dressed. It describes *man*.

- What is the prepositional phrase in sentence (3)? _____

  Which word does it describe? _____

PRACTICE 1   Underline the prepositional phrases in the following sentences.

1. Bill collected some interesting facts about human biology.

2. Human eyesight is sharpest at midday.

3. In extreme cold, shivering produces heat, which can save lives.

4. A pound of body weight equals 3,500 calories.

5. Each of us has a distinguishing odor.

6. Fingernails grow fastest in summer.

7. One of every ten people is left-handed.

8. The human body contains approximately ten pints of blood.

9. Beards grow more rapidly than any other hair on the human body.

10. Most people with an extra rib are men.

PRACTICE 2

In pairs or small groups, look at this photograph. Describe it by writing at least ten sentences using prepositional phrases.

EXAMPLES: She holds *onto a rope.*
The blue sea lies *beneath her.*

B.   Troublesome Prepositions: IN, ON, and LIKE

IN/ON for Time

Use *in* before seasons of the year, before months not followed by specific dates, and before years that do not include specific dates.

(1) *In the summer,* some of us like to lie around in the sun.

(2) No classes will meet *in January.*

(3) Rona was a student at Centerville Business School *in 2004.*

Use *on* before days of the week, before holidays, and before months if a date follows.

> (4) *On Thursday*, the gym was closed for renovations.
>
> (5) The city looked deserted *on Christmas Eve*.
>
> (6) We hope to arrive in Burlington *on October 3*.

IN/ON for Place

In means *inside of*.

> (1) My grandmother slept *in the spare bedroom*.
>
> (2) The exchange student spent the summer *in Sweden*.

On means *on top of* or *at a particular place*.

> (3) The spinach pie *on the table* is for tonight's book discussion group meeting.
>
> (4) Dr. Helfman lives *on Marblehead Road*.

LIKE

Like is a preposition that means *similar to*. Therefore, it is followed by an object (usually a noun or a pronoun).

> (1) *Like you*, I prefer watching films on DVD rather than going to a crowded movie theater.

Do not confuse *like* with *as* or *as if*. *As* and *as if* are subordinating conjunctions.* They are followed by a subject and a verb.

> (2) *As the instructions explain*, insert flap B into slit B before folding the bottom in half.
>
> (3) Robert sometimes acts *as if he has never made a mistake*.

PRACTICE 3

Fill in the correct prepositions in the following sentences. Be especially careful when using *in*, *on*, and *like*.

1. To celebrate America's one hundredth birthday, _____ July 4, 1876, the French decided to give a special statue _____ their "sister country."

---

* For more work on subordinating conjunctions, see Chapter 15.

2. Sculptor Frederic-Auguste Bartholdi sailed _____ America, seeking support _____ the ambitious project.

3. Bartholdi was awed _____ America's vastness as he traveled _____ redwood forests, _____ prairies, and _____ mountains.

4. _____ Egypt he had seen huge monuments _____ the pyramids and the Sphinx, and he wanted to honor liberty _____ a structure as majestic as those.

5. His monument would be so big that visitors would be able to walk _____ it and climb _____ a staircase _____ its top.

6. Funded _____ the French, Bartholdi finally built his statue _____ a woman raising her torch _____ the sky.

7. _____ many delays, a newspaper urged American citizens to help pay for the statue's base; money poured _____ , and the base was erected _____ Bedloe's Island _____ New York Harbor.

8. The Statue of Liberty was not shipped _____ France _____ America _____ 1885, and then it took six months to mount her _____ the foundation.

9. One million people and hundreds of ships gathered _____ the rain and fog to see the statue unveiled _____ October 28, 1886.

10. Today, Lady Liberty still rises 305 feet _____ the harbor, lighting the darkness _____ her torch and symbolizing freedom _____ the globe.

The Statue of Liberty's arm and torch under construction in a Paris studio

AP Images/Agence Papyrus

EXPLORING ONLINE

To learn more, look up "Statue of Liberty" on your favorite search engine. Can you answer these questions? 1. What famous person designed the metal skeleton, or scaffolding, that holds up Lady Liberty? 2. In how many pieces was the Statue of Liberty shipped from France?

C. Prepositions in Common Expressions

Prepositions often are combined with other words to form certain expressions—groups of words, or phrases, in common use. These expressions can sometimes be confusing. Below is a list of some troublesome expressions. If you are in doubt about others, consult a dictionary.

Common Expressions with Prepositions	
Expression	**Example**
acquainted with	He became *acquainted with* his duties.
addicted to	I am *addicted to* chocolate.
agree on (a plan)	They finally *agreed on* a sales strategy.
agree to (another's proposal)	Did she *agree to* their demands?
angry about or at (a thing)	The subway riders are *angry about* (or *at*) the delays.
angry with (a person)	The manager seems *angry with* Jake.
apply for (a position)	You should *apply for* this job.
approve of	Does he *approve of* the proposed budget?
consist of	The plot *consisted of* both murder and intrigue.
contrast with	The red lettering *contrasts* nicely *with* the gray stationery.
convenient for	Is Friday *convenient for* you?
correspond with (write)	My daughter *corresponds with* a pen pal in India.
deal with	How do you *deal with* friends who always want to borrow your notes?
depend on	He *depends on* your advice.
differ from (something)	A diesel engine *differs from* a gasoline engine.
differ with (a person)	On that point, I *differ with* the medical technician.
different from	His account of the accident is *different from* hers.
displeased with	She is *displeased with* all the publicity.
fond of	We are all *fond of* Sam's grandmother.
grateful for (something)	Tia was *grateful for* the two test review sessions.
grateful to (someone)	We are *grateful to* the plumber for repairing the leak on Sunday.

identical with or to	This watch is *identical with (or to)* hers.
interested in	George is *interested in* modern art.
interfere with	Does the party *interfere with* your study plans?
object to	She *objects to* the increase in the state sales tax.
protect against	This vaccine *protects* people *against* the flu.
reason with	Don't *reason with* a hungry pit bull.
reply to	Did the newspaper editor *reply to* your letter?
responsible for	Omar is *responsible for* marketing.
shocked at	We were *shocked at* the damage to the buildings.
similar to	That popular song is *similar to* another one I know.
specialize in	The shop *specializes in* clothing for large men.
succeed in	Gandhi *succeeded in* freeing India from British rule.
take advantage of	Let's *take advantage of* that two-for-one paperback book sale.
worry about	I no longer *worry about* my manager's moods.

PRACTICE 4

Circle the correct expressions in these sentences.

1. Most people need time to adjust to a new environment that (differs with, differs from) what is familiar and comfortable.

2. For example, entering a new college or country requires that a person (deal with, deal in) strange sights, customs, and values.

3. The difficulty of the adjustment period (depends on, depends with) the individual.

4. The process of cultural adjustment (consists in, consists of) four predictable stages.

5. During the enjoyable "honeymoon stage," a person is (interested on, interested in) the new place.

6. He or she settles in and gets (acquainted with, acquainted to) the new surroundings.

7. In the second stage, however, the excitement wears off, and the person might (worry of, worry about) not fitting in.

8. In this "conflict stage," people struggle to understand behaviors and expectations (different from, different with) those in their native country or hometown.

9. In the third, so-called critical stage, some (take advantage on, take advantage of) the opportunity and immerse themselves in the foreign culture.

10. Others feel (displeased with, displeased in) their experience and spend more time with people who share their customs.

11. During the final stage, the recovery stage, those who (deal about, deal with) their experience as an adventure usually begin to feel more at ease.

12. They (succeed on, succeed in) adapting to their new home.

Chapter Highlights

- **Prepositions are words like** *at*, *from*, *in*, **and** *of*. **A prepositional phrase contains a preposition and its object:**

  The tree *beneath my window* has lost its leaves.

- **Be careful of the prepositions** *in*, *on*, **and** *like*:

  I expect to graduate *in* June.
  I expect to graduate *on* June 10.

  The Packards live *in* Tacoma.
  The Packards live *on* Farnsworth Avenue.

  Like my father, I am a Dodgers fan.

- **Prepositions are often combined with other words to form fixed phrases:**

  convenient for, different from, reason with

Proofreading Strategy

If preposition errors are one of your error patterns, try this strategy. Using the feedback you've received from instructors and tutors who know your writing, **record the five prepositions that give you the most trouble** on your Personal Error Patterns Chart.

Carefully scan your writing for each of these five prepositions. If you are using a computer, use the *"Find"* feature to locate these words in your draft. Then **make sure that you have used each of these prepositions correctly.**

In
~~On~~ the United States, citizens celebrate Independence Day ~~in~~ July 4 ~~with~~ parades, picnics, and fireworks. *(on)*

WRITING AND PROOFREADING ASSIGNMENT

A friend or relative of yours has come to spend a holiday week in your city. He or she has never been there before and wants advice on sightseeing. In complete sentences, write directions for one day's sightseeing. Make sure to explain why you think this person would enjoy visiting each particular spot.

Organize your directions according to time order—that is, what to do first, second, and so on. Use transitional expressions like *then*, *after*, and *while* to indicate time order. Try to work in a few of the expressions listed in Part C. Proofread for your five most troublesome prepositions.

CHAPTER REVIEW

Proofread this essay for preposition errors. Cross out the errors and correct them above the lines.

Science Babe: What's in a Name?

(1) Deborah Berebichez grew up at Mexico City in a traditional family. (2) One day she told her parents that she wanted to be a mathematician. (3) They were shocked of this idea and did not approve about their daughter studying math. (4) "Then you will never find a man to marry with you," they declared. (5) Deborah, however, did not worry of being too smart to find a husband. (6) Instead, she searched for colleges with the best math and science programs.

(7) In 2005, Dr. Berebichez became the first Mexican woman to earn a PhD about physics at California's Stanford University. (8) In addition to science, she had always been interested on communication. (9) Knowing that many people are afraid about math and science, she wished they could see these subjects as a fascinating and important part off everyday life. (9) In particular, she dreamed on teaching this view to the next generation of girls.

(10) Now Dr. Berebichez is igniting new interest in science from speaking tours, radio and television appearances, and Web videos of titles like "The Physics of High Heels." (11) Who knew that a 110-pound woman wearing stiletto high heels puts more pressure for the ground than a 6,000-pound elephant? (12) Showing that scientists, as well as science, can be interesting and fun, she goes with the name of Science Babe. (13) Perhaps the Science Babe is telling her parents and others that science and feminine appeal can exist during the same person.

EXPLORING ONLINE

<http://a4esl.org/q/h/vm/prepos01.html> Interactive quiz: Select the right prepositions for each sentence.

<http://a4esl.org/q/j/ck/mc-prepositions.html> Test your preposition intuition with this 52-question quiz.

<http://grammar.ccc.commnet.edu/grammar/quizzes/cross/cross_prep3.htm> Crossword puzzle: Have you mastered prepositions?

 View an integrated eBook and chapter-specific interactive learning tools, including flashcards, quizzes, videos, and extra help tracking and correcting your Personal Error Patterns, in your Basic Writing CourseMate, accessed through <www.cengagebrain.com>.

UNIT 5

Writing Assignments

As you complete each writing assignment, remember to perform these steps:

- Write a clear, complete topic sentence.

- Use freewriting, brainstorming, or clustering to generate ideas for the body of your paragraph, essay, or speech.

- Arrange your best ideas in a plan.

- Revise for support, unity, coherence, and exact language.

- Proofread for grammar, punctuation, and spelling errors.

Writing Assignment 1 *Imagine yourself going global.* Have you ever imagined leaving your familiar culture in the United States to study, work, or volunteer abroad? If you could live for one year anywhere in the world, where would you go and to what task or cause would you devote yourself? Would you want to focus on doing humanitarian work or on developing your knowledge, career, or language skills? Describe your dream destination and the work you would want to do there. Proofread for the correct use of nouns, pronouns, adjectives, adverbs, and prepositions.

Writing Assignment 2 *Explain your job.* Explain what you do—your duties and responsibilities—to someone who knows nothing about your kind of work but is interested in it. In your first sentence, sum up the work you do. Then name the equipment you use and tell how you spend an average working day. Explain the rewards and drawbacks of your job. Finally, proofread for the correct use of nouns, pronouns, adjectives, adverbs, and prepositions.

Writing Assignment 3 *Give an award.* When we think of awards, we generally think of awards for the most home runs or the highest grade average. However, Cal Ripken Jr. of the Baltimore Orioles became famous because he played in a record number of consecutive games. In other words, his award was for *showing up*, for *being there*, for *constancy*. Write a speech for an awards dinner in honor of someone who deserves recognition for this kind of constancy. Perhaps your parents deserve the award, or your spouse, or the law enforcement officer in your neighborhood. Be specific in explaining why this person deserves the award. You might try a humorous approach. Proofread your speech for the correct use of nouns, pronouns, adjectives, adverbs, and prepositions.

Writing Assignment 4 *Discuss your future.* Imagine yourself ten years from now; how will your life be different? Pick one major way in which you expect it will have changed. You may want to choose a difference in your income, your marital status, your idea of success, or anything else that is important to you. Your first sentence should state this expected change. Then explain why this change will be important to you. Proofread for the correct use of nouns, pronouns, adjectives, adverbs, and prepositions.

UNIT 5

Review

Proofreading

Proofread the following essay for the incorrect use of nouns, pronouns, adjectives, adverbs, and prepositions. Cross out errors and correct them above the lines. (You should find twenty-six errors.)

The Last Frontier

(1) When the government of Brazil opened the Amazon rain forest for settlement on the 1970s, they created the last frontier on Earth. (2) Many concerned man and woman everywhere now fear that the move has been a disasters for the land and for the people.

(3) The most large rain forest in the world, the Amazon rain forest has been hit real hard. (4) The government built highways to make it more easy for poor people to get to the land, but the roads also made investors interested to the forest. (5) Lumber companies chopped down millions of tree. (6) Ranchers and settlers theirselves burned the forest to make room for cattle and crops. (7) All this activities have taken their toll: in one area, which is the size of Colorado, three-quarters of the rain forest has already been destroyed. (8) Many kinds of plants and animals have been lost forever.

(9) As the rain forest itself, the Indians who live there are threatened by these wholesale destruction. (10) Ranchers, miners, loggers, and settlers have moved onto Indian lands. (11) Contact with the outside world has changed the Indians' traditional way of life. (12) A few Indian tribe have made economic and political gains; many tribes have totally disappeared, however.

(13) Many of the settler are not doing very good either. (14) People have poured into the region too rapid, and the government is unable to provide the needed services.

Brazilian rain forest being burned for farm-land. Every minute of every day, 150 acres of rain forest are destroyed.

(15) Small villages have become crowded cities, diseases (especially malaria) have spread, and lawlessness is common. (16) Worse of all, the soil beneath the rain forest is not fertile. (17) After a few years, the settlers' land, it is worthless. (18) As the settlers go into debt, businesses take advantage for the situation by buying land quick and exploiting it bad.

(19) Can the situation in the rain forest improve? (20) Although the Brazilian government has been trying to preserve those forest, thousands of fires are still set every year to clear land for cattle grazing, planting, and building. (21) On the more hopeful side, however, scientists have discovered fruits in the rain forest that are extreme high in vitamins and proteins. (22) Those fruits would be much better crops for the rain forest than the corn, rice, and beans that farmers are growing there now. (23) The world watches nervous. (24) Will the Earth's preciousest rain forest survive?

Transforming

Change the subject of this paragraph from singular (*the hybrid*) to plural (*hybrids*), changing every *the car* to *cars*, every *it* to *they*, and so forth. Make all necessary verb and other changes. Write your revisions above the lines.

(1) The hybrid automobile is gaining popularity worldwide, especially in the United States, Europe, and Japan. (2) It is powered by a combination of gasoline and a rechargeable electric battery instead of gasoline alone. (3) Admirers of the hybrid like its excellent gas mileage and the fact that it is less polluting than conventional cars. (4) Although a hybrid car, truck, or SUV will not solve our global warming problem, it will help reduce the emission of gases harmful to our environment. (5) In the future, this vehicle may be supplanted by a car powered by hydrogen fuel cells or other technologies. (6) But for now, it is probably the most environmentally friendly car on the road.

UNIT 5

Writers' Workshop

Tell How Someone Changed Your Life

Strong writing flows clearly from point to point so that a reader can follow easily. In your class or group, read this essay, aloud if possible. As you read, pay special attention to organization.

Stephanie

(1) There are many people who are important to me. However, the most important person is Stephanie. Stephanie is my daughter. She has changed my life completely. She has changed my life in a positive way.

(2) Stephanie is only five years old, but she has taught me the value of education. When I found out that I was pregnant, my life changed in a positive way. Before I got pregnant, I didn't like school. I went to school just to please my mom, but I wasn't learning anything. When I found out that I was pregnant, I changed my mind about education. I wanted to give my baby the best of this world. I knew that without a good education, I wasn't going anywhere, so I decided to get my life together.

(3) Stephanie taught me not to give up. I remember when she was trying to walk, and she fell down. She didn't stop but kept on going until she learned how to walk.

(4) In conclusion, you can learn a lot from babies. I learned not to give up. Stephanie is the most important person in the whole world to me. She has changed me in the past, and she will continue to change me in the future.

Claudia Huezo, student

1. How effective is this essay?

   _____ Clear thesis statement?   _____ Good support?

   _____ Logical organization?   _____ Effective conclusion?

296

2. Claudia Huezo has organized her essay very well: introduction and thesis statement, two supporting paragraphs, conclusion. Is the main idea of each supporting paragraph clear? Does each have a good topic sentence?

3. Is each supporting paragraph developed with enough facts and details? If not, what advice would you give the writer for revising, especially for reworking paragraph (3)?

4. This student has picked a wonderful subject and writes clearly—two excellent qualities. However, did you find any places where short, choppy, or repetitious sentences could be improved?

    If so, point out one or two places where Huezo might cross out or rewrite repetitious language (where she says the same thing twice in the same words). Point out one or two places where she might combine short sentences for variety.*

5. Proofread for grammar and spelling. Do you spot any error patterns this student should watch out for?

Writing and Revising Ideas

1. Tell how someone changed your life.

2. Discuss two reasons why education is (is not) important.

Before you write, plan or outline your paragraph or essay so that it will be clearly organized (see Chapter 3, Part E, and Chapter 4, Part B). As you revise, pay special attention to the order of ideas and to clear, concise writing without needless repetition (see Chapter 4, Part C).

---

* Cross out paragraph 2, sentence 2, and paragraph 4, sentence 2. Combine paragraph 4, sentences 2 and 3. Combine paragraph 2, sentences 4 and 5.

Unit 6

Revising for Consistency and Parallelism

This unit will teach you some easy but effective ways to add style to your writing. In this unit, you will

- Make sure your verbs and pronouns are consistent
- Use a secret weapon of many writers—parallel structure
- Vary the lengths and types of your sentences
- Learn proofreading strategies to find and correct your own errors

Spotlight on Writing

This writer uses balanced words and phrases to describe a popular celebration in her culture. If possible, read the paragraph aloud.

Quinceañeras are coming-of-age ceremonies for Latina girls when they turn fifteen (*quince años*, thus, "quinceañera"). They can be highly <u>elaborate</u> and <u>ritualized</u>. Many start with a mass that is kind of like a wedding without the groom. The girl is traditionally dressed in a pink gown, white being reserved for brides. She is blessed by the priest, who also blesses certain symbolic objects: the quinceañera's first <u>set of heels</u>, her <u>crown</u>, her "<u>last doll</u>." These symbolic objects open the party part of the celebration in which her father changes her shoes from flats to heels, her mother crowns her, she receives a last doll from a *madrina* (godmother), and sometimes, like the bride with her bouquet, she tosses this "last doll" into a crowd of screaming little girls who will some day be quinceañeras, too. Now, as a woman, she dances her first public dance as an adult with her *papi*—traditionally, the dance is a waltz—and then a dance that is more specific to the country of origin: a *meringue* for Dominicans, a *danzón* for Cubans. Throughout this ritual she is accompanied by a "court" of 14 couples, representing her 14 years, as well as her escort, who will be handed the young lady after the men in her family (father, grandfather, brothers, sometimes a dozen uncles!) have danced with her.

Julia Alvarez, excerpted from an interview found at
<http://us.penguingroup.com/static/html/features/alvarez.html>

- Describing the *quinceañera*, this writer employs two techniques you will learn in this unit. First, she uses *one verb tense consistently* all the way through.

- She also uses *balanced pairs or series of words*: *elaborate* and *ritualized* (underlined) are both adjectives. The next underlined words are all nouns: *set* of heels, *crown*, *doll*.

- Can you find any other balanced pairs or series of words?

Writing Ideas

- *A ritual or custom you know well*
- *An aspect of your cultural heritage that you value (or that your parents valued)*

CHAPTER 24

Consistent Tense

Consistent tense means using the same verb tense whenever possible within a sentence or paragraph. As you write and revise, avoid shifting from one tense to another—for example, from present to past—without a good reason for doing so.

(1) **Inconsistent tense:**	We *were* seven miles from shore. Suddenly, the sky *turns* dark.
(2) **Consistent tense:**	We *were* seven miles from shore. Suddenly, the sky *turned* dark.
(3) **Consistent tense:**	We *are* seven miles from shore. Suddenly, the sky *turns* dark.

- The sentences in (1) begin in the past tense with the verb *were* but then shift into the present tense with the verb *turns*. The tenses are inconsistent because both actions are occurring at the same time.

- The sentences in (2) are consistent. Both verbs, *were* and *turned*, are in the past tense.

- The sentences in (3) are also consistent. Both verbs, *are* and *turns*, are in the present tense.

Of course, you should use different verb tenses in a sentence or paragraph if they convey the meaning you want to express.

(4) Two years ago, I *wanted* to be a chef, but now I *am studying* forestry.

- The verbs in sentence (4) accurately show the time relationship: In the past, I *wanted* to be a chef, but now I *am studying* forestry.

As you proofread your papers for tense consistency, ask yourself: Have I unthinkingly moved from one tense to another, from past to present, or from present to past?

PRACTICE 1   Underline the verbs in these sentences. Then correct any tense inconsistencies above the line.

> *got*
> **EXAMPLE:**   As soon as I get out of bed, I did fifty pushups.
> **or**
> *do*
> As soon as I get out of bed, I did fifty pushups.

1. We were walking near the lake when a large moose appears just ahead.

2. When Bill asks the time, the cab driver told him it was after six.

3. The woman on the red bicycle was delivering newspapers while she is enjoying the morning sunshine.

4. Dr. Choi smiled and welcomes the next patient.

5. The Oklahoma prairie stretches for miles, flat and rusty red. Here and there, an oil rig broke the monotony.

6. They were strolling down Main Street when the lights go out.

7. My cousins questioned me for hours about my trip. I describe the flight, my impressions of Paris, and every meal I ate.

8. We started cheering as he approaches the finish line.

9. If Terry takes short naps during the day, she didn't feel tired in the evening.

10. Yesterday, we find the book we need online. We ordered it immediately.

11. Whenever I attempt the tango, I am looking goofy, not sexy.

12. My roommate saves money for three years and then took the trip of a lifetime to Vietnam and Cambodia.

13. An afternoon protein shake can provide an energy boost and kept a person from overeating later in the day.

14. As Cal opens the door, we all broke into song.

Chapter Highlights

- **In general, use the same verb tense within a sentence or a paragraph:**

    She *sings* beautifully, and the audience *listens* intently.

    or

    She *sang* beautifully, and the audience *listened* intently.

- **However, at times different verb tenses are required because of meaning:**

    He *is* not *working* now, but he *spent* sixty hours behind the counter last week.

Proofreading Strategy

To proofread for inconsistent tense (confusing tense changes), go through your draft and **underline or highlight every verb**.

Identify the tense of every verb. Whenever the tense *changes*, is there a good reason for change? Here is an example:

PAST-CORRECT

In 2008, Dawn completed her two-year degree in culinary arts. After graduating,

PAST-CORRECT   PRESENT-WRONG

she got a job as a chef in a Jacksonville restaurant. She decides to open her own

PRESENT-CORRECT

restaurant in 2009 and now owns two popular downtown eateries.

In this example, the past tense works well because the writer is describing past events. The last sentence, however, should shift from past tense (*decided* in 2009) to present tense (now *owns* two restaurants).

WRITING AND PROOFREADING ASSIGNMENT

Suppose that you have been asked for written advice on what makes a successful family. Your adult child, an inexperienced friend, or a sibling has asked you to write down some words of wisdom on what makes a family work. Using your own family as an example, write your suggestions for making family life as nurturing, cooperative, and joyful as possible. You may draw on your family's experience to give examples of pitfalls to avoid or of positive behaviors and attitudes. Revise for consistent tense.

CHAPTER REVIEW

Read each of these paragraphs for consistent tense. Correct any inconsistencies by changing the tense of the verbs. Write your corrections above the lines.

A. (1) It was 1954. (2) Eight-year-old Jack Horner discovered his first dinosaur fossil as he roams the dry hills near Shelby, Montana. (3) His discovery sparks a lifelong passion for dinosaurs and science. (4) Horner struggled with school work and only later learns that he had dyslexia, yet he earns a degree in paleontology, the study of prehistoric life forms. (5) Horner and his team overturned many theories about dinosaurs. (6) For instance, he finds clusters of dinosaur nests and realizes that dinosaur mothers were fierce protectors of their young. (7) He located the largest *Tyrannosaurus Rex* on record. (8) When his team dug up a whole group of *T. rex* skeletons, he concludes that the *T. rex* isn't the dreaded solitary killer of popular imagination but rather a scavenger roaming in packs. (9) Dr. Horner's fame grew. (10) He advises director Steven Spielberg on all three *Jurassic Park* films. (11) In 2009, Horner announces plans to grow a live dinosaur from DNA, a real-life Jurassic Park idea that critics called dangerous and unethical. (12) Today, by visiting schools and hosting a television science show, Horner hoped to inspire other children to question, explore, and love science.

B.   (1) Self-confidence is vital to success both in childhood and in adulthood. (2) With self-confidence, children knew that they are worthwhile and that they have important goals. (3) Parents can teach their children self-confidence in several ways. (4) First, children needed praise. (5) When they drew, for example, parents can tell them how beautiful their drawings are. (6) The praise lets them know they had talents that other people admire. (7) Second, children required exposure to many different experiences. (8) They soon found that they need not be afraid to try new things. (9) They realized that they can succeed as well at chess as they do at basketball. (10) They discovered that a trip to a museum to examine medieval armor is fascinating or that they enjoy taking a class in pottery. (11) Finally, it was very important to treat children individually. (12) Sensitive parents did not compare their children's successes or failures with those of their brothers or sisters, relatives, or friends. (13) Of course, parents should inform children if their behavior or performance in school needs improvement. (14) Parents helped children do better, however, by showing them how much they have accomplished so far and by suggesting how much they can and will accomplish in the future.

C.   (1) Like many ancient Greek myths, the story of Narcissus provided psychological insight and vocabulary still relevant today. (2) Although Narcissus was a mere mortal, this conceited young man believes himself to be as handsome as the gods. (3) Many young women fall in love with him, including a pretty nymph* named Echo. (4) When Narcissus rejected her affections, Echo sinks into heartbreak. (5) She faded into the landscape until the only thing left is the echo of her voice. (6) The youth's outrageous vanity infuriated the goddess Nemesis.** (7) She decides to teach Narcissus a lesson and dooms him to fall

---

* nymph: a minor nature goddess
** Nemesis: goddess of divine vengeance and retribution

Narcissus, 1597–1599, as imagined by the painter Caravaggio. Oil on canvas, 110 × 92 cm.

What would a twenty-first-century Narcissus look like?

Photo credit: Scala/Art Resource, NY.

in love with his own image. (8) As he passed by Echo's pond, he glimpses himself in the water and falls in love with his own reflection. (9) For days, Narcissus lay lovesick on the bank, pining hopelessly for his own eyes, lips, and curls, until he dies. (10) From the ashes of his funeral pyre growns a white flower now known as the narcissus. (11) The story of this arrogant young man also gave modern psychology the term *narcissist*, a person so admiring of himself that he cannot love others.

EXPLORING ONLINE

<http://owl.english.purdue.edu/owl/resource/601/08> Good review of tense consistency.

<http://aliscot.com/bigdog/consist_exercise.htm> Big Dog's self-test on the verbs.

<http://www.towson.edu/ows/exercisetenseconsistency3.htm> Interactive quiz. This one is difficult. Test yourself.

 View an integrated eBook and chapter-specific interactive learning tools, including flashcards, quizzes, videos, and extra help tracking and correcting your Personal Error Patterns, in your Basic Writing CourseMate, accessed through <www.cengagebrain.com>.

CHAPTER 25

Consistent Person

Consistent **person** means using the same person or personal pronoun throughout a sentence or a paragraph. As you write and revise, avoid confusing shifts from one person to another. For example, don't shift from *first person* (*I, we*) or *third person* (*he, she, it, they*) to *second person* (*you*).*

> (1) **Inconsistent person**: College *students* soon see that *you* are on *your* own.
>
> (2) **Consistent person**: College *students* soon see that *they* are on *their* own.
>
> (3) **Consistent person**: In college, *you* soon see that *you* are on *your* own.

- Sentence (1) shifts from the third person plural *students* to the second person *you* and *your*.

- Sentence (2) uses the third person plural consistently. *They* and *their* now clearly refer to *students*.

- Sentence (3) is also consistent, using the second person *you* and *your* throughout.

PRACTICE 1

Correct any inconsistencies of person in these sentences. If necessary, change the verbs to make them agree with any new subjects. Make your corrections above the lines.

EXAMPLE: Each hiker should bring ~~your~~ *his or her* own lunch.

1. Touria treats me like family when I visit her. She always makes you feel at home.

2. I love to go dancing. You can exercise, work off tension, and have fun, all at the same time.

3. If a person has gone to a large high school, you may find a small college a welcome change.

4. When Lee and I drive to work at 6 a.m., you see the city waking up.

5. Every mechanic should make sure they have a good set of tools.

---

* For more work on pronouns, see Chapter 21.

6. People who want to buy cars today are often stopped by high prices. You aren't sure how to get the most for your money.

7. Do each of you have his or her own e-mail address?

8. Many people mistakenly think that your vote doesn't really count.

9. A teacher's attitude affects the performance of their students.

10. It took me three years to decide to enroll in college; in many ways, you really didn't know what you wanted to do when you finished high school.

11. Each person should seek a type of exercise that you enjoy.

12. The students in my CSI class were problem solvers; he loved a challenge.

13. If that is your heart's desire, she should pursue it.

Chapter Highlights

- **Use the same personal pronoun throughout a sentence or a paragraph:**

  When *you* apply for a driver's license, *you* may have to take a written test and a driving test.

  When a *person* applies for a driver's license, *he or she* may have to take a written test and a driving test.

Proofreading Strategy

You, *your*, *they*, and *their* are probably the most misused personal pronouns. If pronoun agreement is one of your error patterns, **color code *you*, *your*, *they*, and *their* in your draft**. If you are using a computer, use the "*Find*" feature to locate these words.

Every time you spot one of these pronouns in your writing, **draw an arrow to its antecedent**. If the **antecedent is plural**, make sure the **pronoun is plural**. If the **antecedent is singular**, make sure the **pronoun is singular**. Here is an example:

they

Job seekers must create an excellent resume if you want a potential employer to

them   *his or her*

call you for an interview. Each candidate must highlight their special strengths.

WRITING AND PROOFREADING ASSIGNMENT

In small groups, write as many endings as you can think of for this sentence: "You can (cannot) tell much about a person by . . ." You might write, "the way he or she dresses," "the way he or she styles his or her hair," or "the place he or she is from." Each group member should write down every sentence.

Then let each group member choose one sentence and write a short paragraph supporting it. Use people in the news or friends as examples to prove your point. When you finish drafting, proofread to make sure you have used the first, second, or third person correctly. When everyone is finished, exchange papers, locate all *you* and *they* pronouns and check each other's work for consistent person.

CHAPTER REVIEW

Correct the inconsistencies of person in these paragraphs. Then make any other necessary changes. Write your corrections above the lines.

A.   (1) When exam time comes, do you become anxious because you aren't sure how to study for tests? (2) They may have done all the work for their courses, but you still don't feel prepared. (3) Fortunately, he can do some things to make taking tests easier. (4) They can look through the textbook and review the material one has underlined. (5) You might read the notes you have taken in class and highlight or underline the main points. (6) A person can think about some questions the professor may ask and then try writing answers. (7) Sometimes, they can find other people from your class and form a study group to compare class notes. (8) The night before a test, they shouldn't drink too much coffee. (9) They should get a good night's sleep so that your mind will be as sharp for the exam as your pencil.

B.   (1) The sport of mountain biking began in northern California in the 1970s. (2) Some experienced cyclists began using his or her old one-speed fat-tire bikes to explore dirt roads and trails. (3) You began by getting car rides up one of the mountains and pedaling their bikes down. (4) Then they began cycling farther up the mountain until he and she were pedaling to the top. (5) Those cyclists eventually started designing bikes to fit our sport. (6) By the end of the 1970s, road bike manufacturers decided you would join the action. (7) By the mid-1980s, mountain biking had become a national craze, and sales of mountain bikes were exceeding sales of road bikes.

(8) Today, mountain bikers pay about $1,000 for bikes that have everything we need for riding on rough trails: front-wheel shock absorbers, twenty-four gears that shift easily, a

lightweight frame, flexible wheels, and even a full-suspension frame. (9) Cyclists ride your bikes everywhere; some of their favorite places are South Dakota's Badlands, Colorado's ski resorts, and Utah's Canyonlands National Park. (10) You compete in mountain bike races all over the world. (11) To top this off, in 1996 some of you competed in the first Olympic mountain bike race, outside Atlanta, Georgia. (12) The course, which had tightly spaced trees and large rocks, included steep climbs and sharp descents with surprise jumps. (13) What were those early "inventors" thinking as he and she watched that first Olympic race?

EXPLORING ONLINE

<http://www.powa.org/editing/six-problem-areas.html?start=5> Review and then complete Activity 4.16: Rewrite the paragraph in consistent first person (*I* or *we*) and then in third person (*he/she* or *they*).

<http://grammar.ccc.commnet.edu/grammar/cgi-shl/quiz.pl/consistency_quiz.htm> Interactive quiz: Test your pronoun IQ.

 View an integrated eBook and chapter-specific interactive learning tools, including flashcards, quizzes, videos, and extra help tracking and correcting your Personal Error Patterns, in your Basic Writing CourseMate, accessed through <www.cengagebrain.com>.

CHAPTER 26

Parallelism

A: Writing Parallel Constructions

B: Using Parallelism for Special Effects

A. Writing Parallel Constructions

This chapter will show you an excellent way to add clarity and smoothness to your writing. Which sentence in each pair sounds better to you?

> (1) Jennie is an artist and flies planes also.
> (2) Jennie is *an artist* and *a pilot*.
>
> (3) He slowed down and came sliding. The winning run was scored.
> (4) He *slowed* down, *slid*, and *scored* the winning run.

- Do sentences (2) and (4) sound smoother and clearer than sentences (1) and (3)?

- Sentences (2) and (4) balance similar words or phrases to show similar ideas.

This technique is called *parallelism* **or** *parallel structure*. **The italicized parts of (2) and (4) are** *parallel*. **When you use** *parallelism*, **you repeat similar parts of speech or phrases to express similar ideas.**

| **Jennie is** | an artist . . . a pilot |
| **He** | slowed . . . slid . . . scored |

- Can you see how *an artist* and *a pilot* are parallel? Both words in the pair are singular nouns.

- Can you see how *slowed, slid,* and *scored* are parallel? All three words in the series are verbs in the past tense.

Now let's look at two more pairs of sentences. Note which sentence in each pair contains parallelism.

(5) The car was big, had beauty, and it cost a lot.

(6) The car was *big, beautiful,* and *expensive.*

(7) They raced across the roof, and the fire escape is where they came down.

(8) They raced *across the roof* and *down the fire escape.*

● In sentence (6), how are *big, beautiful,* and *expensive* parallel words?

_____

● In sentence (8), how are *across the roof* and *down the fire escape* parallel phrases?

_____

Try This Try this parallelism test: Does each word or phrase complete the sentence in the same balanced way, with the same part of speech? If so, it is parallel. Test sentence: *The car was big, beautiful, and a Chevy Tahoe.*

The car was *big*.   YES (adjective)

The car was *beautiful*.   YES (adjective)

The car was *a Chevy Tahoe*.   NO (noun—replace with an adjective)

Certain special constructions require parallel structure:

(9) The room is *both* light *and* cheery.

(10) You *either* love geometry *or* hate it.

(11) Tanya *not only* plays the guitar *but also* sings.

(12) Richard would *rather* fight *than* quit.

● Each of these constructions has two parts:

both . . . and   not only . . . but also

(n)either . . . (n)or   rather . . . than

● The words, phrases, or clauses following each part must be parallel:

light . . . cheery   plays . . . sings

love . . . hate   fight . . . quit

Parallelism is an excellent way to add smoothness and power to your writing. Use it in pairs or in a series of ideas, balancing a noun with a noun, an *-ing* verb with an *-ing* verb, a prepositional phrase with a prepositional phrase, and so on.

PRACTICE 1   Circle the element that is *not* parallel in each list.

EXAMPLE: blue

red

(colored like rust)

purple

1. rowing
   jogging
   runner
   lifting weights

2. my four dogs
   out the door
   across the yard
   under the fence

3. painting the kitchen
   cans of paint
   several brushes
   one roller

4. persistent
   strong-willed
   work
   optimistic

5. opening his mouth to speak
   toward the audience
   smiling with anticipation
   leaning against the table

6. music shops
   clothing stores
   buying a birthday present
   electronics shops

7. dressed for the office
   laptop computer
   leather briefcase
   cellular phone

8. We shop for fruits at the market.
   We buy enough food to last a week.
   We are baking a cake tonight.
   We cook healthy meals often.

PRACTICE 2

Rewrite each sentence, using parallelism to accent the similar ideas.

EXAMPLE: Do you believe that gratitude and feeling happy are related?

Rewrite: *Do you believe that gratitude and happiness are related?*

1. Many people believe that they will be happy once they have money, they are famous, married to a spouse, or working at a good job.

   Rewrite: _____

   _____

2. Psychologist Martin Seligman found that gratitude is a key ingredient of happiness, and the "gratitude visit" was his invention.

   Rewrite: _____

   _____

3. First, you think of a person who was truly helpful to you, and then a "gratitude letter" is written by you to that person.

   Rewrite: _____

   _____

4. In this letter, explain sincerely and with specifics why you are grateful.

   Rewrite: _____

   _____

5. Then visit this person and reading your letter aloud.

   Rewrite: _____

   _____

6. According to Seligman, the ritual is moving, powerful, and there is a lot of emotion.

   Rewrite: _____

   _____

7. Seligman says people feel happier if they focus on the positive aspects of the past rather than being negative.

   Rewrite: _____

   _____

8. Gratitude visits, he believes, increase how intense, length, and frequency of positive memories.

   Rewrite: _____

   _____

9. In addition, they tend to inspire the receivers of thanks to become giving of thanks.

   Rewrite: _____

   _____

10. One gratitude visit leads to another, creating a chain of appreciation and also to make everyone feel more content.

    Rewrite: _____

    _____

PRACTICE 3

Fill in the blanks in each sentence with parallel words or phrases of your own. Be creative. Take care that your sentences make sense and that your parallels are truly parallel.

EXAMPLE: I feel _____ *rested* _____ and _____ *happy* _____.

1. Ethan's favorite colors are _____ and

   _____.

2. The day of the storm, we _____, and they

   _____.

3. Her attitude was strange. She acted as if _____

   and as if _____.

4. I like people who _____ and who

    _____.

5. Some married couples _____, whereas others

    _____.

6. Harold _____, but I just

    _____.

7. To finish this project, work _____ and

    _____.

8. _____ and _____

    relax me.

9. We found _____, _____,

    and _____ on the beach.

10. They might want to _____ or to

    _____.

B. Using Parallelism for Special Effects

By rearranging the order of a parallel series, you can sometimes add a little drama or humor to your sentences. Which of these two sentences is more dramatic?

> (1) Bharati is a wife, a mother, and a black belt in karate.
>
> (2) Bharati is a wife, a black belt in karate, and a mother.

- If you chose sentence (1), you are right. Sentence (1) saves the most surprising item—*a black belt in karate*—for last.

- Sentence (2), on the other hand, does not build suspense but gives away the surprise in the middle.

   You can also use parallelism to set up your readers' expectations and then surprise them with humor.

> (3) Mike Hardware was the kind of private eye who didn't know the meaning of the word *fear*, who could laugh in the face of danger and spit in the eye of death—in short, a moron with suicidal tendencies.

- Clever use of parallelism made this sentence a winner in the Bulwer-Lytton Contest. Every year, contestants make each other laugh by inventing the first sentence of a bad novel.

PRACTICE 4

On paper or on a computer, write five sentences of your own, using parallel structure. In one or two of your sentences, arrange the parallel elements to build toward a dramatic or humorous conclusion. For ideas, look at Practice 3, but create your own sentences.

Chapter Highlights

- **Parallelism balances similar words or phrases to express similar ideas:**

  He left the gym *tired*, *sweaty*, and *satisfied*.

  Tami not only *finished the exam in record time* but also *answered the question for extra credit*.

  To celebrate his success, Alejandro *took in a show*, *went dancing*, and *ate a late dinner*.

Proofreading Strategy

To proofread for parallelism problems, read through your draft and **find pairs, lists, or series of words, phrases, or clauses.**

Circle or highlight the items in each pair, list, or series. **Test for parallelism** by rewriting to see whether each item could complete the sentence. Here is one example:

teamwork

Being successful in this position requires attention to detail, to work on a team, and the ability to prioritize.

TEST: Being successful in this position requires *attention to detail*	YES	(noun)
requires *to work on a team*	NO	(infinitive)
requires *the ability to prioritize*	YES	(noun)

WRITING AND PROOFREADING ASSIGNMENT

Write a one-paragraph newspaper advertisement to rent or sell your house or apartment. Using complete sentences, let the reader know the number of rooms, their size, and their appearance, and explain why someone would be happy there. Emphasize your home's good points, such as "lots of light" or "closet space galore," but don't hide the flaws. If possible, minimize them while still being honest.

You may want to begin with a general description such as "This apartment is a plant lover's dream." Be careful, though: if you describe only the good features or exaggerate, readers may think, "It's too good to be true." Use parallel structure to help your sentences read more smoothly. As you proofread, test for correct parallelism.

CHAPTER REVIEW

This essay contains both correct and faulty parallel constructions. Revise the faulty parallelism. Write your corrections above the lines. You should make eleven corrections.

Chinese Medicine in the United States

(1) When diplomatic relations between the United States and mainland China were restored in 1972, acupuncture was one import that sparked America's imagination and

made people interested. (2) In the United States today, the most popular form of Chinese medicine is acupuncture.

(3) Acupuncture involves the insertion of thin, sterile, made of stainless steel needles at specific points on the body. (4) Chinese medical science believes that the *chi,* or life force, can be redirected by inserting and by the manipulation of these needles. (5) They are inserted to just below the skin and are either removed quickly or leave them in for up to forty minutes. (6) In addition, the acupuncturist can twirl them, heat them, or charging them with a mild electrical current. (7) Acupuncture can reduce pain for those suffering from allergies, arthritis, backache, or with a toothache. (8) It also has helped in cases of chronic substance abuse, anxiety, and for depressed people.

(9) Chinese medicine has grown in popularity and become important in America. (10) Thirty-five schools in the United States teach Chinese acupuncture. (11) Forty-four states have passed laws that regulate or for licensing the practice of acupuncture. (12) Since 1974, the federal government has authorized several studies of acupuncture's effectiveness and how reliable it is. (13) Although research has failed to explain how acupuncture works, it has confirmed that it does work. (14) The studies also suggest that acupuncture should continue to be tested and using it.

EXPLORING ONLINE

<http://aliscot.com/bigdog/parallel_exercise.htm> Take Big Dog's parallelism test.

<http://grammar.ccc.commnet.edu/grammar/cgi-shl/quiz.pl/parallelism_quiz .htm> Interactive quiz: Click on the sentence that uses parallelism correctly.

<http://grammar.ccc.commnet.edu/grammar/quizzes/niu/niu10.htm> Interactive quiz: Which sentence in each group has parallelism errors?

 View an integrated eBook and chapter-specific interactive learning tools, including flashcards, quizzes, videos, and extra help tracking and correcting your Personal Error Patterns, in your Basic Writing CourseMate, accessed through <www.cengagebrain.com>.

UNIT 6

Writing Assignments

As you complete each writing assignment, remember to perform these steps:

- Write a clear, complete topic sentence.
- Use freewriting, brainstorming, or clustering to generate ideas for the body of your paragraph, essay, or speech.
- Arrange your best ideas in a plan.
- Revise for support, unity, coherence, and exact language.
- Proofread for grammar, punctuation, and spelling errors.

Writing Assignment 1 *Pay a gratitude visit.* Experts like Dr. Martin Seligman claim that people who let themselves feel and express gratitude are happier than people who do not. Do your own research. 1. Pick a person who has been kind or helpful to you but whom you have never properly thanked. 2. Write a letter to this person, discussing specifically, in concrete terms, why you feel grateful to him or her. 3. Arrange a visit to the object of your gratitude and—in person—read your letter aloud. 4. Then write a one-paragraph report on how the two of you felt about the experience. Are the experts right? Revise for consistent tense and person; use parallelism to make your sentences read smoothly.

Writing Assignment 2 *Send an e-mail of praise or complaint to a company.* What recent purchase either pleased or disappointed you? Use a search engine to find the website of this product's manufacturer. Locate the Contact Us or Customer Support page of the website, and write an e-mail that explains specifically what you like or dislike about the product. Before you click Send, proofread for the correct use of nouns, pronouns, adjectives, adverbs, and prepositions. Be sure to print a copy or send one to your instructor.

Writing Assignment 3 *Write about a celebration.* Reread Julia Alvarez's paragraph about the quinceañera, page 299 at the beginning of this unit. Notice how the author uses parallelism as she describes the steps in this ceremony and their meaning. Plan and write a paragraph or short essay about a ceremony or celebration from your cultural tradition. Brainstorm for rich details so that your reader can visualize the steps in this ceremony. Select the best details, arrange them, and write for a diverse audience. Take a break before you revise, looking for opportunities to use parallelism to underscore pairs or series of actions or steps. Be sure you use one consistent verb tense, either past or present.

Writing Assignment 4 *Review a restaurant.* You have been asked to review the food, service, and atmosphere at a local restaurant. Your review will appear in a local newspaper and will have an impact on the success or failure of this eating establishment. Tell what you ordered, how it tasted, and why you would or would not recommend this dish. Note the service: was it slow, efficient, courteous, rude, or generally satisfactory? Is the restaurant one in which customers can easily carry on a conversation, or is there too much noise? Is the lighting good or poor? Include as much specific detail as you can. Revise for consistent tense and person.

UNIT 6
Review

Proofreading

A. We have changed this student's composition so that it contains inconsistent tenses and faulty parallelism. Proofread for these errors, and correct them above the lines. (You should find fourteen errors.)

My Thoughts on Failure

(1) What brought me to this college was my dream of becoming a physician's assistant. (2) When I arrive on campus, I already had good study habits. (3) I know that my curriculum required hard work, and some of the subject matter was tedious and difficult to learn. (4) I also knew that biology was one of the hardest subjects. (5) But one day, my first thoughts of failure sneak into my brain when I overhear other students talking about Biology 23. (6) They said the course was so hard that few students last term even pass it. (7) Soon I heard testimonials from students who either fail Bio 23 or withdrew because they were failing. (8) I begin to doubt my own abilities. (9) What if I fail, too? (10) I need the course to achieve my dream.

(11) I realized that I am scaring myself with negative thoughts. (12) Instead, I focused on my goal of becoming a physician's assistant. (13) I pushed all my fears to the back of my mind and registered for Bio 23. (14) Once I enter the class, I study all the material day and night. (15) I took every pop quiz and test and poured my best effort into every assignment. (16) In the end, I pass with a B. (17) This experience increased my self-confidence because I turn my fear into victory by trying.

Jacqueline Dixon, student

B. Proofread the following essay for inconsistent person and faulty parallelism. Correct the errors above the lines. (You should find thirteen errors.)

True Colors

(1) One day in 1992, the life of Californian John Box changed radically for the second time. (2) That day, John drove four hours to buy a new wheelchair that would allow you to play tennis. (3) Years before, a motorcycle accident had left both his legs paralyzed, but John refused to surrender his love of sports. (4) Instead, he turned anger into being determined. (5) Now a weekend wheelchair athlete, John wanted a better, lighter chair, and one that was faster. (6) When he arrived at the wheelchair manufacturer, however, the salespeople ignored him as if his disability made him invisible.

(7) Back home, furious and feeling frustration, John and his brother Mike decided to design one's own sports wheelchair. (8) The result inspired them to start a company

John Box, wheelchair
athlete and founder of
Colours Wheelchair

and name her Colours. (9) Colours Wheelchair sells high-performance chairs with edgy names like Hammer, Avenger, Swoosh, and one is called Boing. (10) John Box, the company's president, hires other "wheelers," and he or she often contribute new product ideas. (11) The company also sponsors seventy-five wheelchair athletes. (12) In fact, Aaron Fotheringham, a wheelchair skateboarder, became the first human to perform a somersault flip in a wheelchair when he was just fourteen years old.

(13) Today John Box and his brother not only want to expand his or her successful company but also in educating the public about disability. (14) "A person doesn't lose their personality by becoming disabled," declares John. (15) The disabled, he says, can be funny, brilliance, pregnant, competing, sexy, or none of the above, just like everyone else.

EXPLORING ONLINE

Visit the Colours Wheelchair website and examine the photos, video, and presentation of disabled people. What is the message this website is sending? Do these images of the disabled differ from other images you have seen?

UNIT 6

Writers' Workshop

Shift Your Audience and Purpose

Playing with the idea of audience and purpose can produce some interesting writing—such as writing to your car to persuade it to keep running until finals are over. Likewise, writing as if you are someone else can be a learning experience.

In your class or group, read this unusual essay, aloud if possible.

A Fly's-Eye View of My Apartment

(1) Hey, are you guys ready? Today is Armageddon!* When you enter this door, remember, you're not getting out alive. She's a pretty tough lady. Oh, and don't forget to eat all you can. The kids are always dropping crumbs. You can make it through the night if you stay on the ceilings. Whatever you do, stay out of the peach room that is always humid. Once the door is shut, you're trapped. Try not to be noticed on the cabinets in the room where the smells come from. There is nothing interesting in the room with the big screen, but the room with the large bed can be rather stimulating if you stay on the walls.

(2) She won't get tired of us until about 6 p.m.; that is usually around dinnertime. She switches around, using different swatters, so you never really know what to look for. When you hear the gospel music, start looking out. She gets an enormous amount of energy from this music, and her swats are accurate, which means they're deadly. It kills me how she becomes so baffled about how we get in since she has screens on the windows. Little does she know that it's every time she opens the front door.

(3) Well, I think she's ready to leave for work. I hear the lock. To a good life, fellows. See you in heaven—and remember to give her hell!

Tanya Peck, student

---

* Armageddon: a final battle between forces of good and evil.

1. How effective is Tanya Peck's essay?

   _____ Interesting subject?   _____ Good supporting details?

   _____ Logical organization?   _____ Effective conclusion?

2. This writer cleverly plays with the notions of speaker, audience, and purpose. Who is Peck pretending to be as she writes? Whom is she addressing and for what purpose?

3. The writer/speaker refers to the "pretty tough lady" of the house. Who is that lady? How do you know?

4. Peck divides her essay into two main paragraphs and a brief conclusion. Because of her unusual subject, the paragraphs do not have topic sentences. However, does each paragraph have a clear main idea? What is the main idea of paragraph (1)? Of paragraph (2)?

5. Underline any details or sentences that you especially liked—for example, in paragraph (2), the clever idea that the fly realizes that gospel music (for some mysterious reason) energizes the woman with the swatter. Can you identify the rooms described in paragraph (1)?

6. The essay concludes by playing with the terms *heaven* and *hell*. Do you find this effective—or offensive? Are these words connected to *Armageddon* in the introduction? How?

7. Proofread for any grammar or spelling errors.

Writing and Revising Ideas

1. Write a _____'s-eye view (dog, cat, flea, canary, goldfish, ant, roach) of your home.

2. Describe an important moment in history as if you were there.

Before you write, read about audience and purpose in Chapter 1, Part B. Prewrite and plan to get an engaging subject. As you revise, pay special attention to keeping a consistent point of view; really try to imagine what that person (or other creature) would say in those circumstances.

Mastering Mechanics

Even the best ideas may lose their impact if the writer doesn't know how to capitalize and punctuate correctly. In this unit, you will

- Learn when—and when not—to capitalize
- Recognize when—and when not—to use commas
- Find out how to use apostrophes
- Learn how to quote the words of others in your writing
- Learn proofreading strategies to find and correct your own errors

Spotlight on Writing

In this humorous paragraph on a serious subject, the writer correctly uses capital letters, commas, apostrophes, and quotation marks. As you will learn in this unit, knowing these rules will add clarity to your writing and improve your grades. Read this paragraph aloud.

My daughter, Olivia, who just turned three, has an imaginary friend whose name is Charlie Ravioli. Olivia is growing up in Manhattan, and so Charlie Ravioli has a lot of local traits: he lives in an apartment "on Madison and Lexington," he dines on grilled chicken, fruit, and water, and having reached the age of seven and a half, he feels, or is thought, "old." But the most peculiarly local thing about Olivia's imaginary playmate is this: he is always too busy to play with her. She holds her toy cell phone up to her ear, and we hear her talk into it. "Ravioli? It's Olivia . . . It's Olivia. Come and play? OK. Call me. Bye." Then she snaps it shut and shakes her head. "I always get his machine," she says. Or she will say, "I spoke to Ravioli today." "Did you have fun?" my wife and I ask. "No. He was busy working. On a television" (leaving it up in the air if he repairs electronic devices or has his own talk show).

Adam Gopnik, "Bumping Into Mr. Ravioli," *The New Yorker*

- This writer describes his daughter's imaginary playmate as someone too busy to play! Why do you think Olivia has invented a playmate like Ravioli? Where did she learn about cell conversations, phone machines, and busyness?

- Does this paragraph point out a modern problem? If so, is it a big-city problem or a problem that exists in many places? What is the solution?

Writing Ideas

- *Taking time to play*
- *A time when "child's play" taught you something important*

CHAPTER 27

Capitalization

Here are the basic rules of capitalization:

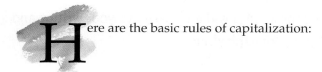

1. | nationality, race, language, religion | *Capitalize* → | American, African American, French, Latino, Protestant, Jewish, Catholic, Muslim, Buddhist, and so forth |

- This group is *always capitalized*.

2. | names of persons, countries, states, cities, places, streets, bodies of water, and so forth |

Capitalize → Bill Morse, New Zealand, Texas, Denver, Golden Gate Bridge, Jones Street, Pacific Ocean, and so forth

but → a person, a country, a large state, a city, a bridge, an ocean, and so forth

- If you name a specific person, state, city, street, or body of water, *capitalize;* if you don't, use small letters.

3. | buildings, organizations, institutions |

Capitalize → Art Institute of Chicago, Apollo Theater, National Council of La Raza, Johnson City Library, Smithson University, and so forth

but → a museum, a famous theater, an activist group, a library, an old school, and so forth

- If you name a specific building, group, or institution, *capitalize;* if you don't, use small letters.

4. historic events, periods, documents

Capitalize → the Spanish-American War, the Renaissance, the Constitution, and so forth

but → a terrible war, a new charter, and so forth

- If you name a specific historical event, period, or document, *capitalize;* if you don't, use small letters.

5. months, days, holidays

Capitalize → June, Monday, the Fourth of July, and so forth

but → summer, fall, winter, spring

- *Always capitalize* months, days, and holidays; use small letters for the seasons.

6. professional and civil titles

Capitalize → Dr. Smith, Professor Greenstein, Judge Alvarez, and so forth

but → the doctor, the professor, the judge, and so forth

- If you name the doctor, judge, and so forth, *capitalize;* if you don't, use small letters.

7. family names

Capitalize → Uncle Xavier, Grandmother Stein, Cousin Emma, Mother, Grandfather, and so forth

but → an uncle, the grandmother, our cousin, my mother, and so for

- If you name a relative or use *Mother, Father, Grandmother,* or *Grandfather* as a name, *capitalize;* however, if one of these words is preceded by the word *a, an,* or *the,* a possessive pronoun, or an adjective, use a small letter.

8. brand names

Capitalize → Greaso hair oil, Quick drafting ink, and so forth

- *Capitalize* the brand name but not the type of product.

9. geographic locations

Capitalize → the East, the Northwest, the South, and so forth

but → east on the boulevard

● If you mean a geographic location, *capitalize;* if you mean a direction, use small letters.

10. academic subjects

Capitalize → Mathematics 51, Sociology 11, English Literature 210, and so forth

but → a tough mathematics course, an A in sociology, a course in English literature, and so forth

● If you use the course number, *capitalize;* if you don't, use small letters. Remember to capitalize languages and countries, however.

11. Titles of books, poems, plays, films

Capitalize → *Pride and Prejudice,* "Ode to a Bat," *Fences, Women on the Edge of a Nervous Breakdown,* and so forth

● *Capitalize* the first letter of words in titles except for *a, an,* and *the;* prepositions; and coordinating conjunctions. However, always capitalize the first letter of the *first* and *last* words of the title.

PRACTICE 1

Capitalize where necessary.

EXAMPLE: Dr. richard carmona went from high school dropout to Surgeon General
of the united states.

1. Richard carmona grew up in a poor puerto rican family in harlem, new york.

2. He started skipping classes in middle school and dropped out of dewitt clinton high school at age seventeen.

3. Carmona worked at dull, low-paying jobs until a conversation with a young man on leave from the u.s. army changed his life.

4. This soldier inspired him to join the military in 1967, and Carmona soon found himself working as a medic in vietnam.

5. He joined the green berets, earning two purple hearts for his brave service.

Dr. Richard Carmona speaks with children about health and wellness.

6. Carmona returned to america determined to become a doctor, so he enrolled at bronx community college.

7. He says that he owes his career to that college and to several of its professors— including michael steuerman and richard kor, who inspired him to succeed.

8. Carmona went on to earn degrees in biology and chemistry; he attended medical school at the university of california, graduating first in his class in three years instead of four.

9. Even after becoming a trauma surgeon and professor at the university of arizona, he continued to use his military training and knowledge of special operations.

10. This crime-fighting doctor joined the SWAT team for the pima county sheriff's department in 1986.

11. Carmona made headlines in 1992 when he dangled out of a helicopter to rescue a person stranded on the side of a cliff, an event that inspired a television movie.

12. In 1999, he stopped at a traffic accident in tucson, arizona; saw a hostage taker holding a woman at gunpoint; and shot the suspect.

13. Less than a year after the terrorist attacks of september 11, 2001, president george w. bush selected dr. carmona for the country's top medical post, noting his knowledge of law enforcement, bioterrorism, and emergency preparedness.

14. The second latino to be named to the u.s. post, surgeon general Carmona thanked the president in both spanish and english.

15. Senator john mccain said in the u.s. congress that carmona is "the embodiment of the american dream."

Chapter Highlights

- **Capitalize nationalities, languages, races, and religions:**

  Asian, French, Caucasian, Baptist

- **Capitalize specific countries, states, cities, organizations, and buildings:**

  Belgium, Utah, Akron, United Nations, the White House

- **Capitalize months, days, and holidays, but not seasons:**

  November, Friday, Labor Day, summer

- **Capitalize professional titles only when a person is named:**

  Mayor Gomez, the mayor, Superintendent Alicia Morgan

- **Capitalize brand names, but not the type of product:**

  Dawn dishwashing detergent

- **Capitalize geographic locations, but not directions:**

  the West, west of the city

- **Capitalize academic subjects only when they are followed by a course number:**

  History 583, psychology

- **Capitalize titles of books, poems, plays, and films:**

  The House on Mango Street, "The Raven," *Rent, The Perfect Storm*

Proofreading Strategy

Incorrect use of capital and lowercase letters can confuse your readers. If capitalization is one of your error patterns, try this:

1. Proofread your entire draft once, **searching for any proper nouns** (names of specific people, places, and things). Circle or color code every proper noun and capitalized word.

2. Now check to **make sure that you have correctly capitalized** each one. This student coded his proper nouns yellow:

   Community College

   In August, I will begin attending Northern Virginia community college, where I will

   math,

   take classes in Math, English, and psychology.

"Community college" is part of the college's name and must be capitalized whereas "math" is not a *specific* math course, so it needs no capital.

WRITING AND PROOFREADING ASSIGNMENT

Is your vacation usually a disaster or a success? Describe a particularly memorable vacation—either bad or good—in which you learned something about how to plan or enjoy a vacation.

In your first sentence, tell what you learned. Explain what went right and what went wrong. Be sure to name the places you visited and the sights you saw. You will probably want to arrange events in time order. Proofread for correct capitalization.

CHAPTER REVIEW

Proofread the following essay for errors in capitalization; correct the errors above the lines.

The Strange Career of Deborah Sampson

(1) Few Soldiers have had a stranger army career than Deborah Sampson. (2) Sampson disguised herself as a man so that she could fight in the revolutionary war. (3) Born on december 17, 1760, she spent her early years in a Town near plymouth, massachusetts. (4) Her Father left his large family, however, and went to sea when Sampson was seven years old. (5) After living with a Cousin and then with the widow of a Minister, sampson became a servant in a wealthy family.

(6) Household tasks and hard outdoor work built up her physical strength. (7) She was taller than the average Man and more muscular than the average Woman. (8) Therefore, she was able to disguise herself successfully. (9) Sampson enlisted in the continental army on may 20, 1782, under the name of robert shurtleff.

(10) Sampson fought in several Battles and was wounded at least twice. (11) One story says that she took a bullet out of her own leg with a penknife to avoid seeing a Doctor. (12) However, after the surrender of the british, Sampson's regiment was sent to philadelphia, where she was hospitalized with a high fever and lost consciousness. (13) At the Hospital, dr. Barnabas Binney made the discovery that ended Sampson's army life. (14) She was honorably discharged by general henry knox at west point on october 28, 1783.

(15) Officially female again, Sampson returned to Massachusetts and eventually married a Farmer named benjamin gannett. (16) The story of Sampson's adventures spread; in 1797, a book titled *the female review* was published about her. (17) When Sampson decided to earn money by telling her own story, she became the first american woman to be paid as a Public Speaker. (18) She gave her first talk at the federal street theatre in boston in march 1802 and

toured until september. (19) Her health was poor, however, and she could not continue her appearances.

(20) In 1804, paul revere, who was a neighbor of the gannetts, wrote to a member of the united states congress. (21) He asked for a pension for this Soldier who had never been paid and was still suffering from her war wounds. (22) Congress granted deborah sampson gannett a pension of four dollars a month.

(23) Deborah Sampson died in sharon, Massachusetts, in april 1827. (24) Her story inspired the People of her own time and continues to inspire People today. (25) Two plays have been written about her: *she was there* and *portrait of deborah.* (26) On veterans day in 1989, a life-size bronze statue was dedicated in front of the sharon public library to honor her.

EXPLORING ONLINE

<http://grammar.ccc.commnet.edu/grammar/cgi-shl/par_numberless_quiz.pl/caps_quiz.htm> Interactive quiz: Capitalize as needed.

<http://a4esl.org/q/j/ck/ed-caps.html> Proofread for "caps" errors and correct them; then electronically check your work.

 View an integrated eBook and chapter-specific interactive learning tools, including flashcards, quizzes, videos, and extra help tracking and correcting your Personal Error Patterns, in your Basic Writing CourseMate, accessed through <www.cengagebrain.com>.

Commas

The comma is a pause. It gives your reader a chance to stop for a moment to think about where your sentence has been and where it is going, and to prepare to read on.

Although this chapter covers basic uses of the comma, always keep this generalization in mind: If there is no reason for a comma, leave it out!

A. Commas After Items in a Series

(1) I like apples, oranges, and pears.

● What three things do I like? _____, _____, and _____

Use commas to separate three or more items in a series.

(2) We will walk through the park, take in a film, and visit a friend.

● What three things will we do? _____, _____, and _____

(3) She loves to explore new cultures sample different foods and learn foreign languages.

- In sentence (3), what are the items in the series? _____, _____, and _____
- Punctuate sentence (3).

However, if you want to join three or more items with *and* or *or* between the items, do not use commas.

(4) She plays tennis *and* golf *and* softball.

- Note that commas are not used in sentence (4).

PRACTICE 1

Punctuate these sentences correctly.

1. I can't find my shoes my socks or my hat!
2. Sylvia Eric and James have just completed a course in welding.
3. Over lunch, they discussed new accounts marketing strategy and motherhood.
4. Frank is in Florida Bob is in Brazil and I am in the bathtub.
5. On Sunday, we repaired the porch cleaned the basement and shingled the roof.
6. The exhibit will include photographs diaries and love letters.
7. Spinning kickboxing and tai chi have become very popular recently.
8. Paula hung her coat on the hook Oscar draped his jacket over her coat and Ruby threw her scarf on top of the pile.

PRACTICE 2

On paper or on a computer, write three sentences, each containing three or more items in a series. Punctuate them correctly.

B. Commas After Introductory Phrases

(1) By the end of the season, our local basketball team will have won thirty games straight.

- *By the end of the season* introduces the sentence.

An introductory phrase is usually followed by a comma.

(2) On Thursday we left for Hawaii.

However, a very short introductory phrase, like the one in sentence (2), need not be followed by a comma.

PRACTICE 3   Punctuate these sentences correctly. One sentence is already punctuated correctly.

1. During the rainstorm we huddled in a doorway.
2. Every Saturday at 9 p.m. she carries her telescope to the roof.
3. After their last trip Fred and Nita decided on separate vacations.
4. The first woman was appointed to the U.S. Supreme Court in 1981.
5. By the light of the moon we could make out a dim figure.
6. During the coffee break George reviewed his psychology homework.
7. In the deep end of the pool he found three silver dollars.
8. In almost no time they had changed the tire.

PRACTICE 4   On paper or on a computer, write three sentences using introductory phrases. Punctuate them correctly.

C. Commas for Direct Address

(1) Bob, you must leave now.

(2) You must, Bob, leave now.

(3) You must leave now, Bob.

(4) Don't be surprised, old buddy, if I pay you a visit very soon.

- In sentences (1), (2), and (3), *Bob* is the person spoken to; he is being *addressed directly*.
- In sentence (4), *old buddy* is being *addressed directly*.

The person addressed directly is set off by commas wherever the direct address appears in the sentence.

PRACTICE 5   Circle the person or persons directly addressed, and punctuate the sentences correctly.

1. I am happy to inform you Mr. Forbes that you are the father of twins.
2. We expect to return on Monday Miguel.
3. It appears my friend that you have won two tickets to the opera.
4. Get out of my roast you mangy old dog.
5. Tom it's probably best that you sell the old car at a loss.
6. If I were you Hilda I would wait to make the phone call until we are off the highway.
7. Bruce it's time you learned to operate the lawn mower!
8. I am pleased to announce ladies and gentlemen that Beyoncé is our surprise guest tonight.

PRACTICE 6   On paper or on a computer, write three sentences using direct address. Punctuate them correctly.

D. Commas to Set Off Appositives

(1) The Rialto, a new theater, is on Tenth Street.

● *A new theater* describes *the Rialto*.

(2) An elderly man, my grandfather walks a mile every day.

● What group of words describes *my grandfather*?

_____

(3) They bought a new painting, a rather beautiful landscape.

● What group of words describes *a new painting*?

_____

● *A new theater*, *an elderly man*, and *a rather beautiful landscape* are called *appositives*.

An *appositive* is a group of words that renames a noun or pronoun and gives more information about it. The appositive can appear at the beginning, middle, or end of a sentence. An appositive is usually set off by commas.

PRACTICE 7

Circle the appositive, and punctuate the sentences correctly.

1. That door the one with the X on it leads backstage.

2. A short man he decided not to pick a fight with the basketball player.

3. Hassim my friend from Morocco will be staying with me this week.

4. My nephew wants to go to Mama's Indoor Arcade a very noisy place.

5. George Eliot a nineteenth-century novelist was a woman named Mary Ann Evans.

6. A very close race the election for mayor wasn't decided until 2 a.m.

7. On the Fourth of July my favorite holiday my high school friends get together for an all-day barbecue.

8. Dr. Bawa a specialist in tribal music always travels with a digital recorder.

PRACTICE 8

On paper or on a computer, write three sentences using appositives. Punctuate them correctly.

E. Commas for Parenthetical Expressions

(1) By the way, I think that you're beautiful.

(2) I think, by the way, that you're beautiful.

(3) I think that you're beautiful, by the way.

- *By the way* modifies or qualifies the entire sentence or idea.
- It is called a **parenthetical expression** because it is a side remark, something that could be placed in parentheses: *(By the way) I think that you're beautiful.*

Set off a parenthetical expression with commas.

Here is a partial list of parenthetical expressions:

as a matter of fact	in fact
believe me	it seems to me
I am sure	it would seem
I assure you	to tell the truth

PRACTICE 9

Circle the parenthetical expressions in the sentences below; then punctuate them correctly.

1. Believe me Felice has studied hard for her law boards.

2. He possesses it would seem an uncanny gift for gab.

3. It was I assure you an accident.

4. To tell the truth I just put a treadmill in your basement.

5. Her supervisor by the way will never admit when he is wrong.

6. A well-prepared résumé as a matter of fact can help you get a job.

7. He is in fact a black belt.

8. To begin with you need a new carburetor.

PRACTICE 10

On paper or on a computer, write three sentences using parenthetical expressions. Punctuate them correctly.

F. Commas for Dates

(1) I arrived on Monday, March 20, 2009, and found that I was in the wrong city.

- Note that commas separate the different parts of the date.
- Note that a comma follows the last item in the date.

(2) She saw him on Wednesday and spoke with him.

However, a one-word date (*Wednesday* or *1995*) preceded by a preposition (*in*, *on*, *near*, or *from*, for example) is not followed by a comma unless there is some other reason for it.

PRACTICE 11

Punctuate these sentences correctly. Not every sentence requires additional punctuation.

1. By Tuesday October 6 he had outlined the whole history text.

2. Thursday May 8 is Hereford's birthday.

3. She was born on January 9, 1985 in a small Iowa town.

4. He was born on July 4 1976 the two-hundredth anniversary of the Declaration of Independence.

5. Do you think we will have finished the yearbook by May?

6. On January 24 1848 James Wilson Marshall found gold in California.

7. My aunt is staying with us from Tuesday to Friday.

8. Charles Schulz's final *Peanuts* comic strip was scheduled for February 13 2000 the day on which he died.

PRACTICE 12

On paper or on a computer, write three sentences using dates. Punctuate them correctly.

G. Commas for Addresses

(1) We just moved from 11 Landow Street, Wilton, Connecticut, to 73 James Street, Charleston, West Virginia.

- Commas separate different parts of an address.
- A comma generally follows the last item in an address, usually a state (*Connecticut*).

(2) Julio Perez *from* Queens was made district sales manager.

However, a one-word address preceded by a preposition (*in*, *on*, *at*, *near*, or *from*, for example) is not followed by a comma unless there is another reason for it.

(3) Julio Perez, Queens, was made district sales manager.

Commas are required to set off a one-word address if the preposition before the address is omitted.

PRACTICE 13   Punctuate these sentences correctly. Not every sentence requires additional punctuation.

1. Their address is 6 Great Ormond Street London England.

2. Seattle Washington faces the Cascade Mountains.

3. That package must be sent to 30 West Overland Street Phoenix Arizona.

4. We parked on Marble Lane, across the street from the bowling alley.

5. His father now lives in Waco Texas but his sister has never left Vermont.

6. How far is Kansas City Kansas from Independence Missouri?

7. The old watch factory at 43 North Oak Street Scranton Pennsylvania has been condemned by the building inspector.

8. Foster's Stationery 483 Heebers Street Plainview sells special calligraphy pens.

PRACTICE 14   On paper or on a computer, write three sentences using addresses. Punctuate them correctly.

H. Commas for Coordination and Subordination

Chapters 14 and 15 cover the use of commas with coordinating and subordinating conjunctions. This is a brief review.

> (1) Enzio enjoys most kinds of music, but heavy metal gives him a headache.
>
> (2) Although the weather bureau had predicted rain, the day turned out bright and sunny.
>
> (3) The day turned out bright and sunny although the weather bureau had predicted rain.

- In sentence (1), a comma precedes the coordinating conjunction *but*, which joins two independent ideas.

- In sentence (2), a comma follows the dependent idea because it precedes the independent idea.

- Sentence (3) does not require a comma because the independent idea precedes the subordinate one.

Use a comma before coordinating conjunctions—*and*, **but**, **for**, *nor*, *or*, **so**, **or** *yet*—**that join two independent ideas.**

Use a comma after a dependent idea only when the dependent idea precedes the independent one; do not use a comma if the dependent idea follows the independent one.

PRACTICE 15   Punctuate correctly. Not every sentence requires additional punctuation.

EXAMPLE: Because scrapped cars create millions of tons of ~~waste~~ *waste,* recycling auto parts has become an important issue.

1. Today new cars are made from many old parts and manufacturers are trying to increase the use of recycled materials from old cars.

2. Scrapped cars can be easily recycled because they consist mostly of metals.

3. After these cars are crushed magnets draw the metals out of them.

4. However, the big problem in recycling cars is the plastic they contain.

5. Although plastic can be recycled the average car contains about twenty kinds of plastic.

6. Separating the different types of plastic takes much time but companies are developing ways to speed up the process.

7. Still, new cars need to be made differently before recycling can truly succeed.

8. Their parts should detach easily and they should be made of plastics and metals that can be separated from each other.

9. As we develop more markets for the recycled auto parts new cars may soon be 90 percent recycled and recyclable.

10. Our environment will benefit and brand-new cars will really be more than fifty years old!

PRACTICE 16

On paper or on a computer, write three sentences, one with a coordinating conjunction, one beginning with a subordinating conjunction, and one with the subordinating conjunction in the middle.

Chapter Highlights

- **Commas separate three or more items in a series:**

    He bought a ball, a bat, and a fielder's glove.

- **Unless it is very short, an introductory phrase is followed by a comma:**

    By the end of January, I'll be in Australia.

- **Commas set off the name of a person directly addressed:**

    I think, Aunt Betty, that your latest novel is a winner.

- **Commas set off appositives:**

    My boss, the last person in line in the cafeteria, often forgets to eat lunch.

- **Commas set off parenthetical expressions:**

    My wife, by the way, went to school with your sister.

- **Commas separate the parts of a date or an address, except for a one-word date or an address preceded by a preposition:**

    On April 1, 1997, I was in a terrible blizzard.

    I live at 48 Trent Street, Randolph, Michigan.

    She works in Tucson as a plumber.

- **A comma precedes a coordinating conjunction that joins two independent ideas:**

    We had planned to see a movie together, but we couldn't agree on one.

- **If a dependent idea precedes the independent idea, it is followed by a comma; if the independent idea comes first, it is not followed by a comma:**

    Although I still have work to do, my project will be ready on time.

    My project will be ready on time although I still have work to do.

Proofreading Strategy

Armed with the eight comma rules, you can proofread effectively for comma errors.

1. **Circle or highlight every comma** in your draft. This forces your eye and brain to focus on every one of them. If you are writing on a computer, use the *"Find"* feature to locate all your commas.

2. For every comma, ask, ***Does one of the eight comma rules explain why this comma needs to be here?*** If you aren't sure, review the rules in the Chapter Highlights. Make any needed corrections, like this:

C (introductory phrase)
Unlike our planet's Northern Hemisphere, the Southern Hemisphere contains fewer
X (*not* a series—remove comma)   C (series)   C (series)
land masses, and more water. The South Pacific Ocean, South Atlantic Ocean,
C (series)
Indian Ocean, and various seas cover almost 81 percent of Earth's southern half.

WRITING AND PROOFREADING ASSIGNMENT

We live in what is often called "the age of invention" because of rapid advances in technology, communication, and medicine. Which modern invention has meant the most to *you*, and why? You might choose something as common as disposable diapers or as sophisticated as a special feature of a personal computer.

In the first sentence, name the invention. Then, as specifically as possible, discuss why it means so much to you. Proofread for the correct use of commas.

CHAPTER REVIEW

Proofread the following essay for comma errors—either missing commas or commas used incorrectly. Correct the errors above the lines.

Treetop Crusader

(1) On December 18, 1999 Julia Butterfly Hill's feet touched ground for the first time in more than two years. (2) She had just climbed down from the top, of an ancient tree in Humboldt County California. (3) The tree a thousand-year-old redwood was named Luna. (4) Hill had climbed 180 feet up Luna on December 10 1997 for what she thought would be a protest of two or three weeks.

(5) Hill's action was intended to stop Pacific Lumber a division of the Maxxam Corporation from cutting down old-growth forests. (6) The area immediately next to Luna, had already been stripped of trees. (7) Because nothing was left to hold the soil to the mountain a huge part of the hill had slid into the town of Stafford California. (8) Many homes had been destroyed.

Julia Hill and Luna

(9) During her long tree-sit, Hill endured incredible hardships. (10) For more than two years she lived on a tiny platform eighteen stories off the ground. (11) El Niño storms almost destroyed her with ferocious winds razor-sharp rain and numbing cold. (12) She once wore two pairs of socks booties two pairs of thermal ski pants two thermal shirts a wool sweater two windbreakers a raincoat gloves and two hats to keep from freezing to death during a storm. (13) In addition to enduring nature's hardships Hill withstood life-threatening torment from the logging company. (14) She was harassed by helicopters various sieges and interference with receiving supplies. (15) Of course she also endured loneliness sometimes paralyzing fear and always deep sorrow for the destruction around her.

(16) Only twenty-three at the beginning of her tree-sit Hill eventually became both world famous and very knowledgeable about ancient forests. (17) At the top of Luna she used a cell phone a pager and a daily engagement planner. (18) She was trying to protect the tree itself to slow down all logging in the area and to raise public awareness. (19) She gave hundreds of phone interviews and answered hundreds of letters.

(20) Hill's action was dramatically successful; Luna was eventually saved from destruction.

(21) When Hill returned to normal life she wrote a book *The Legacy of Luna: The Story of a Tree, a Woman, and the Struggle to Save the Redwoods.* (22) Julia Butterfly Hill is now a writer a poet and an activist. (23) She is a frequent speaker at environmental conferences she helped found the Circle of Life Foundation for preserving all life and she has received many honors and awards.

EXPLORING ONLINE

<http://owl.english.purdue.edu/exercises/3/5/15> Quiz with answers: Where have all the commas gone?

<http://chompchomp.com/hotpotatoes/commas01.htm> Interactive quiz: Put those comma rules into action at Grammar Bytes.

<http://grammar.ccc.commnet.edu/grammar/quizzes/comma_quiz.htm> Interactive quiz: Add commas to this essay about basektball and score!

 View an integrated eBook and chapter-specific interactive learning tools, including flashcards, quizzes, videos, and extra help tracking and correcting your Personal Error Patterns, in your Basic Writing CourseMate, accessed through <www.cengagebrain.com>.

CHAPTER 29

Apostrophes

A: Using the Apostrophe for Contractions

B: Defining the Possessive

C: Using the Apostrophe to Show Possession
(in Words That Do Not Already End in -*S*)

D: Using the Apostrophe to Show Possession
(in Words That Already End in -*S*)

The apostrophe is a small mark that greatly confuses many people. The apostrophe has just two important uses, and this chapter will help you master both of them.

A. Using the Apostrophe for Contractions

A contraction combines two words into one.

> do + not = don't
> should + not = shouldn't
> I + have = I've

● Note that an apostrophe (') replaces the omitted letters: "o" in *don't* and *shouldn't* and "ha" in *I've*.

BE CAREFUL: *Won't* is an odd contraction because it cannot be broken into parts in the same way the previous contractions can.

> will + not = won't

PRACTICE 1   Write these words as contractions.

1. you + are = _____

2. who + is = _____

3. was + not = _____

4. she + will = _____

5. can + not = _____

6. it + is = _____

7. I + am = _____

8. will + not = _____

342

PRACTICE 2

Proofread this paragraph for incorrect or missing apostrophes in contractions. Write each corrected contraction above the lines.

(1) For musicians and music lovers in the twenty-first century, its a small world. (2) Musicians whove grown up in Asia, for instance, arent influenced by just Asian musical traditions anymore. (3) Hip-hops a perfect example of musical globalization. (4) Its inspired musicians all over the world, something the first American rappers couldnt have foreseen. (5) Many hip-hop artists in other countries, however, dont like the focus on money and sex in much of American hip-hop. (6) For example, Korean performers like Jo PD and Drunken Tiger are proud that theyre forces for social justice. (7) Many hip-hop stars from New Zealand are Pacific Islanders or Maori tribal people whove developed world-class skills and fight oppression with music. (8) In Senegal, politically active rappers claim that theyre responsible for toppling an oppressive government in the 2000 elections. (9) Sister Fa, whose Senegalese, raps in French about arranged marriages and the oppression of women. (10) Some South American hip-hop stars also have embraced a lifestyle thats committed to social justice. (11) Brazilian rappers, for example, do'nt perform just music; they also perform community service, teaching youth wholl spread the word about social change, music, and art.

Members of this all-girl Iraqi rap group, Rap Curse, learned their moves from satellite TV.

EXPLORING ONLINE

<http://www.hiphoparchive.org/> Explore The Hiphop Archive. Click "Hiphop University" to tap the research on this musical form. Topics on the site include global hip-hop, conferences and events, information on particular artists and groups, and women in hip-hop (watch the trailer for *Say My Name*, a film on this subject).

PRACTICE 3

On paper or a computer, write five sentences using an apostrophe in a contraction.

B. Defining the Possessive

A *possessive* is a word that shows that someone or something owns someone or something else.

PRACTICE 4

In the following phrases, who owns what?

> **EXAMPLE:** "The hat of the man" means _the man owns the hat_____.

1. "The camera of Judson" means _____.
2. "The hopes of the people" means _____.
3. "The thought of the woman" means _____.
4. "The trophies of the home team" means _____.
5. "The ideas of that man" means _____.

C. Using the Apostrophe to Show Possession (in Words That Do Not Already End in -S)

| (1) the hands of my father | becomes | (2) my father's hands |

- In phrase (1), who owns what? _____
- In phrase (1), what is the *owner word*? _____
- How does the owner word show possession in phrase (2)?

  _____

- Note that what is owned, *hands*, follows the owner word.

  If the *owner word* (possessive) does not end in -*s*, add an apostrophe and an -*s* to show possession.

PRACTICE 5

Change these phrases into possessives with an apostrophe and an -*s*. (Note that the owner words do not already end in -*s*.)

> **EXAMPLE:** the friend of my cousin =   _my cousin's friend_

1. the eyes of Rona = _____
2. the voice of the coach = _____

3. the ark of Noah = _____

4. the technology of tomorrow = _____

5. the jacket of someone = _____

PRACTICE 6   Add an apostrophe and an -s to show possession in these phrases.

1. Judy briefcase

2. the diver tanks

3. Murphy Law

4. Bill decision

5. somebody umbrella

6. everyone dreams

7. your daughter sandwich

8. last month prices

9. that woman talent

10. anyone guess

PRACTICE 7   On paper or on a computer, write five sentences. In each, use an apostrophe and an -s to show ownership. Use owner words that do not already end in -s.

D. Using the Apostrophe to Show Possession (in Words That Already End in -S)

> (1) the uniforms of the pilots   becomes   (2) the pilots' uniforms

● In phrase (1), who owns what? _____

● In phrase (1), what is the *owner word*? _____

● How does the owner word show possession in phrase (2)?

_____

● Note that what is owned, *uniforms*, follows the owner word.

If the *owner word* (possessive) ends in -s, add an apostrophe after the -s to show possession.*

PRACTICE 8   Change these phrases into possessives with an apostrophe. (Note that the owner words already end in -s.)

EXAMPLE: the helmets of the players =   *the players' helmets*

1. the farm of my grandparents = _____

2. the kindness of my neighbors = _____

3. the dunk shots of the basketball players = _____

4. the music of The Stone Temple Pilots = _____

5. the trainer of the horses = _____

_____

* Some writers add an 's to one-syllable proper names that end in -s: *James's book*.

PRACTICE 9

Add either *'s* or *'* to show possession in these phrases. BE CAREFUL: Some of the owner words end in *-s* and some do not.

1. the models faces
2. the model face
3. the captain safety record
4. the children room
5. the runner time
6. Boris radio

7. my niece two iPods
8. your parents anniversary
9. the men locker room
10. three students exams
11. several contestants answers
12. Mr. Jones band

PRACTICE 10

Rewrite each of the following pairs of short sentences as *one* sentence by using a possessive.

EXAMPLE: Joan has a friend. The friend comes from Chile.

Joan's friend comes from Chile.

1. Rusty has a motorcycle. The motorcycle needs new brakes.

_____

2. The nurses had evidence. The evidence proved that the doctor was not careless.

_____

3. Ahmad has a salary. The salary barely keeps him in peanut butter.

_____

4. Lee has a job. His job in the Complaint Department keeps him on his toes.

_____

5. José has a bad cold. It makes it hard for him to sleep.

_____

6. Jessie told a joke. The joke did not make us laugh.

_____

7. John Adams had a son. His son was the first president's son to also become president of the United States.

_____

_____

8. My sisters have a daycare center. The daycare center is open seven days a week.

_____

9. The twins have a goal. Their goal is to learn synchronized swimming.

_____

10. Darren has a thank-you note. The thank-you note says it all.

_____

PRACTICE 11

Proofread this paragraph. Above the lines, correct any missing or incorrectly used apostrophes in possessives. BE CAREFUL: some owner words end in -s and some do not.

(1) Apple Computers' founder, Steven Jobs, is one of the industrys greatest innovators—and survivors. (2) Jobs first position, in the 1970s, was designing computer games for Atari. (3) Then he saw a friends' home-built computer. (4) Jobs convinced this friend, Steve Wozniak, to go into business with him. (5) At first, the partners built computers in the Jobs familys garage. (6) Their companys name came from the story of Isaac Newton, who supposedly formulated his great theory of gravity when he watched an apple fall from a tree. (7) The mens' small computers were a huge success. (8) In 1984, they launched the Macintosh, which simplified peoples interactions with their computers by replacing typed commands with clicks. (9) But then, Job's luck changed. (10) After some poor management decisions, he was fired by Apples' board of directors. (11) Despite public failure, he started over. (12) Ironically, his new company was bought by Apple ten years later. (13) As Apple's leader once again, Jobs soon captured consumer's attention with the revolutionary iPod music player and iTunes software. (14) Jobs latest blockbuster products are the iPhone and the iPad. (15) This mans' success flows not just from farsighted ideas but from a willingness to learn failures lessons and begin again.

PRACTICE 12

On paper or on a computer, write six sentences that use an apostrophe to show ownership—three using owner words that do not end in -s and three using owner words that do end in -s.

BE CAREFUL: Apostrophes show possession by nouns. As the following chart indicates, possessive pronouns do not have apostrophes.

Possessive Pronouns	
Singular	**Plural**
my book, mine	our book, ours
your book, yours	your book, yours
his book, his	their book, theirs
her book, hers	
its book, its	

Do not confuse *its* (possessive pronoun) with *it's* (contraction for *it is* or *it has*) or *your* (possessive pronoun) with *you're* (contraction for *you are*).*

---

* See Chapter 33 for work on words that look and sound alike.

REMEMBER: Use apostrophes for contractions and possessive nouns only. Do not use apostrophes for plural nouns (*four marbles*), verbs (*he hopes*), or possessive pronouns (*his, hers, yours, its*).

Chapter Highlights

- **An apostrophe can indicate a contraction:**

  We're glad you could come.

  They *won't* be back until tomorrow.

- **A word that does not end in** -*s* **takes an** *'s* **to show possession:**

  Is that *Barbara's* coat on the sofa?

  I like *Clint Eastwood's* movies.

- **A word that ends in** -*s* **takes just an** *'* **to show possession:**

  That store sells *ladies'* hats with feathers.

  I depend on my *friends'* advice.

Proofreading Strategy

Knowing the two main uses of apostrophes—contractions and possessives—will help you avoid the mistake of sticking apostrophes where they don't belong, for instance, into plural nouns or possessive pronouns like *hers* or *its*.

Go through your draft and **highlight every word that contains an apostrophe**. If you are using a computer, use the *"Find"* feature to locate all apostrophes in your draft.

For every apostrophe, you should be able to answer YES to one of two questions:

Is this apostrophe used to form a contraction?

Is this apostrophe used to indicate possession?

Example: Ronald didn't realize that the children's toy's weren't in the box.

To find **missing apostrophes**, highlight all words ending in -*s*. If the word is a plural, leave it alone. If the word is a possessive noun, add an apostrophe.

Example: When the coachs whistle blew, the swimmers dove into the pool.

WRITING AND PROOFREADING ASSIGNMENT

Assume that you are writing to apply for a position as a teacher's aide. You want to convince the school principal that you would be a good teacher, and you decide to do this by describing a time when you taught a young child—your own child, a younger sibling, or a friend's child—to do something new.

In your topic sentence, briefly state who the child was and what you taught him or her. What made you want to teach this child? Was the experience easier or harder than you expected? How did you feel afterward? Proofread for the correct use of apostrophes.

CHAPTER REVIEW

Proofread this paragraph for apostrophe errors—missing apostrophes and apostrophes used incorrectly. Correct the errors above the lines.

The Magic Fastener

(1) Its hard to remember the world without Velcro. (2) Shoelaces had to be tied; jackets' had to be zipped and did'nt make so much noise when they were loosened. (3) We have a Swiss engineers' curiosity to thank for todays changes. (4) On a hunting trip in 1948, Georges de Mestral became intrigued by the seedpods that clung to his clothing. (5) He knew that they we're hitching rides to new territory by fastening onto him, but he could'nt tell how they were doing it. (6) He examined the seedpods to find that their tiny hooks were catching onto the threads of his jacket. (7) The idea of Velcro was born, but the actual product wasnt developed overnight. (8) It took eight more years' before Georges de Mestrals invention was ready for the market. (9) Today, Velcro is used on clothing, on space suits, and even in artificial hearts. (10) Velcro not only can help keep a skier warm but can also save a persons' life.

EXPLORING ONLINE

<http://grammar.ccc.commnet.edu/GRAMMAR/quizzes/apostrophe_quiz2.htm> Test your expertise with this "Catastrophes of Apostrophic Proportions" Quiz.

<http://grammar.ccc.commnet.edu/grammar/cgi-shl/par_numberless_quiz.pl/plurals_quiz.htm> Review plurals and possessives in this challenging interactive quiz.

 View an integrated eBook and chapter-specific interactive learning tools, including flashcards, quizzes, videos, and extra help tracking and correcting your Personal Error Patterns, in your Basic Writing CourseMate, accessed through <www.cengagebrain.com>.

CHAPTER 30

Direct and Indirect Quotations

A: Defining Direct and Indirect Quotations

B: Punctuating Simple Direct Quotations

C: Punctuating Split Quotations

D: Ending Direct Quotations

A. Defining Direct and Indirect Quotations

> (1) John said that he was going.
>
> (2) John said, "I am going."

● Which sentence gives the *exact words* of the speaker, John?

_____

● Why is sentence (2) called a *direct quotation*?

_____

● Why is sentence (1) called an *indirect quotation*?

_____

● Note that the word *that* introduces the *indirect quotation*.

PRACTICE 1

Write *D* in the blank at the right if the sentence uses a *direct quotation*. Write *I* in the blank at the right if the sentence uses an *indirect quotation*.

1. She said that she was thirsty. _____

2. Rita asked, "Which is my laptop?" _____

3. Ruth insisted that one turkey would feed the whole family. _____

4. The students shouted, "Get out of the building! It's on fire!" _____

5. "This is silly," she said, sighing. _____

6. I suggested that Rod's future was in the catering business. _____

B. Punctuating Simple Direct Quotations

Note the punctuation:

> (1) Rafael whispered, "I'll always love you."

- Put a comma before the direct quotation.
- Put quotation marks around the speaker's exact words.
- Capitalize the first word of the direct quotation.
- Put the period *inside* the end quotation marks.

  Of course, the direct quotation may come first in the sentence:

> (2) "I'll always love you," Rafael whispered.

- List the rules for a direct quotation written like the sentence above:

  _____

  _____

  _____

PRACTICE 2

Rewrite these simple direct quotations, punctuating them correctly.

1. He yelled answer the phone!

   Rewrite: _____

2. The usher called no more seats in front.

   Rewrite: _____

3. My back aches she repeated dejectedly.

   Rewrite: _____

4. Examining the inside cover, Pierre said this book was printed in 1879.

   Rewrite: _____

5. A bug is doing the backstroke in my soup the man said.

   Rewrite: _____

C. Punctuating Split Quotations

Sometimes one sentence of direct quotation is split into two parts:

> (1) "Because it is 2 a.m.," he said, "you had better go."

- *He said* is set off by commas.

- The second part of the quotation—*you had better go*—begins with a small letter because it is part of one directly quoted sentence.

> (2) "Because it is 2 a.m. . . . you had better go."

A direct quotation can also be broken into separate sentences:

> (3) "It is a long ride to San Francisco," he said. "We should leave early."

- Because the second part of the quotation is a separate sentence, it begins with a capital letter.
- Note the period after *said*.

    BE CAREFUL: If you break a direct quotation into separate sentences, be sure that both parts of the quotation are complete sentences.

PRACTICE 3

Rewrite these split direct quotations, punctuating them correctly.

1. Before the guests arrive she said let's relax.

   Rewrite: _____

2. Don't drive so fast he begged I get nervous.

   Rewrite: _____

3. Although Mort is out shellfishing Fran said his hip boots are on the porch.

   Rewrite: _____

4. Being the youngest in the family she said has its advantages.

   Rewrite: _____

5. This catalog is fantastic the clerk said and you can have it for free.

   Rewrite: _____

PRACTICE 4

On paper or on a computer, write three sentences using split quotations.

D. Ending Direct Quotations

A sentence can end in any of three ways:

- with a period (.)
- with a question mark (?)
- with an exclamation point (!)

The period is *always* placed inside the end quotation marks:

> (1) He said, "My car cost five thousand dollars."

The question mark and the exclamation point go before or after the quotation marks—depending on the sense of the sentence.

---

(2) He asked, "Where are you?"

(3) Did he say, "I am thirty-two years old"?

(4) She yelled, "Help!"

- The question mark in sentence (2) is placed before the end quotation marks because the direct quotation is a question.

- The question mark in sentence (3) is placed after the end quotation marks because the direct quotation itself *is not a question*.

Note that sentence (2) can be reversed:

---

(5) "Where are you?" he asked.

- Can you list the rules for the exclamation point used in sentence (4)?

  _____

  _____

Note that sentence (4) can be reversed:

---

(6) "Help!" she yelled.

PRACTICE 5

Rewrite these direct quotations, punctuating them correctly.

1. Marlena asked is that your Humvee.

   Rewrite: _____

2. Did Shenoya make the team he inquired.

   Rewrite: _____

3. Be careful with that mirror she begged the movers.

   Rewrite: _____

4. The truck driver shouted give me a break.

   Rewrite: _____

5. Did she say I wouldn't give my social security number to that telemarketer?

   Rewrite: _____

   _____

Chapter Highlights

- **A direct quotation requires quotation marks:**

  Benjamin Franklin said, "There never was a good war or a bad peace."

- **Both parts of a split quotation require quotation marks:**

  "It isn't fair," she argued, "for us to lose the money for the after-school programs."

- **When a direct quotation is split into separate sentences, begin the second sentence with a capital letter:**

  "It's late," he said. "Let's leave in the morning."

- **Always place the period inside the end quotation marks:**

  He said, "Sometimes I talk too much."

- **A question mark or an exclamation point can be placed before or after the end quotation marks, depending on the meaning of the sentence:**

  She asked, "Where were you when we needed you?"

  Did she say, "Joe looks younger without his beard"?

Proofreading Strategy

If quotation marks give you trouble, use this strategy.

1. **Scan your draft** for sentences in which you give **someone's exact words**.

2. **Check these sentences** for correct use of commas, quotation marks, and capitalization.

3. For every quotation mark before the quoted words start, **make sure that you have provided the end quotation mark.**

   Gwendolyn just texted, "Can you meet me for coffee?"

WRITING AND PROOFREADING ASSIGNMENT

Write a note to someone with whom you have had an argument. Your goal is to get back on friendly terms with this person. In your first sentence, state this goal, asking for his or her open-minded attention. Then tell him or her why you think a misunderstanding occurred and explain how you think conflict might be avoided in the future. Refer to the original argument by using both direct and indirect quotations. When you are finished drafting, proofread for the correct use of quotation marks; be careful with *all* punctuation.

CHAPTER REVIEW

Proofread this essay for direct and indirect quotations. Punctuate the quotations correctly and make any other necessary changes above the lines.

Satchel Paige

(1) Some people say that the great pitcher Leroy Paige was called Satchel because of his big feet. (2) Paige himself said I got the nickname as a boy in Mobile before my feet grew. (3) He earned money by carrying bags, called satchels, at the railroad station. (4) I figured out a way to make more money by carrying several bags at a time on a pole he said. (5) Other boys began shouting at him that he looked like a satchel tree. (6) The name stuck.

(7) Unfortunately, for most of Paige's long pitching career, major league baseball excluded African-American players. (8) However, Satchel Paige pitched impressively in the black leagues and in tours against white teams. (9) In 1934, he won a thirteen-inning, one-to-nothing pitching duel against the white pitcher Dizzy Dean and a team of major league all-stars. (10) My fast ball admitted Dean looks like a change of pace alongside of that little bullet old Satchel shoots up to the plate!

(11) After Jackie Robinson broke the major league color barrier in 1948, Satchel Paige took his windmill windup to the Cleveland Indians. (12) He became the oldest rookie in major league history. (13) Some people said that he was too old, but his record proved them wrong. (14) His plaque in the Baseball Hall of Fame reads he helped pitch the Cleveland Indians to the 1948 pennant.

(15) Satchel Paige pitched off and on until he was sixty years old. (16) When people asked how he stayed young, he gave them his famous rules. (17) Everyone remembers the last one. (18) Don't look back he said. (19) Something might be gaining on you.

EXPLORING ONLINE

<http://www.dailygrammar.com/371to375.shtml> Practice with answers: Place quotation marks and capitalize correctly.

<http://grammar.ccc.commnet.edu/grammar/quizzes/quotes_quiz.htm> Challenging interactive quiz: Think hard and punctuate.

 View an integrated eBook and chapter-specific interactive learning tools, including flashcards, quizzes, videos, and extra help tracking and correcting your Personal Error Patterns, in your Basic Writing CourseMate, accessed through <www.cengagebrain.com>.

CHAPTER 31

Putting Your Proofreading Skills to Work

Proofreading is the important final step in the writing process. After you have planned and written a paragraph or an essay, you must **proofread**, carefully checking each sentence for correct grammar, punctuation, and capitalization. Proofreading means applying everything you have learned in Units 2 through 7. Is every sentence complete? Do all your verbs agree with their subjects? Have you mistakenly written any comma splices or sentence fragments?

This chapter gives you the opportunity to practice proofreading skills in real-world situations. As you proofread the paragraphs and essays that follow, you must look for any—and every—kind of error, just as you would in the real world of college or work. The first five practices tell you what kinds of errors to look for. If you have trouble, go back to the chapters listed and review the material. The final practices, however, give you no clues at all, so you must put your proofreading skills to the real-world test.

- Before you proofread, review your **Personal Error Patterns Chart** that you learned to keep in Chapter 6. Take special care to proofread for the errors you tend to make.

- Use the **proofreading strategies** that work best for you. In this book, you have practiced strategies like reading out loud as you look for errors, reading from the bottom up, and color highlighting. Apply your favorite strategies here!

- Examine the proofreading checklist at the end of this chapter for a quick reminder of what to look for.

- Keep a **dictionary** handy. If you are not sure of the spelling of a word, look it up.

PRACTICE 1

Proofread this paragraph, correcting any errors above the lines. (You should find seventeen individual errors.) To review, see these chapters:

Chapter 11	past participle verb errors
Chapter 16	run-on sentences and comma splices
Chapter 20	errors in forming plural nouns
Chapter 23	preposition errors

(1) Bono is an unusual superstar. (2) Instead of going in shopping spree and polishing his ego, he travels the world, using his fame to empower others. (3) Bono was born Paul Hewson at Ireland. (4) Young friends there nicknamed him *Bonovox,* which means "good voice" in Latin. (5) The *vox* was dropped, *Bono* stuck. (6) Bono became the lead singer of the Irish rock band U2. (7) Using music to send a message of love and peace, U2 has sell more than 100 million album worldwide and has won twenty-two Grammy Awards. (8) Yet perhaps Bono's greatest influence is not the sound of his voice crooning U2 songs under the heads of fans. (9) Rather, it is his work for human beings on need. (10) Bono has use his celebrity to turn the media's attention to Africa, where the lives of millions are being destroy by AIDS and starvation. (11) Frightening numbers of African child are already AIDS orphans, social structures in Africa are breaking down. (12) Bono urges the United States and other nations to relieve the crippling debt of African nations, one of the factor that keeps them unable to afford AIDS drugs and prevention programs. (13) He has work with former President Clinton, Oprah, and others to make the love he sings about become reality. (14) Bono has received many award for this humanitarian work he was even nominate for the Nobel Peace Prize.

PRACTICE 2

Proofread this paragraph, correcting any errors above the lines. (You should find twelve individual errors.) To review, see these chapters:

Chapter 8   sentence fragments
Chapter 10   past tense errors
Chapter 22   adjective and adverb errors
Chapter 26   parallelism

(1) Can exercise make us smarter? (2) Vigorous exercise tones muscles, aids weight loss, and the heart is strengthened. (3) But, according to recent studies, aerobic workouts also increase brainpower. (4) In one experiment, students at the University of Illinois memorized letters. (5) Then picked those letters from a list. (6) Next, the students were divided into three groups. (7) For thirty minutes, some sat quiet, some run on a treadmill, and weight lifting was done by some. (8) After a thirty-minute rest period. (9) The students taked the letter test again. (10) Every time, the group who runned on the treadmill was

more quicker and more accurate than the other two groups. (11) Studies of laboratory mice in Taiwan reinforced these results. (12) The rodents who worked out strenuously on tiny treadmills performed complex mental tasks more effective than mice who raced at their own pace. (13) Examining the animals' brains under a microscope (14) Scientists found positive changes in the brain cells of those who exercised harder. (15) They concluded that the greatly increased blood flow during aerobic exercise carries growth-promoting chemicals to the brain. (16) Hard, aerobic exercise, it seems. (17) Benefits both body *and* mind.

PRACTICE 3

Proofread this paragraph, correcting any errors above the lines. (You should find sixteen individual errors.) To review, see these chapters:

Chapter 8	sentence fragments
Chapter 11	past participle verb errors
Chapter 16	run-ons and comma splices
Chapters 20 and 29	plural and possessive errors

(1) Christiane Amanpour is one of the most respected foreign correspondents in the world, but she calls herself an "accidental journalist." (2) Because she never intended to become one. (3) Her native Iran had no freedom of the press, journalism did not interest her. (4) Christiane attended high school in England. (5) Then the revolution in Iran brought

ABC news anchor Christiane Amanpour on assignment in the Middle East

chaos to her family, her fathers money was froze, the families fund were very tight. (6) Christianes' sister dropped out of journalism college in London, Christiane took her place for the sole reason of saving the tuition money. (7) Soon she was hook on reporting. (8) After graduating from the University of Rhode Island, she applied for a job at a new cable station. (9) Called CNN. (10) She longed to write news story's and go overseas but was mock by her boss, who said she didn't have the right looks and that her name was difficult to pronounce. (11) Amanpour worked hard and hid her frustration with doing routine task. (12) Like bringing people coffee. (13) Every time a new job opened at CNN, she applied for it. (14) Her big break was being send to Germany and the Gulf War. (15) With gunfires and rockets around her, she reported the news with intelligence and heart. (16) Today Amanpour says it is not so bad that some people "always try to knock your dreams." (17) This gives you the chance, she believes, to prove that you are strong enough to keep going.

PRACTICE 4

Proofread this paragraph, correcting any errors above the lines. (You should find twenty individual errors.) To review, see these chapters:

Chapter 8   sentence fragments
Chapter 9   subject/verb agreement errors
Chapter 28   comma errors
Chapter 29   apostrophe errors

(1) Every spring and summer, storm chaser's spreads out across the Midwestern part of the United States known as Tornado Alley. (2) Armed with video cameras maps and radios. (3) These lovers of violent weather follows huge weather systems called supercells, which sometimes produces tornadoes. (4) On a good day, a storm chaser may find a supercell. (5) And get close enough to film the brief, destructive life of a tornado. (6) Some joins the storm-chasing tours offered every summer by universities or private companies. (7) Others learn what they can from Internet websites and sets off on their own to hunt tornadoes. (8) Storm chasing can be very dangerous. (9) A large tornado spins winds between 125 and 175 mph, tearing roofs off houses, ripping limbs from trees, and overturning cars. (10) The greatest danger comes from airborne branches boards shingles and glass hurtling through the air like deadly weapons. (11) Even if a supercell don't spawn tornadoes. (12) It often

produces winds over 50 mph, heavy rain, large hail, and intense lightning. (13) Most storm chasers avoids these risks by racing out of a tornados' path before it gets too close. (14) Despite or perhaps because of these dangers, dramatized in the 1996 movie *Twister*. (15) Storm chasing remains popular. (16) Fans claim that few things in life matches the thrill of discovering a tornado and witnessing the power of nature.

PRACTICE 5

Proofread this paragraph, correcting any errors above the lines. (You should find seventeen individual errors.) To review, see these chapters:

Chapter 21   pronoun agreement errors
Chapter 22   adjective/adverb errors
Chapter 27   capitalization errors
Chapter 28   comma errors

(1) A secret society called SSSSH is gaining agents across the country. (2) To become a secret agent, one must simply perform a well deed for someone else without taking credit for it or letting them know who did it. (3) The group was inspired by a young Ohioan named hal reichle (pronounced "Rike-el"), a graduate of hiram college who had a habit of quiet helping people. (4) After Hal's death in a helicopter crash during the gulf War some friends started paying tribute to the fallen soldier by "pulling Reichles." (5) That is, they would do small or large good deeds, leaving only a card that said, "You are the recipient of an anonymously good deed done in the name of Hal Reichle." (6) The group called themselves SSSSH, or Secret Society of Serendipitous* Service to Hal. (7) After several newspapers wrote about the secret society, schoolchildren and people in other states began to pull Reichles theirselves. (8) If an agent wants to report, they can write about the deed performed—without a signature or return address, of course—to Hal Reichle, P.O. Box 375 Hiram ohio 44234. (9) Alternatively, anyone whom wants to report a good deed anonymously can go to ‹http://thehiramcollege.net/ssssh/deedideas.html›, tell how they Pulled a Reichle, and press Send.

_____

* serendipitous: unexpectedly lucky

PRACTICE 6   Proofread this essay, correcting any errors above the lines.

Crime-Fighting Artist

(1) Jeanne Boylan helps capture Americas most wanted criminals but she's not a police officer or a detective. (2) Instead, she is an artist who draws the faces of suspects, base only on her gentle conversations with victim's and eyewitnesses. (3) Her portraits are so lifelike and accurate that she has became famous for drawing nearly mirror images of criminals. (4) Boylan's sketches often leads to arrests. (5) She drew the Unabomber in his sunglasses and hooded sweatshirt, the kidnapper-murderer of twelve-year-old Polly Klaas, and Timothy McVeigh. (6) Who bombed Oklahoma City's Federal Building. (7) Once doubtful, FBI officials and police now calls on Boylan in almost every major case.

(8) Boylan decided to become a sketch artist after she was the victim of a crime. (9) The police, following standard procedure, asked her to describe her attackers' faces, then they showed her mug shots of criminals. (10) Hoping that she would recognize the suspects. (11) Boylan sensed that this was the wrong approach to help her mind remember. (12) She realized that the authorities leading questions—questions like "Did he have a moustache? Was he wearing glasses?"—clutter the victim's mind with details that might not be true. (13) At the same time, the subconscious mind is trying to avoid reliving a traumatic experience consequently, memories easily become distorted.

Boylan's sketch (left) and a photo of the Unabomber, Ted Kaczynski.

(14) Boylan developed a very different method for coaxing images from victims and witnesses. (15) What distinguishes her method from others, she says, is that she *listens.* (16) She takes her time. (17) Talking for hours with eyewitnesses to a crime. (18) She does not pressure them to recall the color of a suspect's eyes or what the shape of his nose was. (19) Instead, she asks about their daily lives and interests, here and there asking nonleading questions about what they saw. (20) Slowly and careful, she guides people back through their confusion and pain to the moment when they seen or felt something that they desperately want to forget. (21) She asks them to describe whole shapes, forms, and textures rather than specific details. (22) She sometimes gives children Play-Doh to mold as they explore their memories. (23) As they draw closer and closer to the terrifying images seared into their minds. (24) Boylan watches, listens, and sketching. (25) "What people see," she says, "is evidence as fragile and valuable as a fingerprint. (26) And it should be protected with as much care."

(27) Many have claimed that Boylan's method, a blend of art, psychology, and human compassion, are a unique gift. (28) Boylan insists, though, that her technique can be teach. (29) "What I do is no great mystery she says. (30) "It has to do with allowing someone the freedom and the time to remember. (31) It has to do with the human heart."

PRACTICE 7   Proofread this essay, correcting any errors above the lines.

Quiet, Please!

(1) America is loud. (2) Horns and sirens pierces the air, car stereos pump out loud music. (3) Cell phones rings, shriek, or trumpets the owner's noise of choice. (4) Construction equipments, lawnmowers, and leaf blowers buzz and roar into the public space. (5) Restaurant and movie theater manager's often seem to link loudness with cultural cool. (6) Sounds are measured in decibels, with the human voice measuring about 60 decibels, the sound of a car is about 80 decibels. (7) According to the U.S. Environmental Protection Agency, 70 decibels is a safe daily average. (8) Here is the problem: the level of noise that many of us hear every day are far above this.

(9) The sound of a food blender, for example, measures 90 decibels. (10) Many leaf blower exceed 115 decibels, and a jet taking off is 120 decibels of ear-blasting noise. (11) All of this racket are taking it's toll on us both physically and in psychological ways. (12) According to the American Speech-Language-Hearing Association (ASHA), 28 million U.S. citizens have already suffer hearing loss from too much noise. (13) Furthermore, loud noise raises blood pressure increases stress hormone levels, and deprives us of sleep. (14) Noise pollution also increases aggression and even violence and harms concentration and learning. (15) One study found that New york children in classrooms that faced the train tracks were almost a year behind children taught in more quieter parts of the same school.

(16) In Europe, noise pollution has been taken serious for years. (17) Now in the United States, organizations like the Noise Pollution Clearinghouse is trying to raise awareness of the problem and promote solutions. (18) Members of this organization believes that just as smoke or toxins in the air are not acceptable, neither is loud noise. (19) They are working for new laws. (20) To enforce our right to peace and quiet.

Chapter Highlights

- **Know your error patterns.** In Chapter 6, you learned how to recognize and chart your **personal error patterns**, the mistakes—such as sentence fragments or apostrophes—you tend to make. Before you proofread, review your **Personal Error Patterns Chart.** Take special care to proofread for these errors.

- **Use the proofreading strategies that work best *for you.*** In Chapter 6 and throughout the book, you have learned and practiced many strategies—like reading out loud, reading from the bottom up, and color highlighting. Put your favorite strategies to work.

- **Know where to find help.** If you need more help with recognizing and eliminating your personal error patterns, consult print sources, such as this book; online resources, such as the *Grassroots* student website, the Exploring Online websites listed at the end of each chapter, or the OWLs you have bookmarked; and expert people, such as the staff of your college's writing lab.

Proofreading Strategy

A proofreading checklist like the one below can be an effective tool for remembering what to look for when reviewing your writing.

Proofreading Checklist

- ☐ Check for sentence fragments, comma splices, and run-on sentences.
- ☐ Check for verb errors: present tense -*s* endings (verb agreement), past tense -*ed* endings, past participles, and tense consistency.
- ☐ Check for incorrect singular and plural nouns, incorrect pronouns, confused adjectives and adverbs, and incorrect prepositions.
- ☐ Check all punctuation: commas, apostrophes, semicolons, quotations marks.
- ☐ Check all capitalization.
- ☐ Check spelling and look-alikes/sound-alikes.
- ☐ Check for omitted words and typos.
- ☐ Check layout, format, titles, dates, and spacing.
- ☐ Check for all personal error patterns.

WRITING AND PROOFREADING ASSIGNMENT

How have you strengthened your writing skills by taking this course? If possible, look back at a paper you wrote early in the term, and reflect on how you have developed as a writer. Write one or more paragraphs in which you describe the concepts and skills you have learned that have improved your writing the most.

Apply what you have learned throughout this course to produce an error-free paper. Use this opportunity to practice consulting your Personal Error Patterns Chart, applying your favorite proofreading strategies, and using a proofreading checklist to find and rid your writing of mistakes.

EXPLORING ONLINE

<http://owl.english.purdue.edu/owl/resource/561/01/> Proofreading guide.

<http://a4esl.org/q/j/vm/mc-stockmarket.html> Interactive quiz: Correct a mix of errors and learn about the stock exchange.

<http://jcomm.uoregon.edu/~russial/grammar/grambo.html> Test of the Emergency Grammar System. Challenge yourself and have fun.

 View an integrated eBook and chapter-specific interactive learning tools, including flashcards, quizzes, videos, and extra help tracking and correcting your Personal Error Patterns, in your Basic Writing CourseMate, accessed through <www.cengagebrain.com>.

UNIT 7

Writing Assignments

As you complete each writing assignment, remember to perform these steps:

● Write a clear, complete topic sentence.

● Use freewriting, brainstorming, or clustering to generate ideas for the body of your paragraph, essay, letter, or commercial.

● Arrange your best ideas in a plan.

● Revise for support, unity, coherence, and exact language.

● Proofread for grammar, punctuation, and spelling errors.

Writing Assignment 1 *Discuss an unusual friendship.* Have you ever had or witnessed a truly unusual friendship—for instance, between two people many years apart in age, between people from different social worlds who bonded because of a shared hobby or problem, or between a human being and an animal? Select one such unusual friendship and capture its essence in writing. How did the friendship start? What do you think bonded the two friends? Be as specific as possible so that the reader will understand this special relationship. Proofread carefully for correct use of capitals, commas, apostrophes, and quotation marks.

Writing Assignment 2 *Write a letter to compliment or to complain.* Write a letter to a store manager or a dean, to praise an especially helpful salesperson or a particularly good teacher. If you are not feeling complimentary, write the opposite: a letter of complaint about a salesperson or an instructor. State your compliment or complaint, describing what occurred and explaining why you are pleased or displeased. Remember, how well your letter is written will contribute to the impression you make. Proofread carefully for the correct use of capitals, commas, apostrophes, and quotation marks.

Writing Assignment 3 *Create a print ad.* You and several classmates considering careers in advertising have been asked to create a print ad for a magazine, newspaper, or billboard. You must sell one product or idea of your choice—anything from a brand of jeans to a cell phone to a good cause, like recycling or becoming a foster parent. Your goal is to capture people's attention with a strong picture and then persuade them with a few well-chosen words. Sketch and draft your ad; don't let punctuation errors get in the way of your message. For online help step by step, visit this website: <http://adbusters.org/spoofads/printad/>.

Writing Assignment 4 *Revise a quotation.* Pick a quotation from the Quotation Bank at the end of this book, and alter it to express something new. For example, you might want to change "Insanity is hereditary—you get it from your children" to "Insanity is learned—you get it from going to school." Be as serious or as humorous as you would like. Prove that your quotation is valid, arguing from your own or others' experience. Proofread carefully for the correct use of capitals, commas, apostrophes, and quotation marks.

UNIT 7

Review

Proofreading

A. Proofread the following business letter for incorrect or missing capitals, commas, apostrophes, and quotation marks. Correct all errors above the lines. (You should find thirty-one individual errors.)

99 somers street

Northfield, ohio 44056

january 11, 2011

weird walts Discount Store

Main office

akron, Ohio 44313

Dear sir or Madam:

On january 5, 2011 I ordered a Panasonic forty-two-inch plasma flat-screen television with a remote control from your store at 1101 Lakeland avenue medina ohio. The model number is TH42PX20UP. When your delivery man brought the set to my home yesterday, he seemed impatient. He urged me to sign before I had a chance to open the box unpack it or examine the equipment. In fact, he said, "Listen, buddy Ive got five more deliveries, and Im out of here whether you open the box or not. To my dismay I later discovered that the hand-held remote control was missing.

Please send me this remote control immediately. I purchased this panasonic in time to use it at my Super-bowl party. Obviously, my friends and I need the remote control. For years now I have been a loyal customer of Weird Walts and will appreciate your prompt attention to this matter. thank you.

Sincerely your's,

Milton rainford

B. Proofread the following essay for incorrect or missing capitals, commas, apostrophes, and quotation marks. Correct the errors above the lines. (You should find thirty-two individual errors.)

Most Valuable

(1) One of baseballs most feared sluggers, José albert Pujols was name greatest player of the decade by ESPN in 2010. (2) Talent, luck, and hard work helped him realize his dreams. (3) Pujols was born on January 16 1980 in Santo domingo. (4) The son of a well-known Dominican pitcher, he was raised by his grandmother. (5) Although they were poor, Pujols' was Happy. (6) Playing ball in the dusty fields of the dominican republic he dreamed of a career in the majors. (7) When he was 16 the family moved to the united states and settled in Independence Missouri. (8) Alberts' obsessions were learning english and playing amazing baseball on the Fort Osage high school team.

(9) His work ethic and skills attracted scouts, and in 1999 he was drafted by the St. Louis cardinals. (10) In 2001 Pujols was voted the National Leagues top rookie player, with a .329 batting average 194 hits and 130 runs batted in. (11) He helped carry the Cardinals to a world series title in 2006.

(12) According to Sparky Anderson, whos managed many elite players, Before he's done, we might be saying hes the best of them all." (13) A strong faith in God spurs Pujols to give back through the Pujols family Foundation. (14) Because his wifes child has Down syndrome, they support this cause. (15) In addition, Pujol's foundation helps underprivileged children in his beloved dominican republic. (16) More than all his baseball awards, Pujols treasures a 2008 Roberto Clemente Award for his foundations work.

Writers' Workshop

Explain a Cause or an Effect

Examining causes and effects is a useful skill, both in college and at work. This student's thoughtful essay looks at the effects of school pressure to "speak like an American." In your group or class, read it aloud if possible. As you read, pay attention to the causes and effects he describes.

In America, Speak Like an American

(1) Many teachers tell immigrant students to lose their accents and "speak like an American." They mean well. They want the children to succeed. However, this can also encourage children to be ashamed of who they are and give up their heritage.

(2) When I was in fourth grade, I was sent to a class for "speech imperfections." Apparently, I had a Spanish accent. The class wasn't so bad, it taught us to say "chair" instead of "shair" and "school" instead of "eschool." It was so important for me to please the teacher, I did practically everything she asked. She told us things like "The bums on the street have accents, that's why they're not working." I abandoned my roots and my culture and embraced "America." I learned about Stonewall Jackson and William Shakespeare. Soon Ponce de León and Pedro Calderón de la Barca were just memories at the back of my mind. I listened to country music and rock because this was "American."

(3) I can't remember when it happened, but suddenly I found myself listening to Spanish love songs. They were great! They were so sincere, the lyrics were beautiful. While turning the radio dial one day, I stopped at a Hispanic radio station. It was playing salsa. "Holy smokes," I thought to myself. All the instruments were synchronized so tightly. The horn section kept accenting the singer's lines. All of a sudden, my hips started swaying, my feet started tapping,

and I stood up. And then the horror. I couldn't dance to this music, I had never learned how. There I was, a Puerto Rican boy, listening to Puerto Rican music but unable to dance the typical Puerto Rican way.

(4) Anger flared through me as I remembered my fourth-grade teacher. I was also upset with my parents, in their zeal to have me excel, they kept me from my roots as a first-generation Hispanic American. But that was years ago. I have searched for my Latin heritage. I've found beautiful music, wonderful literature, and great foods. I now associate with "my people" as well as with everyone else, and I am learning the joys of being Sam Rodriguez, Puerto Rican.

Sam Rodriguez, student

1. How effective is Sam Rodriguez's essay?

   _____ Clear main idea?   _____ Good supporting details?

   _____ Logical organization?   _____ Effective conclusion?

2. Does the essay have a *thesis statement*, one sentence that states the main idea of the entire essay? Which sentence is it?

3. In paragraph (2), the writer says that he "abandoned [his] roots." In his view, what caused him to do this?

4. Underline the lines and ideas you find especially effective and share them with your group or class. Try to understand exactly why you like a word or sentence. For example, in paragraph (3), we can almost experience the first time the writer really *hears* salsa—the instruments, the horns accenting the singer's lines, his tapping feet and swaying hips.

5. As the writer gets older, he realizes he has lost too much of his heritage. At first he is angry (short-term effect), but what long-term effect does this new understanding have on him?

6. What order does this writer follow throughout the essay?

7. This fine essay is finished and ready to go, but the student makes the same punctuation error five different times. Can you spot and correct the error pattern that he needs to watch out for?

Writing and Revising Ideas

1. What does it mean to "become American"?

2. Write about something important that you gave up and explain why you did so.

Plan carefully, outlining your paragraph or essay before you write. State your main idea clearly and plan your supporting ideas or paragraphs. As you revise, pay special attention to clear organization and convincing, detailed support.

UNIT 8

Improving Your Spelling

Some people are naturally better spellers than others, but anyone can become a better speller. In this unit, you will

- Master six basic spelling rules
- Learn to avoid common look-alike/sound-alike errors
- Learn proofreading strategies to find and correct your own errors

Spotlight on Writing

No spelling errors mar this writer's memory of summer mornings years ago. If possible, read the paragraph aloud.

Summer, when I was a boy in Brooklyn, was a string of <u>intimacies</u>, a sum of small knowings, and almost none of them cost money. Nobody ever <u>figured</u> out a way to charge us for morning, and morning then was the <u>beginning</u> of everything. I was an altar boy in the years after the war, up in the morning before most other people for the long walk to the church on the hill. And I would watch the sun rise in Prospect Park—first a rumor, then a <u>heightened</u> light, something unseen and immense melting the hard, early darkness; then suddenly there was a molten ball, <u>screened</u> by the trees, about to climb to a scalding noon. The sun would dry the dew on the grass of the park, soften the tar, bake the rooftops, brown us on the <u>beaches</u>, make us sweat, force us out of the tight small flats of the tenements.

Pete Hamill, "Spaldeen Summers"

- Through his choice and arrangement of words, this writer helps us see and feel the park at sunrise. He also has avoided the six most common types of spelling errors. The underlined words are all spelled correctly. If you don't know why, read on.

Writing Ideas

- *Morning in a particular place (a desert, a suburb, an all-night bar, a mountaintop, and so forth)*
- *An experience of "awe" or wonder*

CHAPTER 32

Spelling

A. Suggestions for Improving Your Spelling

One important ingredient of good writing is accurate spelling. No matter how interesting your ideas are, your writing will not be effective if your spelling is incorrect.

Tips for Improving Your Spelling

1. **Look closely at the words on the page.** Use any tricks you can to remember the right spelling. For example, "Argument has no *e* because I lost the *e* during an argument" or "*Believe* has a *lie* in it."

2. **Use a dictionary.** Even professional writers frequently check spelling in a dictionary. As you write, underline the words you are not sure of and look them up when you write your final draft. If locating words in the dictionary is a real problem for you, consider a "poor speller's dictionary." Ask your professor to recommend one.

3. **Use a spell checker.** If you write on a computer, make a habit of using the spell checker. See Part B for tips and cautions about spell checkers.

4. **Keep a list of the words you misspell.** Look over your list whenever you can and keep it handy as you write.

5. **Look over corrected papers for misspelled words** (often marked *sp*)**.** Add these words to your list. Practice writing each word three or four times.

6. **Test yourself.** Have a friend dictate words from your list or from this chapter or use flashcards; computerized flashcards can be helpful.

7. **Review the basic spelling rules explained in this chapter.** Take time to learn the material; don't rush through the entire chapter all at once.

8. **Study the spelling list on pages 380–381,** and test yourself on those words.

9. **Read through Chapter 33, "Look-Alikes/Sound-Alikes,"** for commonly confused words (*their, there,* and *they're,* for instance). The practices in that chapter will help you eliminate some common spelling errors from your writing.

B. Computer Spell Checkers

If you write on a computer, always run the spell checker as part of your proofreading process. A spell checker picks up certain spelling errors and gives you alternatives for correcting them. Your program might also highlight misspelled words as you write.

What a spell checker cannot do is *think.* If you have written one correctly spelled word instead of another—*if* for *it,* for example—the spell checker cannot bring that error to your attention. If you have written *then* for *than,* the spell checker cannot help.* To find such errors, you must always proofread your paper *after* running the spell checker.

PRACTICE 1

In a small group, read this poem, which "passed" spell check. Above the lines, correct the errors that the spell checker missed.

My righting is soup eerier

Too yore pay purr this thyme.

Iran my SA threw spell check,

Each sill able an rime.

Two bad, ewe awe full righters,

Fore ewe probe lee en vee me.

My verb all cents muss bee immense,

four aye right sew quick lee.

Eye donut kneed a textbook.

I through it inn the lake.

The pro fey sore rote big read Marx.

Their muss bee sum miss take!

C. Spotting Vowels and Consonants

To learn some basic spelling rules, you must know the difference between vowels and consonants. Refer to the following chart.

> The **vowels** are *a, e, i, o,* and *u.*
> The **consonants** are *b, c, d, f, g, h, j, k, l, m, n, p, q, r, s, t, v, w, x,* and *z.*
> **The letter *y* can be either a vowel or a consonant, depending on its sound:**
>
> | happy | shy |
> | young | yawn |

---

* For questions about words that sound the same but are spelled differently, check Chapter 33, "Look-Alikes/Sound-Alikes."

- In both *happy* and *shy*, *y* is a vowel because it has a vowel sound: an *ee* sound in *happy* and an *i* sound in *shy*.

- In both *young* and *yawn*, *y* is a consonant because it has the consonant sound of *y*.

PRACTICE 2

Write *V* for vowel or *C* for consonant in the space over each letter. Be careful of the *y*.

EXAMPLE:

C	C	V	C	C	V
s	t	a	r	r	y

1.
_	_	_	_	_
t	h	e	r	e

3.
_	_	_	_
r	e	l	y

5.
_	_	_	_	_	_
h	i	d	d	e	n

2.
_	_	_	_
j	u	m	p

4.
_	_	_	_
y	a	m	s

6.
_	_	_	_	_	_
s	i	l	v	e	r

D. Doubling the Final Consonant (in Words of One Syllable)

When you add a suffix, or ending, that begins with a vowel (like -ed, -ing, -er, -est) to a word of one syllable, double the final consonant *if* the last three letters of the word are consonant-vowel-consonant, or *cvc*.

mop + ed = mopped	swim + ing = swimming
burn + er = burner	thin + est = thinnest

- *Mop*, *swim*, and *thin* all end in *cvc*; therefore, the final consonants are doubled.
- *Burn* does not end in *cvc*; therefore, the final consonant is not doubled.

PRACTICE 3

Which of the following words double the final consonant? Check to see whether the word ends in *cvc*. Double the final consonant if necessary; then add the suffixes *-ed* and *-ing*.

	Word	Last Three Letters	-ed	-ing
EXAMPLES:	drop	cvc	dropped	dropping
	boil	vcc	boiled	boiling
1.	plan			
2.	brag			
3.	dip			
4.	sail			
5.	stop			

PRACTICE 4

Which of the following words double the final consonant? Check for *cvc*. Then add the suffixes *-er* or *-est*.

	Word	Last Three Letters	-er	-est
EXAMPLES:	hot	cvc	hotter	hottest
	cool	vvc	cooler	coolest

1.	tall	_____ _____ _____
2.	short	_____ _____ _____
3.	fat	_____ _____ _____
4.	slim	_____ _____ _____
5.	wet	_____ _____ _____
6.	quick	_____ _____ _____

E. Doubling the Final Consonant (in Words of More Than One Syllable)

When you add a suffix that begins with a vowel to a word of more than one syllable, double the final consonant *if*

(1) the last three letters of the word are *cvc*, *and*

(2) the accent or stress is on the *last* syllable.

> begin + ing = beginning
>
> patrol + ed = patrolled

- *Begin* and *patrol* both end in *cvc*.
- In both words, the stress is on the last syllable: *be-gin´, pa-trol´*. (Pronounce the words aloud and listen for the correct stress.)
- Therefore, *beginning* and *patrolled* double the final consonant.

> gossip + ing = gossiping
>
> visit + ed = visited

- *Gossip* and *visit* both end in *cvc*.
- However, the stress is **not** on the last syllable: *gos´-sip, vis´-it*.
- Therefore, *gossiping* and *visited* do not double the final consonant.

PRACTICE 5

Which of the following words double the final consonant? First, check for *cvc*. Then check for the final stress and add the suffixes *-ed* and *-ing*.

	Word	Last Three Letters	*-ed*	*-ing*
EXAMPLES:	repel	*cvc*	*repelled*	*repelling*
	enlist	*vcc*	*enlisted*	*enlisting*
1.	occur	_____	_____	_____
2.	happen	_____	_____	_____
3.	polish	_____	_____	_____
4.	commit	_____	_____	_____
5.	offer	_____	_____	_____
6.	prefer	_____	_____	_____

7. exit _____ _____ _____

8. travel _____ _____ _____

9. wonder _____ _____ _____

10. omit _____ _____ _____

PRACTICE 6

Which words in parentheses double the final consonant? First, check for *cvc*. Then add the suffixes *-ed* and *-ing*. In words of two or more syllables, check for the final stress.

Hayao Miyazaki, Movie Magician

(1) Many Americans are just _____ to learn about Hayao Miyazaki,
(begin + ing)

one of the world's greatest animators. (2) Born in Tokyo in 1941, Miyazaki

_____ college just as the arts of *manga* (Japanese comics) and *anime* (animated
(attend + ed)

movies) were _____ in Japan. (3) After _____ his degree, he was
(bud + ing)   (get + ing)

_____ a job in an animation studio. (4) With his _____ ability to
(offer + ed)   (stun + ing)

draw and his creative mind, Miyazaki _____ the work.
(enjoy + ed)

(5) Soon he was not only _____ animes, but also _____,
(draw + ing)   (invent + ing)

_____, and _____ them. (6) With director Isao Takahata, he
(plan + ing)   (direct + ing)

Princess Mononoke, one
of Miyazaki's strong girl
heroines

_____ a new film studio, Studio Ghibli. (7) By _____ his own
           (open + ed)   (run + ing)

company, he could realize his vision, _____ the anime in new directions.
                                              (shift + ing)

   (8) Above all, Miyazaki is _____ to _____ with children in
                                    (commit + ed)   (film + ing)

mind. (9) With clear colors and imaginative plots, his movies are _____ in
                                                                          (root + ed)

_____, not logic. (10) Films like _My Neighbor Totoro_, _Princess Mononoke_, and
     (feel + ing)

Ponyo have _____ themes such as courage, environmental awareness, and
                  (explore + ed)

the bonds of love. (11) The idea for his film _Spirited Away_ _____ to Miyazaki
                                                                       (occur + ed)

when he had _____ _____ for a while and _____ with a
                (stop + ed)   (work + ing)   (stay + ed)

friend who had a 10-year-old daughter. (12) The filmmaker _____ to make a
                                                                   (vow + ed)

movie that _____ to little girls. (13) In fact, his heroines are often strong girls,
               (appeal + ed)

some _____ superpowers and some not.
         (possess + ing)

   (14) To make a film, Miyazaki begins without even _____ the story, which
                                                               (know + ing)

then develops through the drawings. (15) The results have _____ him to the top
                                                                   (propel + ed)

ranks of animated filmmakers, _____ him many awards and millions of fans, first
                                       (win + ing)

in Japan and then the world over.

F. Dropping or Keeping the Final _E_

When you add a suffix that begins with a vowel (like _-able_, _-ence_, **or** _-ing_**), drop
the final** _e_.

When you add a suffix that begins with a consonant (like _-less_, _-ment_, **or** _-ly_**),
keep the final** _e_.

> write + ing = writing   pure + ity = purity

- _Writing_ and _purity_ both drop the final _e_ because the suffixes _-ing_ and _-ity_ begin
  with vowels.

> hope + less = hopeless   advertise + ment = advertisement

- _Hopeless_ and _advertisement_ keep the final _e_ because the suffixes _-less_ and _-ment_
  begin with consonants.

  Here are some exceptions to memorize:

argument	courageous	knowledgeable	simply
awful	judgment	manageable	truly

PRACTICE 7   Add the suffix shown to each word.

EXAMPLES: come + ing = _____*coming*_____

rude + ness = _____*rudeness*_____

1. blame + less = _____
2. guide + ance = _____
3. debate + ing = _____
4. motive + ation = _____
5. sincere + ly = _____
6. desire + able = _____
7. argue + ment = _____
8. home + less = _____

9. response + ible = _____
10. rejoice + ing = _____
11. awe + ful = _____
12. manage + er = _____
13. judge + ment = _____
14. fame + ous = _____
15. grieve + ance = _____
16. arrange + ing = _____

G. Changing or Keeping the Final Y

When you add a suffix to a word that ends in -*y*, change the *y* to *i* if the letter before the *y* is a consonant.

Keep the final *y* if the letter before the *y* is a vowel.

> happy + ness = happiness   delay + ed = delayed

- The *y* in *happiness* is changed to *i* because the letter before the *y* is a consonant, *p*.
- However, the *y* in *delayed* is not changed to *i* because the letter before it is a vowel, *a*.

When you add -*ing* to words ending in *y*, always keep the *y*.

> copy + ing = copying   delay + ing = delaying

Here are some exceptions to memorize:

day + ly = daily   pay + ed = paid

lay + ed = laid   say + ed = said

When the final *y* is changed to *i*, add -*es* instead of -*s*.

> fly + es = flies   candy + es = candies
>
> marry + es = marries   story + es = stories

PRACTICE 8   Add the suffix shown to each of the following words.

EXAMPLES: vary + ed = _____*varied*_____

buy + er = _____*buyer*_____

1. cry + ed = _____
2. mercy + ful = _____
3. worry + ing = _____
4. say + ed = _____
5. juicy + er = _____

6. enjoy + able = _____
7. clumsy + ness = _____
8. wealthy + est = _____
9. day + ly = _____
10. merry + ly = _____

PRACTICE 9

Add the suffixes in parentheses to each word.

1. lively (er) _____
       (est) _____
       (ness) _____
2. beauty (fy) _____
       (ful) _____
       (es) _____
3. healthy (er) _____
       (est) _____
       (ly) _____

4. study (es) _____
      (ous) _____
      (ing) _____
5. busy (ness) _____
      (er) _____
      (est) _____
6. try (es) _____
      (ed) _____
      (al) _____

PRACTICE 10

Add the suffix shown to each word in parentheses. Write the correctly spelled word in each blank.

Winter Blues

(1) Although Kim _____ (try + ed) to ignore her feelings, she always felt _____ (hungry + er), _____ (sleepy + er), _____ (angry + er), and _____ (lonely + er) during the winter months. (2) As part of her _____ (deny + al), she went about her _____ (busy + ness) as usual, but she knew that she no longer found life as _____ (pleasure + able) as before.

(3) Then one day she read a _____ (fascinate + ing) magazine article about a medical condition called *seasonal affective disorder*, or *SAD*. (4) Kim _____ (immediate + ly) saw the _____ (similarity + es) between her yearly mood changes and the symptoms that people with SAD _____ (display + ed). (5) She learned that winter SAD is a kind of depression triggered _____ (primary + ly) by lack of _____ (expose + ure) to light—by insufficient sunshine, inadequate indoor light at home or work, or even by _____ (mercy + lessly) cloudy weather.

(6) _____ (Happy + ly), Kim discovered that three or four kinds of treatment are available. (7) The most severe cases—people who sleep more than fourteen hours a day and still feel _____ (fatigue + ed), for example—are usually cured by light therapy given in a clinic

or at home under a doctor's care. (8) Taking medication, _____ , or

_____ one's diet often brings _____ relief. (9) Kim did some
    (change + ing)   (notice + able)

research on the Web and found a list of SAD clinics, _____ , and support.
                                               (guide + ance)

(10) Attending a light-therapy clinic near her home, she soon experienced her

_____ winter in years.
    (healthy + est)

(Above text shows "(exercise + ing)" under the first blank in sentence (8).)

H. Choosing *IE* or *EI*

Write *i* before *e*, except after *c*, or in any *ay* sound like *neighbor*:

> niece, believe, conceive, weigh

- *Niece* and *believe* are spelled *ie*.
- *Conceive* is spelled *ei* because of the preceding *c*.
- *Weigh* is spelled *ei* because of its *ay* sound.

   However, words with a *shen* sound are spelled with an *ie* after the *c*: *ancient,
conscience, efficient, sufficient.*

   Here are some exceptions to memorize:

either	height	seize	their
foreign	neither	society	weird

PRACTICE 11   Pronounce each word out loud. Then fill in the blanks with either *ie* or *ei*.

1. f __ __ ld
2. w __ __ ght
3. n __ __ ther
4. w __ __ rd
5. ch __ __ f

6. s __ __ ze
7. rec __ __ ve
8. br __ __ f
9. h __ __ ght
10. ach __ __ ve

11. effic __ __ nt
12. v __ __ n
13. th __ __ r
14. for __ __ gn
15. cash __ __ r

I. Commonly Misspelled Words

Below is a list of commonly misspelled words. They are words that you probably use daily in speaking and writing. Each word has a trouble spot, the part of the word that is often spelled incorrectly. The trouble spot is in bold type.

   Two tricks to help you learn these words are (1) to copy each word twice, underlining the trouble spot, and (2) to copy the words on flashcards and have someone else test you. If possible, consult this list while or after you write.

1. a**c**ross	7. behavi**o**r	13. de**s**cribe	19. eig**hth**
2. add**r**ess	8. calend**a**r	14. desp**e**rate	20. embarra**ss**
3. an**sw**er	9. car**ee**r	15. diff**e**rent	21. envir**on**ment
4. arg**u**ment	10. cons**ci**ence	16. disa**pp**oint	22. exa**gg**erate
5. ath**l**ete	11. crow**ded**	17. disa**pp**rove	23. famil**ia**r
6. begin**n**ing	12. defin**i**te	18. does**n't**	24. fina**lly**

25. government
26. grammar
27. height
28. **il**legal
29. immed**iately**
30. import**ant**
31. int**eg**ration
32. int**ell**igent
33. inte**re**st
34. inte**r**fere
35. jew**el**ry
36. jud**g**ment
37. knowle**dg**e
38. main**tain**
39. mathematics
40. meant
41. nec**ess**ary
42. ner**vous**
43. occasion
44. opin**ion**
45. optimist
46. particular
47. **per**form
48. **per**haps
49. perso**nn**el
50. possess
51. possible
52. **prefer**
53. pre**ju**dice
54. privil**ege**
55. pro**bably**
56. **psychology**
57. pursue
58. reference
59. **rhythm**
60. ridic**ulous**
61. sep**ar**ate
62. sim**i**lar
63. **since**
64. speech
65. stren**gth**
66. success
67. **sur**prise
68. **taught**
69. temperature
70. tho**rough**
71. though**t**
72. tire**d**
73. until
74. weig**ht**
75. written

Personal Spelling List

In your notebook, keep a list of words that *you* misspell. Add words to your list from corrected papers and from the exercises in this chapter. First, copy each word as you misspelled it, underlining the trouble spot; then write the word correctly. Use the following form. Study your list often.

	As I Wrote It	Correct Spelling
1.	*dissappointed*	*disappointed*
2.		
3.		

Chapter Highlights

- **Double the final consonant in one-syllable words that end in *cvc*:**
  hop/hopped   tan/tanning

- **Double the final consonant in words of more than one syllable if they end in *cvc* and if the stress is on the last syllable:**
  begin/beginning   prefer/preferred

- **Keep the final *e* when adding a suffix that begins with a consonant:**
  hope/hopeful   time/timely

- **Drop the final *e* when adding a suffix that begins with a vowel:**
  hope/hoping   time/timer

- **Keep the final *y* when adding a suffix if the letter before the *y* is a vowel:**
  buy/buying   delay/delayed

- **Change the *y* to *i* when adding a suffix if the letter before the *y* is a consonant:**
  snappy/snappiest   pity/pitiful

- **Write *i* before *e*, except after *c*, or in any *ay* sound like *neighbor*:**
  believe, niece, *but* receive, weigh

- **Remember that there are exceptions to all of these rules. Check a dictionary whenever you are uncertain.**

Proofreading Strategy

If poor spelling is one of your error patterns, keep your Personal Spelling List of errors and a dictionary beside you as you write.

1. Use the **bottom-up proofreading technique**. Read your draft sentence by sentence from the last sentence to the first. This will help you see possible misspellings and typos more easily.

2. Ask **someone who is a good speller** to read your draft and help you spot any misspellings and typos. Then correct these yourself; this will help you learn correct spellings. Tutors in your college's writing lab or classmates who have a good eye for errors can be excellent sources of help.

WRITING AND PROOFREADING ASSIGNMENT

Success can be defined in many ways. In a small group, discuss what the term *success* means to you. Is it a rewarding career, a happy family life, lots of money?

Now pick the definition that most appeals to you and write a paragraph explaining what success is. You may wish to use people in the news or friends to support your main idea. Proofread your work for accurate spelling, especially the words covered in this chapter. Finally, exchange papers and read each other's work. Did your partner catch any spelling errors that you missed?

CHAPTER REVIEW

Proofread this essay for spelling errors. Correct the errors above the lines.

A Precious Resource

(1) Many people have pleasant memorys of recieving their first library card or chooseing books for the first time at a local public library. (2) Widely recognized as a priceless resource, the public library is defined just as you might expect: a collection of books and other materials supported by the public for public use.

(3) Several New England towns claim the honor of contributeing the first public money for a library. (4) However, the first such library of meaningful size and influence—the first fameous public library—originated in Boston, Massachusetts, in 1854. (5) The Boston Public Library, with its useful refrence collection and its policy of circulateing popular books, set the pattern for all public librarys subsequently created in the United States and Canada. (6) By the end of the nineteenth century, many state goverments were beginning to raise taxes to support libraries. (7) They beleived that public libraries had an extremely importent role to play in helping people pursue knowlege and continue thier education. (8) Although

The beautiful Library of Congress in Washington, D.C., offers the public an array of services and resources. Explore online at ‹**http://www.loc.gov/index.html**›.

© PictureNet/CORBIS

public libaries today have much the same goal, they now offer a truely admireable number of resources and services. (9) These include story hours for children, book discussion clubs for adults, intresting lectures, art exhibits, literacy classes, and most recently, computer training and guideance.

(10) Technology, of course, has transformed the management of the public library as well as the way the library is used. (11) The bigest changes—today's computerized catalogs, searchable databases, and Internet access—would definately have gone beyond the wildest dreams of even the most commited early public libary supporters.

EXPLORING ONLINE

‹http://grammar.ccc.commnet.edu/grammar/cgi-shl/quiz20.pl/spelling_quiz3.htm› Interactive quiz: Add endings to these words.

‹http://owl.english.purdue.edu/exercises/4/20/43› Is that *ei* or *ie*? Take the test and check your answers.

 View an integrated eBook and chapter-specific interactive learning tools, including flashcards, quizzes, videos, and extra help tracking and correcting your Personal Error Patterns, in your Basic Writing CourseMate, accessed through ‹www.cengagebrain.com›.

CHAPTER 33

Look-Alikes/ Sound-Alikes

A/An/And

1. *A* **is used before a word beginning with a consonant or a consonant sound.**

   a man   *a* house   *a* union (the *u* in *union* is pronounced like the consonant *y*)

2. *An* **is used before a word beginning with a vowel (*a, e, i, o, u*) or a silent *h*.**

   an igloo   *an* apple   *an* hour (the *h* in *hour* is silent)

3. *And* **joins words or ideas.**

   Theo *and* Brad are taking the same biology class.
   He is very honest, *and* most people respect him.

PRACTICE 1

Fill in *a*, *an*, or *and*.

1. Don Miller has used each summer vacation to try out _____ different career choice.

2. Last summer, he worked in _____ law office, filling in for _____ administrative assistant on leave.

3. One lawyer was impressed by how carefully Don worked _____ suggested that Don consider _____ law career.

4. Don returned to school in the fall _____ talked to his adviser about becoming _____ paralegal.

5. _____ paralegal investigates the facts of cases, prepares documents, _____ does other background work for lawyers.

6. With his adviser's help, Don found _____ course of study to prepare for this career.

7. Next summer, he hopes to work for _____ public interest law firm _____ to learn about environmental law.

8. He is happy to have found _____ interesting career _____ looks forward to making _____ difference.

Accept/Except

1. *Accept* **means "to receive."**

   Please *accept* my apologies.   I *accepted* his offer of help.

2. *Except* **means "other than" or "excluding."**

   Everyone *except* Ron thinks it's a good idea.

PRACTICE 2   Fill in forms of *accept* or *except*.

1. Did Steve _____ the collect call from his brother?

2. Mr. Francis will _____ the package in the mailroom.

3. All of our friends attended the wedding _____ Meg.

4. The athlete proudly _____ his award.

5. Every toddler _____ my daughter enjoyed the piñata party.

6. _____ for Jean, we all had tickets for the movie.

7. The tornado left every building standing _____ for the barn.

8. Everyone _____ Ranjan was willing to _____ the committee's decision.

Been/Being

1. *Been* **is the past participle form of** *to be*. *Been* **is usually used after the helping verb** *have*, *has*, **or** *had*.

   I *have been* to that restaurant before.

   She *has been* in Akron for ten years.

2. *Being* **is the** *-ing* **form of** *to be*. *Being* **is usually used after the helping verbs** *is*, *are*, *am*, *was*, **and** *were*.

   They *are being* helped by the salesperson.

   Rhonda *is being* courageous and independent.

PRACTICE 3   Fill in *been* or *being*.

1. The children have _____ restless all day.

2. What good films are _____ shown on television tonight?

3. We have _____ walking in circles!

4. I haven't _____ in such a good mood for a week.

5. This building is _____ turned into a community center.

6. His last offer has _____ on my mind all day.

7. Which elevator is _____ inspected now?

8. Because you are _____ honest with me, I will admit that I have _____ in love with you for years.

Buy/By

1. *Buy* **means "to purchase."**
She *buys* new furniture every five years.

2. *By* **means "near," "before," or "by means of."**
He walked right *by* and didn't say hello.
By sunset, we had finished the harvest.
We prefer traveling *by* bus.

PRACTICE 4

Fill in *buy* or *by*.

1. Did you _____ that computer, or did you rent it?

2. These tracks on the trail were made _____ a deer.

3. He stood _____ the cash register and waited his turn to _____ a cheeseburger.

4. She finds it hard to walk _____ a bookstore without going in to browse.

5. It's better to stick with your budget than to _____ that ten-seater couch.

6. Please answer this letter _____ October 10.

7. Pat trudged through the storm to _____ a Sunday paper.

8. The dishes _____ the sink need to be put away.

Fine/Find

1. *Fine* **means "good" or "well." It can also mean "a penalty."**
He wrote a *fine* analysis of the short story.
She paid a $10 *fine*.

2. *Find* **means "to locate."**
I can't *find* my red suspenders.

PRACTICE 5

Fill in *fine* or *find*.

1. The library charges a large _____ for overdue videotapes.

2. As soon as we _____ your lost suitcase, we'll send it to you.

3. Can you _____ me one of these in an extra-large size?

4. Harold made a _____ impression on the assistant buyer.

5. By tonight, I will be feeling _____ .

6. My father gave me good advice: "When you _____ good friends, stick with them."

It's/Its

1. *It's* **is a contraction of** *it is* **or** *it has*. **If you cannot substitute** *it is* **or** *it has* **in the sentence, you cannot use** *it's*.

   It's a ten-minute walk to my house.   *It's* been a nice party.

2. *Its* **is a possessive and shows ownership.**

   The bear cub rolled playfully on *its* side.

   Industry must do *its* share to curb inflation.

PRACTICE 6   Fill in *it's* or *its*.

1. If _____ not too much trouble, drop the package off on your way home.

2. _____ been hard for him to accept the fact that he can no longer play ball.

3. The *Daily News* reporter was lucky because the jury reached _____ verdict just before her deadline.

4. _____ been a long time since I had a real vacation.

5. _____ a chocolate cake with your Social Security number in pink frosting.

6. My family is at _____ best when there is work to be done.

7. _____ impossible to open this window.

8. Although I hate shoveling the walk, I am happy _____ been a good year for winter sports.

9. _____ sad to see that seagull huddled in the sand.

10. If _____ not flying, perhaps _____ wing is hurt.

Know/Knew/No/New

1. *Know* **means "to have knowledge or understanding."** *Knew* **is the past tense of the verb** *to know*.

   Carl *knows* he has to finish by 6 p.m.

   The police officer *knew* the quickest route to the pier.

2. *No* **is a negative.**

   He is *no* longer dean of academic affairs.

3. *New* **means "fresh" or "recent."**

   I like your *new* belt.

PRACTICE 7   Fill in *know*, *knew*, *no*, or *new*.

1. We will need _____ wiring to handle those powerful air conditioners.

2. She didn't _____ the lid was loose.

3. I _____ I need to find _____ jokes because no one laughs when I tell my old ones.

4. Because she _____ the answer, she won a pool table and a popcorn machine.

5. Because you really _____ the _____ material, why don't you take the final early?

6. Charlene thinks there's _____ way we can do it, but I _____ we'll be speaking Italian by June.

7. Arnold _____ that he shouldn't have eaten that third dessert.

8. We have _____ way of knowing how well you scored on the civil service examination.

9. He didn't _____ whether the used equipment came with a guarantee.

10. I wish I _____ then what I _____ now.

Lose/Loose

1. *Lose* **means "to misplace" or "not to win."**
    Be careful not to *lose* your way on those back roads.
    George hates to *lose* at cards.

2. *Loose* **means "ill fitting" or "too large."**
    That's not my size; it's *loose* on me.

PRACTICE 8   Fill in *lose* or *loose*.

1. Because the plug is _____ in the socket, the television keeps blinking on and off.

2. A professional team has to learn how to win and how to _____ gracefully.

3. If Irene doesn't tighten that _____ hubcap, she will _____ it.

4. I like wearing _____ clothing in the summer.

5. Before these pants shrank in the dryer, they were too _____.

6. Act now, or you will _____ your opportunity to get that promotion.

7. She won't _____ those mittens again because I've clipped them onto her jacket.

8. I'm surprised you didn't _____ those _____ quarters.

Mine/Mind

1. *Mine* **is a possessive and shows ownership.**
    This is your umbrella, but where is *mine*?

2. *Mind* **means "intelligence." It can also be a verb meaning "to object" or "to pay attention to."**
    What's on your *mind*?   I don't *mind* if you come late.

PRACTICE 9

Fill in *mine* or *mind*.

1. Her road test is tomorrow; _____ was yesterday.

2. Will Doris _____ if we spend the evening talking about our days in boot camp?

3. Sherlock put his _____ to work and solved the mystery.

4. Please _____ your manners when we meet the king.

5. Please don't interrupt us; we really _____ when someone breaks our train of thought.

6. My _____ is made up; I want to switch my major from accounting to marketing.

7. Don't _____ him; he always snores in public.

8. "That toy is _____," whined Tim, "and I do _____ if you take it!"

Past/Passed

1. *Past* **is that which has already occurred; it is over with.**
   His *past* work has been satisfactory.
   Never let the *past* interfere with your hopes for the future.

2. *Passed* **is the past tense of the verb** *to pass***.**
   She *passed* by and nodded hello.

PRACTICE 10

Fill in *past* or *passed*.

1. He asked for the butter, but I absentmindedly _____ him the mayonnaise.

2. Forget about failures in the _____ and look forward to success in the future.

3. The police car caught up to the truck that had _____ every other car on the road.

4. I have _____ this same corner every Saturday morning for a year.

5. Wasn't that woman who just _____ us on a motorcycle your Aunt Sally?

6. In the _____, Frieda and Carolyn used to talk on the phone once a week.

7. Your _____ attendance record was perfect.

8. Don knew he had _____ the test, but he had never received such a high grade in the _____.

Quiet/Quit/Quite

1. *Quiet* **means "silent, still."**
   The woods are *quiet* tonight.

2. *Quit* **means "to give up" or "to stop doing something."**
   Last year, I *quit* smoking.

3. *Quite* **means "very" or "exactly."**

   She was *quite* tired after playing soccer for two hours.

   That's not *quite* right.

PRACTICE 11 Fill in *quiet, quit,* or *quite*.

1. When it comes to expressing her feelings, Tonya is _____ vocal.

2. I can't concentrate when my apartment is too _____ .

3. Selling belly chains can be _____ amusing.

4. Please be _____ ; I'm trying to listen to the news.

5. If she _____ now, she will risk losing her vacation pay.

6. Dwight asked the crew to be absolutely _____ while the magicians performed.

7. Don't _____ when the going gets rough; just increase your efforts and succeed.

8. I have the general idea, but I don't _____ understand all the details.

9. This usually _____ library is now _____ noisy.

10. She _____ whistling when people in the line began to stare at her.

Rise/Raise

1. *Rise* **means "to get up by one's own power." The past tense of** *rise* **is** *rose.* **The past participle of** *rise* **is** *risen.*

   The sun *rises* at 6 a.m.

   Daniel *rose* early yesterday.

   He has *risen* from the table.

2. *Raise* **means "to lift an object" or "to grow or increase." The past tense of** *raise* **is** *raised.* **The past participle of** *raise* **is** *raised.*

   Raise your right hand.

   She *raised* the banner over her head.

   We have *raised* $1,000.

PRACTICE 12 Fill in forms of *rise* or *raise*.

1. When the moon _____ , we'll be able to see the path better.

2. During the meeting, she _____ the possibility of a strike.

3. The jet _____ off the runway and roared into the clouds.

4. Bud would like to _____ early, but usually he wakes, turns over, and goes back to sleep.

5. Can you _____ corn in this soil?

6. He couldn't _____ from his chair because of the chewing gum stuck to his pants.

7. My boss has unexpectedly _____ my salary.

8. I felt foolish when I accidentally _____ my voice in the quiet
concert hall.

9. The loaves of homemade bread have _____ .

10. He _____ to his feet and shuffled out the door.

Sit/Set

1. *Sit* **means "to seat oneself." The past tense of** *sit* **is** *sat*. **The past
participle of** *sit* **is** *sat*.

   Sit up straight!

   He *sat* down on the porch and fell asleep.

   She has *sat* reading that book all day.

2. *Set* **means "to place" or "to put something down." The past tense of** *set*
is *set*. **The past participle of** *set* **is** *set*.

   Don't *set* your books on the dining room table.

   She *set* the package down and walked off without it.

   He had *set* the pot on the stove.

PRACTICE 13   Fill in forms of *sit* or *set*.

1. Marcy _____ her glasses on the seat next to her.

2. Please _____ there; the dentist will see you in ten minutes.

3. _____ the cans of paint in the corner, please.

4. My grandfather always _____ in that overstuffed, red-and-blue plaid chair.

5. Please _____ that box of clothes by the door.

6. _____ down, and let me _____ this Hawaiian feast before you.

7. I would have _____ your bracelet on the counter, but I was afraid
someone might walk off with it.

8. We have always _____ in the first row, but tonight I want to
_____ at the back of the auditorium.

Suppose/Supposed

1. *Suppose* **means "to assume" or "to guess." The past tense of** *suppose* **is**
supposed. **The past participle of** *suppose* **is** *supposed*.

   Brad *supposes* that the teacher will give him an A.

   We all *supposed* she would win first prize.

   I had *supposed* Dan would win.

2. *Supposed* **means "should have"; it is followed by** *to*.

   He is *supposed* to meet us after class.

   You were *supposed* to wash and wax the car.

   REMEMBER: When you mean *ought* or *should*, always use the *-ed* ending—
supposed.

PRACTICE 14 Fill in *suppose* or *supposed*.

1. How do you _____ he will get himself out of this mess?

2. My father-in-law was _____ to arrive last night.

3. I _____ I'll find my car keys in my other pants.

4. Why do you _____ that cereal is so expensive?

5. You are not _____ to open the presents until your birthday.

6. Diane was _____ to check the bus schedule.

7. Where do you _____ he bought that gold lamé shirt?

8. What are we _____ to do with these three-by-five-inch cards?

9. Frank _____ that Meredith would meet him for dinner.

10. I _____ Ron is willing to shovel the snow this time.

Their/There/They're

1. *Their* **is a possessive pronoun and shows ownership.**
   They couldn't find *their* wigs.   *Their* children are charming.

2. *There* **indicates a location.**
   I wouldn't go *there* again.   Put the lumber down *there*.

3. *There* **is also a way of introducing a thought.**
   There is a fly in my soup.
   There are two ways to approach this problem.

4. *They're* **is a contraction:** *they* + *are* = *they're*. **If you cannot substitute** *they are* **in the sentence, you cannot use** *they're*.
   They're the best poems I have read in a long time.
   If *they're* coming, count me in.

PRACTICE 15 Fill in *their*, *there*, or *they're*.

1. If you move over _____, I can get everyone into the picture.

2. _____ are three ways to mix paint, all of which are messy.

3. If _____ here, we can set out the food.

4. That is _____ hot air balloon way up _____.

5. _____ preparing for a hot, sticky summer.

6. Is _____ a faster route to Topeka?

7. _____ never on time when it comes to paying _____ cell phone bills.

8. _____ products contain no sugar and no preservatives.

9. Is _____ a wrench in the toolbox?

10. Because _____ so quiet, I suppose _____ asleep.

Then/Than

1. *Then* **means "next" or "at that time."**

   First, we went to the theater, and *then* we went for pizza.

   I was a heavyweight boxer *then*.

2. *Than* **is used in a comparison.**

   She is a better student *than* I.

PRACTICE 16   Fill in *then* or *than*.

1. Carlos works harder _____ anyone else in this office.

2. San Francisco has colder winters _____ San Diego.

3. Get your first paycheck; _____ think about moving into your own apartment.

4. It's often better to forgive someone _____ to carry a grudge.

5. If you receive straight A's this semester, will you _____ apply for a scholarship?

6. You asked me a question and _____ interrupted me before I could answer.

7. This red convertible gets more miles to the gallon _____ any other car on the lot.

8. Now I'm ready for marriage; _____ , I was confused.

Threw/Through

1. *Threw* **is the past tense of the verb** *to throw.*

   Charleen *threw* the ball into the bleachers.

2. *Through* **means "in one side and out the other" or "finished."**

   He burst *through* the front door laughing.

   If you are *through* eating, we can leave.

PRACTICE 17   Fill in *threw* or *through*.

1. I went _____ my notes, but I couldn't find any reference to Guatemala.

2. He _____ the pillow on the floor and plopped down in front of the television.

3. Gail _____ her raincoat over her head and ran out into the storm.

4. You go _____ that door to get to the dean's office.

5. If you are _____ with that reference material, I would like to take a look at it.

6. We can always see _____ their tricks.

To/Too/Two

1. *To* **means "toward."**

   We are going *to* the stadium.

2. *To* **can also be combined with a verb to form an infinitive.**

   Where do you want *to* go for lunch?

3. *Too* **means "also" or "very."**

   Roberto is going to the theater *too*.   They were *too* bored to stay awake.

4. *Two* **is the number 2.**

   Ms. Palmer will teach *two* new accounting courses this term.

PRACTICE 18   Fill in *to, too,* or *two.*

1. If you want _____ enroll in college this fall, you will need
   _____ letters of recommendation.

2. It will be _____ awkward _____ leave the dinner before
   the dessert is served.

3. He likes _____ sing at parties _____ .

4. It's _____ early _____ go _____
   the theater.

5. That dance step may be _____ advanced for me right now.

6. Yamaris and I have _____ design _____ outfits by Friday if we
   want _____ enter the fashion competition.

7. We traveled _____ the Grand Canyon _____ try white-water
   rafting.

8. It's _____ much trouble _____ make my own salad dressing.

9. She _____ likes _____ watch professional wrestling.

10. We saw _____ undercover agents talking quietly _____
    the bartender.

Use/Used

1. *Use* **means "to make use of." The past tense of** *use* **is** *used.* **The past
   participle of** *use* **is** *used.*

   Why do you *use* an iPhone?

   He *used* the wrong paint in the bathroom.

   I have *used* that brand of toothpaste myself.

2. *Used* **means "in the habit of" or "accustomed"; it is followed by** *to.*

   I am not *used to* getting up at 4 a.m.   They got *used to* the good life.

   REMEMBER: When you mean *in the habit of* or *accustomed,* always use the *-ed*
   ending—*used.*

PRACTICE 19   Fill in *use* or *used*.

1. Terry is _____ to long bus rides.

2. It may take a few days to get _____ to this high altitude.

3. Do you know how to _____ a digital camera?

4. Vera hopes to get _____ to her grumpy father-in-law.

5. Carlotta and Roland still _____ the laundromat on the corner.

6. We _____ the self-service pump; the gas was cheaper.

7. Feel free to _____ my telephone if you need to make a call.

8. You'll get _____ to it.

9. My grandmother does not _____ her e-mail account because she has
   never gotten _____ to it.

10. Never get _____ to failure; always expect success.

Weather/Whether

1. *Weather* **refers to atmospheric conditions.**
   In June, the *weather* in Spain is lovely.

2. *Whether* **implies a question.**
   Whether you pass is up to you.

PRACTICE 20   Fill in *weather* or *whether*.

1. Rainy _____ makes me lazy.

2. Be sure to tell the employment agency _____ you plan to take the job.

3. You never know _____ Celia will be happy or sad.

4. Good _____ always brings joggers to the park.

5. Flopsy didn't know _____ to eat the carrot or the lettuce first.

6. Please check to see _____ the printer needs a new ink cartridge.

7. The real estate agent must know by 10 a.m. _____ you intend to rent
   the house.

8. _____ the _____ cooperates or not, we're going to
   the beach.

Where/Were/We're

1. *Where* **implies place or location.**
   Where have you been all day?   Home is *where* you hang your hat.

2. *Were* **is the past tense of** *are*.
   We *were* on our way when the hurricane hit.

3. *We're* **is a contraction:** *we* + *are* = *we're*. **If you cannot substitute** *we are* **in the sentence, you cannot use** *we're*.

We're going to leave now.

Because *we're* in the city, let's go to the galleries.

PRACTICE 21

Fill in *where*, *were*, or *we're*.

1. The desk was emptied, but _____ not sure who did it.

2. _____ did you put the remote control?

3. Ted and Gloria _____ childhood sweethearts.

4. When you _____ in South America, _____ did your poodles stay?

5. Virginia is not _____ I was born.

6. The librarians _____ very helpful in showing us _____ to find the latest information.

7. _____ you surprised to learn that _____ commercial fishermen?

8. The clouds _____ blocking the sun in exactly the spot _____ we _____ sitting.

9. Everyone needs a peaceful hideaway, a place _____ he or she can be absolutely alone.

10. _____ _____ going, sir, is a question _____ not about to answer.

Whose/Who's

1. *Whose* **implies ownership and possession.**

Whose term paper is that?

2. *Who's* **is a contraction of** *who is* **or** *who has*. **If you cannot substitute** *who is* **or** *who has*, **you cannot use** *who's*.

Who's knocking at the window?

Who's seen my new felt hat with the green bows?

PRACTICE 22

Fill in *whose* or *who's*.

1. _____ ready for an adventure?

2. _____ CDs are scattered all over the floor?

3. We found a puppy in the vacant lot, but we don't know _____ it is.

4. _____ that playing the saxophone?

5. He's a physician _____ diagnosis can be trusted.

6. Grace admires the late Marian Anderson, _____ singing always moved her.

7. I'm not sure _____ coming and _____ not.

8. _____ been eating all the chocolate chip cookies?

Your/You're

1. *Your* **is a possessive and shows ownership.**

   Your knowledge is astonishing!

2. *You're* **is a contraction:** *you + are = you're.* **If you cannot substitute** *you are* **in the sentence, you cannot use** *you're.*

   You're the nicest person I know.

PRACTICE 23   Fill in *your* or *you're.*

1. Is that _____ iPod or mine?

2. If _____ tired, take a nap.

3. Does _____ daughter like her new telescope?

4. I hope _____ teammates haven't forgotten the code words.

5. If _____ in a rush, we can mail _____ scarves to you.

6. _____ foreman was just transferred.

7. Please keep _____ Saint Bernard out of my rose garden.

8. _____ in charge of _____ finances from now on.

9. When _____ optimistic about life, everything seems to go right.

10. Let me have _____ order by Thursday; if it's late, _____ not likely to receive the merchandise in time for the holidays.

Chapter Highlights

Some words look and sound alike. Below are a few of them:

● **it's/its**

   It's the neatest room I ever saw.

   Everything is in *its* place.

● **their/they're/there**

   They found *their* work easy.

   They're the best actors I have ever seen.

   Put the lumber down *there.*

● **then/than**

   I was a heavyweight boxer *then.*

   He is a better cook *than* I.

- **to/too/two**

  We are going *to* the stadium.

  No one is *too* old to learn.

  I bought *two* hats yesterday.

- **whose/who's**

  Whose Italian dictionary is this?

  I'm not sure *who's* leaving early.

- **your/you're**

  Is *your* aunt the famous mystery writer?

  You're due for a promotion and a big raise.

Proofreading Strategy

If you tend to confuse the *look-alikes/sound-alikes*, **keep your Personal Error Patterns Chart updated** with the specific words you misuse, such as *their* and *there*, *affect* and *effect*, and *your* and *you're*.

Every time you proofread, **search your draft for every one of these words**. If you are using a computer, use the *"Find"* feature to locate them. Then double-check the meaning of the sentence to make sure that you've used and spelled the word correctly.

WRITING AND PROOFREADING ASSIGNMENT

Look back through this chapter and make a list of the look-alikes that most confuse you. List at least five pairs or clusters of words. Then use them all correctly in a paper about a problem on your campus or in your neighborhood (such as a lack of public parks or playgrounds, too much drug or alcohol use, or a gulf between computer haves and have-nots). Try to use every word on your look-alikes list and proofread to make sure you have spelled everything correctly.

CHAPTER REVIEW

Proofread this essay for look-alike/sound-alike errors. Write your corrections above the lines.

Rapper with a Difference

(1) If you're concept of hip-hop music is gang fights, drugs, the fast life, and negative views of women, than perhaps you haven't heard of Wyclef Jean. (2) Like many rappers, Jean is committed to making music with powerful lyrics and driving rhythms. (3) However, this

Activist Wyclef Jean works the phones for SOS Help Haiti, 2010

Haitian-born former Fugee sends a very different message and lives a quiter lifestyle than many hip-hop artists do.

(4) Unlike some hip-hop music—named "gangsta rap" for it's glorification of violence—Jean's songs celebrate nonviolence and understanding. (5) For example, in his fourth solo album, *The Preacher's Son*, Jean shares his vision of a peaceful world were everyone gets along. (6) He believes that if people can set and talk, they can work though almost anything. (7) Wyclef pleads for an end to dangerous feuds between rappers, such as the clashes between 50 Cent and Ja Rule, Jay-Z and Nas, and the passed rivalry, kept alive in music, between Tupac Shakur and Notorious B.I.G., both gunned down in there prime.

(8) Jean also differs from other rappers in his calm lifestyle. (9) While many hip-hop celebrities live the high life, traveling with bodyguards and a posse of companions, the down-to-earth Jean insists on strolling the streets by himself. (10) He says he does not want to become disconnected from reality buy cutting himself off from it. (11) So its not unusual to see Jean standing on a street corner talking with a homeless person or bonding with a young thug who tried to rob him moments before.

(12) Now Jean is been seen as a role model by a new generation of hip-hop artists and fans. (13) One of his passions is Clef's Kids, an after-school music program, for music is a vehicle to his higher goal of changing the world. (14) Jean's preacher father, now deceased, use to urge him to study theology, too which Jean replied, "I am just a messenger in a different way."

EXPLORING ONLINE

<http://grammar.ccc.commnet.edu/grammar/cgi-shl/quiz.pl/spelling_add1.htm>
Interactive quiz: Choose the correctly spelled words.

<http://grammar.ccc.commnet.edu/grammar/cgi-shl/quiz.pl/lie_lay_quiz.htm>
Interactive quiz: Practice *lie/lay*, *sit/set*.

<http://a4esl.org/q/h/homonyms.html> Practice sound-alikes, like *night/knight*, that may confuse ESL students. Pick easy, medium, or difficult, and test yourself.

 View an integrated eBook and chapter-specific interactive learning tools, including flashcards, quizzes, videos, and extra help tracking and correcting your Personal Error Patterns, in your Basic Writing CourseMate, accessed through <www.cengagebrain.com>.

UNIT 8

Writing Assignments

As you complete each writing assignment, remember to perform these steps:

- Write a clear, complete topic sentence.
- Use freewriting, brainstorming, or clustering to generate ideas for the body of your paragraph, essay, letter, or review.
- Arrange your best ideas in a plan.
- Revise for support, unity, coherence, and exact language.
- Proofread for grammar, punctuation, and spelling errors.

Writing Assignment 1 *Express your opinion.* Write a letter to either a newspaper editor or an elected official (a mayor, governor, or senator, for example) in which you suggest one solution to a particular problem, such as illegal immigration or gun control. For topic ideas and information, visit Yahoo's directory of websites on current issues and causes at <http://dir.yahoo.com/Society_and_Culture/Issues_and_Causes/> or SpeakOut.com at <http://speakout.com/activism/issues/>. State your opinion in your topic sentence or thesis statement, and present at least three reasons in support of your opinion. Consider actually mailing your letter to the recipient, but not before you proofread for spelling errors that would weaken your writing.

Writing Assignment 2 *Solve a problem.* You have identified what you consider to be a problem in your place of employment. When you go to your supervisor, you are asked to write up your concerns and to suggest a solution. Begin first by describing the problem, and then give background information, including what you suspect are the causes of the problem. Then offer suggestions for solving it. End with some guidelines for evaluating the success of the changes. In your concluding sentence, thank your supervisor for his or her consideration of your letter. Don't let typos or mistaken look-alikes/sound-alikes detract from your ideas. Proofread for accurate spelling!

Writing Assignment 3 *Review a movie.* Your college newspaper has asked you to review a movie. Pick a popular film that you especially liked or disliked. In your first sentence, name the film and state whether you recommend it. Explain your evaluation by discussing two or three specific reasons for your reactions to the picture. Describe as much of the film as is necessary to make your point, but do not retell the plot. Proofread for accurate spelling. Consider posting your review at <http://www.movievine.com/> or <http://www.franksreelreviews.com>.

Writing Assignment 4 *Describe a family custom.* Most families have customs that they perform together. These customs often help strengthen the bond that the members of the family feel toward each other. A custom might be eating Sunday dinner together, going to religious services, celebrating holidays in a special way, or even holding a family council to discuss difficulties and concerns. Write about a custom in your family that is especially meaningful. Of what value has this custom been to you or other members of the family? Proofread for accurate spelling.

Review

Proofreading

The following essay contains a number of spelling and look-alike/sound-alike errors. First, underline the misspelled or misused words. Then write each correctly spelled word above the line. (You should find thirty-eight errors.)

Everyday Angel

(1) On January 2, 2007, construction worker Wesley Autry and his too young daugters were standing on a New York City subway platform waiting for the train. (2) Suddenly, a twenty-year-old student standing nearby suffered a siezure and tumbled onto the subway tracks. (3) Autry saw the headlights of an approaching train and realized that the young men was about to be run over right in front of the children. (4) Leapping onto the rails, Autry pulled the strugling student down into the shallow drainage ditch between the tracks and pined him their while one train and than another rumbled over them with about two inchs to spare. (5) The next day, national and international headlines proclaimed Autry to be an "angle," a "superman," a "hero," and "one in a million." (6) Autry explained simply, "I just tryed to do the right thing."

(7) But his action began a nationel arguement about how far one should go to help others. (8) People couldn't help wondering if they themselfs would make a similer split-second decision to risk they're own lives for a total stranger. (9) Was Autry's act truely a one-in-a-million occurence? (10) After all, pychologists and sociologists point out that people quiet often fail to act in a emergancy because of the "bystander effect." (11) Bystander effect is the tendency to do nothing in a crisis because one assumes that someone else will take any nesessary action.

(12) On the other hand, Autry's bravery inspirred people worldwide. (13) CNN reconized him as an "everyday hero," and in 2007, *Time* magazine

named him one of 100 poeple "whose power, talent or moral example is transforming the world." (14) Some went so far as to honor his selfless behavor buy giving him awards, scholarships for his children, cash, and free trips. (15) Others gained new confidence in they're own ability to peform a dareing rescue. (16) In one poll, most New Yorkers beleived that they would probly jump off a ferry boat to save a child who had fallen overboard, try to stop a mugger from steeling an elderly women's money, and even run into a burning building to save someone traped inside.

EXPLORING ONLINE

<http://www.rd.com/heroes-stories-of-bravery> Visit the *Reader's Digest* Heroes and True Stories of Bravery website, read about others' heroic deeds, and post a story about a hero in your community.

UNIT 8

Writers' Workshop

Examine Positive (or Negative) Values

One good way to develop a paragraph or essay is by supporting the topic sentence or the thesis statement with three points. A student uses this approach in the following essay. In your group or class, read her work, aloud if possible.

Villa Avenue

(1) The values I learned growing up on Villa Avenue in the Bronx have guided me through thirty-five years and three children. Villa Avenue taught me the importance of having a friendly environment, playing together, and helping people.

(2) Villa Avenue was a three-block, friendly environment. I grew up on the middle block. The other ones were called "up the block" and "down the block." Mary's Candy Store was up the block. It had a candy counter and soda fountain on the left and on the right a jukebox that played three songs for twenty-five cents. My friends and I would buy candy, hang out, and listen to the Beatles and other music of the sixties. A little down from Mary's on the corner was Joey's Deli. When you walked into Joey's, different aromas would welcome you to a world of Italian delicacies. Fresh mozzarella in water always sat on the counter, with salami, pepperoni, and imported provolone cheese hanging above. On Sundays at Joey's, my father would buy us a black-and-white cookie for a weekly treat.

(3) On Villa Avenue, everyone helped everyone else. Everybody's doors were open, so if I had to go to the bathroom or needed a drink of water, I could go to a dozen different apartments. If my parents had to go somewhere, they would leave me with a friend. When people on the block got sick, others went to the store for them, cleaned for them, watched their kids, and made sure they had food to eat. If someone died, everyone mourned and pitched

in to help with arrangements. When I reflect on those days, I realize that the way the mothers looked out for each other's children is like your modern-day play group. The difference is that our play area was "the block."

(4) The whole street was our playground. We would play curb ball at the intersection. One corner was home plate, and the other ones were the bases. Down the block where the street was wide, we would play Johnny on the Pony with ten to fifteen kids. On summer nights, it was kick the can or hide and seek. Summer days we spent under an open fire hydrant. Everyone would be in the water, including moms and dads. Sometimes the teenagers would go to my Uncle Angelo's house and get a wine barrel to put over the hydrant. With the top and bottom of the barrel off, the water would shoot twenty to thirty feet in the air and come down on us like a waterfall.

Loretta M. Carney, student

1. How effective is Loretta Carney's essay?

   _____ Clear main idea?   _____ Good supporting details?

   _____ Logical organization?   _____ Effective conclusion?

2. What is the main idea of the essay? Can you find the thesis statement, one sentence that states this main idea?

3. The writer states that Villa Avenue taught her three values. What are they? Are these clearly explained in paragraphs 2, 3, and 4? Are they discussed in the same order in which the thesis statement presents them? If not, what change would you suggest?

4. Does this essay *conclude* or just stop? What suggestions would you make to the writer for a more effective conclusion?

5. Proofread Carney's essay. Do you see any error patterns that she should watch out for?

Writing and Revising Ideas

1. Describe a place or person that taught you positive (or negative) values.

2. Do places like Villa Avenue exist anymore? Explain why you do or do not think so.

See Chapter 5 for help with planning and writing. You might wish to present your topic with three supporting points, the way Loretta Carney does. As you revise, pay close attention to writing a good thesis sentence and supporting paragraphs that contain clear, detailed explanations.

Reading Selections and Quotation Bank

Reading Selections

Reading Strategies for the Writer

The reading selections that follow were chosen to interest you, inspire you, and make you think. Many deal with issues you face at college, at work, or at home. Your instructor may ask you to read a selection and be prepared to discuss it in class or to write a composition or journal entry about it. The more carefully you read these selections, the better you will be able to think, talk, and write about them. Below are eight strategies that can help you become a more active and effective reader.

1. **Preview the reading selection.** Before you begin to read, scan the whole article to get a sense of the author's main idea and supporting points. First read the title, headnote, and any subtitles; next, quickly read the first and last paragraphs. This should give you a fairly clear idea of the author's subject and point of view. Finally, skim the whole selection, looking for the main supporting ideas. Previewing will increase your enjoyment and understanding as you read.

2. **Underline important ideas.** It is easy to forget what you have read, even though you have recently read it. Underlining or highlighting what you consider the main ideas will help you later to remember and discuss what you have read. Some students number the main points in order to understand the development of the author's ideas.

3. **Write your reactions in the margins.** If you strongly agree or disagree with an idea, write *yes* or *no* next to it. Record other questions and comments also, as if you were having a conversation with the author. Writing assignments will often ask you to respond to a particular idea or situation in a selection. Having already noted your reactions in the margins will help you focus your thinking and your writing.

4. **Prepare questions.** You will occasionally come across material that you cannot follow. Reread the passage. If you still have questions, place a question mark in the margin to remind you to ask a classmate or the instructor for an explanation.

5. **Circle unfamiliar words.** If you come across a new word that makes it difficult to follow what the author is saying, look it up immediately, jot the definition in the margin, and go back to reading. If, however, you can sense the meaning from the context—how the word fits the sentence—just circle it and, when you have finished the selection, consult a dictionary.

6. **Note effective or powerful writing.** If a particular line strikes you as especially important or moving, underline or highlight it. You may wish later to quote it in your written assignment. Be selective, however, in what you mark. *Too much* annotation can make it hard to focus on what is important when you discuss the selection in class or write about it.

7. **Vary your pace.** Some selections can be read quickly because you already know a great deal about the subject or because you find the material simple and direct. Other selections may require you to read slowly, pausing between

sentences. Guard against the tendency to skim when the going gets tough: more difficult material will usually reward your extra time and attention.

8. **Reread.** If you expect to discuss or write about a selection, one reading is usually not enough. Budget your time so you will be able to give the selection a second or third reading. You will be amazed at how much more you can get from the selection as you reread. You may understand ideas that were unclear the first time around. In addition, you may notice significant new points and details: perhaps you will change your mind about ideas you originally agreed or disagreed with. Rereading will help you discuss and write more intelligently and will increase your reading enjoyment.

The following essay has been marked by a student. Your own responses to this essay would, of course, be different. Examining how this essay was annotated may help you annotate other selections in this book and read more effectively in your other courses.

Daring to Dream Big

Diane Sawyer

I see her on TV—she's a top journalist.

A beauty contest?

I like this comparison—my dad is my island.

I was seventeen years old, a high school senior in Louisville, Kentucky, representing my state in the 1963 America's Junior Miss competition in Mobile, Alabama. In the midst of it all, there was one person who stood at the center—at least my psychological center—someone I viewed as an island in an ocean of anxiety. She was one of the judges, a well-known writer, a woman whose sea-gray eyes fixed on you with laser penetration. Her name was Catherine Marshall.

During the rehearsal on the last day of the pageant, the afternoon before it would all end, several of us were waiting backstage when a pageant official said Catherine Marshall wanted to speak with us. We gathered around. Most of us were expecting a last-minute pep talk, but we were surprised.

Wow, this is interesting. Being a beauty queen is not enough.

Main idea? DREAM BIG. Many of my friends don't set high goals for themselves. Do I? Aspired = aimed

She fixed her eyes upon us. "You have set goals for yourselves. I have heard some of them. But I don't think you have set them high enough. You have talent and intelligence and a chance. I think you should take those goals and expand them. Think of the most you could do with your lives. Make what you do matter. Above all, dream big."

It was not so much an instruction as a dare. I felt stunned. This woman I admired so much was disappointed in us—not by what we were but by how little we (aspired) to be.

Good question: How would I answer it? Should I dream bigger?

I won the America's Junior Miss contest that year. I graduated in 1967 with a BA degree in English and a complete lack of inspiration about what I should do with it. I went to my father. "What is it that you enjoy doing most?" he asked.

"Writing," I replied slowly. "And working with people. And being in touch with what's happening in the world."

He thought for a moment. "Did you ever consider television?"

Marshall's speech really motivated Sawyer to act.

At that time there were few if any women journalists on television. The idea of being a pioneer in the field sounded like dreaming big. That's how I came to get up my nerve and go out to convince the news director at Louisville's WLKY-TV to let me have a chance.

revelation = discovery

He gave it to me. For the next two and a half years I worked as a combination weather and news reporter. Eventually, though, I began to feel restless. I'd wait for the (revelation,) the sign pointing in the direction of the Big Dream. What I didn't realize is what Catherine Marshall undoubtedly knew all along—that the dream is not the destination but the journey.

I never thought of it this way.

Today I'm coeditor of CBS's *Sixty Minutes*. I keep a suitcase packed at all times so that I can fly out on assignment at a moment's notice. When I go out into the world, I can almost hear a wonderful woman prodding me with her fiery challenge to stretch farther and, no matter how big the dream, to dream a little bigger still. God, she seems to be saying, can forgive failure, but not failing to try.

This story makes me think of the importance of good role models—a good writing topic?

I'm inspired! Should I go for it and be a dentist instead of a dental assistant?

Mrs. Flowers
Maya Angelou

Maya Angelou (born Marguerite Johnson) is one of America's best-loved poets and the author of *I Know Why the Caged Bird Sings*. In this book, her life story, she tells of being raped when she was eight years old. Her response to the traumatic experience was to stop speaking. In this selection, Angelou describes the woman who eventually threw her a "life line."

1   For nearly a year, I sopped around the house, the Store, the school and the church, like an old biscuit, dirty and inedible. Then I met, or rather got to know, the lady who threw me my first life line.

2   Mrs. Bertha Flowers was the aristocrat of Black Stamps. She had the grace of control to appear warm in the coldest weather, and on the Arkansas summer days it seemed she had a private breeze which swirled around, cooling her. She was thin without the taut[1] look of wiry people, and her printed voile[2] dresses and flowered hats were as right for her as denim overalls for a farmer. She was our side's answer to the richest white woman in town.

3   Her skin was a rich black that would have peeled like a plum if snagged, but then no one would have thought of getting close enough to Mrs. Flowers to ruffle her dress, let alone snag her skin. She didn't encourage familiarity. She wore gloves too.

4   I don't think I ever saw Mrs. Flowers laugh, but she smiled often. A slow widening of her thin black lips to show even, small white teeth, then the slow effortless closing. When she chose to smile on me, I always wanted to thank her. The action was so graceful and inclusively benign.[3]

5   She was one of the few gentlewomen I have ever known and has remained throughout my life the measure of what a human being can be . . .

6   One summer afternoon, sweet-milk fresh in my memory, she stopped at the Store to buy provisions. Another Negro woman of her health and age would have been expected to carry the paper sacks home in one hand, but Momma said, "Sister Flowers, I'll send Bailey up to your house with these things."

7   She smiled that slow dragging smile. "Thank you, Mrs. Henderson. I'd prefer Marguerite though." My name was beautiful when she said it. "I've been meaning to talk to her, anyway." They gave each other age-group looks.

---

1. taut: tight, tense
2. voile: a light, semi-sheer fabric
3. benign: kind, gentle

Momma said, "Well, that's all right then. Sister, go and change your dress. You 8
going to Sister Flowers's." . . .

There was a little path beside the rocky road, and Mrs. Flowers walked in front 9
swinging her arms and picking her way over the stones.

She said, without turning her head, to me, "I hear you're doing very good 10
school work, Marguerite, but that it's all written. The teachers report that they
have trouble getting you to talk in class." We passed the triangular farm on our
left, and the path widened to allow us to walk together. I hung back in the separate
unasked and unanswerable questions.

"Come and walk along with me, Marguerite." I couldn't have refused even 11
if I wanted to. She pronounced my name so nicely. Or more correctly, she spoke
each word with such clarity that I was certain a foreigner who didn't understand
English could have understood her.

"Now no one is going to make you talk—possibly no one can. But bear in 12
mind, language is man's way of communicating with his fellow man and it is language alone which separates him from the lower animals." That was a totally new
idea to me, and I would need time to think about it.

"Your grandmother says you read a lot. Every chance you get. That's good, 13
but not good enough. Words mean more than what is set down on paper. It takes
the human voice to infuse[4] them with the shades of deeper meaning."

I memorized the part about the human voice infusing words. It seemed so 14
valid and poetic.

She said she was going to give me some books and that I not only must read 15
them. I must read them aloud. She suggested that I try to make a sentence sound
in as many different ways as possible.

"I'll accept no excuse if you return a book to me that has been badly handled." 16
My imagination boggled at the punishment I would deserve if in fact I did abuse
a book of Mrs. Flowers's. Death would be too kind and brief.

The odors in the house surprised me. Somehow I had never connected Mrs. 17
Flowers with food or eating or any other common experience of common people.
There must have been an outhouse, too, but my mind never recorded it.

The sweet scent of vanilla met us as she opened the door. 18

"I made tea cookies this morning. You see, I had planned to invite you for 19
cookies and lemonade so we could have this little chat. The lemonade is in the
icebox."

It followed that Mrs. Flowers would have ice on an ordinary day, when most 20
families in our town bought ice late on Saturdays only a few times during the summer to be used in the wooden ice-cream freezers.

She took the bags from me and disappeared through the kitchen door. I looked 21
around the room that I had never in my wildest fantasies imagined I would see.
Browned photographs leered or threatened from the walls and the white, freshly
done curtains pushed against themselves and against the wind. I wanted to gobble
up the room entire and take it to Bailey, who would help me analyze and enjoy it.

"Have a seat, Marguerite. Over there by the table." She carried a platter cov- 22
ered with a tea towel. Although she warned that she hadn't tried her hand at baking sweets for some time, I was certain that like everything else about her the
cookies would be perfect.

They were flat round wafers, slightly browned on the edges and butter-yellow 23
in the center. With the cold lemonade they were sufficient for childhood's lifelong
diet. Remembering my manners, I took nice little lady-like bites off the edges. She
said she had made them expressly for me and that she had a few in the kitchen that

> *"I was liked, and what a difference it made. I was respected not as Mrs. Henderson's grandchild or Bailey's sister but for just being Marguerite Johnson."*

---

4. infuse: to fill or penetrate

I could take home to my brother. So I jammed one whole cake in my mouth and the rough crumbs scratched the insides of my jaws, and if I hadn't had to swallow, it would have been a dream come true.

As I ate she began the first of what we later called "my lessons in living." She said that I must always be intolerant of ignorance but understanding of illiteracy. That some people, unable to go to school, were more educated and even more intelligent than college professors. She encouraged me to listen carefully to what country people called mother wit. That in those homely sayings was couched the collective[5] wisdom of generations. 24

When I finished the cookies she brushed off the table and brought a thick, small book from the bookcase. I had read *A Tale of Two Cities* and found it up to my standards as a romantic novel. She opened the first page and I heard poetry for the first time in my life. 25

"It was the best of times and the worst of times . . ." Her voice slid in and curved down through and over the words. She was nearly singing. I wanted to look at the pages. Were they the same that I had read? Or were there notes, music, lined on the pages, as in a hymn book? Her sounds began cascading[6] gently. I knew from listening to a thousand preachers that she was nearing the end of her reading, and I hadn't really heard, heard to understand, a single word. 26

"How do you like that?" 27

It occurred to me that she expected a response. The sweet vanilla flavor was still on my tongue and her reading was a wonder in my ears. I had to speak. 28

I said, "Yes ma'am." It was the least I could do, but it was the most also. 29

"There's one more thing. Take this book of poems and memorize one for me. Next time you pay me a visit, I want you to recite." 30

I have tried often to search behind the sophistication of years for the enchantment I so easily found in those gifts. The essence escapes but its aura[7] remains. To be allowed, no, invited, into the private lives of strangers, and to share their joys and fears, was a chance to exchange the Southern bitter wormwood[8] for . . . a hot cup of tea and milk with Oliver Twist.[9] 31

I was liked, and what a difference it made. I was respected not as Mrs. Henderson's grandchild or Bailey's sister but for just being Marguerite Johnson. 32

Childhood's logic never asks to be proved (all conclusions are absolute). I didn't question why Mrs. Flowers had singled me out for attention, nor did it occur to me that Momma might have asked her to give me a little talking to. All I cared about was that she had made tea cookies for *me* and read to *me* from her favorite book. It was enough to prove that she liked me. 33

Discussion and Writing Questions

1. Angelou vividly describes Mrs. Flowers's appearance and style (paragraphs 2–5). What kind of woman is Mrs. Flowers? What words and details convey this impression?
2. What strategies does Mrs. Flowers use to reach out to Marguerite?
3. What does Marguerite's first "lesson in living" include (paragraph 24)? Do you think such a lesson could really help a young person live better or differently?

---

5. collective: gathered from a group
6. cascading: falling like a waterfall
7. aura: a special quality or air around something or someone
8. wormwood: something harsh or embittering
9. Oliver Twist: a character from a novel by Charles Dickens

4. In paragraph 31, the author speaks of her enchantment at receiving gifts from Mrs. Flowers. Just what gifts did Mrs. Flowers give her? Which do you consider the most important gift?

Writing Assignments

1. Has anyone ever thrown you a lifeline when you were in trouble? Describe the problem or hurt facing you and just what this person did to reach out. What "gifts" did he or she offer you (attention, advice, and so forth)? Were you able to receive them?

    If you prefer, write about a time when you helped someone else. What seemed to be weighing this person down? How were you able to help?

2. Mrs. Flowers read aloud so musically that Marguerite "heard poetry for the first time in [her] life." Has someone ever shared a love—of a sport, gardening, or history, for example—so strongly that you were changed? What happened and how were you changed?

3. Many people have trouble speaking up—in class, at social gatherings, even to one other person. Can you express your thoughts and feelings as freely as you would like in most situations? What opens you up, and what shuts you up?

Superman and Me

Sherman Alexie

Growing up on the Spokane Indian Reservation, Sherman Alexie and his classmates were "expected to fail." This essay tells the story of how the author refused to fail and instead found his true calling as a writer and poet. In 2010, Alexie's *War Dances* won the Pen/Faulkner Fiction Award, and his movie *Smoke Signals* has become a classic.

I learned to read with a Superman comic book. Simple enough, I suppose. I cannot recall which particular Superman comic book I read, nor can I remember which villain he fought in that issue. I cannot remember the plot, nor the means by which I obtained the comic book. What I can remember is this: I was three years old, a Spokane Indian boy living with his family on the Spokane Indian Reservation in eastern Washington State. We were poor by most standards, but one of my parents usually managed to find some minimum-wage job or another, which made us middle-class by reservation standards. I had a brother and three sisters. We lived on a combination of irregular paychecks, hope, fear and government surplus food.

My father, who is one of the few Indians who went to Catholic school on purpose, was an avid[1] reader of westerns, spy thrillers, murder mysteries, gangster epics, basketball player biographies and anything else he could find. He bought his books by the pound at Dutch's Pawn Shop, Goodwill, Salvation Army, and Value Village. When he had extra money, he bought new novels at supermarkets, convenience stores and hospital gift shops. Our house was filled with books. They were stacked in crazy piles in the bathroom, bedrooms and living room. In a fit of unemployment-inspired creative energy, my father built a set of bookshelves and soon filled them with a random assortment of books about the Kennedy assassination, Watergate, the Vietnam War and the entire twenty-three-book series of

---

1. avid: enthusiastic and eager

Author Sherman Alexie taught himself to read with Superman comics.

the Apache westerns. My father loved books, and since I loved my father with an aching devotion, I decided to love books as well.

I can remember picking up my father's books before I could read. The words themselves were mostly foreign, but I still remember the exact moment when I first understood, with a sudden clarity,[2] the purpose of a paragraph. I didn't have the vocabulary to say "paragraph," but I realized that a paragraph was a fence that held words. The words inside a paragraph worked together for a common purpose. They had some specific reason for being inside the same fence. This knowledge delighted me. I began to think of everything in terms of paragraphs. Our reservation was a small paragraph within the United States. My family's house was a paragraph, distinct from the other paragraphs of the LeBrets to the north, the Fords to our south and the Tribal School to the west. Inside our house, each family member existed as a separate paragraph but still had genetics[3] and common experiences to link us. Now, using this logic, I can see my changed family as an essay of seven paragraphs: mother, father, older brother, the deceased sister, my younger twin sisters and our adopted little brother.

At the same time I was seeing the world in paragraphs, I also picked up that Superman comic book. Each panel, complete with picture, dialogue and narrative was a three-dimensional paragraph. In one panel, Superman breaks through a door. His suit is red, blue and yellow. The brown door shatters into many pieces. I look at the narrative above the picture. I cannot read the words, but I assume it tells me that "Superman is breaking down the door." Aloud, I pretend to read the words and say, "Superman is breaking down the door." Words, dialogue, also float out of Superman's mouth. Because he is breaking down the door, I assume he says, "I am breaking down the door." Once again, I pretend to read the words and say aloud, "I am breaking down the door." In this way, I learned to read.

This might be an interesting story all by itself. A little Indian boy teaches himself to read at an early age and advances quickly. He reads "Grapes of Wrath" in kindergarten when other children are struggling through "Dick and Jane." If he'd

3

4

5

2. clarity: clear understanding
3. genetics: characteristics and traits passed from parents to their children

been anything but an Indian boy living on the reservation, he might have been called a prodigy.[4] But he is an Indian boy living on the reservation and is simply an oddity.[5] He grows into a man who often speaks of his childhood in the third-person, as if it will somehow dull the pain and make him sound more modest about his talents.

"A smart Indian is a dangerous person."

A smart Indian is a dangerous person, widely feared and ridiculed by Indians and non-Indians alike. I fought with my classmates on a daily basis. They wanted me to stay quiet when the non-Indian teacher asked for answers, for volunteers, for help. We were Indian children who were expected to be stupid. Most lived up to those expectations inside the classroom but subverted[6] them on the outside. They struggled with basic reading in school but could remember how to sing a few dozen powwow[7] songs. They were monosyllabic[8] in front of their non-Indian teachers but could tell complicated stories and jokes at the dinner table. They submissively[9] ducked their heads when confronted by a non-Indian adult but would slug it out with the Indian bully who was ten years older. As Indian children, we were expected to fail in the non-Indian world. Those who failed were ceremonially accepted by other Indians and appropriately pitied by non-Indians.

I refused to fail. I was smart. I was arrogant. I was lucky. I read books late into the night, until I could barely keep my eyes open. I read books at recess, then during lunch, and in the few minutes left after I had finished my classroom assignments. I read books in the car when my family traveled to powwows or basketball games. In shopping malls, I ran to the bookstores and read bits and pieces of as many books as I could. I read the books my father brought home from the pawnshops and secondhand. I read the books I borrowed from the library. I read the backs of cereal boxes. I read the newspaper. I read the bulletins posted on the walls of the school, the clinic, the tribal offices, the post office. I read junk mail. I read auto-repair manuals. I read magazines. I read anything that had words and paragraphs. I read with equal parts joy and desperation. I loved those books, but I also knew that love had only one purpose. I was trying to save my life.

Despite all the books I read, I am still surprised I became a writer. I was going to be a pediatrician.[10] These days, I write novels, short stories and poems. I visit schools and teach creative writing to Indian kids. In all my years in the reservation school system, I was never taught how to write poetry, short stories or novels. I was certainly never taught that Indians wrote poetry, short stories and novels. Writing was something beyond Indians. I cannot recall a single time that a guest teacher visited the reservation. There must have been visiting teachers. Who were they? Where are they now? Do they exist? I visit the schools as often as possible. The Indian kids crowd the classroom. Many are writing their own poems, short stories and novels. They have read my books. They have read many other books. They look at me with bright eyes and arrogant wonder. They are trying to save their lives. Then there are the sullen[11] and already defeated Indian kids who sit in the back rows and ignore me with theatrical precision. The pages of their notebooks are empty. They carry neither pencil nor pen. They stare out the window. They refuse and resist. "Books," I say to them. "Books," I say. I throw my weight

6

7

8

---

4. prodigy: a child with exceptional talents
5. oddity: an unusual person or thing
6. subverted: undercut, defied
7. powwow: an Indian social gathering
8. monosyllabic: speaking only in one-syllable words
9. submissively: without resistance; obediently
10. pediatrician: a doctor who treats children
11. sullen: in a bad mood and silent

against their locked doors. The door holds. I am smart. I am arrogant. I am lucky. I am trying to save our lives.

Discussion and Writing Questions

1. Why would a smart Indian be a "dangerous person, widely feared and ridiculed" (paragraph 6)? Why would non-Indians adopt this opinion? Why would Indian children adopt this self-defeating idea?
2. What does the author mean when he writes in paragraph 7, "I was trying to save my life"? What point is he making about reading books and educating oneself?
3. Based on Alexie's story, what inner characteristics or outward support does a person need to break free of stereotypes and dead ends and forge a path to success?
4. In paragraph 3, the author uses the metaphor that "a paragraph was a fence that held words." Does this metaphor help you understand what a paragraph does? How would you explain a paragraph?

Writing Assignments

1. Sherman Alexie writes about an activity—reading—that gave him strength and hope during a very painful time in his life. Write a composition describing an activity, tool, or person that gives you strength and hope for your future.
2. Has there ever been a time in your life when someone *expected* you to fail? If so, who was it, what happened, and how did you react?
3. Have you ever been rejected or even ridiculed by your peers for making an unpopular decision or taking an unpopular action? Why did you defy the group's wishes and choose to go your own way?

Hot Dogs and Wild Geese

Firoozeh Dumas

More than 31 million people who live in the United States were born in other countries, and most of them did not speak English very well—or at all—when they first came here. As Iranian-born writer Firoozeh Dumas illustrates with her family's story, learning English is not only confusing but often downright hilarious. This essay appears in her book, *Funny in Farsi*.

Moving to America was both exciting and frightening, but we found great comfort in knowing that my father spoke English. Having spent years regaling[1] us with stories about his graduate years in America, he had left us with the distinct impression that America was his second home. My mother and I planned to stick close to him, letting him guide us through the exotic American landscape that he knew so well. We counted on him not only to translate the language but also to translate the culture, to be a link to this most foreign of lands. He was to be our own private Rosetta stone.[2]

---

1. regaling: entertaining
2. Rosetta stone: carved stone tablet, the key to translating ancient Egyptian writing

Once we reached America, we wondered whether perhaps my father had confused his life in America with someone else's. Judging from the bewildered looks of store cashiers, gas station attendants, and waiters, my father spoke a version of English not yet shared with the rest of America. His attempts to find a "vater closet"[3] in a department store would usually lead us to the drinking fountain or the home furnishings section. Asking my father to ask the waitress the definition of "sloppy Joe" or "Tater Tots" was no problem. His translations, however, were highly suspect. Waitresses would spend several minutes responding to my father's questions, and these responses, in turn, would be translated as "She doesn't know." Thanks to my father's translations, we stayed away from hot dogs, catfish, and hush puppies, and no amount of caviar[4] in the sea would have convinced us to try mud pie.

We wondered how my father had managed to spend several years attending school in America yet remain so utterly befuddled[5] by Americans. We soon discovered that his college years had been spent mainly in the library, where he had managed to avoid contact with all Americans except his engineering professors. As long as the conversation was limited to vectors,[6] surface tension, and fluid mechanics, my father was Fred Astaire[7] with words. But one step outside the scintillating[8] world of petroleum engineering and he had two left tongues.

My father's only other regular contact in college had been his roommate, a Pakistani who spent his days preparing curry. Since neither spoke English but both liked curries, they got along splendidly. The person who had assigned them together had probably hoped they would either learn English or invent a common language for the occasion. Neither happened.

> *"After searching fruitlessly for elbow grease, I asked the salesclerk for help."*

My father's inability to understand spoken English was matched only by his efforts to deny the problem. His constant attempts at communicating with Americans seemed at first noble and adventurous, then annoying. Somewhere between his thick Persian accent and his use of vocabulary found in pre–World War II British textbooks, my father spoke a private language. That nobody understood him hurt his pride, so what he lacked in speaking ability, he made up for by reading. He was the only person who actually read each and every document before he signed it. Buying a washing machine from Sears might take the average American thirty minutes, but by the time my father had finished reading the warranties, terms of contracts, and credit information, the store was closing and the janitor was asking us to please step aside so he could finish mopping the floor.

My mother's approach to learning English consisted of daily lessons with Monty Hall and Bob Barker.[9] Her devotion to *Let's Make a Deal* and *The Price Is Right*[10] was evident in her newfound ability to recite useless information. After a few months of television viewing, she could correctly tell us whether a coffeemaker cost more or less than $19.99. How many boxes of Hamburger Helper, Swanson's TV dinners, or Turtle Wax could one buy without spending a penny more than twenty dollars? She knew that, too. Strolling down the grocery aisle, she rejoiced in her celebrity sightings—Lipton tea! Campbell's tomato soup! Betty Crocker Rich & Creamy Frosting! Every day, she would tell us the day's wins and

2

3

4

5

6

---

3. "vater closet": *water closet,* the British term for *bathroom*
4. caviar: fancy fish eggs
5. befuddled: confused
6. vectors: mathematical quantities
7. Fred Astaire: American dancer and film star of the 1930s, 1940s, and 1950s
8. scintillating: sparkling, brilliant
9. Monty Hall and Bob Barker: early television game show hosts
10. *Let's Make a Deal* and *The Price Is Right:* television game shows that began in the 1960s and 1970s

losses on the game shows. "He almost won the boat, but the wife picked curtain number two and they ended up with a six-foot chicken statue." The bad prizes on *Let's Make a Deal* sounded far more intriguing than the good ones. Who would want the matching La-Z-Boy recliners when they could have the adult-size crib and high-chair set?

My mother soon decided that the easiest way for her to communicate with Americans was to use me as an interpreter. My brother Farshid, with his schedule full of soccer, wrestling, and karate, was too busy to be recruited for this dubious[11] honor. At an age when most parents are guiding their kids toward independence, my mother was hanging on to me for dear life. I had to accompany her to the grocery store, the hairdresser, the doctor, and every place else that a kid wouldn't want to go. My reward for doing this was the constant praise of every American we encountered. Hearing a seven-year-old translate Persian into English and vice versa made quite an impression on everyone. People lavished[12] compliments on me. "You must be very, very smart, a genius maybe." I always responded by assuring them that if they ever moved to another country, they, too, would learn the language. (What I wanted to say was that I wished I could be at home watching *The Brady Bunch*[13] instead of translating the qualities of various facial moisturizers.) My mother had her own response to the compliments: "Americans are easily impressed."   **7**

I always encouraged my mother to learn English, but her talents lay elsewhere. Since she had never learned English in school, she had no idea of its grammar. She would speak entire paragraphs without using any verbs. She referred to everyone and everything as "it," leaving the listener wondering whether she was talking about her husband or the kitchen table. Even if she did speak a sentence more or less correctly, her accent made it incomprehensible. "W" and "th" gave her the most difficulty. As if God were playing a linguistic[14] joke on us, we lived in "Veetee-er" (Whittier), we shopped at "Veetvood" (Whitwood) Plaza, I attended "Leffingvell" School, and our neighbor was none other than "Valter Villiams."   **8**

Despite little progress on my mother's part, I continually encouraged her. Rather than teach her English vocabulary and grammar, I eventually decided to teach her entire sentences to repeat. I assumed that once she got used to speaking correctly, I could be removed, like training wheels, and she would continue coasting. I was wrong.   **9**

Noticing some insects in our house one day, my mother asked me to call the exterminator. I looked up the number, then told my mother to call and say, "We have silverfish in our house." My mother grumbled, dialed the number, and said, "Please come rrright a-vay. Goldfeeesh all over dee house." The exterminator told her he'd be over as soon as he found his fishing pole.   **10**

A few weeks later, our washing machine broke. A repairman was summoned and the leaky pipe was quickly replaced. My mother wanted to know how to remove the black stain left by the leak. "Y'all are gonna hafta use some elbow grease," he said. I thanked him and paid him and walked with my mother to the hardware store. After searching fruitlessly[15] for elbow grease, I asked the sales-clerk for help. "It removes stains," I added. The manager was called.   **11**

---

11. dubious: doubtful, questionable
12. lavished: heaped or poured
13. *The Brady Bunch:* an early 1970s television sitcom
14. linguistic: relating to language
15. fruitlessly: without success

Once the manager finished laughing, he gave us the disappointing explana- 12
tion. My mother and I walked home empty-handed. That, I later learned, is what
Americans call a wild-goose chase.

Now that my parents have lived in America for thirty years, their English has 13
improved somewhat, but not as much as one would hope. It's not entirely their
fault; English is a confusing language. When my father paid his friend's daughter
the compliment of calling her homely, he meant she would be a great housewife.
When he complained about horny drivers, he was referring to their tendency to
honk. And my parents still don't understand why teenagers want to be cool so
they can be hot.

I no longer encourage my parents to learn English. I've given up. Instead, I'm 14
grateful for the wave of immigration that has brought Iranian television, newspapers, and supermarkets to America. Now, when my mother wants to ask the
grocer whether he has any more eggplants in the back that are a little darker and
more firm, because the ones he has out aren't right for *khoresht bademjun*, she can
do so in Persian, all by herself. And for that, I say hallelujah, a word that needs no
translation.

Discussion and Writing Questions

1. Why was Dumas so sure that her father would guide the family easily through
   the mysteries of American life (paragraph 1)? Why was he, in fact, so little help
   (paragraph 2)? How do you guess that he translated the words *hot dogs, catfish,
   hush puppies,* and *mud pie* so that his family refused to eat these foods?
2. The author humorously describes the weird skills her mother learned by
   watching so much American television. What did the mother learn?
3. In paragraph 7, Dumas writes, "At an age when most parents are guiding their
   kids toward independence, my mother was hanging on to me for dear life." If
   a child of immigrants must serve as a translator for his or her parents, parent-
   child roles sometimes can be reversed. Is this a problem?
4. Dumas uses funny examples to show how confusing English can be. If English
   was not your first language, what words or aspects of American culture
   especially confused you? What was funniest (or most frustrating)?

Writing Assignments

1. The United States, with its many races and ethnic groups, has been called a
   "melting pot." In a group with several classmates, decide whether the United
   States is more like a *melting pot* (where various ingredients melt together into
   one soup or goo), a *salad* (where different ingredients are tossed together but
   keep their separate flavors), or a *grocery store shelf* (where many foods in sealed
   containers do not mix). Write a paper presenting your own ideas.
2. Have you ever found yourself in a place where you did not understand the
   "rules"? This place might be a new country, a new school, a new job, or the
   dinner table of your future in-laws. Describe the challenges you faced in this
   strange new world and tell how you dealt with them. Use humor if you wish.
3. Does your town have ethnic shops, markets, restaurants, or neighborhoods that
   you have never explored? Choose one place that you would like to learn more
   about and visit there, chat with people, and perhaps have something to eat.
   Take notes on the sights, sounds, smells, and details; then write a vivid account
   of your adventure.

Beauty Is Not Just Smaller Than Life

Leonard Pitts Jr.

America's standard of female beauty, writes Leonard Pitts Jr., is now that "svelte look common to heroin addicts and supermodels." In this *Miami Herald* column, he examines this obsession and its consequences. For insightful commentary on American society, Pitts won the Pulitzer Prize in 2004.

1. It may be the ultimate weight loss plan: no diet, no exercise, no surgery, no pills. Just a little digital wizardry. Point and click here, point and click there, and unwanted pounds melt magically away—from your photographed image, that is.

2. This is what the British edition of *GQ* magazine recently did, altering photographs of actress Kate Winslet—without her knowledge or permission, she says—to give her that svelte[1] look common to heroin addicts and supermodels. Winslet has responded angrily. "This is me," she says. "Like it or lump it. . . . I'm not a twig, and I refuse to be one. I'm happy with the way I am."

3. Let the church say amen.

4. Winslet, it should be pointed out, is not what we delicately describe as a "plus-sized woman." She's just a woman with womanly curves, some of which she displayed quite openly in her star-making turn as Rose in *Titanic*.

5. I wish I had a convenient theory for when and why womanly curves became a bad thing, wish I could explain our fascination with a kind of woman who does not, as a rule, exist in nature: stick legs, sunken cheeks, waist in to here, chest out to there.

6. It was not always thus. I mean, by those standards, sex symbols of an earlier era would never have heard the first wolf whistle. Marilyn Monroe was not, after all, a bean pole. And that famous pinup of Betty Grable,[2] which, we are told, inspired the GIs to go out and win World War II, did not show a woman who had missed many meals.

7. By contrast, a 1997 *Psychology Today* article reported on a researcher who had quantified[3] the fact that Playboy centerfolds and Miss America contestants—purported[4] icons[5] of feminine physical perfection—had been getting skinnier over the years.

8. Our perception of beauty has changed. And if you're wondering why that matters, it's because our girls are watching. Watching and learning from all this how it is they should be. Much of what they have learned has proven dangerous if not deadly to body and spirit.

9. Approximately 5 million to 10 million women and girls (and 1 million boys and men) suffer from eating disorders—primarily anorexia and bulimia—which are sometimes fatal. That same *Psychology Today* recounted the results of a body image survey of 4,000 women and men. Almost 90 percent of the women wanted to lose weight.

10. Score one for pop culture. I mean, one of its primary functions is to make us dissatisfied with what we are, make us want what it is selling. Right now, it's

> *"I wish I had a convenient theory for when and why womanly curves became a bad thing."*

---

1. svelte: slender
2. Betty Grable: a popular American movie star of the 1930s–1950s
3. quantified: put in numerical form
4. purported: supposed
5. icons: symbols

selling the canard[6] that the average supermodel's body is achievable or even desirable for the average girl. And girls are getting sick, even dying, as a result.

There are those feminists who would argue that the solution is for men to stop objectifying[7] women, but their reasoning flies in the face of human nature. If somebody hadn't objectified somebody else, none of us would be here to argue about it. And anyone who doesn't think women fantasize about a masculine ideal has never seen a soap opera or romance novel. 11

I'm not out to stop—as if I could!—the endless mating dance of male and female. I'd just like to see something done to protect our girls and women from its more insidious[8] effects. Just like to see the gatekeepers of media become more conscientious about depicting the beauty of women and girls in all its dimensions. 12

Not just breasts, but brains, heart, humor, compassion, love. 13

It is a pipe dream, yes. So I guess those of us who care about such things will have to be satisfied with concentrating on those girls closest to us—our daughters, our nieces, our sisters and friends—and exhorting[9] them to value themselves for *all* the things they are. 14

I tell my adolescent daughter that there's going to come a day when someone will seek to evaluate her by the same cold, meat-market standards by which *GQ* evaluated Kate Winslet. I hope, when that day comes, she has enough love for herself to respond as Winslet did. 15

"This is me. Like it or lump it." 16

For the record, Kate: Like it. Like it a lot. 17

Discussion and Writing Questions

1. Pitts opens his essay by telling how the magazine *GQ* digitally altered photographs of Kate Winslet. Why do you think he starts this way? Is it an effective introduction?
2. In paragraphs 5–8, Pitts discusses America's changing ideal of female beauty from womanly curves to "stick legs and sunken cheeks." What examples of this shift does he give? Can you think of other examples?
3. What solution does Pitts propose to protect girls and women from the media's obsession with thinness (paragraphs 14–15)? Do you think this strategy will be effective? What else can be done to make young women value themselves for more than their physical appearance?
4. Do you agree that one of the main functions of pop culture is to "make us dissatisfied with what we are" (paragraph 10)? Why would this be so?

Writing Assignments

1. Have you or someone you know ever tried to achieve our society's beauty ideal, even got plastic surgery or developed an eating disorder? Tell the story of your own or someone else's quest for the perfect body.
2. Most of the world's societies actually prefer curvy or even plump women to skinny women. It is the Western world that celebrates the "svelte look common to heroin addicts and supermodels" (paragraph 2). Do you think that the majority's attitude is preferable to that of the Western world? Why?

---

6. canard: a false or misleading story
7. objectifying: regarding as an object
8. insidious: harmful in a hidden or sneaky way
9. exhorting: urging

3. Some photographers and editors alter photographs to manipulate the viewers' perceptions or "improve the shot." In your opinion, is this a problem? When does it become a problem? For examples, including the *GQ* Winslet cover, visit <http://www.frankwbaker.com/isbmag.htm> and <http://www.frankwbaker.com/isbnews.htm>.

A Day in the Life of an Emergency Room Nurse

Beve Stevenson, RN, BN

Beve Stevenson is a veteran emergency nurse who has worked emergency rooms in Calgary, Alberta, Canada, and in a trauma helicopter. She is also a stand-up comedian, writer, and motivational speaker who believes that comedy is the perfect antidote to a high-stress job. Here she describes her work day in a busy urban hospital.

1 As I enter the hospital through the ER entrance, I assess the overall mood of the waiting room. Is everyone patient and quiet, or is the frustration palpable?[1] I change into my comfy scrubs and secure my stethoscope around my neck as I mentally prepare for my day.

2 I survey the work environment that only an ER nurse could consider normal: patients of all shapes, sizes, and colors in various states of undress, illness, and lucidity.[2] There is a cacophony[3] of loud voices, crying children, gurneys[4] and people darting about in a frantic dance. Continuing through the ER hallway, I can easily hear conversations of physicians behind the curtains with their patients. "You did this . . . how?" "How long have your teeth been itchy?" "With a fork?"

"What brings you to hospital?"
"A cab."

3 "What brings you to hospital?"

4 "A cab."

5 I am relieved not to be assigned to triage[5] today. Increased patient volumes and acuity,[6] bed and nursing shortages, not to mention agonizingly long waiting times, have made triage the bane[7] of the ER nurse's existence. The triage nurse, otherwise known as "The Bag in the Bubble," assumes the brunt[8] of waiting room abuse and acts as detective, counselor, organizer, diplomat, gatekeeper, interpreter, and sometimes magician too. No one taught us any of this in nursing school.

6 "Why do you want to see the doctor today?"

7 "None of your *?&% business!"

8 For twelve hours, I will be responsible for everything that happens in my six-bed area. I will assess and treat twenty-five patients with seemingly every kind of illness or trauma. Two will go to the OR, one will lose her baby, and another will go to heaven. I will witness the effects of domestic abuse. I will calm a frightened child and his parents, then dodge a few punches and the occasional poorly aimed spitball. I will peel off socks that haven't been removed for a year and not be surprised by what is beneath. I will start dozens of IVs, produce mounds of

---

1. palpable: obvious
2. lucidity: state of mental clarity
3. cacophony: harsh mixture of sounds
4. gurneys: rolling carts for patient transport
5. triage: process of determining and prioritizing patients' medical needs
6. acuity: awareness, sharpness
7. bane: something that brings misery or difficulty
8. brunt: the main impact

Emergency room staff at a city hospital tend a critcially ill patient.

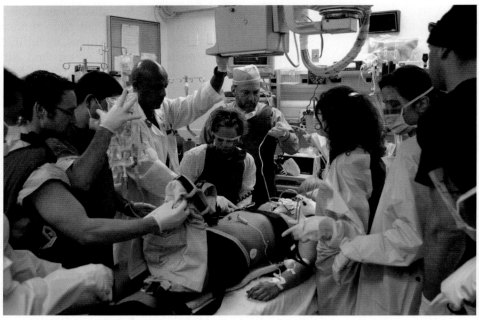

paperwork, and fix at least one computer problem. I will give multiple medications, initiate a blood transfusion, assist with a fracture reduction, then arrange for Home Care. For thirty minutes, a man will insist, with almost religious fervor,[9] that he is unconscious. I will tidy up after a herd of messy medical students. I will print labels, wipe brows and bums, collect blood samples, and educate new immigrants on the proper use of Tylenol. I will convince a teenager that her horoscope is not an effective method of birth control. I will constantly reassess my patients' conditions, making sure to alert the physician if someone deteriorates. Somehow, I will find time to ease my patients' fears by telling a few jokes. I will encourage the use of helmets, teach crutch walking and proper wound care. And that is just *today*.

Having *ER*[10] on television has helped in one way; I can now communicate great thirst after work by ordering a STAT[11] margarita. But often patients confuse TV for reality. Haven't they noticed that there aren't any wildly good-looking doctors like George Clooney or Noah Wiley working here? No physicians smooch with gorgeous nurses in the bedpan room. I've never seen a doctor rush out to the ambulance bay—that is, except to get a Coke out of the machine. And no patient's problem can be fixed in just one hour, ever.   9

On a short break, several nurses meet in the staff room for some "Vitamin C."   10
I take mine black. Here we are free to discuss typical ER subjects like festering[12] wounds while we eat. There's almost always a plate of old, greasy "share food" that could easily double as a food-poisoning lab. Why do health-care professionals eat this stuff?

Often the shift's most difficult skill is not the tough IV start, but plain old communication. Blend several languages, cultural and generational differences; mix in   11

---

9. fervor: emotional intensity
10. *ER*: a television drama about an emergency room
11. STAT: medical expression meaning "immediately, without delay"
12. festering: infected

anxiety, fear, missing teeth, intoxication, speech impediments,[13] dementia, igno- rance, and embarrassment. Add a dash of medical jargon,[14] and soon everyone is confused beyond belief. Imagine the loud assessment of the severely hearing- impaired patient; everyone within earshot cannot help but learn much more than they wanted to, including the play-by-play of a rectal examination.

By shift's end, I'm totally exhausted, my hands raw from washing, my voice 12 hoarse, and my feet screaming in agony. When I stop at the grocery store on my way home, I notice how a woman's ankles literally *flow* over the sides of her shoes. I know that her Lasix[15] dose is sub-therapeutic, just as I know the man behind me is an asthmatic who still smokes. I cannot seem to turn off this constant assessment of everyone around me.

At a party in the evening, gore-curious guests who work "normal" jobs and 13 whose trauma experience is likely limited to occasional mishaps with the office stapler, interrogate me about my work. I cannot divulge[16] what truly transpired, nor do they really want to know even if they think they do. One guest launches into the gory details of her recent surgical procedure, even offering to show me her abscess.[17] I decline.

Despite all of this, I am proud to be an Emergency Nurse. Now, where is my 14 STAT margarita?

Discussion and Writing Questions

1. Did any specifics about this nurse's day surprise you? What details did you find most effective?
2. If you went to the emergency room where the author works, would you want her to be your nurse? Why or why not? In your opinion, what are the qualities of a good nurse?
3. Do you think that a sense of humor is important in most workplaces today? Give specific examples that support your opinion.
4. Reread paragraph 8, aloud if possible, underlining examples of *parallelism*. What effect does the author's use of parallel words have on her description of her many daily tasks?

Writing Assignments

1. Write your own "Day in the Life . . ." composition. Complete the title as you wish (for example, *of a Single Mother, a Soldier in Afghanistan, a Fast Food Worker, a Video Gamer,* and so on). Use time order and many specific details to show the reader exactly what that day is like.
2. What are your main sources of stress at work, at home, or at school? How do you cope with these stresses? Use humor if you wish.
3. The author writes in paragraph 10 that "patients often confuse TV for reality." Give examples of television shows that lead viewers to form misconceptions about certain professions, such as law enforcement, medicine, or teaching. How do the characters in the show differ from the real professionals?

---

13. impediments: difficulties
14. jargon: words used in a specific profession
15. Lasix: medication for water retention
16. divulge: reveal
17. abscess: area of infected tissue and pus

You Can Take This Job and . . . Well, It Might Surprise You

Ana Veciana-Suarez

If you won a lottery jackpot, what would you do? Buy a house? Take a trip? Quit your job? Not so fast, cautions Ana Veciana-Suarez. According to this *Miami Herald* columnist, there are some very good reasons to keep right on working.

Have you heard about the part-time letter carrier who won the $183 million jackpot in Maryland? She will collect more than $76 million after state and federal taxes, making her one of the largest individual winners in U.S. lottery history. **1**

And she bought the ticket on a *whim*.[1] **2**

I read about Bernadette Gietka's good fortune just as I was about to begin a grueling[2] workday that consisted of catching up from vacation while juggling new assignments. She reminded me of all the other lottery winners I had heard about, lucky people made suddenly wealthy (and confused) by happenstance.[3] There was the California software consultant who had a $7 million winning ticket stuffed in her purse for two months. And one Nebraska couple who ended up buying the jackpot after the wife had had a bad day at work. **3**

As my mother used to say, *"La suerte es loca y a cualquiera le toca."* Luck is crazy and it can touch anybody. (Believe me, it sounds better in Spanish.) **4**

I'm not much of a player, and gambling, in one form or another, holds little attraction. Life itself, with its tribulations[4] and surprises, is risky enough for me. But belief in steady nose-to-the-grindstone economic growth has never stopped me from daydreaming. So in a biting moment of anxiety, I schlepped[5] on over to the grocery store to buy a lottery ticket for the next drawing. You never know; you just never know. **5**

> *"For better or for worse, work provides structure, imposes routine. It gives us an identity."*

Like most people, my friends and I entertain ourselves by coming up with ways to spend money we don't have. (And money we do have.) It is one of those futile[6] exercises that, done right and not too flippantly,[7] can help you focus on priorities, what truly matters to you when money is taken out of the equation. **6**

What would I do with a sudden windfall?[8] Take a trip. Buy a house on the beach. Make sure my family is well taken care of. You know, the usual. I don't know if I would quit my job, however. **7**

You would? Well, don't be so sure. Gietka, for one, plans to continue making her rounds. **8**

We complain about work, curse our bosses, practice Oscar-winning monologues[9] to deliver when we finally walk out of the sweatshop, but most of us would keep punching that time clock. According to a recent Opinion Research Corporation poll, 70 percent of us would go right on working even if the fiscal gods smiled on us. In fact, we're so wedded to our jobs that only 5 percent would go on a vacation and 3 percent would actually splurge on shopping. I think I know why. **9**

---

1. whim: sudden impulse
2. grueling: difficult, exhausting
3. happenstance: accident or twist of fate
4. tribulations: troubles
5. schlepped: dragged or moved clumsily
6. futile: useless
7. flippantly: without much thought or care
8. windfall: unexpected good fortune
9. monologues: long speeches made by one person

For better or for worse, work provides structure, imposes routine. It gives us 10 an identity. How many party conversations, after all, start with: "What do you do for a living?" Work is often social, the place we share stories about spouses and children and each other. Boardroom, factory, or cubicle, it is the prime venue[10] and source of juicy gossip.

But there's something more, too. Though we think we never have enough of 11 it, we also suspect, somewhere in the deep recesses[11] of our conniving,[12] greedy little hearts, that money, lots and lots of it, isn't all that it's cracked up to be. We nod knowingly when we hear about co-workers who sue each other over lottery winnings. We tsk-tsk when news reports tell us about a couple splitting up over the winning numbers. And we recognize, if only momentarily, that a weekly paycheck is paradoxically[13] both enslaving and liberating. Just ask your unemployed neighbor.

My mother was right: crazy, fickle luck. It arrives in many guises[14] and some- 12 times in the shape of a pay stub.

Discussion and Writing Questions

1. Veciana-Suarez begins this article with three examples of recent lottery winners (paragraphs 1–3). Who are they? Do you think these winners' stories sum up the statement "Luck is crazy and it can touch anybody"?
2. Have you ever dreamed of winning the lottery? What would you do if you won $10 million? Explain why you would—or would not—quit your job.
3. What benefits of working, besides a paycheck, does the author discuss (paragraph 10)? Can you think of other benefits that a job provides? Do all jobs offer such benefits, or do only some jobs?
4. In paragraph 6, Veciana-Suarez says that daydreaming about how to spend lottery winnings "can help you focus on priorities, what truly matters to you when money is taken out of the equation." Is this true? List the three most important things you would do if you won $10 million. Does this list help you understand what truly matters to you?

Writing Assignments

1. The odds of winning a multimillion-dollar lottery are about one in 13.98 million, yet millions of people exchange their hard-earned cash for lottery tickets every week. Discuss the reasons why so many people play when the odds are so much against them. Use examples from your own or a friend's experience.
2. The author writes that "we suspect, somewhere in the deep recesses of our conniving, greedy little hearts, that money, lots and lots of it, isn't all that it's cracked up to be" (paragraph 11). What is more important than money? Write a composition in which you answer this question.
3. Describe three or four of the most important *benefits* of being employed. Draw on your own experiences or the experiences of people you know for examples or stories that support your points.

---

10. venue: setting
11. recesses: interior spaces
12. conniving: scheming
13. paradoxically: seeming to go against common sense, yet true
14. guises: forms

The Gift

Courtland Milloy

Help sometimes comes from unexpected places. This newspaper story describes the generosity of a friend whose gift saved someone's life—and baffled most people who knew him. As you read, ask yourself how you would have acted in his place.

1   When Jermaine Washington entered the barbershop, heads turned and clippers fell silent. Customers waved and nodded, out of sheer respect. With his hands in the pockets of his knee-length, black leather coat, Washington acknowledged them with a faint smile and quietly took a seat.

2   "You know who that is?" barber Anthony Clyburn asked in a tone reserved for the most awesome neighborhood characters, such as ball players and ex-cons.

3   A year and a half ago, Washington did something that still amazes those who know him. He became a kidney donor, giving a vital organ to a woman he described as "just a friend."

4   "They had a platonic[1] relationship," said Clyburn, who works at Jake's Barber Shop in Northeast Washington. "I could see maybe giving one to my mother, but just a girl I know? I don't think so."

5   Washington, who is 25, met Michelle Stevens six years ago when they worked for the D.C. Department of Employment Services. They used to have lunch together in the department cafeteria and chitchat on the telephone during their breaks.

6   "It was nothing serious, romance-wise," said Stevens, who is 23. "He was somebody I could talk to. I had been on the kidney donor waiting list for 12 months and I had lost all hope. One day, I just called to cry on his shoulder."

7   Stevens told Washington how depressing it was to spend three days a week, three hours a day, on a kidney dialysis machine.[2] She said she suffered from chronic fatigue and blackouts and was losing her balance and her sight. He could already see that she had lost her smile.

8   "I saw my friend dying before my eyes," Washington recalled. "What was I supposed to do? Sit back and watch her die?"

9   Stevens's mother was found to be suffering from hypertension[3] and was ineligible to donate a kidney. Her 14-year-old sister offered to become a donor, but doctors concluded that she was too young.

10   Stevens's two brothers, 25 and 31, would most likely have made ideal donors because of their relatively young ages and status as family members. But both of them said no.

11   So did Stevens's boyfriend, who gave her two diamond rings with his apology.

12   "I understood," Stevens said. "They said they loved me very much, but they were just too afraid."

13   Joyce Washington, Jermaine's mother, was not exactly in favor of the idea, either. But after being convinced that her son was not being coerced,[4] she supported his decision.

14   The transplant operation took four hours. It occurred in April 1991, and began with a painful X-ray procedure in which doctors inserted a metal rod into Wash-

> "I had been on the kidney donor waiting list for 12 months and I had lost all hope. One day, I just called to cry on his shoulder."

---

1. platonic: nonromantic
2. kidney dialysis machine: a machine that filters waste material from the blood when the kidneys fail
3. hypertension: high blood pressure
4. coerced: pressured

ington's kidney and shot it with red dye. An incision nearly 20 inches long was made from his groin to the back of his shoulder. After the surgery he remained hospitalized for five days.

Today, both Stevens and Washington are fully recovered. Stevens, a graduate of Eastern High School, is studying medicine at the National Educational Center. Washington still works for D.C. Employment Services as a job counselor. 15

"I jog and work out with weights," Washington said. "Boxing and football are out, but I never played those anyway." 16

A spokesman for Washington Hospital Center said the Washington-to-Stevens gift was the hospital's first "friend-to-friend" transplant. Usually, it's wife to husband, or parent to child. But there is a shortage of even those kinds of transplants. Today, more than 300 patients are in need of kidneys in the Washington area. 17

"A woman came up to me in a movie line not long ago and hugged me," Washington said. "She thanked me for doing what I did because no one had come forth when her daughter needed a kidney, and the child died." 18

About twice a month, Stevens and Washington get together for what they call a gratitude lunch. Since the operation, she has broken up with her boyfriend. Seven months ago, Washington got a girlfriend. Despite occasional pressure by friends, a romantic relationship is not what they want. 19

"We are thankful for the beautiful relationship that we have," Stevens said. "We don't want to mess up a good thing." 20

To this day, people wonder why Washington did it. To some of the men gathered at Jake's Barber Shop not long ago, Washington's heroics were cause for questions about his sanity. Surely he could not have been in his right mind, they said. 21

One customer asked Washington where he had found the courage to give away a kidney. His answer quelled[5] most skeptics[6] and inspired even more awe. 22

"I prayed for it," Washington replied. "I asked God for guidance and that's what I got." 23

Discussion and Writing Questions

1. Long after Jermaine Washington donated a kidney to Michelle Stevens, his friends were still amazed by what he did. Why did they find his action so surprising?
2. Washington says, "What was I supposed to do? Sit back and watch her die?" (paragraph 8). Yet Stevens's brothers and her boyfriend did not offer to donate a kidney. Do you blame them? Do you understand them?
3. In what ways has Stevens's life changed because of Washington's gift? Consider her physical status, her social life, her choice of profession, her "gratitude lunches" with Washington, and so on.
4. According to Washington, where did he find the courage to donate a kidney? How did his action affect his standing in the community? How did it affect other aspects of his life?

Writing Assignments

1. Have you ever been unusually generous—or do you know someone who was? Describe that act of generosity. Why did you—or the other person—do it? How did your friends or family react?

---

5. quelled: quieted
6. skeptics: people who doubt or question

2. Do you have or does anyone you know have a serious medical condition? Describe the situation. How do or how can friends help? Can strangers help in any way?

3. Stevens and Washington do not have or want a romantic relationship. "We don't want to mess up a good thing," Stevens says (paragraph 20). Does romance "mess things up"? Write about a time when a relationship changed—either for better or for worse—because romance entered the picture.

Quitting Hip-Hop

Michaela Angela Davis

Hip-hop music is "the talking drum of our time," declares Michaela Angela Davis in this article for *Essence* magazine. She wonders, however, whether too many hip-hop artists are beating out the wrong kinds of messages. In this article, Davis shares her personal struggle with this question.

I am a 40-year-old fly girl.[1] My 13-year-old daughter, Elenni, and I often look for the same next hot thing—that perfect pair of jeans, a she's-gotta-have-it shoe, the ultimate handbag, and the freshest new sound in music, which is, more often than not, hip-hop. Though we are nearly three decades apart in age, we both feel that hip-hop is the talking drum of our time; it teaches us and represents us. But, just as some of our African ancestors sold their people to European slave traders for a few used guns and porcelain plates, it seems as if the images of women of color in much of today's hip-hop music have been sold off to a greedy industry for a few buckets of "ice"[2] and a stack of "cheese."[3]

Recently while watching a new video in which yet another half-dressed girl gyrated[4] and bounced, Elenni turned to me and asked, "Why can't that girl just have on a cute pair of jeans with a halter top? Why does she always have to have on booty shorts? And why can't she just dance instead of grinding on the hood of a car? What does that have to do with the song?" I had no easy answers. Although the images of the women were both demeaning and predictable, the beats were undeniably hot. Therein lies the paradox[5] at the heart of my beef with hip-hop: songs that make you bounce can carry a message far and wide, irrespective of what that message is. And far too often the message is that most young women of color are "bitches" or "hoes." I was backed into a corner, forced to choose between my love for hip-hop and my need to be respected and to pass the ideals of self-respect on to my daughter. No contest.

> "I was backed into a corner, forced to choose between my love for hip-hop and my need to be respected."

Look, I'm no finger-wagging conservative outsider. I was one of the founding editors of *Vibe*, the first national magazine dedicated to hip-hop music, style, and culture, so it's really hard for me to hate. I also worked as a fashion stylist, helping to create looks for everyone from LL Cool J to Mary J. Later I landed at *Honey*, a magazine for young urban women, and eventually became its editor-in-chief. I wouldn't have had my career if it weren't for hip-hop culture. And that goes for lots of black folks. In addition to its music, hip-hop has journalism, film, fashion,

---

1. fly girl: slang for a pretty, stylish woman
2. "ice": slang for diamonds
3. "cheese": slang for money
4. gyrated: moved in a spiral
5. paradox: contradiction

and other lucrative[6] by-products that have employed and empowered hundreds, if not thousands, of us. So clearly I'm not one of those out-of-touch mothers who won't listen to current music or who espouse[7] corny clichés like "In my day, we knew what real music was."

Today is my day, too. And the danger with what's currently going on in hip-hop is not as simple as a mere generation gap. Increasingly, the male-dominated industry tends to view women as moneymakers (as in the kind you shake). Few of us are in a position to be decision makers. As a result of this imbalance, many popular hip-hop CDs and videos feature a brand of violence and misogyny[8] that is as lethal as crack and as degrading as apartheid.[9] And though I would love to maintain my "flyest mom ever" status, my daughter's self-esteem and that of every young sister in the world is at risk. I'm willing to risk my public image to help recover theirs. If there's not a shift in how the hip-hop industry portrays women, then our 20-year relationship is officially O-V-E-R.

I've since found creative ways to deal with my daughter's dilemma and my heartbreaking breakup: I ask Elenni why she likes a song, then I suggest alternative artists who might have a similar vibe. We look for videos that feature more progressive acts like Floetry, Jean Grae, and Talib Kweli. We listen to classics such as Public Enemy and MC Lyte, so she knows that hip-hop does have a positive history. We also participate in other urban-culture activities that affirm and satisfy us, like art exhibits, poetry slams, and yes, shoe shopping.

It's not going to be easy, leaving hip-hop behind. But I can no longer merely take what it dishes out and blame it on the boogie. The cost is just too great.

Discussion and Writing Questions

1. What does the author like and respect about hip-hop music? What does she strongly dislike about it? Specifically, what caused the author's "heartbreaking breakup" with hip-hop (paragraph 5)?
2. Do you listen to hip-hop? Do you agree with Davis that much of today's hip-hop is degrading to women and often violent? If so, what effects might this have on young women and young men? Does this message prevent both genders from "dreaming big," as Diane Sawyer urges (page 408)?
3. An effective argument establishes the credibility of both the writer and any experts whose opinions are included. Is this author a credible authority on the subject of hip-hop? Where in the essay does she reveal her credentials?
4. Hip-hop artists in countries like Korea, Senegal, and Brazil don't rap about money and sex, as many American performers do. Instead, they use their music to fight oppression and encourage social justice. Do you think that American hip-hop music would be as popular if it focused on similar subjects?

Writing Assignments

1. What kind of music do you enjoy? What do you like most about this style of music? What does it give you?
2. Michaela Angela Davis, like most parents, wants to nurture her child's self-esteem and protect her from the negative messages of pop culture. Choose one

---

6. lucrative: profitable
7. espouse: adopt or follow
8. misogyny: hatred of women
9. apartheid: the official policy of racial discrimination that existed in South Africa before 1994

gender, describe the risks faced by young men or women today, and describe the best way that parents can nurture and protect them.

3. In paragraph 3, Davis credits hip-hop with providing careers for many black people. How, in your opinion, has hip-hop music and culture *positively* affected America? Use specific examples and details to support your argument.

Stuff

Richard Rodriguez

Do you—like many Americans—own a lot of stuff? Do the things you buy bring brief or lasting pleasure? San Francisco writer Richard Rodriguez wonders whether our relationship to material possessions sets us up for disappointment. Rodriguez is an editor at the *Pacific News* service; he has authored three books and numerous essays and articles.

I come often to this huge building to do much of my shopping. It's called Costco. There are warehouse stores like this all over the country where you can buy most anything you need and you buy it in bulk, cheap.

A revolution is going on in American shopping habits. Two generations ago Americans went to their corner store where everyone knew the name of the man behind the counter and where toward the end of the month our grandmothers would ask to charge the milk and the bread. And then the suburbs created the supermarket with its Muzak[1] and its wide aisles and its 20 varieties of breakfast cereal. Now we don't go to the corner drugstore. Nor do we shop at a small nursery run by the lady who knows all about roses. We shop at places with names like Drug Barn and Plant World and Shoe Universe.

Every choice is available to us, and the prices are low, but no one knows your name and there is no Muzak. It's wonderful coming here to Costco. The well-to-do shop here along with immigrant families. Everyone's basket is full. You don't get a bottle of mineral water; you buy a case. You don't get a roll of toilet paper; you get a gigantic package that will last most families several months. You can buy tires at Costco, as well as Pampers and bananas. So people buy and buy and buy. And, yet, despite all the buying there is something oddly unmaterialistic about shopping in places plain as a warehouse.

We Americans often criticize ourselves for being materialistic. In fact, we take little pleasure in things, preferring to fill our lives with stuff. Only rarely do we dare a materialism that delights in the sensuality of the material world. In the 1950s, for example, we gave the world wonderful, wide-bodied cars with lots of chrome and fins like angels—the rare American instance of the materialism of the senses. We leave it, normally, to other cultures to teach us about materialism.

I remember years ago in London a friend of mine urging me to go into Fortnum and Mason's, the fancy food store, go in and buy just one piece of chocolate, he said, and think about that chocolate all day, and when you eat it tonight, eat it slowly, very slowly.

Americans don't eat slowly. We taught the world how to eat on the run, and we treasure food, convenience food, that doesn't take much thinking about, which

> *"We end up surrounded by stuff and regret."*

---

1. Muzak: the name for easy-listening or "elevator" music played in retail stores and other companies

A family from Bhutan and
all its possessions

is why in the end we don't have very much to say about the smell of a piece of
chocolate.

To this day I remember the weight and the smells of the first books I ever   7
owned. I can still remember the texture of paper in the first novel I ever got from
the library. Now we can order our books on the Internet without first holding them
in our hands or fingering the paper. Now Americans watch TV and order jewelry
or dolls or whatever on the 24-hour shopping channels. People buy from catalogs
without first trying the sweater on and testing its color against their skin.

There are no windows at Costco.   8

In an earlier, more sweetly materialistic America, our parents used to win-   9
dow shop. People would stop on a busy street, peer at the mannequins in the
shop windows. Here in San Francisco there are still downtown department stores
where one can see elaborate window displays, but who has the time to window
shop?

Despite the many dollars we spend, I think we are less materialistic now than   10
at any time in our history. We are not much interested in the shape of an orange
or the weight of a book, or the dark scent of a chocolate. We buy appliances off a
rack, and we throw them away when they no longer work. Nothing gets repaired
in America. Nothing we own grows old. We buy in bulk. We are surrounded by
choices. There is little we desire. We end up surrounded by stuff and regret. We
take the huge bag of chocolates home, and we end up eating too many.

Discussion and Writing Questions

1. Why does Rodriguez begin his essay with the example about shopping at
   Costco? How do stores like Costco help prove his point about Americans and
   material things?

2. Do you agree with Rodriguez that other cultures can teach Americans about healthy materialism? What example does he provide as evidence? Can you think of other examples?

3. In your opinion, is it good or bad to be surrounded by too many choices? What are the advantages of having many choices? What are the advantages of having few choices?

4. In his famous poem "The World Is Too Much with Us," English poet William Wordsworth wrote that "getting and spending, we lay waste our powers." In other words, we squander our energy on making money and spending it. Do you agree? If so, what might humans be able to accomplish if we weren't spending so much time and effort on working and buying?

Writing Assignments

1. Describe a time when you immersed yourself in and truly savored a specific sensual experience—a moonlit swim, a delicious meal, a slow stroll down your favorite street, or the like. Describe this experience, including details about what you saw, smelled, tasted, touched, and heard.

2. Which of your possessions are crucial to your happiness? What things do you own now that you could live without? What possessions do you lack that you believe will make you happier?

3. In 1993, photographer Peter Menzel asked "statistically average" families in different countries to pose in front of their houses with every possession they owned. In a group with four of five classmates, carefully observe and discuss the photo on page 431 of a family and all its possessions. From this family's home, location, and possessions, can you make any guesses about its values, daily life, or priorities? Is this family like or different from families you know?

Another Road Hog with Too Much Oink

Dave Barry

Humorist Dave Barry is the author of more than two dozen books, but he admits that not one of them contains useful information. Until 2005, his Pulitzer-Prize-winning humor column appeared in over 500 newspapers. In his spare time, Barry is a candidate for President of the United States. If elected, he promises to seek the death penalty for whoever made Americans install low-flow toilets. In the following essay, he takes on America's love of gigantic sport utility vehicles (SUVs).

If there's one thing this nation needs, it's bigger cars. That's why I'm excited that Ford is coming out with a new mound o' metal that will offer consumers even more total road-squatting mass than the current leader in the humongous[1]-car category, the popular Chevrolet Suburban Subdivision—the first passenger automobile designed to be, right off the assembly line, visible from the Moon.

I don't know what the new Ford will be called. Probably something like the "Ford Untamed Wilderness Adventure." In the TV commercials, it will be shown splashing through rivers, charging up rocky mountainsides, swinging on vines, diving off cliffs, racing through the surf, and fighting giant sharks hundreds of feet beneath the ocean surface—all the daredevil things that cars do in Sport Utility

———————————

1. humongous: huge

*"We're not certain why they disappeared, but archeologists speculate
that it may have had something to do with their size."*

"In the real world, of course, nobody drives a sport utility vehicle in the forest, because the last thing you want is squirrels pooping on it."

Vehicle Commercial World, where nobody ever drives on an actual road. In fact, the interstate highways in Sport Utility Vehicle Commercial World, having been abandoned by humans, are teeming[2] with deer, squirrels, birds, and other wildlife species that have fled from the forest to avoid being run over by nature seekers in multi-ton vehicles barreling through the underbrush at 50 miles per hour.

In the real world, of course, nobody drives sport utility vehicles in the forest, because when you have paid upward of $40,000 for a transportation investment, the last thing you want is squirrels pooping on it. No, if you want a practical "off-road" vehicle, you get yourself a 1973 American Motors Gremlin, which combines the advantage of not being worth worrying about with the advantage of being so ugly that poisonous snakes flee from it in terror.

In the real world, what people mainly do with their sport utility vehicles, as far as I can tell, is try to maneuver[3] them into and out of parking spaces. I base this statement on my local supermarket, where many of the upscale patrons drive Chevrolet Subdivisions. I've noticed that these people often purchase just a couple of items—maybe a bottle of diet water and a two-ounce package of low-fat dried carrot shreds—which they put into the back of their Subdivisions, which have approximately the same cargo capacity, in cubic feet, as Finland. This means there is plenty of room left over back there in case, on the way home, these people decide to pick up something else, such as a herd of bison.

Then comes the scary part: getting the Subdivision out of the parking space. This is a challenge, because the driver apparently cannot, while sitting in the driver's seat, see all the way to either end of the vehicle. I drive a compact car, and on a number of occasions I have found myself trapped behind a Subdivision backing

3

4

5

2. teeming: filled
3. maneuver: move skillfully

directly toward me, its massive metal butt looming[4] high over my head, making me feel like a Tokyo pedestrian looking up at Godzilla.[5]

I've tried honking my horn, but the Subdivision drivers can't hear me, because they're always talking on cellular phones the size of Chiclets ("The Bigger Your Car, the Smaller Your Phone," that is their motto). I don't know who they're talking to. Maybe they're negotiating with their bison suppliers. Or maybe they're trying to contact somebody in the same area code as the rear ends of their cars, so they can find out what's going on back there. All I know is, I'm thinking of carrying marine flares, so I can fire them into the air as a warning to Subdivision drivers that they're about to run me over. Although frankly I'm not sure they'd care if they did. A big reason why they bought a sport utility vehicle is "safety," in the sense of, "you, personally, will be safe, although every now and then you may have to clean the remains of other motorists out of your wheel wells."

Anyway, now we have the new Ford, which will be *even larger* than the Subdivision, which I imagine means it will have separate decks for the various classes of passengers, and possibly, way up in front by the hood ornament, Leonardo DiCaprio showing Kate Winslet[6] how to fly. I can't wait until one of these babies wheels into my supermarket parking lot. Other motorists and pedestrians will try to flee in terror, but they'll be sucked in by the Ford's powerful gravitational field and become stuck to its massive sides like so many refrigerator magnets. They won't be noticed, however, by the Ford's driver, who will be busy whacking at the side of his or her head, trying to dislodge[7] his or her new cell phone, which is the size of a single grain of rice and has fallen deep into his or her ear canal.

And it will not stop there. This is America, darn it, and Chevrolet is not about to just sit by and watch Ford walk away with the coveted title of Least Sane Motor Vehicle. No, cars will keep getting bigger: I see a time, not too far from now, when upscale suburbanites will haul their overdue movies back to the video-rental store in full-size, 18-wheel tractor-trailers with names like The Vagabond.[8] It will be a proud time for all Americans, a time for us to cheer for our country. We should cheer loud, because we'll be hard to hear, inside the wheel wells.

Discussion and Writing Questions

1. What is Barry's point of view about huge sport utility vehicles (paragraph 1)? What lines tell you this? Barry often exaggerates to get a laugh and to make a point. Can you point to examples of this technique?
2. What passages or details in the essay do you find particularly funny? Look for experiences to which you relate, vivid word use, exaggerations, or lines that create humorous mental pictures.
3. In paragraph 6, Barry says that safety is a big reason why people claim to buy SUVs. Do you agree with their reasoning? What are some other reasons why so many Americans choose to drive giant vehicles?
4. Barry ends his essay with a prediction that American vehicles will get even bigger (paragraph 8). What does he predict will soon happen? Although the essay is humorous, it makes a serious point. Does the last line underscore this point?

---

4. looming: appearing to be huge and towering
5. Godzilla: a fictional monster that menaced cities in Japanese films
6. Leonardo DiCaprio, Kate Winslet: stars of the film *Titanic*
7. dislodge: remove something stuck
8. vagabond: a wandering person

Writing Assignments

1. Fill in the blank in this sentence: "If there's one thing this nation needs, it's
_____ ." Then take a stand, perhaps humorous, as Barry has, about
something else Americans crave: fancy cell phones, brand-name clothing, even
plastic surgery. Or try a serious approach, arguing for more youth centers,
"hybrid" automobiles, or some other goal.
2. Write a response to Dave Barry's criticisms of SUVs and their owners. Defend
these vehicles by giving reasons why people *should* drive them. Take a humorous
or serious approach, as you wish.
3. Barry suggests that we Americans like our possessions big. What are some
other things, besides vehicles, that we continue to super-size? What do you
think this trend reveals about Americans?

Montgomery, Alabama, 1955

Rosa Parks

A refusal to give up her seat in a segregated bus pushed Rosa Parks into the spotlight
of the civil rights movement. In this excerpt from *Rosa Parks: My Story*, the Medal of
Freedom winner tells what really happened.

When I got off from work that evening of December 1, I went to Court Square   1
as usual to catch the Cleveland Avenue bus home.[1] I didn't look to see who was
driving when I got on, and by the time I recognized him, I had already paid my
fare. It was the same driver who had put me off the bus back in 1943, twelve years
earlier. He was still tall and heavy, with red, rough-looking skin. And he was still
mean-looking. I didn't know if he had been on that route before—they switched
the drivers around sometimes. I do know that most of the time if I saw him on a
bus, I wouldn't get on it.

I saw a vacant seat in the middle section of the bus and took it. I didn't even   2
question why there was a vacant seat even though there were quite a few people
standing in the back. If I had thought about it at all, I would probably have figured
maybe someone saw me get on and did not take the seat but left it vacant for me.
There was a man sitting next to the window and two women across the aisle.

The next stop was the Empire Theater, and some whites got on. They filled   3
up the white seats, and one man was left standing. The driver looked back and
noticed the man standing. Then he looked back at us. He said, "Let me have those
front seats," because they were the front seats of the black section. Didn't anybody
move. We just sat right where we were, the four of us. Then he spoke a second
time: "Y'all better make it light on yourselves and let me have those seats."

The man in the window seat next to me stood up, and I moved to let him pass   4
by me, and then I looked across the aisle and saw that the two women were also
standing. I moved over to the window seat. I could not see how standing up was
going to "make it light" for me. The more we gave in and complied,[2] the worse
they treated us.

---

1. home: Parks lived in Montgomery, the capital of Alabama, when racial segregation
was legal.
2. complied: acted in accordance with the rules

I thought back to the time when I used to sit up all night and didn't sleep   5
and my grandfather would have his gun right by the fireplace, or if he had his
one-horse wagon going anywhere, he always had his gun in the back of the wagon.
People always say that I didn't give up my seat because I was tired, but that isn't
true. I was not tired physically, or no more tired than I usually was at the end of a
working day. I was not old, although some people have an image of me as being
old then. I was forty-two. No, the only tired I was, was tired of giving in.

*"The only tired
I was, was tired
of giving in."*

The driver of the bus saw me still sitting there, and he asked was I going to   6
stand up. I said, "No." He said, "Well, I'm going to have you arrested." Then I said,
"You may do that." These were the only words we said to each other. I didn't even
know his name, which was James Blake, until we were in court together. He got
out of the bus and stayed outside for a few minutes, waiting for the police.

As I sat there, I tried not to think about what might happen. I knew that any-   7
thing was possible. I could be manhandled or beaten. I could be arrested. People
have asked me if it occurred to me then that I could be the test case the NAACP[3]
had been looking for. I did not think about that at all. In fact, if I had let myself
think too deeply about what might happen to me, I might have gotten off the bus.
But I chose to remain.

Discussion and Writing Questions

1. How had Parks been treated on buses before this particular bus incident? How
    had she reacted before?
2. What does the bus driver mean by "make it light on yourselves" (paragraph 3)?
    What does Parks think about her seatmates' decision to stand up?
3. Paragraph 5 describes the actual moment of deliberation when Parks is deciding
    whether to stand up. What determined her decision? What factors were not
    important?
4. Why does the author conclude, "In fact if I had let myself think too deeply
    about what might happen to me, I might have gotten off the bus" (paragraph
    7)? Parks takes full responsibility for her action, however. What two words
    indicate that?

Writing Assignments

1. Have you known someone who protested an injustice? What were the circum-
    stances? Describe the circumstances, along with your reaction. Then discuss
    how your view of the event has changed (or not changed) over time.
2. Parks maintains that the public's understanding of her motivation (she was old
    and tired) is simply not true. She thus draws attention to the difference between
    how others may see us and how we see ourselves. Have you ever acted in a
    specific way, only to have others describe your actions differently? Write about
    your experience.
3. Do you have a complaint about college life? In a letter to your school newspaper,
    try to imitate Parks's low-key style as you describe the problem and suggest a
    solution.

---

3. NAACP: National Association for the Advancement of Colored People

In This Arranged Marriage, Love Came Later

Shoba Narayan

Although arranged marriages are common in many parts of the world, most Americans believe that the best marriages start with falling in love. In this essay, an American-educated journalist from India discusses her decision to let her family find her a husband.

We sat around the dining table, my family and I, replete[1] from yet another home-cooked South Indian dinner. It was my younger brother, Shaam, who asked the question.

"Shoba, why don't you stay back here for a few months? So we can try to get you married."

Three pairs of eyes stared at me across the expanse of the table. I sighed. Here I was, at the tail end of my vacation after graduate school. I had an airplane ticket to New York from Madras, India, in ten days. I had accepted a job at an artists' colony in Johnson, Vermont. My car, and most of my possessions, were with friends in Memphis.

"It's not that simple," I said. "What about my car . . . ?"

"We could find you someone in America," my dad replied. "You could go back to the States."

They had thought it all out. This was a plot. I glared at my parents accusingly.

Oh, another part of me rationalized, why not give this arranged-marriage thing a shot? It wasn't as if I had a lot to go back to in the States. Besides, I could always get a divorce.

Stupid and dangerous as it seems in retrospect,[2] I went into my marriage at twenty-five without being in love. Three years later, I find myself relishing my relationship with this brilliant, prickly man who talks about the yield curve and derivatives,[3] who prays when I drive, and who tries valiantly to remember names like Giacometti, Munch, Kandinsky.[4]

My enthusiasm for arranged marriages is that of a recent convert. True, I grew up in India, where arranged marriages are common. My parents' marriage was arranged, as were those of my aunts, cousins, and friends. But I always thought I was different. I blossomed as a foreign fellow in Mount Holyoke College where individualism was expected and feminism encouraged. As I experimented with being an American, I bought into the American value system.

I was determined to fall in love and marry someone who was not Indian. Yet, somehow, I could never manage to. Oh, falling in love was easy. Sustaining it was the hard part.

Arranged marriages in India begin with matching the horoscopes of the man and the woman. Astrologers look for balance . . . so that the woman's strengths balance the man's weaknesses and vice versa. Once the horoscopes match, the two

---

1. replete: filled to satisfaction
2. in retrospect: looking back
3. yield curve and derivatives: technical terms from finance
4. Giacometti, Munch, Kandinsky: great twentieth-century artists

families meet and decide whether they are compatible. It is assumed that they are of the same religion, caste,[5] and social stratum.[6]

While this eliminates risk and promotes homogeneity,[7] the rationale is that the personalities of the couple provide enough differences for a marriage to thrive. Whether or not this is true, the high statistical success rate of arranged marriages in different cultures—90 percent in Iran, 95 percent in India, and a similar high percentage among Hasidic Jews in Brooklyn, and among Turkish and Afghan Muslims—gives one pause.   12

Although our families met through a mutual friend, many Indian families meet through advertisements placed in national newspapers.   13

My parents made a formal visit to my future husband's house to see whether Ram's family would treat me well. My mother insists that "you can tell a lot about the family just from the way they serve coffee." The house had a lovely flower garden. The family liked gardening. Good.   14

Ram's mother had worked for the United Nations on women's-rights issues. She also wrote humorous columns for Indian magazines. She would be supportive. She served strong South Indian coffee in the traditional stainless steel tumblers instead of china; she would be a balancing influence on my youthful radicalism.   15

Ram's father had supported his wife's career even though he belonged to a generation of Indian men who expected their wives to stay home. Ram had a good role model. His sister was a pediatrician in Fort Myers. Perhaps that meant he was used to strong, achieving women.   16

November 20, 1992. Someone shouted, "They're here!" My cousin Sheela gently nudged me out of the bedroom into the living room.   17

"Why don't you sit down?" a voice said.   18

I looked up and saw a square face and smiling eyes anxious to put me at ease. He pointed me to a chair. Somehow I liked that. The guy was sensitive and self-confident.   19

He looked all right. Could stand to lose a few pounds. I liked the way his lips curved to meet his eyes. Curly hair, commanding voice, unrestrained laugh. To my surprise, the conversation flowed easily. We had a great deal in common, but his profession was very different from mine. He had an MBA from the University of Michigan and had worked on Wall Street before joining a financial consulting firm.   20

Two hours later, Ram said, "I'd like to get to know you better. Unfortunately, I have to be back at my job in Connecticut, but I could call you every other day. No strings attached, and both of us can decide where this goes, if anywhere."   21

I didn't dislike him.   22

He called ten days later. We talked about our goals, dreams, and anxieties.   23

"What do you want out of life?" he asked me one day. "Come up with five words, maybe, of what you want to do with your life." His question intrigued me. "Courage, wisdom, change," I said, flippantly.[8] "What about you?"   24

"Curiosity, contribution, balance, family, and fun," he said. In spite of myself, I was impressed.   25

One month later, he proposed and I accepted. Our extended honeymoon in Connecticut was wonderful. On weekends, we took trips to Mount Holyoke, where I showed him my old art studio, and to Franconia Notch in New Hampshire, where we hiked and camped.   26

> *"Stupid and dangerous as it seems in retrospect, I went into my marriage at twenty-five without being in love."*

---

5. caste: one of four social classes in India
6. stratum: level
7. homogeneity: sameness, similarity
8. flippantly: lightly, thoughtlessly

It was in Taos, New Mexico, that we had our first fight. Ram had arranged for a surprise visit to the children's summer camp where I used to work as a counselor. We visited my old colleagues with their Greenpeace T-shirts and New Age commune mentality. Ram, with his clipped accent, neatly pressed clothes, and pleasant manners, was so different. What was I doing with this guy? On the car trip to the airport, I was silent. "I think, perhaps, we might have made a mistake," I said slowly. The air changed.   27

"Your friends may be idealistic, but they are escaping their lives, as are you," he said. "We are married. Accept it. Grow up!"   28

He had never spoken to me this harshly before, and it hurt. I didn't talk to him during the entire trip back to New York.   29

That fight set the pattern of our lives for the next several months. In the evening, when Ram came home, I would ignore him or blame him for bringing me to Connecticut.   30

Two years into our marriage, something happened. I was ashamed to realize that while I had treated Ram with veiled dislike, he had always tried to improve our relationship. I was admitted to the journalism program at Columbia, where, at Ram's insistence, I had applied.   31

Falling in love, for me, began with small changes. I found myself relishing a South Indian dish that I disliked, mostly because I knew how much he loved it. I realized that the first thing I wanted to do when I heard some good news was to share it with him. Somewhere along the way, the "I love you, too" that I had politely parroted[9] in response to his endearments had become sincere.   32

My friends are appalled[10] that I let my parents decide my life partner; yet, the older they get, the more intrigued they are. I am convinced that our successful relationship has to do with two words: tolerance and trust. In a country that emphasizes individual choice, arranged marriages require a familial web for them to work. For many Americans, that web doesn't exist.   33

As my friend Karen said, "How can I get my parents to pick out my spouse when they don't even talk to each other?"   34

Discussion and Writing Questions

1. Why did the author agree to an arranged marriage?
2. What factors did her family consider as they matched her with a husband? Which of these factors do you think are important predictors of success in marriage? Which, if any, seem unimportant?
3. How did Shoba Narayan know, after two years, that she was falling in love? If you have ever fallen in love, how was your experience similar or different?
4. What might be the disadvantages, or even risks, of an arranged marriage?

Writing Assignments

1. Soon after they met, Ram asked Shoba what words she would choose to express what she wanted in life. She said, "Courage, wisdom, change." Ram chose "curiosity, contribution, balance, family, and fun." What three to five words would you select in answer to Ram's question? Choose your words carefully; then explain why each one is important to you.

---

9. parroted: repeated mindlessly
10. appalled: shocked

2. Marriage in the United States usually occurs after two people "fall in love." Of course, more than 50 percent of marriages in this country end in divorce. Discuss three reasons why marriage that is based on first falling in love is or is not a good idea.

3. Would you consider letting your relatives pick your marriage partner? Take a stand, presenting the two or three most important reasons why you would or would not consider such a move.

A Homemade Education

Malcolm X

Sometimes a book can change a person's life. In this selection, Malcolm X, the influential and controversial black leader who was assassinated in 1965, describes how, while he was in prison, a dictionary set him free.

It was because of my letters that I happened to stumble upon starting to acquire some kind of homemade education. 1

I became increasingly frustrated at not being able to express what I wanted to convey in letters that I wrote, especially those to Mr. Elijah Muhammad.[1] In the street, I had been the most articulate hustler out there—I had commanded attention when I said something. But now, trying to write simple English, I not only wasn't articulate, I wasn't even functional. How would I sound writing in slang, the way I would *say* it, something such as, "Look, daddy, let me pull your coat about a cat. Elijah Muhammad—" 2

Many who today hear me somewhere in person, or on television, or those who read something I've said, will think I went to school far beyond the eighth grade. This impression is due entirely to my prison studies. 3

It had really begun back in the Charlestown Prison, when Bimbi first made me feel envy of his stock of knowledge. Bimbi had always taken charge of any conversation he was in, and I had tried to emulate[2] him. But every book I picked up had few sentences which didn't contain anywhere from one to nearly all of the words that might as well have been in Chinese. When I just skipped those words, of course, I really ended up with little idea of what the book said. So I had come to the Norfolk Prison Colony still going through only book-reading motions. Pretty soon, I would have quit even these motions, unless I had received the motivation that I did. 4

I saw that the best thing I could do was get hold of a dictionary—to study, to learn some words. I was lucky enough to reason also that I should try to improve my penmanship. It was sad. I couldn't even write in a straight line. It was both ideas together that moved me to request a dictionary along with some tablets and pencils from the Norfolk Prison Colony school. 5

I spent two days just riffling[3] uncertainly through the dictionary's pages. I'd never realized so many words existed! I didn't know *which* words I needed to learn. Finally, just to start some kind of action, I began copying. 6

---

1. Elijah Muhammad: founder of the Muslim sect Nation of Islam
2. emulate: copy
3. riffling: thumbing through

In my slow, painstaking, ragged handwriting, I copied into my tablet every-   7
thing printed on that first page, down to the punctuation marks.

I believe it took me a day. Then, aloud, I read back, to myself, everything I'd   8
written on the tablet. Over and over, aloud, to myself, I read my own handwriting.

I woke up the next morning, thinking about those words—immensely proud   9
to realize that not only had I written so much at one time, but I'd written words
that I never knew were in the world. Moreover, with a little effort, I also could
remember what many of these words meant. I reviewed the words whose meanings I didn't remember. Funny thing, from the dictionary first page right now, that
"aardvark" springs to my mind. The dictionary had a picture of it, a long-tailed,
long-eared burrowing African mammal, which lives off termites caught by sticking out its tongue as an anteater does for ants.

I was so fascinated that I went on—I copied the dictionary's next page. And   10
the same experience came when I studied that. With every succeeding page, I also
learned of people and places and events from history. Actually, the dictionary is
like a miniature encyclopedia. Finally, the dictionary's A section had filled a whole
tablet—and I went on into the B's. That was the way I started copying what eventually became the entire dictionary. It went a lot faster after so much practice helped
me pick up handwriting speed. Between what I wrote in my tablet, and writing
letters, during the rest of my time in prison I would guess I wrote a million words.

I suppose it was inevitable that as my word-base broadened, I could for the   11
first time pick up a book and read and now begin to understand what the book
was saying. Anyone who has read a great deal can imagine the new world that
opened. Let me tell you something: from then until I left that prison, in every free
moment I had, if I was not reading in the library, I was reading on my bunk. You
couldn't have gotten me out of books with a wedge. Between Mr. Muhammad's
teachings, my correspondence, my visitors—usually Ella and Reginald—and my
reading of books, months passed without my even thinking about being imprisoned. In fact, up to then, I never had been so truly free in my life.

> "I saw that the best thing I could do was get hold of a dictionary— to study, to learn some words."

Discussion and Writing Questions

1. Malcolm X says that in the streets he had been the "most articulate hustler" of all, but that in writing English he "not only wasn't articulate, [he] wasn't even functional" (paragraph 2). What does he mean?
2. What motivated Malcolm X to start copying the dictionary? What benefits did he gain from doing this?
3. What does Malcolm X mean when he says that until he went to prison, he "never had been so truly free in [his] life" (paragraph 11)?
4. Have you ever seen the 1992 film *Malcolm X*? If so, do you think the film's prison scenes showed how strongly Malcolm X was changed by improving his writing skills?

Writing Assignments

1. Choose three entries on a dictionary page and copy them. Then describe your experience. What did you learn? Can you imagine copying the entire dictionary? How do you feel about what Malcolm X accomplished? Where do you think he got the motivation to finish the task?
2. Malcolm X's inner life changed completely because of the dictionary he copied. Write about a time when a book, a story, a person, or an experience changed your life.

3. Have you ever wished that you had a better vocabulary? Learning new words is a process that pays off quickly if you keep at it. For one week, learn and practice a new word every day, perhaps using the following useful vocabulary website with a year's worth of great words. Then write an evaluation of your experiment to share with the class. Go to <http://grammar.ccc.commnet.edu/grammar/definition_list.htm>.

The Power to Shine

Deborah Rosado Shaw

We all have voices in our heads that tell us how we should feel about ourselves. In this selection from *Chicken Soup for the Latino Soul*, Deborah Rosado Shaw describes how winning an award caused her to question what the negative voices had always told her.

Anyone who saw me standing at the podium during the awards ceremony that June day would have called me a success. At thirty-five, I was the founder and sole owner of a multimillion-dollar business. I traveled the country speaking to businesspeople. I had three beautiful sons and was prosperous enough not to need to work another day in my life. But I had spent so much of my early life feeling lost and powerless that I wasn't able to savor my own good fortune.

As a girl, growing up poor in the South Bronx, I wasn't sure what success looked like, but I was pretty sure it didn't look like me. There was no chubby, freckled, bespectacled[1] Puerto Rican girl in any movie I'd ever seen or book I'd ever read—nor had I ever heard of a Latino CEO[2] or scholar. And there weren't too many successes on view outside my window either. The women I saw were worn-out domestics[3] and shop clerks, carrying groceries to their walk-ups,[4] trying to scrape together enough energy to make it through another day. Without realizing what I was doing, I began putting together a model for myself from bits and pieces of those around me—that one's straight back, and this one's spirit—a kind of rag doll I kept by my side.

As I grew up and moved out into the world, I worked hard to overcome the impoverishment of my childhood years. But early versions of myself were stacked inside me like Russian dolls: the four-year-old who was beaten up the first day of school because she was mistaken for white; the frightened teenager at a South Bronx high school where police stood in riot gear;[5] the college freshman at Wellesley whose roommate requested to be moved because she didn't want to room with a kid from the ghetto. I couldn't get rid of them entirely, nor did I want to. They were part of me, reminders of where I was from, although I made sure to keep them hidden. Then completely by chance, at seventeen, I landed a job as a customer-service clerk at a company that made umbrellas and tote bags. Eventually, I decided I wanted to move into sales, but the company turned down

"Who do you think you are? What's a ghetto girl like you doing here?"

---

1. bespectacled: wearing glasses
2. CEO: abbreviation for Chief Executive Officer
3. domestics: hired household servants
4. walk-ups: apartments above the ground floor in buildings that have no elevators
5. riot gear: protective clothing and equipment worn by law enforcement officers

Deborah Rosado Shaw

my request. Not to be deterred,[6] I called in sick one day so that I could call on the Museum of Natural History, a potential customer. I left there with a huge order and a new customer. After I brought the order to the office, I met with the company president and asked, "Are you guys gonna let me sell now or what?"

They did. After working for that company for a few years, I had enough money to step out on my own. My company, Umbrellas Plus, continued to grow and expand, landing several major retail accounts. Eventually, I relocated to New Jersey to be closer to the industry action. One day as I was flipping through a magazine, I came across an announcement for the Women of Enterprise Awards sponsored by Avon and the SBA.[7] The award was given to women business owners who had overcome significant odds to build a successful enterprise. It sounded right up my alley. As I filled out the essay questions, it occurred to me that this kind of award might bring me smack up against my carefully constructed identity, but I completed the application anyhow. A month later I opened a notice from Avon, read the first word—*Congratulations!*—and whooped out loud.

The day of the awards luncheon, I felt like Cinderella as I walked into the legendary Waldorf-Astoria, surrounded by well-wishers. But once I was seated in the hotel's grand ballroom, looking around at the crystal chandeliers, the linen tablecloths and the impeccably[8] dressed crowd, I grew increasingly anxious. When it was my turn to speak, my ears roared and my legs shook as I made my way to the podium. The old voices I had battled all my life came thundering back at me: *Who do you think you are? What's a ghetto girl like you doing here?*

4

5

---

6. deterred: discouraged or prevented from
7. SBA: abbreviation for Small Business Administration
8. impeccably: without any flaws

And then an amazing thing happened. A vision of an old woman with a bucket   6
and rag flashed before me: a widow who spoke no English, whose only option had
been to leave her children and homeland to work as a domestic in the United States.
That woman was my great-grandmother, Juanita. You see, my great-grandmother
had left Puerto Rico and found a job at a large, fancy hotel in New York—this
hotel, the Waldorf-Astoria. She had worked on her knees, in this very building. As
I looked out over the audience, I felt such a connection to Mama Juanita, her spirit
of fortitude[9] and resolve, and all the other women who came before me, women
who worked hard without knowing how it would affect future generations. If they
could push through their fears and achieve so much, then so could I.

For the first time publicly, I shared, with pride, my true story, not a sani-   7
tized[10] version. As I gave that speech, I came to terms with where I came from and
where I was going. To this day, whenever I feel discouraged, I think of my great-
grandmother Juanita and how she scrubbed floors on her knees so that one day, I
might shine.

Discussion and Writing Questions

1. In paragraph 2, the author says that she put together "a model for myself from
   bits and pieces of those around me." What does she mean? If you created a
   similar model for yourself, what features or qualities would you include? Who
   would be your specific example for each one?
2. In paragraph 3, the author uses illustration to develop the idea that experiences
   of her youth shaped who she is today. What are three or four experiences—
   positive, negative, or a combination—that affected your developing sense of
   your own identity? What did each one teach you to believe about yourself?
3. Has someone—a friend, relative, or co-worker—ever paved the way for you
   so that you might shine? How did this individual contribute to your personal
   success?
4. The author thinks of her great-grandmother Juanita when she's feeling
   discouraged. What thoughts or activities help you revive your own sense of
   purpose and motivation when you encounter an obstacle to a goal?

Writing Assignments

1. Tell the story of a time when you received an award or recognition that made
   you proud. What was your accomplishment, and what did you receive for it? If
   there was a ceremony, describe in vivid detail what happened at that event.
2. Contrast where you come from and where you're going. Select three aspects
   of your life that you expect to change significantly once you complete your
   education and begin achieving your career goals, and explain how they will
   differ from your current circumstances.
3. Have you ever had to push through fear in order to accomplish a goal? What
   strategies did you use? Explain to readers who are facing a similar situation
   what they can do to conquer their anxiety and achieve success.

---

9. fortitude: mental and emotional strength
10. sanitized: made more acceptable by removing unpleasant features

Playing a Violin with Three Strings

Jack Riemer

When Jack Riemer attended a concert by the famous violinist Itzhak Perlman, he and the rest of the audience felt lucky just to hear one of Perlman's dazzling musical performances. But then the unexpected happened. In this article for the *Houston Chronicle*, Riemer tells the story.

1   On November 18, 1995, Itzhak Perlman, the violinist, came on stage to give a concert at Avery Fisher Hall at Lincoln Center in New York City. Anyone who has ever been to a Perlman concert knows that getting on stage is no small achievement for him.

2   He was stricken with polio[1] as a child, and so he has braces on both legs and walks with the aid of two crutches. To see him walk across the stage one step at a time, painfully and slowly, is an unforgettable sight. He walks painfully, yet majestically,[2] until he reaches his chair. Then he sits down, slowly, puts his crutches on the floor, undoes the clasps on his legs, tucks one foot back, and extends the other foot forward. Then he bends down and picks up the violin, puts it under his chin, nods to the conductor, and proceeds to play.

3   By now, audience members are used to this ritual. They sit quietly while he makes his way across the stage to his chair. They remain reverently[3] silent while he undoes the clasps on his legs. They wait until he is ready to play.

"We could hear it snap—it went off like gunfire across the room. There was no mistaking what that sound meant."

4   But this time, something went wrong. Just as he finished the first few bars, one of the strings on his violin broke. We could hear it snap—it went off like gunfire across the room. There was no mistaking what that sound meant. There was no mistaking what he had to do. People who were there that night thought to themselves: "We figured that he would have to get up, put on the clasps again, pick up the crutches, and limp his way off stage—to either find another violin or else find another string for this one."

5   But he didn't. Instead, he waited a moment, closed his eyes, and then he played with such passion and such power and such purity as we had never heard before. Of course, anyone knows that it is impossible to play a symphonic[4] work with just three strings. I know that, and you know that, but that night Itzhak Perlman refused to know that. We could see him modulating,[5] changing, recomposing the piece in his head. At one point, it sounded like he was de-tuning the strings to get new sounds from them that they had never made before.

6   When he finished, there was an awesome silence in the room. And then people rose and cheered. There was an extraordinary outburst of applause from every corner of the auditorium. We were all on our feet, screaming and cheering, doing everything we could to show how much we appreciated what he had done.

7   He smiled, wiped the sweat from his brow, raised his bow to quiet us, and then he said, not boastfully, but in a quiet, pensive,[6] reverent tone, "You know, sometimes it is the artist's task to find out how much music he can still make with what he has left."

---

1. polio: a viral disease that disabled or killed many people until a polio vaccine was created in 1955
2. majestically: with greatness and dignity
3. reverently: with feelings of awe and respect
4. symphonic: meant for a large musical orchestra
5. modulating: adjusting or adapting
6. pensive: deeply thoughtful

The violinist Itzhak
Perlman in performance

What a powerful line that is. It has stayed in my mind ever since I heard it.   8
And who knows? Perhaps that is the definition of life—not just for artists but for
all of us. Perhaps our task in this shaky, fast-changing, bewildering world in which
we live is to make music, at first with all that we have, and then, when that is no
longer possible, to make music with what we have left.

Discussion and Writing Questions

1. The first three paragraphs vividly describe Perlman as he walks onto the stage,
   sits, and prepares to play. What words or details especially capture the process?
   Why do you think the author devotes so many words to this description?
2. Why do you think the author compares the violin string's snapping to "gunfire"
   (paragraph 4)? What do the concertgoers expect to happen next? Why are they
   so amazed when instead Perlman improvises—when he changes the music in
   his head to fit his new situation?
3. Can you draw any conclusions about Perlman's personality or character from
   the description of his physical appearance, actions, and words? What does this
   man seem to believe is important?
4. In paragraph 8, what do you think Riemer means when he writes that perhaps
   Perlman's words apply to all of us—that our task "is to make music, at first
   with all that we have, and then, when that is no longer possible, to make music
   with what we have left"? Does this relate to you or to anyone you know?

Writing Assignments

1. Sometimes things that go wrong can lead us down new—and better—paths.
   Itzhak Perlman, for example, gave one of his most amazing performances after

a violin string broke. Write about someone who has turned a loss, an illness, or a disability into a strength.

2. Discuss a memorable musical concert or performance that you attended—any kind of music, any number of performers. Think of an opening that will capture your readers' attention, perhaps describing in detail, as Riemer does, how the performer(s) came onstage. Then try to capture in words what made the performance so unforgettable.

3. Write about a time when you (or someone else) had to improvise under pressure. Think of a situation that did not go as you had planned—during work, college, or leisure time. What happened, and what did you do in response? Would you behave differently today?

The Jacket

Gary Soto

Fifth and sixth grades are years of identity formation and intense self-consciousness. Not fitting in or wearing the right clothes can turn embarrassment into agony. Award-winning Mexican-American writer and filmmaker Gary Soto tells the story of a jacket that made him feel so ugly it damaged his young life.

1   My clothes have failed me. I remember the green coat that I wore in fifth and sixth grades when you either danced like a champ or pressed yourself against a greasy wall, bitter as a penny toward the happy couples.

2   When I needed a new jacket and my mother asked what kind I wanted, I described something like bikers wear: black leather and silver studs with enough belts to hold down a small town. We were in the kitchen, steam on the windows from her cooking. She listened so long while stirring dinner that I thought she understood for sure the kind I wanted. The next day when I got home from school, I discovered draped on my bedpost a jacket the color of day-old guacamole.[1] I threw my books on the bed and approached the jacket slowly, as if it were a stranger whose hand I had to shake. I touched the vinyl sleeve, the collar, and peeked at the mustard-colored lining.

3   From the kitchen mother yelled that my jacket was in the closet. I closed the door to her voice and pulled at the rack of clothes in the closet, hoping the jacket on the bedpost wasn't for me but my mean brother. No luck. I gave up. From my bed, I stared at the jacket. I wanted to cry because it was so ugly and so big that I knew I'd have to wear it a long time. I was a small kid, thin as a young tree, and it would be years before I'd have a new one. I stared at the jacket, like an enemy, thinking bad things before I took off my old jacket whose sleeves climbed halfway to my elbow.

4   I put the big jacket on. I zipped it up and down several times, and rolled the cuffs up so they didn't cover my hands. I put my hands in the pockets and flapped the jacket like a bird's wings. I stood in front of the mirror, full face, then profile, and then looked over my shoulder as if someone had called me. I sat on the bed, stood against the bed, and combed my hair to see what I would look like doing

---

1. guacamole: a dip made from avocadoes

something natural. I looked ugly. I threw it on my brother's bed and looked at it for a long time before I slipped it on and went out to the backyard, smiling a "thank you" to my mom as I passed her in the kitchen. With my hands in my pockets I kicked a ball against the fence, and then climbed it to sit looking into the alley. I hurled orange peels at the mouth of an open garbage can and when the peels were gone, I watched the white puffs of my breath thin to nothing.

I jumped down, hands in my pockets, and in the backyard on my knees I teased   5
my dog, Brownie, by swooping my arms while making birdcalls. He jumped at me and missed. He jumped again and again, until a tooth stuck deep, ripping an L-shaped tear on my left sleeve. I pushed Brownie away to study the tear as I would a cut on my arm. There was no blood, only a few loose pieces of fuzz. Damn dog, I thought, and pushed him away hard when he tried to bite again. I got up from my knees and went to my bedroom to sit with my jacket on my lap, with the lights out.

That was the first afternoon with my new jacket. The next day I wore it to sixth   6
grade and got a D on a math quiz. During the morning recess Frankie T., the playground terrorist, pushed me to the ground and told me to stay there until recess was over. My best friend, Steve Negrete, ate an apple while looking at me, and the girls turned away to whisper on the monkey bars. The teachers were no help: they looked my way and talked about how foolish I looked in my new jacket. I saw their heads bob with laughter, their hands half-covering their mouths.

Even though it was cold, I took off the jacket during lunch and played kickball   7
in a thin shirt, my arms feeling like Braille from goose bumps. But when I returned to class I slipped the jacket on and shivered until I was warm. I sat on my hands, heating them up, while my teeth chattered like a cup of crooked dice. Finally warm, I slid out of the jacket but a few minutes later put it back on when the fire bell rang. We paraded out into the yard where we, the sixth graders, walked past all the other grades to stand against the back fence. Everybody saw me. Although they didn't say out loud, "Man, that's ugly," I heard the buzz-buzz of gossip and even laughter that I knew was meant for me.

And so I went, in my guacamole jacket. So embarrassed, so hurt, I wouldn't   8
even do my homework. I received C's on quizzes, and forgot the state capitals and the rivers of South America, our friendly neighbor. Even the girls who had been friendly blew away like loose flowers to follow the boys in neat jackets.

I wore that thing for three years until the sleeves grew short and my forearms   9
stuck out like the necks of turtles. All during that time no love came to me—no little dark girl in a Sunday dress she wore on Monday. At lunchtime I stayed with the ugly boys who leaned against the chain link fence and looked around with propellers of grass spinning in our mouths. We saw the girls walk by alone, saw couples, hand in hand, their heads like bookends pressing air together. We saw them and spun our propellers so fast our faces were blurs.

I blame that jacket for those bad years. I blame my mother for her bad taste   10
and her cheap ways. It was a sad time for the heart. With a friend I spent my sixth grade year in a tree in the alley, waiting for something good to happen to me in that jacket, which had become the ugly brother who tagged along with me wherever I went. And it was about that time I began to grow. My chest puffed up with muscle and, strangely, a few more ribs. Even my hands, those fleshy hammers, showed bravely through the cuffs, the fingers already hardening for the coming fights. But the L-shaped rip on the left sleeve got bigger, bits of stuffing coughed out from its wound after a hard day of play. I finally Scotch-taped it closed, but in rain or cold weather the tape peeled off like a scab and more stuffing fell out until that sleeve shriveled into a palsied arm. That winter the elbows began to crack and whole chunks of green began to fall off. I showed the cracks to my mother, who always seemed to be at the stove with steamed up glasses, and she said there were

"I stared at the jacket. I wanted to cry because it was so ugly and so big that I knew I'd have to wear it a long time."

children in Mexico who would love that jacket. I told her that this was America and yelled that Debbie, my sister, didn't have a jacket like mine. I ran outside, ready to cry, and climbed the tree by the alley to think bad thoughts and watch my breath puff white and disappear.

But whole pieces still casually flew off my jacket when I played hard, read quietly, or took vicious spelling tests at school. When it became so spotted that my brother began to call me "camouflage," I flung it over the fence into the alley. Later, however, I swiped the jacket off the ground and went inside to drape it across my lap and mope. 11

I was called to dinner: steam silvered my mother's glasses as she said grace; my brother and sister with their heads bowed made ugly faces at their glasses of powdered milk. I gagged too, but eagerly ate big rips of buttered tortilla that held scooped-up beans. Finished, I went outside with my jacket across my arm. It was a cold sky. The faces of clouds were piled up, hurting. I climbed the fence, jumping down with a grunt. I started up the alley and soon slipped into my jacket, that green ugly brother who breathed over my shoulder that day and ever since. 12

Discussion and Writing Questions

1. In the first paragraph, the author says that his clothes—including the green jacket—have failed him. What do you think he expected his clothes to do? Do clothes really have such power?
2. Describe the author's relationship to his mother, based on this essay. How do they view each other?
3. The author blames his "bad years" (paragraph 10) on the green jacket. What specific details and memories reveal how the jacket negatively impacted his life? Do you think he misinterpreted the behaviors of his friends, classmates, and teachers that he describes in paragraphs 6–8?
4. Soto uses many similes[2] and metaphors.[3] In fact, the essay ends with a metaphor of the jacket as a "green ugly brother" breathing over his shoulder then—and now. What does he mean? Why is this happening now?

Writing Assignments

1. Tell the story of a time when some aspect of your physical appearance—perhaps an injury, your size or weight, or a piece of clothing—changed your perception of yourself positively or negatively. What changed?
2. Brain research has shown that emotions can interfere with learning. Has an emotion such as fear, embarrassment, or anger ever affected your ability to concentrate, learn, or perform? What happened, and how did you deal with the situation?
3. What does your clothing tell the world about you? Do you dress differently in different settings, such as school, work, and social events? What messages about yourself do you communicate through your clothing styles in each of these settings?

---

2. simile: a comparison using *like* or *as* (*danced like a champ . . . bitter as a penny*, paragraph 1)
3. metaphor: a comparison without these words (*my jacket, that green ugly brother*, last paragraph)

Four Directions

Amy Tan

Have you ever possessed a certain skill or strength, and then, as you grew, lost it? Amy Tan, a Chinese-American novelist who lives in San Francisco, writes about a young chess player who seemed unbeatable—at age ten.

1   I was ten years old. Even though I was young, I knew my ability to play chess was a gift. It was effortless, so easy. I could see things on the chessboard that other people could not. I could create barriers to protect myself that were invisible to my opponents. And this gift gave me supreme confidence. I knew at exactly what point their faces would fall when my seemingly simple and childlike strategy would reveal itself as a devastating and irrevocable[1] course. I loved to win.

2   And my mother loved to show me off, like one of my many trophies she polished. She used to discuss my games as if she had devised the strategies.

3   "I told my daughter, 'Use your horses to run over the enemy,'" she informed one shopkeeper. "She won very quickly this way." And of course, she had said this before the game—that and a hundred other useless things that had nothing to do with my winning.

4   To our family friends who visited she would confide, "You don't have to be so smart to win chess. It is just tricks. You blow from the North, South, East, and West. The other person becomes confused. They don't know which way to run."

5   I hated the way she tried to take all the credit. And one day I told her so, shouting at her on Stockton Street, in the middle of a crowd of people. I told her she didn't know anything, so she shouldn't show off. She should shut up. Words to that effect.

6   That evening and the next day she wouldn't speak to me. She would say stiff words to my father and brothers, as if I had become invisible and she was talking about a rotten fish she had thrown away but which had left behind its bad smell.

7   I knew this strategy, the sneaky way to get someone to pounce back in anger and fall into a trap. So I ignored her. I refused to speak and waited for her to come to me.

8   After many days had gone by in silence, I sat in my room, staring at the sixty-four squares of my chessboard, trying to think of another way. And that's when I decided to quit playing chess.

9   Of course I didn't mean to quit forever. At most, just for a few days. And I made a show of it. Instead of practicing in my room every night, as I always did, I marched into the living room and sat down in front of the television with my brothers, who stared at me, an unwelcome intruder. I used my brothers to further my plan; I cracked my knuckles to annoy them.

10   "Ma!" they shouted. "Make her stop. Make her go away."

11   But my mother did not say anything.

12   Still I was not worried. But I could see I would have to make a stronger move. I decided to sacrifice a tournament that was coming up in one week. I would refuse to play in it. And my mother would certainly have to speak to me about this. Because the sponsors and the benevolent associations[2] would start calling her, asking, shouting, pleading to make me play again.

---

1. irrevocable: impossible to cancel or halt
2. benevolent associations: charities

And then the tournament came and went. And she did not come to me, crying, "Why are you not playing chess?" But I was crying inside, because I learned that a boy whom I had easily defeated on two other occasions had won. 13

I realized my mother knew more tricks than I had thought. But now I was tired of her game. I wanted to start practicing for the next tournament. So I decided to pretend to let her win. I would be the one to speak first. 14

"I am ready to play chess again," I announced to her. I had imagined she would smile and then ask me what special thing I wanted to eat. 15

But instead, she gathered her face into a frown and stared into my eyes, as if she could force some kind of truth out of me. 16

"Why do you tell me this?" she finally said in sharp tones. "You think it is so easy. One day quit, next day play. Everything for you is this way. So smart, so easy, so fast." 17

"I said I'll play," I whined. 18

"No!" she shouted, and I almost jumped out of my scalp. "It is not so easy anymore." 19

I was quivering, stunned by what she said, in not knowing what she meant. And then I went back to my room. I stared at my chessboard, its sixty-four squares, to figure out how to undo this terrible mess. And after staring like this for many hours, I actually believed that I had made the white squares black and the black squares white, and everything would be all right. 20

And sure enough, I won her back. That night I developed a high fever, and she sat next to my bed, scolding me for going to school without my sweater. In the morning she was there as well, feeding me rice porridge flavored with chicken broth she had strained herself. She said she was feeding me this because I had the chicken pox and one chicken knew how to fight another. And in the afternoon, she sat in a chair in my room, knitting me a pink sweater while telling me about a sweater that Auntie Suyuan had knit for her daughter June, and how it was most unattractive and of the worst yarn. I was so happy that she had become her usual self. 21

But after I got well, I discovered that, really, my mother had changed. She no longer hovered over[3] me as I practiced different chess games. She did not polish my trophies every day. She did not cut out the small newspaper item that mentioned my name. It was as if she had erected[4] an invisible wall and I was secretly groping each day to see how high and how wide it was. 22

At my next tournament, while I had done well overall, in the end the points were not enough. I lost. And what was worse, my mother said nothing. She seemed to walk around with this satisfied look, as if it had happened because she had devised this strategy. 23

I was horrified. I spent many hours every day going over in my mind what I had lost. I knew it was not just the last tournament. I examined every move, every piece, every square. And I could no longer see the secret weapons of each piece, the magic within the intersection of each square. I could see only my mistakes, my weaknesses. It was as though I had lost my magic armor. And everybody could see this, where it was easy to attack me. 24

Over the next few weeks and later months and years, I continued to play, but never with that same feeling of supreme confidence. I fought hard, with fear and desperation. When I won, I was grateful, relieved. And when I lost, I was filled with growing dread, and then terror that I was no longer a prodigy,[5] that I had lost the gift and had turned into someone quite ordinary. 25

When I lost twice to the boy whom I had defeated so easily a few years before, I stopped playing chess altogether. And nobody protested. I was fourteen. 26

"It was as though I had lost my magic armor."

---

3. hovered over: paid close attention to
4. erected: built
5. prodigy: a person with enormous talents in a particular area

Discussion and Writing Questions

1. Why did the child and her mother fight? Do you think the mother really wanted "all the credit" for herself (paragraph 5)? Why did she refuse to speak to the child after their argument?
2. The mother and daughter almost seem locked in a chess match of their own after their argument. What do you think is happening between them? Does the daughter's age—adolescence—have anything to do with it?
3. Why do you suppose the narrator says she had lost more than the last tournament, she had lost her "magic armor" (paragraph 24)?
4. The narrator says that "nobody protested" when she gave up chess permanently at age fourteen (paragraph 26). Do you think people might have protested if she were a boy? Why or why not?

Writing Assignments

1. Did you possess a talent or strength as a young person that you later lost? What happened? What caused you to change?
2. Adolescence is for most people a time of enormous change, and change often produces great anxiety. Was there an incident in your adolescence that caused you such anxiety—because you or your surroundings were somehow changing? Describe this incident.
3. Research suggests that once they reach adolescence, many girls give up asserting themselves—in sports, in class, and in student government, for example—because they feel pressure to be "feminine." Do you think this is true? Discuss why or why not, using yourself or a young woman you know as an example.

The Hidden Life of Bottled Water

Liza Gross

Consumers buy more bottled water than ever, believing that they are satisfying their thirst with something healthy. In fact, they might be better off just turning on the tap, according to this writer for *Sierra*, a magazine devoted to conservation and the environment.

"Consumers spent more than $4 billion on bottled water last year, but is bottled really better?"

1 Americans used to turn on their faucets when they craved a drink of clear, cool water. Today, concerned about the safety of water supplies, they're turning to the bottle. Consumers spent more than $4 billion on bottled water last year, establishing the fount[1] of all life as a certifiably hot commodity. But is bottled really better?

2 You might think a mountain stream on the label offers some clue to the contents. But sometimes, to paraphrase Freud, a bottle is just a bottle. "Mountain water could be anything," warns Connie Crawley, a health and nutrition specialist at the University of Georgia. "Unless the label says it comes from a specific source, when the manufacturer says 'bottled at the source,' the source could be the tap."

3 Yosemite brand water comes not from a bucolic[2] mountain spring but from deep wells in the undeniably less picturesque Los Angeles suburbs, and Everest sells water drawn from a municipal source in Corpus Christi, Texas—a far cry

---

1. fount: source
2. bucolic: rural

from the pristine[3] glacial peaks suggested by its name. As long as producers meet the FDA's[4] standards for "distilled" or "purified" water, they don't have to disclose the source.

Even if the water does come from a spring, what's in that portable potable[5] may be *less* safe than what comes out of your tap. Bottled water must meet the same safety standards as municipal-system water. But while the EPA[6] mandates daily monitoring of public drinking water for many chemical contaminants, the FDA requires less comprehensive testing only once a year for bottled water. Beyond that, says Crawley, the FDA "usually inspects only if there's a complaint. Yet sources of bottled water are just as vulnerable to surface contamination as sources of tap water. If the spring is near a cattle farm, it's going to be contaminated."

Let's assume your store-bought water meets all the safety standards. What about the bottle? Because containers that sit for weeks or months at room temperature are ideal breeding grounds for bacteria, a bottle that met federal safety standards when it left the plant might have unsafe bacteria levels by the time you buy it. And because manufacturers aren't required to put expiration dates on bottles, there's no telling how long they've spent on a loading dock or on store shelves. (Bacteria also thrive on the wet, warm rim of an unrefrigerated bottle, so avoid letting a bottle sit around for too long.) But even more troubling is what may be leaching[7] from the plastic containers. Scientists at the FDA found traces of bisphenol A—an endocrine[8] disruptor that can alter the reproductive development of animals—after 39 weeks in water held at room temperature in large polycarbonate containers (like that carboy[9] atop your office water cooler).

Wherever you get your water, *caveat emptor*[10] should be the watchword. If you're simply worried about chlorine or can't abide its taste, fill an uncapped container with tap water and leave it in the refrigerator overnight; most of the chlorine will vaporize. If you know your municipal water is contaminated, bottled water can provide a safe alternative. But shop around. The National Sanitation Foundation (NSF) independently tests bottled water and certifies producers that meet FDA regulations and pass unannounced plant, source, and container inspections. And opt for glass bottles—they don't impart the taste and risks of chemical agents and they aren't made from petrochemicals.[11]

To get information on bottled-water standards—or to find out what's in the water you buy—contact the Food and Drug Administration, (888) INFO-FDA, <http://www.fda.gov/>. For information on your tap water, call the EPA's Safe Drinking Water Hotline, (800) 426-4791, <http://www.epa.gov/safewater>.

Discussion and Writing Questions

1. Why might tap water be safer than bottled water?
2. Even if bottled water meets all safety standards, what other problems can affect its quality?
3. According to the author, how can consumers ensure that the bottled water they buy is, in fact, safe spring water?
4. What is the author suggesting about the American public and bottled water? What is she trying to accomplish by writing this article? Does she succeed?

---

3. pristine: pure
4. FDA's: Food and Drug Administration's
5. potable: a beverage that is safe to drink
6. EPA: Environmental Protection Agency
7. leaching: dissolving, draining away
8. endocrine: hormonal
9. carboy: oversized bottle
10. *caveat emptor:* a warning in Latin meaning "buyer beware"
11. petrochemicals: compounds derived from petroleum or natural gas

Writing Assignments

1. Check a campus location that sells bottled water (vending machine, cafeteria, campus store). Which brand of bottled water is sold? Contact the Food and Drug Administration (see Gross's last paragraph) to find out what information the federal government has collected on that brand. Is it spring water? Tap water from another location? Safe to drink? What ingredients does it contain? Have any problems been associated with it? Report your findings in a letter to the campus newspaper.

2. Study the contents label of one of your favorite snacks. What are the ingredients? Consult a dictionary to "translate" those ingredients. Does your appetite diminish as a result? Describe the snack, including what you thought its ingredients were and what the ingredients really are. Conclude with a recommendation for other consumers.

3. Gross suggests that perhaps the public has been fooled by the bottled-water industry. What other products do people buy without really needing them? Find an ad for one such product and describe how it works—how it creates a need where there is none. Attach the ad to your description.

Emotional Intelligence

Daniel Goleman

How important to a person's success is IQ—that is, his or her score on an intelligence test? According to a widely read book, other personality traits and skills are even more important than IQ. The author, Daniel Goleman, calls these traits and skills *emotional intelligence*. How would you rate your emotional IQ?

It was a steamy afternoon in New York City, the kind of day that makes people sullen[1] with discomfort. I was heading to my hotel, and as I stepped onto a bus, I was greeted by the driver, a middle-aged man with an enthusiastic smile.   1

"Hi! How're you doing?" he said. He greeted each rider in the same way.   2

As the bus crawled uptown through gridlocked traffic, the driver gave a lively commentary: there was a terrific sale at that store . . . a wonderful exhibit at this museum . . . had we heard about the movie that just opened down the block? By the time people got off, they had shaken off their sullen shells. When the driver called out, "So long, have a great day!" each of us gave a smiling response.   3

That memory has stayed with me for close to twenty years. I consider the bus driver a man who was truly successful at what he did.   4

Contrast him with Jason, a straight-A student at a Florida high school who was fixated[2] on getting into Harvard Medical School. When a physics teacher gave Jason an 80 on a quiz, the boy believed his dream was in jeopardy.[3] He took a butcher knife to school, and in a struggle the teacher was stabbed in the collarbone.   5

How could someone of obvious intelligence do something so irrational? The answer is that high IQ does not necessarily predict who will succeed in life. Psychologists agree that IQ contributes only about 20 percent of the factors that deter-   6

---

1. sullen: gloomy
2. fixated: rigidly focused
3. jeopardy: danger

mine success. A full 80 percent comes from other factors, including what I call *emotional intelligence.*

Following are some of the major qualities that make up emotional intelligence, and how they can be developed: 7

1. Self-awareness. The ability to recognize a feeling as it happens is the keystone of emotional intelligence. People with greater certainty about their emotions are better pilots of their lives. 8

Developing self-awareness requires tuning in to . . . gut feelings. Gut feelings can occur without a person being consciously aware of them. For example, when people who fear snakes are shown a picture of a snake, sensors on their skin will detect sweat, a sign of anxiety, even though the people say they do not feel fear. The sweat shows up even when a picture is presented so rapidly that the subject has no conscious awareness of seeing it. 9

Through deliberate effort we can become more aware of our gut feelings. Take someone who is annoyed by a rude encounter for hours after it occurred. He may be oblivious[4] to his irritability and surprised when someone calls attention to it. But if he evaluates his feelings, he can change them. 10

Emotional self-awareness is the building block of the next fundamental of emotional intelligence: being able to shake off a bad mood. 11

2. Mood Management. Bad as well as good moods spice life and build character. The key is balance. 12

We often have little control over *when* we are swept by emotion. But we can have some say in *how long* that emotion will last. Psychologist Dianne Tice of Case Western Reserve University asked more than 400 men and women about their strategies for escaping foul moods. Her research, along with that of other psychologists, provides valuable information on how to change a bad mood. 13

Of all the moods that people want to escape, rage seems to be the hardest to deal with. When someone in another car cuts you off on the highway, your reflexive[5] thought may be, *That jerk! He could have hit me! I can't let him get away with that!* The more you stew, the angrier you get. Such is the stuff of hypertension and reckless driving. 14

What should you do to relieve rage? One myth is that ventilating[6] will make you feel better. In fact, researchers have found that's one of the worst strategies. Outbursts of rage pump up the brain's arousal system, leaving you more angry, not less. 15

A more effective technique is "reframing," which means consciously reinterpreting a situation in a more positive light. In the case of the driver who cuts you off, you might tell yourself: *Maybe he had some emergency.* This is one of the most potent ways, Tice found, to put anger to rest. 16

Going off alone to cool down is also an effective way to defuse anger, especially if you can't think clearly. Tice found that a large proportion of men cool down by going for a drive—a finding that inspired her to drive more defensively. A safer alternative is exercise, such as taking a long walk. Whatever you do, don't waste the time pursuing your train of angry thoughts. Your aim should be to distract yourself. 17

The techniques of reframing and distraction can alleviate[7] depression and anxiety as well as anger. Add to them such relaxation techniques as deep breathing and meditation and you have an arsenal of weapons against bad moods. "Praying," Dianne Tice also says, "works for all moods." 18

---

4. oblivious: totally unaware
5. reflexive: automatic
6. ventilating: "letting off steam," raving
7. alleviate: reduce, make better

3. Self-motivation. Positive motivation—the marshaling[8] of feelings of enthusiasm, zeal, and confidence—is paramount for achievement. Studies of Olympic athletes, world-class musicians, and chess grandmasters[9] show that their common trait is the ability to motivate themselves to pursue relentless training routines.

19

To motivate yourself for any achievement requires clear goals and an optimistic, can-do attitude. Psychologist Martin Seligman of the University of Pennsylvania advised the MetLife insurance company to hire a special group of job applicants who tested high on optimism, although they had failed the normal aptitude test. Compared with salesmen who passed the aptitude test but scored high in pessimism, this group made 21 percent more sales in their first year and 57 percent more in their second.

20

A pessimist is likely to interpret rejection as meaning *I'm a failure; I'll never make a sale.* Optimists tell themselves, *I'm using the wrong approach,* or *That customer was in a bad mood.* By blaming failure on the situation, not themselves, optimists are motivated to make that next call.

21

Your . . . positive or negative outlook may be inborn, but with effort and practice, pessimists can learn to think more hopefully. Psychologists have documented that if you can catch negative, self-defeating thoughts as they occur, you can reframe the situation in less catastrophic terms.

22

4. Impulse Control. The essence of emotional self-regulation is the ability to delay impulse in the service of a goal. The importance of this trait to success was shown in an experiment begun in the 1960s by psychologist Walter Mischel at a preschool on the Stanford University campus.

23

Children were told that they could have a single treat, such as a marshmallow, right now. However, if they would wait while the experimenter ran an errand, they could have two marshmallows. Some preschoolers grabbed the marshmallow immediately, but others were able to wait what, for them, must have seemed an endless twenty minutes. To sustain themselves in their struggle, they covered their eyes so they wouldn't see the temptation, rested their heads on their arms, talked to themselves, sang, even tried to sleep. These plucky kids got the two-marshmallow reward.

24

The interesting part of this experiment came in the follow-up. The children who as four-year-olds had been able to wait for the two marshmallows were, as adolescents, still able to delay gratification in pursuing their goals. They were more socially competent and self-assertive, and better able to cope with life's frustrations. In contrast, the kids who grabbed the one marshmallow were, as adolescents, more likely to be stubborn, indecisive, and stressed.

25

The ability to resist impulse can be developed through practice. When you're faced with an immediate temptation, remind yourself of your long-term goals—whether they be losing weight or getting a medical degree. You'll find it easier, then, to keep from settling for the single marshmallow.

26

5. People Skills. The capacity to know how another feels is important on the job, in romance and friendships, and in the family. We transmit and catch moods from each other on a subtle, almost imperceptible level. The way someone says thank you, for instance, can leave us feeling dismissed, patronized, or genuinely appreciated. The more adroit[10] we are at discerning the feelings behind other people's signals, the better we control the signals we send.

27

The importance of good interpersonal skills was demonstrated by psychologists Robert Kelley of Carnegie-Mellon University and Janet Caplan in a study at Bell Labs in Naperville, Ill. The labs are staffed by engineers and scientists who are

28

---

8. marshaling: gathering together, using
9. chess grandmasters: experts at the game of chess
10. adroit: skilled

all at the apex[11] of academic IQ tests. But some still emerged as stars while others languished.[12]

What accounted for the difference? The standout performers had a network   29
with a wide range of people. When a non-star encountered a technical problem, Kelley observed, "he called various technical gurus and then waited, wasting time while his calls went unreturned. Star performers rarely faced such situations because they built reliable networks *before* they needed them. So when the stars called someone, they almost always got a faster answer."

No matter what their IQ, once again it was emotional intelligence that sepa-   30
rated the stars from the average performers.

Discussion and Writing Questions

1. Goleman names five qualities that contribute to emotional intelligence. What are they?
2. Describe someone you observed recently who showed a high level of emotional intelligence in a particular situation. Then describe someone who showed a low level of emotional intelligence in a particular situation. Which of the five qualities did each person display or lack?
3. Did it surprise you to read that "ventilating" is one of the worst ways to handle rage? Instead, experts suggest several techniques. Suppose you are in the following situation, and your first reaction is anger: *You ask a salesperson for help in choosing an MP3 player. As she walks right past you, she tells you that the boxes and labels will give you all the information you need.* What might you do to calm yourself down?
4. In paragraphs 24 and 25, Goleman discusses a now-famous study of children and marshmallows. What was the point of this study? Why does Goleman say that the most interesting part of the study came later, when the children reached adolescence?

Writing Assignments

1. Write a detailed portrait of a person whom you consider an "emotional genius." Develop your paper with specific examples of his or her skills.
2. Daniel Goleman claims that weak emotional qualities can be strengthened with practice. Choose one of the five qualities (self-awareness, people skills, and so forth) and recommend specific ways a person could improve in that area. Your audience is people who wish to improve their emotional intelligence; your purpose is to help them do so.
3. Review or read "The Gift" on page 426, and evaluate the emotional intelligence of Jermaine Washington. Washington saved a friend's life by giving her one of his kidneys after her two brothers and her boyfriend refused to be donors. Most people in their town still think Washington was "crazy" to make this decision. What do you think? Does he have a high level of emotional intelligence? a low level? Why?

---

11. apex: top, topmost point
12. languished: stayed in one place

Quotation Bank

This collection of wise and humorous statements has been assembled for you to read, enjoy, and use in a variety of ways as you write. You might choose some quotations that you particularly agree or disagree with and use them as the basis of journal entries and writing assignments. When you write a paragraph or an essay, you may find it useful to include a quotation to support a point you are making. You may simply want to read through these quotations for ideas and for fun. As you come across other intriguing statements by writers, add them to the list—or write some of your own.

Learning

Teachers open the door, but you must enter by yourself.
>—CHINESE PROVERB

Only the educated are free.
>—EPICTETUS

The mind is a mansion, but most of the time we are content to live in the lobby.
>—DR. WILLIAM MICHAELS

Pay attention to what they tell you to forget.
>—MURIEL RUKEYSER

Prejudices, it is well known, are most difficult to eradicate from the heart whose soil has never been loosened or fertilized by education; they grow there, firm as weeds among stones.
>—CHARLOTTE BRONTË

The day someone quits school he is condemning himself to a future of poverty.
>—JAIME ESCALANTE

The purpose of a liberal arts education is to liberate the human being to exercise his or her potential to the fullest.
>—BARBARA M. WHITE

Love

We can only learn to love by loving.
>—IRIS MURDOCH

So often when we say "I love you," we say it with a huge "I" and a small "you."
>—ARCHBISHOP ANTHONY

Choose your life's mate carefully. From this one decision will come 90 percent of all your happiness or misery.
>—H. JACKSON BROWNE, JR.

A divorce is like an amputation; you survive, but there's less of you.
> —MARGARET ATWOOD

Gold and love affairs are difficult to hide.
> —SPANISH PROVERB

Marriage is our last best chance to grow up.
> —JOSEPH BARTH

No partner in a love relationship should feel that she has to give up an essential part of herself to make it viable.
> —MAY SARTON

Power without love is reckless and abusive, and love without power is sentimental and anemic.
> —MARTIN LUTHER KING, JR.

Love doesn't just sit there, like a stone, it has to be made, like bread, remade all the time, made new.
> —URSULA K. LE GUIN

To be loved, be lovable.
> —OVID

Work and Success

The best career advice to give the young is, find out what you like doing best and get someone to pay you for doing it.
> —KATHERINE WHILEHAEN

If there is any one secret of success, it lies in the ability to get the other person's point of view and see things from that person's angle as well as from your own.
> —HENRY FORD

If you have built castles in the air, your work need not be lost; that is where they should be. Now put foundations under them.
> —HENRY DAVID THOREAU

I think most of us are looking for a calling, not a job. Most of us, like the assembly line worker, have had jobs that are too small for our spirit.
> —NORA WATSON

A celebrity is a person who works hard all his [or her] life to become well known, then wears dark glasses to avoid being recognized.
> —FRED ALLEN

If at first you don't succeed, skydiving is not for you.
> —FRANCIS ROBERTS

You've got to believe. Never be afraid to dream.
> —GLORIA ESTEFAN

If you aren't fired with enthusiasm, you will be fired with enthusiasm.

> —Vince Lombardi

A good reputation is more valuable than money.

> —Publius

Money is like manure. If you spread it around, it does a lot of good, but if you pile it up in one place, it stinks like hell.

> —Clint W. Murchison

Measure a thousand times and cut once.

> —Turkish Proverb

It is never too late to be what you might have been.

> —George Eliot

Family and Friendship

Making the decision to have a child—it's momentous. It is to decide forever to have your heart go walking around outside your body.

> —Elizabeth Stone

Govern a family as you would fry small fish—gently.

> —Chinese Proverb

Nobody who has not been in the interior of a family can say what the difficulties of any individual in that family may be.

> —Jane Austen

Everything that irritates us about others can lead us to understanding of ourselves.

> —Morton Hunt

A true friend is someone who thinks that you are a good egg even though he knows that you are slightly cracked.

> —Bernard Meltzer

The only way to have a friend is to be one.

> —Ralph Waldo Emerson

Wisdom for Living

It is not easy to find happiness in ourselves, and it is not possible to find it elsewhere.

> —Agnes Reppelier

Regret is an appalling waste of energy; you can't build on it; it is good only for wallowing in.

> —Katherine Mansfield

Smooth seas do not make a skillful sailor.
—AFRICAN PROVERB

Don't be afraid your life will end; be afraid that it will never begin.
—GRACE HANSEN

Flowers grow out of dark moments.
—KORITA KENT

Pick battles big enough to matter, small enough to win.
—JONATHAN KOZOL

A fanatic is one who can't change his [or her] mind and won't change the subject.
—WINSTON CHURCHILL

Take your life into your own hands and what happens? A terrible thing: no one to blame.
—ERICA JONG

My life, my *real life*, was in danger, and not from anything other people might do but from the hatred I carried in my own heart.
—JAMES BALDWIN

No one can make you feel inferior without your consent.
—ELEANOR ROOSEVELT

When you come to a fork in the road, take it.
—YOGI BERRA

Writing

Writing, like life itself, is a voyage of discovery.
—HENRY MILLER

I am a Dominican, hyphen, American. As a writer, I find that the most exciting things happen in the realm of that hyphen—the place where two worlds collide or blend together.
—JULIA ALVAREZ

I think best with a pencil in my hand.
—ANNE MORROW LINDBERGH

Writing is the hardest work in the world not involving heavy lifting.
—PETE HAMILL

I never travel without my diary. One should always have something sensational to read on the train.
—OSCAR WILDE

A professional writer is an amateur who didn't quit.
—RICHARD BACH

Parts of Speech Review

A knowledge of basic grammar terms will make your study of English easier. Throughout this book, these key terms are explained as needed and are accompanied by ample practice. For your convenience and reference, the following is a short review of the eight parts of speech.

Nouns

Nouns are the names of persons, places, things, animals, activities, and ideas.*

Persons:	Ms. Caulfield, Dwayne, accountants
Places:	Puerto Rico, Vermont, gas station
Things:	sandwich, Sears, eyelash
Animals:	whale, ants, Dumbo
Activities:	running, discussion, tennis
Ideas:	freedom, intelligence, humor

Pronouns

Pronouns replace or refer to nouns or other pronouns. The word that a pronoun replaces is called its *antecedent*.**

My partner succeeded; *she* built a better mousetrap!

These computers are amazing; order four of *them* for the office.

Everyone should do *his* or *her* best.

All students should do *their* best.

---

* For more work on nouns, see Chapter 20.
** For more work on pronouns, see Chapter 21.

Pronouns take different forms, depending on how they are used in a sentence. They can be the subjects of sentences (*I, you, he, she, it, we, they*) or the objects of verbs and prepositions (*me, you, him, her, it, us, them*). They also can show possession (*my, mine, your, yours, his, her, hers, its, our, ours, their, theirs*).

Subject:	*You* had better finish on time.
	Did *someone* leave a laptop on the chair?
Object of verb:	Bruno saw *her* on Thursday.
Object of preposition:	That iPad is for *her*.
Possessive:	Did Adam leave *his* sweater on the dresser?

Verbs

Verbs can be either action verbs or linking verbs. Verbs can be single words or groups of words.*

Action verbs show what action the subject of the sentence performs.

> Leila *bought* a French dictionary.
>
> Ang *has opened* the envelope.

Linking verbs link the subject of a sentence with a descriptive word or words. Common linking verbs are *be, act, appear, become, feel, get, look, remain, seem, smell, sound,* and *taste*.

> This report *seems* well organized and complete.
>
> You *have been* quiet this morning.

The **present participle** of a verb is its *-ing* form. The present participle can be combined with some form of the verb *to be* to create the progressive tenses, or it can be used as an adjective or a noun.

Geraldo *was waiting* for the report.	(*past progressive tense*)
The *waiting* taxis lined up at the curb.	(*adjective*)
Waiting for trains bores me.	(*noun*)

The **past participle** of a verb can be combined with helping verbs to create different tenses, it can be combined with forms of *to be* to create the passive voice, or it can be used as an adjective. Past participles regularly end in *-d* or *-ed*, but irregular verbs take other forms (*seen, known, taken*).

---

* For more work on verbs, see Unit 3.

> He *has edited* many articles for us.   (*present perfect tense*)
>
> This report *was edited* by the committee.   (*passive voice*)
>
> The *edited* report reads well.   (*adjective*)

Every verb can be written as an *infinitive: to* plus the *simple form* of the verb.

> She was surprised *to meet* him at the bus stop.

Adjectives

Adjectives describe or modify nouns or pronouns. Adjectives can precede or follow the words they describe.*

> *Several green* chairs arrived today.
>
> Collins Lake is *dangerous* and *deep*.

Adverbs

Adverbs describe or modify verbs, adjectives, or other adverbs.**

> Brandy reads *carefully*.   (*adverb describes verb*)
>
> She is *extremely* tired.   (*adverb describes adjective*)
>
> He wants a promotion *very* badly.   (*adverb describes adverb*)

Prepositions

A **preposition** begins a *prepositional phrase*. A **prepositional phrase** contains a preposition (a word such as *at, in, of,* or *with*), its object (a noun or pronoun), and any adjectives modifying the object.***

Preposition	Object
after	*work*
on	the blue *table*
under	the broken *stairs*

---

* For more work on adjectives, see Chapter 22.

** For more work on adverbs, see Chapter 22.

*** For more work on prepositions, see Chapter 23.

Conjunctions

Conjunctions are connector words.

Coordinating conjunctions (*and, but, for, nor, or, so, yet*) join two equal words or groups of words.*

Shanara is soft-spoken *but* sharp.

Ms. Chin *and* Mr. Warburton attended the technology conference.

He printed out the spreadsheet, *and* Ms. Helfman faxed it immediately.

She will go to Norfolk Community College, *but* she will also continue working at the shoe store.

Subordinating conjunctions (*after, because, if, since, unless,* and so on) join an independent idea with a dependent idea.

Whenever Alexi comes to visit, he takes the family out to dinner.

I haven't been sleeping well *because* I've been drinking too much coffee.

Interjections

Interjections are words such as *ouch* and *hooray* that express strong feeling. They are rarely used in formal writing.

If the interjection is the entire sentence, it is followed by an exclamation point. If the interjection is attached to a sentence, it is followed by a comma.

Hey! You left your wallet on the counter.

Oh, she forgot to send in her tax return.

A Reminder

REMEMBER: Sometimes the same word may be used as a different part of speech.

Terrance *thought* about the problem. (*verb*)

Your *thought* is a good one. (*noun*)

---

* For more work on conjunctions, see Chapters 14 and 15.

Guidelines for Students of English as a Second Language

Count and Noncount Nouns

Count nouns refer to people, places, or things that are separate units. You can often point to them, and you can always count them.

Count Noun	Sample Sentence
computer	The writing lab has ten *computers*.
dime	There are two *dimes* under your chair.
professor	All of my *professors* are at a conference today.
notebook	I carry a *notebook* in my backpack.
child	Why is your *child* jumping on the table?

Noncount nouns refer to things that are wholes. You cannot count them separately. Noncount nouns may refer to ideas, feelings, and other things that you cannot see or touch. Noncount nouns may refer to food or beverages.

Noncount Noun	Sample Sentence
courage	It takes *courage* to study a new language.
equipment	The company sells office *equipment*.
happiness	We wish the bride and groom much *happiness*.
bread	Who will slice this loaf of *bread*?
meat	Do you eat *meat*, or are you a vegetarian?
coffee	The *coffee* turned cold as we talked.

For more noncount nouns, visit <http://grammar.ccc.commnet.edu/grammar/noncount.htm>.

Plurals of Count and Noncount Nouns

Most count nouns form the plural by adding -s **or** -es. Some count nouns have irregular plurals.*

---

* For work on singular and plural nouns, see Chapter 20.

Plurals of Count Nouns

ship/ships	video game/video games
flower/flowers	nurse/nurses
library/libraries	knife/knives
child/children	woman/women

Noncount nouns usually do not form the plural at all. It is incorrect to say *homeworks, equipments,* or *happinesses.*

PRACTICE 1

Write the plural for every count noun. If the noun is a noncount noun, write *no plural.*

1. mountain _____
2. wealth _____
3. forgiveness _____
4. student _____
5. generosity _____

6. man _____
7. assignment _____
8. homework _____
9. knowledge _____
10. bravery _____

Some nouns have both a count meaning and a noncount meaning. Usually, the count meaning is concrete and specific. Usually, the noncount meaning is abstract and general.

Count meaning: All the *lights* in the classroom went out.
Noncount meaning: What is the speed of *light*?

Count meaning: Odd *sounds* came from the basement.
Noncount meaning: The speed of *sound* is slower than the speed of light.

Food and beverages, which are usually noncount nouns, may also have a count meaning.

Count meaning: This store sells *fruits, pies,* and *teas* from different countries.
Noncount meaning: Would you like some more *fruit, pie,* or *tea*?

Articles with Count and Noncount Nouns

Indefinite Articles

The words *a* and *an* are **indefinite articles**. They refer to one *nonspecific* (indefinite) thing. For example, "a man" refers to *any* man, not to a specific, particular man. **The article *a* or *an* is used before a singular count noun.***

Singular Count Noun	With Indefinite Article
question	a question
textbook	a textbook
elephant	an elephant
umbrella	an umbrella

---

* For when to use *an* instead of *a*, see Chapter 33.

The indefinite article *a* or *an* is never used before a noncount noun.

Noncount Noun	Sample Sentence
music	*Incorrect:* I enjoy a music.
	Correct: I enjoy music.
health	*Incorrect:* Her father is in a poor health.
	Correct: Her father is in poor health.
patience	*Incorrect:* Good teachers have a patience.
	Correct: Good teachers have patience.
freedom	*Incorrect:* We have a freedom to choose our courses.
	Correct: We have freedom to choose our courses.

PRACTICE 2

The indefinite article *a* or *an* is italicized in each sentence. Cross out *a* or *an* if it is used incorrectly. If the sentence is correct, write *correct* on the line provided.

1. My friends give me *a* help when I need it. _____

2. The counselor gives her *an* advice about which courses to take. _____

3. *An* honesty is the best policy. _____

4. We have *an* answer to your question. _____

5. They have *an* information for us. _____

Definite Articles

The word *the* is a **definite article.** It refers to one (or more) *specific* (definite) things. For example, "the man" refers not to *any* man but to a specific, particular man. "The men" (plural) refers to specific, particular men. The article *the* also is used after the first reference to a thing (or things). For instance, "I got a new cell phone. The phone has a built-in MP3 player." **The article *the* is used before singular and plural count nouns.**

Definite (*The*) and Indefinite Articles (*A/An*) with Count Nouns

I saw *the* film. (singular; refers to a specific film)

I saw *the* films. (plural; refers to more than one specific film)

I saw *a* film. (refers to any film; nonspecific)

I enjoy seeing *a* good film. (refers to any good film; nonspecific)

I like *a* film that has an important message. (refers to any film that has an important message; nonspecific)

I saw *a* good film. *The* film was about the life of a Cuban singer. (refers to a specific film)

The definite article *the* is used before a noncount noun only if the noun is specifically identified.

Noncount Noun	Sample Sentence
fitness	*Incorrect:* He has *the* fitness. (not identified)
	Correct: He has *the* fitness of a person half his age. (identified)
	Incorrect: The fitness is a goal for many people. (not identified)
	Correct: Fitness is a goal for many people. (not identified, so no *the*)
art	*Incorrect:* I do not understand *the* art. (not identified)
	Correct: I do not understand *the* art in this show. (identified)
	Incorrect: The art touches our hearts and minds. (not identified)
	Correct: Art touches our hearts and minds. (not identified, so no *the*)

PRACTICE 3

The definite article *the* is italicized whenever it appears below. Cross it out if it is used incorrectly. If the sentence is correct, write *correct* on the line provided.

1. She dresses with *the* style.   _____

2. *The* beauty of this building surprises me.   _____

3. This building has *the* beauty of a work of art.   _____

4. *The* courage is an important quality.   _____

5. Alex has *the* wealth but not *the* happiness.   _____

Verb + Gerund

A **gerund** is a noun that is made up of a verb plus *-ing*. The italicized words below are gerunds.

> *Playing* solitaire on the computer helps some students relax.
>
> I enjoy *hiking* in high mountains.

In the first sentence, the gerund *playing* is the simple subject of the sentence.* In the second sentence, the gerund *hiking* is the object of the verb enjoy.** Some common verbs are often followed by gerunds.

---

* For more on simple subjects, see Chapter 7, Part A.

** For more on objects of verbs, see Chapter 21, Part F.

Some Common Verbs That Can Be Followed by a Gerund	
Verb	**Sample Sentence with Gerund**
consider	Would you *consider* **taking** a course in psychology?
discuss	Let's *discuss* **buying** a scanner.
enjoy	I *enjoy* **jogging** in the morning before work.
finish	Abril *finished* **studying** for her physiology exam.
keep	*Keep* **trying** and you will succeed.
postpone	The Brookses *postponed* **visiting** their grandchildren.
quit	Three of my friends *quit* **smoking** this year.

The verbs listed above are *never* followed by an infinitive (*to* + the simple form of the verb).*

> *Incorrect:* Would you consider *to take* a course in psychology?

> *Incorrect:* Let's discuss *to buy* a scanner.

> *Incorrect:* I enjoy *to jog* in the morning before work.

PRACTICE 4   Write a gerund after each verb in the blank space provided.

1. Dave enjoys _____ television in the evening.

2. Have you finished _____ for tomorrow's exam?

3. T.J. is considering _____ to Mexico next month.

4. I have postponed _____ until I receive the results of the test.

5. We are discussing _____ a car.

Preposition + Gerund

A preposition** may be followed by a gerund.

> I forgive you *for* **stepping** on my toe.
>
> Elena believes *in* **pushing** herself to her limits.
>
> We made the flight *by* **running** from one terminal to another.

A preposition is *never* followed by an infinitive (*to* + the simple form of the verb).

> *Incorrect:* I forgive you *for* **to step** on my toe.

> *Incorrect:* Elena believes *in* **to push** herself to her limits.

> *Incorrect:* We made the flight *by* **to run** from one terminal to another.

---

* For more on infinitives, see Chapter 13, Part E.

** For more on prepositions, see Chapter 23.

PRACTICE 5

Write a gerund after the preposition in each blank space provided.

1. We have succeeded in _____ the DVD you wanted.

2. You can get there by _____ left at the next corner.

3. Thank you for _____ those striped socks for me.

4. I enjoy sports like _____ and _____ .

5. Between _____ to school and _____, I have little time

   for _____ .

Verb + Infinitive

Many verbs are followed by the **infinitive** (*to* + the simple form of the verb).

Some Common Verbs That Can Be Followed by an Infinitive	
Verb	**Sample Sentence**
afford	Carla can *afford to buy* a new outfit whenever she wants.
agree	I *agree to marry* you a year from today.
appear	He *appears to be* inspired by his new job.
decide	Will they *decide to drive* across the country?
expect	Jamal *expects to graduate* next year.
forget	Please do not *forget to cash* the check.
hope	My nephews *hope to visit* Santa Fe this year.
intend	I *intend to study* harder this semester than I did last semester.
mean	Did Franco *mean to leave* his lunch on the kitchen table?
need	Do you *need to stop* for a break now?
plan	Justin *plans to go* into advertising.
promise	Sharon has *promised to paint* this wall green.
offer	Did they really *offer to babysit* for a month?
refuse	Haim *refuses to walk* another step.
try	Let's *try to set* up this tent before dark.
wait	On the other hand, we could *wait to camp* out until tomorrow.

PRACTICE 6

Write an infinitive after the verb in each blank space provided.

1. The plumber promised _____ the sink today.

2. My son plans _____ a course in electrical engineering.

3. We do not want _____ late for the meeting again.

4. They refused _____ before everyone was ready.

5. I expect _____ Jorge next week.

Verb + Gerund or Infinitive

Some verbs can be followed by *either* a gerund *or* an infinitive.

<table>
<tr><td colspan="2" align="center">**Some Common Verbs That Can Be Followed
by a Gerund or an Infinitive**</td></tr>
<tr><td align="center">**Verb**</td><td align="center">**Sample Sentence**</td></tr>
<tr><td>begin</td><td>They *began **to laugh**.* (infinitive)</td></tr>
<tr><td></td><td>They *began **laughing**.* (gerund)</td></tr>
<tr><td>continue</td><td>Fran *continued **to speak**.* (infinitive)</td></tr>
<tr><td></td><td>Fran *continued **speaking**.* (gerund)</td></tr>
<tr><td>hate</td><td>Juan *hates **to drive*** in the snow. (infinitive)</td></tr>
<tr><td></td><td>Juan *hates **driving*** in the snow. (gerund)</td></tr>
<tr><td>like</td><td>My daughter *likes **to surf*** the Net. (infinitive)</td></tr>
<tr><td></td><td>My daughter *likes **surfing*** the Net. (gerund)</td></tr>
<tr><td>love</td><td>Phil *loves **to watch*** soccer games. (infinitive)</td></tr>
<tr><td></td><td>Phil *loves **watching*** soccer games. (gerund)</td></tr>
<tr><td>start</td><td>Will you *start **to write*** the paper tomorrow? (infinitive)</td></tr>
<tr><td></td><td>Will you *start **writing*** the paper tomorrow? (gerund)</td></tr>
</table>

PRACTICE 7

For each pair of sentences, first write an infinitive in the space provided. Then write a gerund.

1. a. (infinitive) Ivana hates _____ in long lines.

    b. (gerund) Ivana hates _____ in long lines.

2. a. (infinitive) When will we begin _____ dinner?

    b. (gerund) When will we begin _____ dinner?

3. a. (infinitive) Carmen loves _____ in the rain.

    b. (gerund) Carmen loves _____ in the rain.

4. a. (infinitive) The motor continued _____ noisily.

    b. (gerund) The motor continued _____ noisily.

5. a. (infinitive) Suddenly, the people started _____ .

    b. (gerund) Suddenly, the people started _____ .

Credits

Pages 408–409: Excerpt from Diane Sawyer, "Daring to Dream Big," Guideposts, March 1986 and March 2005, p. 27. Reprinted with permission from Guideposts. Copyright © 1986 by Guideposts. All rights reserved. www.guideposts.org

Page 409–411: "Mrs.Flowers", from I KNOW WHY THE CAGED BIRD SINGS by Maya Angelou, copyright © 1969 and renewed 1997 by Maya Angelou. Used by permission of Random House, Inc., and Virago, an imprint of Little, Brown Book Group.

Pages 412–415: "Superman and Me" by Sherman Alexie, Los Angeles Times, April 19, 1998. Reprinted by permission of Nancy Stauffer Associates.

Pages 415–418: From FUNNY IN FARSI by Firoozeh Dumas, copyright © 2003 by Firoozeh Dumas. Used by permission of Villard Books, a division of Random House, Inc., and Hill Nadell Agency.

Pages 419–420: MIAMI HERALD by Leonard Pitts. Copyright 2003 by MCCLATCHY COMPANY. Reproduced with permission of MCCLATCHY COMPANY in the format Textbook via Copyright Clearance Center.

Pages 421–423: "Beve Stevenson, "A Day in the Life of an ER Nurse," Alberta RN, Oct 2004. Adapted by permission of the author. http://www.beeproductions.ca/articles/Dayinthelife.pdf: Other writings: http://beeproductions.ca/index.html

Pages 424–425: MIAMI HERALD by Ana Veciana-Suarez. Copyright 2003 by MCCLATCHY COMPANY. Reproduced with permission of MCCLATCHY COMPANY in the format Textbook via Copyright Clearance Center.

Pages 426–427: "The Gift" by Courtland Milloy. From The Washington Post, © 1992 The Washington Post. All rights reserved. Used by permission and protected by the Copyright Laws of the United States. The printing, copying, redistribution, or retransmission of the Material without express written permission is prohibited. www.washingtonpost.com

Pages 428–429: Michaela Angela Davis, "Quitting Hip-Hop," Essence, October 2004, Volume 35, issue 6, p. 155. Reprinted by permission of the author.

Pages 430–431: "Stuff" by Richard Rodriguez. Copyright © 1998 by Richard Rodriguez. Originally aired on the NewsHour with Jim Lehrer (PBS) on April 27, 1998. Reprinted by permission of Georges Borchardt, Inc., on behalf of the author.

Pages 432–434: "Another Road Hog with Too Much Oink", copyright © 2000 by Dave Barry, from DAVE BARRY IS NOT TAKING THIS SITTING DOWN by Dave Barry. Used by permission of Crown Publishers, a division of Random House, Inc., and the author.

Pages 435–436: ROSA PARKS: MY STORY by Rosa Parks with Jim Haskins, copyright © 1992 by Rosa Parks. Used by permission of Dial Books for Young Readers, A Division of Penguin Young Readers Group, A Member of Penguin Group (USA) Inc., 345 Hudson Street, New York, NY 10014. All rights reserved.

Pages 437–439: "In This Arranged Marriage, Love Came Later" by Shoba Narayan. Reprinted by permission of The Elizabeth Kaplan Literary Agency.

Pages 440–441: "A Homemade Education", copyright © 1964 by Alex Haley and Malcolm X. Copyright c 1965 by Alex Haley and Betty Shabazz., from THE AUTOBIOGRAPHY OF MALCOLM X by Malcolm X and Alex Haley. Used by permission of Random House, Inc. and The Random House Group Ltd.

Pages 442–444: "The Power to Shine" by Deborah Rosado Shaw from Chicken Soup for the Latino Soul. Reprinted by permission of the author.

Pages 445–446: Jack Riemer, "Playing a Violin with Three Strings," Houston Chronicle, February 10, 2001. Reprinted by permission of Rabbi Jack Riemer.

Pages 447–449: "The Jacket" from The Effects of Knut Hamsun on a Fresno Boy: Recollections and Short Essays, by Gary Soto. Copyright © 1983, 1986, 2000 by Gary Soto. Reprinted by permission of Persea Books, Inc., New York, the Author and Book Stop Literary Agency. All rights reserved.

Pages 450–451: "Four Directions", from THE JOY LUCK CLUB by Amy Tan, copyright © 1989 by Amy Tan. Used by permission of G.P. Putnam's Sons, a division of Penguin Group (USA) Inc., the author and the Sandra Dijkstra Literary Agency.

Pages 452–453: "The Hidden Life of Bottled Water," by Liza Gross, as appeared in Sierra, May/June 1999, pp. 66–67. Reprinted by permission of Sierra.

Pages 454–457: From EMOTIONAL INTELLIGENCE by Daniel Goleman, copyright © 1995 by Daniel Goleman. Used by permission of Bantam Books, a division of Random House, Inc., and Bloomsbury Publishing Plc.

Subject Index

Index of Rhetorical Modes

This index classifies the practices, paragraphs, and essays in this text according to the type of writing pattern, or rhetorical mode, they employ.

Index to the Readings